Eros and the Good

Eros and the Good

wisdom according to nature

James S. Gouinlock

Prometheus Books
59 John Glenn Drive
Amherst, New York 14228-2197

Published 2004 by Prometheus Books

Inquiries should be addressed to
Prometheus Books
59 John Glenn Drive
Amherst, New York 14228–2197
VOICE: 716–691–0133, ext. 207
FAX: 716–564–2711
WWW.PROMETHEUSBOOKS.COM

08 07 06 05 04   5 4 3 2 1

Library of Congress Cataloging-in-Publication Data

Gouinlock, James.
    Eros and the good : wisdom according to nature / James S. Gouinlock.
        p. cm.
    Includes bibliographical references and index.
    ISBN 1–59102–148–0
    1. Ethics. I. Title.

BJ1012.G664 2004
171'.2—dc22

2004001129

Printed in Canada on acid-free paper

I joyfully dedicate this work to my grandchildren,

including any yet unborn at the time of this writing.

Jacob

Connor

Will

Jay

Erik

Freya

Contents

Preface

Wisdom, Plato tells us, is knowledge of what is good for the individual as a whole—taking every need and power of his nature into account. This knowledge is obviously precious; it is the most important that anyone could possess. To acquire it, however, is difficult. It is a quest, reaching out to an examination of things human and divine.

Such a quest has always beckoned to me. That is why I have been drawn, as by a magnet, to the study of philosophy. My hope is not just to know the world in a candid manner but to know it in a way that is at once pertinent to both realism and love of the ideal. I seek realism about the constraints and opportunities of the moral life and knowledge of its possibilities for ideal fulfillment, disciplined and ordered by the contingencies of our natural surroundings. According to all the greatest intellects of the present day, however, it is naive or intolerant to suppose one can distinguish what is higher. Thus we would live without ideals, where self-indulgence and indiscriminate compassion are the only operative norms. I must risk the condescension of such great minds.

I share the view of the Socratic school that, in many ways, the nature of things has lessons for us. Knowledge of them chastens our transient wishes and fanciful desires. There is indeed a discipline, a regimen of sorts, given by nature. In our ignorance of it, we are apt to court folly and failure. With knowledge, and with respect for it, we are more apt to pursue and attain life-affirming goods—goods worthy of celebration and communication. Still, nature's admonitions and invitations have been wrongly deciphered many times, and they have been more often counterfeited than steadily discerned. Hence one must take up the mission boldly but not without trepidation.

Effective pursuit of such a goal presupposes a certain conception of philosophy. It cannot usefully be regarded as a self-enclosed exercise but rather as an inclusive search. One must pursue it as a student of experience in all its variety, force, and nuance, as it is found in conspicuous modes of conduct and numerous media of expression, such as religion and the arts. The philosopher must likewise be a student of human nature, history, and sciences. He strives to distill and appropriate the lessons of all such studies as they might be brought to convergence on matters of large human import. We cannot attain wisdom about the nature of the moral life by mere conceptual analysis, nor can we apprehend forms of ideal life by means of simple intuition. We must, instead, examine the continuities of our being with the real conditions that define its potentialities and limits, so far as we are able, just as Plato studied the whole nature of man and society in his search for the meaning of justice. Philosophy, accordingly, is not a science among sciences. It is the thinking by which the substance of varied forms of experience and inquiry might be distinguished and incorporated into a more inclusive view of things. Such a view is given focus, order, and elaboration in virtue of the distinctive aims of the search. Hardly a nondescript collection of facts, a philosophy would be an integration of information and ideas so far as they are fateful for our self-understanding and aspiration.

Many a mind has been fascinated with the promise of wisdom in an investigation of the realities that circumscribe and inform our existence. I would address such minds. These are the readers I seek: those who have been stirred by the quests of classic philosophic writings—in *The Symposium*, perhaps, or it might be *The Nicomachean Ethics*, *The Critique of Pure Reason*, or *Thus Spoke Zarathustra*, among scores of others. In such works many a soul has found searching responses to the deepest reflections prompted by his existence. The issues are real: what *does* the nature of things hold for us? Many have the desire to look into these matters, hoping for real wisdom, and they pursue them as questions of mortal consequence. Such minds might be found in the university—but not exclusively in departments of philosophy, by any means, while many others are not participants in the academy at all. They are educated and independent inquirers, caught up in varying demands on their energies, while remaining nonetheless seekers of wisdom and virtue. Such is the erotic philosophic spirit, wherever he might be found. I invite him to assess the wisdom in the present attempt—following a Socratic inspiration—at an examined life.

For several reasons, none of them stalwart, philosophers have not proceeded in the Socratic way for many years. One of their common stratagems is to select, or even concoct, but one feature of vital life—reason, perhaps—

and to regard it as all-sufficing in the determination of norms that we would adopt as guides to life, while studiously ignoring the full array of values clamoring for light and power. Other philosophers take equally dysfunctional views. They say, for example, that reality is a mere social construct, determined by nothing but the prejudices that happen to be current in a given milieu. This is a convenient way to legitimate the irresponsible speculations of utopians, who do not wish to endure the disciplines of an obdurate world. Still another group would enter the moral life and command it, having pulled morality, like a rabbit, out of a premoral hat—the mad crusade to deduce an "ought" from an "is." The appropriate sort of study, that of the Socratics, has no such handy shortcuts, but it gives promise of engaging the ideal affinities of the spirit, of eros.

A further obstacle to wisdom is endemic to academic philosophy: the theorists neither begin nor end with a pertinent definition of their subject matter. Morality seems to be conceived as an esoteric or mysterious sort of thing, to be justified by arcane theory. Morality is then without vital continuity with common life yet claims full authority over it. It has become routine, moreover, to center the postulated theory in a way that is marginal to concerns about the vigor or the deterioration of fundamental forms of life. Hence compassion, caring, or sensitivity is supposed to be the heart of morality. This theory is popular in contemporary society, where one can be ever so sensitive and compassionate, while being a cheat and a liar and being irresponsible in the observance of life-sustaining duties. In contrast, I proceed on the assumption, which is essential to human survival and prosperity, that morality comprises precisely those forms of behavior that are necessary for there *to be* a functioning social order. That is why morality is irreplaceably important: it holds society together in some tolerable or even thriving order. To think of it in any other way is to make it the plaything of sentiment and ideology, and it is to neglect the actual limitations and resources inherent in our existence.

When we would examine and criticize the practices within a moral order, we do well to try them neither from the standpoint of uncontaminated theoretical principles nor from a value-free mountain top. We proceed in our capacity as moral beings, such as we variously are, our lives fatefully intermingled in numberless ways, trying to contend with a baffling and resistant world. Just to be a moral being does not commit us to universal principles, but it does commit us to an assessment in terms of elementary moral considerations. The judgments of a moral being might be variously chastened, instructed, and inspired by wisdom according to nature, and in due course they might lead to deeply trustworthy and cherished convictions, and they might enjoy the support of the real world.

To be mired in the schools is not the greatest obstacle to wisdom. It is something more fundamental: normal human incapacity. We have a nearly overwhelming tendency, for example, to see the world in a way that is friendly to our sentimental and pathetic hopes. Even the proudest and most militantly independent minds are apt to succumb. Another weakness is unwittingly to imitate ideas already in currency, no matter how infertile, rather than to seek adequacy in terms dictated by the subject matter itself. Still another is to try to please, to be acceptable—the herd instinct regnant. There are still more, not least of them the temptations of ideology. Given such profoundly corrupting influences, philosophy requires something more than the skills and learning one picks up in school. It requires courage and candor, and a discerning eye for experience, or it is a sham.

The following discussion is not defined by the agendas of prevailing philosophies. In the main, it is better to steer all the way 'round them than to try to turn them into navigable passages. Contemporary preoccupations and reputations will be attended to only insofar as they seem to have achieved canonical status. I pursue an agenda of greater ancestry. My discourse, accordingly, draws mostly upon historic figures, whose impress on moral thought and aspiration has been of perennial moment. It is a discourse, I will add, with its own order and its own pace, so the reader should not become impatient when his every reservation is not attended to at once. The work is a whole, and it will be salutary to consider it as such.

It is concerned with more than philosophic theories. They have import, after all, only insofar as they help us with the conduct of life; otherwise, they can be no more than amusements—and often less. The context of my reflections, then, is not that of theory by itself. I am concerned with ideals of *life*. At the same time, I am haunted by the belief that American civilization is in a perilous state of decay, which advances insidiously—like cancer. That anxiety pervades much of my text. A life that would approximate to the spirit of Socratic excellence is far from our typical thought and practice, yet some semblance to that sort of moral devotion is needful to a gravely faltering culture. The attacks of September 11, to be sure, acted as a shot of moral adrenaline to the American psyche. The reaction is greatly welcome, but can the moral strength of a people endure only by a series of injections? Are they losing their potency over time? What will happen when they cease? The idea of a mere return to the status quo ante—absorption in the self-indulgent and trivial—is anything but reassuring. We cannot evade the question of the sources of moral vigor short of the threat of massive calamity.

A worthwhile philosophy would be conceived in terms of the real processes that might sustain a good and even noble life. Conspicuous among these conditions are universal traits of the natural world, including fateful dispositions of human nature. Such a philosophy, in addition, must include candid observation of our culture and experience, and it must engage in commentary on crucial features of prevailing institutions and beliefs. These traits of contemporary life demand analysis and evaluation as urgently as theories, and they often betray an indifference to the inherent disciplines of man and nature.

I take as my subject matter questions that absorb a reflective and educated mind, but recent thought has succeeded in creating a void where once the life of eros, intelligence, and courage was pondered. I do not mean to leave the void intact. Santayana said that one of life's finer achievements is to share one's ideal values with others, especially with those whom we love. That is what I undertake in these pages. When and if such a sharing occurs, a fragment of ideal immortality has been won. That would be one of the fitting consummations of a philosophic life.

Thousand Julys
Atlanta
September 14, 2003

Acknowledgments

I have meant to write a philosophy that will be beholden to no one, but it is indebted to many. My debts go back to John Herman Randall, Jr., my teacher at Columbia. It is an act of piety for me once more to express my gratitude to him. I have also learned much about how to love wisdom from John Anton, my friend and colleague for many years. Peter Hare and John Lachs are two more whose friendship, advice, and support have been of great help to my thinking and to the writing of this book. My appreciation to all three of them is profound. As a model of intellectual integrity and brilliance I have never known the equal of Richard Herrnstein. It was my joy to have had many conversations with him in years past. I hope that some fraction of his intelligence and courage can be found in the following pages.

I have had some splendid colleagues at Emory. I have learned much from reading the works of both Don Verene and Don Livingston, but I have learned even more from my daily association and conversation with them during the past decades. Each of them made discerning and forceful comments about an early manuscript for this book, and I thank them for that. Another of my fine colleagues at Emory has been Ann Hartle. She also studied the manuscript with much care and discernment. I am grateful for her observations and for her example as a scholar and thinker. Finally, at Emory, I express my thanks to Jim Gustafson and the participants in the interdisciplinary Luce Faculty Seminar on the Idea of Nature. Those sparkling sessions provided an invaluable education on the multiple ways that one can think helpfully about the inclusive realities of our existence.

    With trepidation, I solicited the criticism of John Kekes, knowing that he is an honest and unsparing critic. True to my expectations, he forced me to confront my beliefs and arguments at every turn, and for that I am indebted to him. I likewise express my thanks to Jim Herrnstein. I needed a crash course in probability theory, which he most ably and generously provided. Finally, I am happy to have had the support and guidance of Paul Kurtz, Steven L. Mitchell, and the editors of Prometheus Books. They are helping to sustain fine and honorable traditions in philosophy. I hope that the following chapters will repay their confidence in me.

| 1 |

Introduction

Moral Appraisal

a. THE TRAVAILS OF MORAL PHILOSOPHY

Moral philosophy might be a serious and exciting venture. It might help us to become wise and to give us some insight into the good life. According to one of its earliest practitioners, Socrates, the questions of moral philosophy are the most important that a man can ask and answer. What are these questions, and how does one become qualified to investigate them? They are questions of the nature of man and the world, questions of the nature of the human condition.

These inquiries are currently in a state of near total neglect. In recent generations, virtually no one has taken them up. This failure is due to the peculiarly leaden state of the academic mind. There is a widespread conceit among professors of philosophy that formal training in their discipline makes them qualified moralists, but professors, by and large, are ill suited to being moral philosophers. Their academic environment and professional ambitions almost inevitably turn their thinking to the impertinent. This turn is not deliberate; it happens insensibly. As professional academicians, the subject matter of their reflections is what they have learned in school and what they read in the current technical literature. Like most persons, status and reputation are important to them, and their aim is to do well in their chosen milieu. With scarcely an exception, they write only for each other and are read only by each other. A closed circle of thought is bound to become effete.

The diligent student of academic philosophy succeeds by learning the writings circulating in the profession, analyzing their logic, detecting their inconsistencies, playing them off against one another, and adding a few implications. Put a text before him, and he can analyze its logic, but that is all he can do. His exertions do not and will not make him a moral philosopher. What above all distinguishes the moral philosopher is the will to acquire pertinent knowledge of the world and our place in it, driven by love of the good.

The academy has not proven an apt environment for worldly wisdom, but professors are not the only ones who are reality-aversive, as we shall see. Nor is it true that all moral perplexities are equally in need of guidance from the lessons of existence, though refusal to seek those lessons is the greatest of all failings in moral thought. There are many sources of wisdom in our heritage, but one must appropriate them with reference to the moral life itself. *That* is the primary subject matter.

One of the best ways to think helpfully about the moral life, with its characteristic frustrations and hopes, is to keep steadily in mind the elementary condition of the human race. Homo sapiens first appeared maybe a quarter of a million years ago, the inheritor of about six million years of hominid evolution and hundreds of millions of years of natural selection preceding the hominids, roughly twelve billion years after the big bang. He arrived in very insecure conditions, and virtually every circumstance in his surroundings was of a nature to defeat or support his will in specific ways. Owing to his extraordinary intelligence, he was able to learn that the multiple features of his environment are also signs of other things, with portent for both weal and woe. He then might ally himself deliberately and productively with selected forces of nature. His existence was also of a social nature, and this, too, was ambiguous. Then as now, other members of the species would be competitors, threats in many ways, while others would be accomplices and even friends. The threats would come from both within and outside his own group, and maintaining a secure social order would be the first imperative of life. As societies begin to move beyond the primitive structures of hunting-gathering, it would still be true that the most elementary rule would be loyalty to the group and maintenance of order, but the problem of possible alternatives to the existing manner of life would assert itself as never before. Almost every member of the communal order would have his own urgent sympathies and interests, each of which constitutes at least an implicit demand for recognition and a plea for adjustments in the prevailing regime. Simply for the sake of the cohesiveness and endurance of a society, many of these demands could not be blithely overlooked or suppressed—not in every instance. Indeed, sympathies of comradeship and goodwill would not be entirely absent, so the mutual accommodation of some of these demands would not be unheard of and would even be respected. When such conditions occur, whether in light of the imperatives of social cohesion in a perilous world or of willing concession to urgent interests, a rudimentary form of morality has developed. Above all, the elementary requirements of good conduct must be made clear. The forms of behavior that are necessary for the preservation of associated life—the duties and sacrifices that would sustain a community in all its vicissitudes—these must be discerned, taught, enforced, and celebrated.

In due course, doubtless under unusual conditions, some persons will be moved to give systematic thought to the rules, duties, and aspirations of the group or of some of its members. They will be more poet and prophet than philosopher, and surely they will approach the topic with great bias. No ivory tower theorizing is apt to survive, however. Thought is taken in the context of the endurance and prosperity of the community, comprising passionate and often unruly beings whose goods are always under threat of extinction. This is no environment for sentimental theorizing. We can imagine that men might appropriately ask what form of life is most suitable to the conspicuous contingencies of life: What form of life will most fully answer to the demands of a shared existence for creatures of large appetites, contending with a precarious and sometimes hopeful world? At best, such thinkers will make pertinent generalizations about the typical character of these contingencies and would ask how they conspire to bring down a life, a family, or a civilization or cause them to thrive. They will also study the forces that drive human nature: pride, loyalty, tenderness, love, lust, malice, vengeance, and cruelty, to name some of the most obvious, and greed for wealth, power, status, and reputation. How do these occur and to what effect? No one could be wise who did not have some sense of how such passions shape the order of life and of how we might contend with them, as we must with any natural force. These are some of the questions that would be pursued in a serious moral philosophy, and the investigation might yield helpful proposals for the ordering of life. At its best, it would provide insight into the most gratifying reaches of human nature.

These lessons appear in great epics and religious narratives, populated with gods and other mythical beings who represent natural powers, ideals, and corruptions. The questions addressed by such thinkers can be given answers foolish or sound, but the questions themselves are vital and indispensable. What would be the worth of moral recommendations that were predicated, for example, merely on someone's pleasing intuitions about justice or on another's abstract conception of rationality? Eventually, however, universities are established, and moral thought falls to the keeping of professors. Topics of vital life become cloistered, licensed, monopolized, and scholastic. The moral life is no longer at stake, but professional advancement and reputation are. The subject matter of academic ethics replaces a concern for life itself, and the issues that truly demand inquiry lie fallow. If such loyal soldiers were to come within hailing distance of a truly fertile philosophic idea, most of them would be all but incapable of recognizing it. In practice, meanwhile, moral reality overwhelms moral theory.

This has been a sketchy history, to be sure, but no matter. My aim has been to dramatize the difference between the pertinent and the impertinent in moral thought. Any moral philosophy that is not predicated on an unflinching and thorough analysis of the conditions of human existence will be either worthless or pernicious. In what way or ways is moral philosophy predicated on reality? Indulge me for a moment. I propose an excursion that I trust will turn out to be instructive.

b. Knowing Better

Suppose you were to contemplate taking up a career in a foreign land that is more or less unknown to you. There is much about that place that you will want to learn. What are its customs, for example, regarding the relations of males and females or of young and old? What is the etiquette of relations between superiors and subordinates? How are commercial transactions undertaken? What are the prospects for advancement and prosperity? What is the nature and general level of education and culture? What is the system of justice and law enforcement? How much security of life and possessions might one expect? What rights and obligations can one anticipate? All such questions are of vital importance to you because each will have an effect on the values dear to you, both superficial and profound. Your interest will be not only in your personal fortunes, for you have moral concerns as well. Perhaps you care for the welfare of the young, and you would not willingly participate in a regime that neglected or exploited its children.

You want answers to your questions. You need someone who might know them. You want to avoid anyone who thinks he knows but doesn't, or whose information is incomplete or inaccurate, or whose mind might be a treasury of impertinence and misinformation. A good teacher would also bring your attention to issues that you hadn't thought of but would turn out to be of real consequence. Perhaps you are advised (though you hadn't thought to ask) that political corruption is rampant in this place. In the best of cases, your guide might also tell you of the availability of goods of which you had been unaware: there are (to you) novel religious practices that intimate a level of spirituality that you had not hitherto experienced. The best of guides might go still further: all these conditions about which you are learning are not isolated events. There are costs in resources and effort to bring them into being and sustain them. You might find the costs prohibitive, or they might be astonishingly low. Each of the goods in this society will tend to support or hinder the flourishing of other goods, and you would not know fully and adequately until you found out how these anticipated experiences tended to exclude or reinforce one another. If private property is militantly protected, for example, are masses of people rendered helplessly vulnerable to poverty?

And so your education proceeds. All such learning is crucial to you, so you are hoping for someone who *knows better—who knows better than you and others about the conditions of life in this land.* This knowledge is indispensable for your decision. When you find someone who seems to have it, you listen eagerly to everything he says, reacting gratefully, enthusiastically—or sourly, disappointedly—as each bit of intelligence tells how the features of this habitat will tend to advance or retard your ambitions. Things look better or worse, propitious or disheartening, and your ambitions themselves might undergo change. Some counsel, perhaps, brings you face-to-face with novel and unanticipated conditions, which compete for your affections and will modify them. Your eagerness to amass wealth, it might happen, is diminished in consequence of the discovery that there are drastically needed forms of service that you are uniquely equipped to provide. As your knowledge grows, your evaluation of your plan will undergo such modifications, perhaps of a radical sort. The allegiances to your potential host that you had hitherto entertained might diminish or increase in consequence of your investigations. Thus you address this critical domain of existence.

Finally, you are prepared to make your decision, and you will do so. With the help of knowing better, you have arrived at an important evaluation, and you have made it as well as you could. This entire procedure incorporates no reasoning that pretends to deduce evaluative judgments from declarative ones. The investigation *began* with a swarm of values at stake, and as it progressed, you learned how they would prosper or suffer, or how they might be readjusted in the company of other goods. Priorities change in consequence of appraisal. You know better how the things that you esteem will fare in these once unfamiliar conditions, and some of your habitual estimations will probably have been modified. Indeed, you might even discover the way to experiences even more welcome than you had hoped for. In sum, your choice was predicated upon information concerning the myriad ways in which this change would affect your fate. You *responded* to this critical information. That is what "predicated on an analysis of the conditions of human existence" means: a *response* to vital information, not a deduction from it.

You were challenged with a situation containing a tangle of possibilities fraught with uncertainty, promise, and peril. Any response to the situation is more apt to be to your benefit and less to your misfortune to the extent that you are aware of the actualities and real possibilities that compose it. From that whole palpitating mass of information you can deduce nothing. Your judgment emerged from that situation as a *synthesis*, or *resolution*, of your multiform considerations and reactions. I call the entire process that results in such a resolution an *appraisal*. The resolution or synthesis expressed in a form of words is a *judgment*: "This is what I ought to do," or "That is the best course of action," "This is what I will do," and so forth. A judgment records the outcome of one's appraisal.

A further point of consequence: an appraisal does not carry one fatefully to a single definite decision. Resolution might be conflicted and hesitant. There are uncertainties about the nature of the proposed destination; there are many considerations to be weighed, and they are apt to be indeterminate and ambiguous, and they will contain inherent incompatibilities. It is entirely possible that once the appraisal is over, there will still be ambivalence; we cannot always act with supreme confidence. It is likely that different persons contemplating the same conditions would make different responses. This fact does not, however, give us license to conclude that the procedure is dubious. It might be the best resource available, and quite a good one at that. It would be folly, indeed, to reject a procedure simply on the grounds that it fails to achieve universal certainty and unanimity. If we did so, we would have to reject every method of making up the mind that has ever been conceived.

The little excursion is now over, and it might have seemed a pointless exercise. I propose, however, that the domain of the moral life is analogous to the situation we have just surveyed, and moral deliberation and judgment have no logic different in kind from that of our traveler in foreign places. As each of us tries to make his way through the risks and expectancies of the moral life, we have recourse to no form of inquiry or reasoning that is different in kind from that illustrated above. Whether we are coping with mere daily contingency or asking of the soul what kind of person we really ought to be, our search—short of sophistry and self-deception—must take the form of appraisal. Perhaps this is a startling conclusion. Philosophers, after all, consort with more serious things: moral foundations, principles, universals, ideals, gods, justice, and rationally conclusive systems. I am the last one to disparage moral aspiration and high seriousness, but I want to think about them truthfully.

c. PHILOSOPHIC APPRAISAL

A general account of the conditions from which our normative judgments emerge will teach us more of the nature of evaluative appraisal. In anticipation of substantive discussions to come, this is a topic that must be addressed in some detail. Not surprisingly, we would like to possess unquestionable assurance for our moral convictions. Philosophers as well as others have yearned to discover a source of confidence or certainty. They seek indubitable foundations or some other guarantee, and they wish to escape the waywardness of human passion in the determination of right and wrong. Perhaps this yearning accounts for attachment to the is/ought problem: by logical means to derive an evaluative from a descriptive judgment. By means of an exercise in logic, a prescription of, say, moral obligation will be produced from one or more irreducibly declarative statements. This procedure has a certain appeal. The moral judgments of the race show a dismaying variability and inconsistency. They are repeatedly called into question, and we are easily baffled as to how we can provide them with a decisive defense. We seem not to have the resources to stave off the dreaded moral relativism. "Morals are just a matter of opinion" is whispered everywhere, and soon it is declared brazenly far and wide. Conduct deteriorates; lawlessness flourishes. We have, on the other hand, developed far more confidence in our ability to confirm a descriptive statement; *it* can be determined to be true (or not), so by means of logic, the powerful resources of our cognitive abilities are brought to bear at once on moral questions. The verified descriptive claim, we shall presume, is true regardless of anyone's subjective wishes or prejudices. Unlike moral predilections, it is independent of personal whim and transport; it withstands them. Our knowledge of the nature of things, accordingly, will yield objective prescriptions for conduct. Moral judgments will be deduced from well-ascertained truths, and they will be dependent upon nothing idiosyncratic in the individual.

The feeling that our moral convictions ought to be somehow dependent upon our knowledge of the nature of things is as warranted as any claim in moral philosophy could be, but the belief that the dependency is specified by feats of formal logic is mistaken. The strategy of the logician, which has been a main focus of academic ethics for decades, is not only a failure but wildly impertinent. Truth to tell, obsession with it is fatal to actual moral discernment. I will not survey various attempts to solve the problem. It is defeated simply by the fact that evaluation is not reducible to cognition.[1] The strategy looks a bit slippery if for no other reason than the fact that any statement deduced from a true statement is also true. Accordingly, the moral judgment would be verifiable in its own right without benefit of the alleged deduction. But there are far more serious objections.

If the alleged logic is taken at face value, the descriptive premise is *just* factual—*value neutral*, in the current jargon. It is not a disguised moral judgment, nor does it otherwise conceal one within itself. If the latter were the case, we wouldn't really be performing the desired logic: the premise identifies and expresses, in effect, an existing value or principle. If we acknowledge it as obligatory, we would presumably act in a way to satisfy it, but in any case it is not a free-standing fact, and the question of its origins and validity remains wide open.

In the logic at issue, the premise must be morally indifferent. But maybe it is *selected* for moral reasons, you suggest. If that is what has happened, we are suspicious that another smuggling operation is afoot: the innocent looking factual statement implicitly conveys information assumed to be of moral consequence. Consider this "deduction," for example: "God commands you to love your neighbor as yourself. Therefore, you ought to love your neighbor as yourself." Any believer will subscribe to the resultant prescription. It is by no means a deduction, however. There is no logical entailment. The factual assertion that God commands you to love your neighbor is anything but morally indifferent. The command is issued by one who holds almighty power over your fate and who dispenses inconceivable beatitude or hell contingent upon your obedience. Who could be indifferent to that? In the context of a certain body of religious belief, the declarative statement "God commands you to love your neighbor as yourself" is in fact both threat and promise, and we *respond* to such massive forewarnings. The assertion, "you ought to love your neighbor" is not a logical conclusion. It is an alarm that if you don't love your neighbor, the fiery pit yawns before you, and you will try to obey the command in order to avoid that fate and possibly to gain heaven.

Think of it: Would it not be mad to evaluate an object by reference to some state of affairs that is *without* value? Take the most indifferent collection of facts that you can think of—denuded of any pertinence to the yearnings and terrors of the heart—and make *that* the criterion for everything else. What an idea! It does not comport at all well with the fundamental condition of the human race, as sketched a few moments ago. We are required, in effect, to sweep aside the things that are most dear to us, including our value-laden moral principles and ideals—and all for the sake of some manner of value-neutral fact. Well, we do not and would not leap from a value-free position to an evaluative conclusion. No evaluation begins with a clean slate, and there is no good reason why we should wish it were so. The inquiries of our would-be traveler, for example, were undertaken only because he already had much at stake in venturing abroad. We have a stake, constituted by our existing values, in every situation that we encounter. This is not to say that the ubiquity of valuing is necessarily insidious. Frequently, to be sure, it constitutes unrecognized prejudice, but our values are sometimes openly acknowledged, and they are subject to appraisal.

Philosophers should not torture themselves by trying to found such values on morally indifferent information. The problem, rather, is to discriminate between existing and possible values by considering how variations in them are apt to destroy, enrich, or otherwise modify *one another*. Our generic and continuing task is to *readjust* our existing moral concerns in response to such worldly conditions as we might become cognizant of—including whatever further moral concerns come within our ken. We begin *within* an operating moral context invested with more or less functional values, but they are subject to modification from many sources, including appraisal. Such readjustments occur in many ways, but never by way of deducing evaluative judgments from descriptive premises. A man of moral wisdom will not lightly readjust his well-won values, but that possibility always exists. Philosophic appraisal will prove to be the best means to carry on the readjustments of the moral life with decency, integrity, and even nobility. The means to minimize the effects of human cupidity on our moral judgments is not by somehow deriving them from value-neutral propositions. What keeps our impulses in bounds are, first, the norms inculcated and enforced by a community striving to remain intact and, at best, the cultivation of virtue. These are later topics, however.

The actual and possible interrelations of goods and evils present us with momentous challenges and disciplines. The phenomena of the world, linked or disjoined in countless ways, are attractive and repulsive in myriad fashion. We struggle with objective conditions, subject to limited patterns of rearrangement, that are variously fateful for our existence. In the vague but pertinent expression, we call them values. Part of knowing better, as I have already commented, is to learn of the conditions of their existence and of their mutual harmonies and exclusions.

A more discriminating analysis of values yields conditions that we denominate goods, obligations, and rights, for example, and we use epithets like "evils" or "wrongs" to refer to events that are threatening or abhorrent. The clarifications and applications of such expressions are subject to debate. My point here is to observe that the pertinent subject matter of appraisal is the *interrelations* of these values, not their supposed derivation from evaluatively indifferent states of affairs. All ethical perplexity, all thinking, acting, triumph, failure, and tragedy occur within and in reference to such networks of affective conditions, and nothing counts as a consideration in our deliberations unless it somehow provokes an affection. Nothing else *can* matter. Accordingly: *Beyond immediate reaction, the only way to evaluate a state of affairs is by reference to other valued states of affairs that will occur, be modified, or be excluded contingent upon our action.* This is what happened in the example of receiving the command to love your neighbor. You might have an aversion to the neighbor and a preference for keeping your distance from him, but the consequences of disobedience dwarf all other concerns, so you do your best. Not all goods are on a par, obviously, but the good of any condition is strengthened or diminished only by its relations to the goods of other conditions. This is a process that has varying—but not unlimited—constituents, and it can be undertaken wisely or foolishly.

Any proposed good must prove its worth to your affections, including those of sympathy, benevolence, and a sense of justice. Judging and acting—however assured, ambivalent, or even guilt-ridden—will be a consequence of those real and imagined events that have succeeded in resolving your interest. *That* is your evaluation. There is no essential difference between this courtship of goods and the determination of moral principles and actions in their life-functions. Your appraisal of an existing or proposed moral requirement takes the form of a consideration of its performance in the fabric of the moral life, as you understand it. Your understanding is apt to be deficient in various ways; you need to know better. In addition, of course, your affections might be more or less vicious or depraved in one way or another, but in any event you attempt to determine how the salient requirement would qualify, enhance, or undermine the existing order, constituted in part by exigent moral values. Finally, your acceptance or rejection is contingent upon that appraisal.

Lest one suppose that such an approach can be no better than a lottery, we should be reminded that individuals grow up in communities, the members of which insist on good behavior and encourage the formation of responsible habits. At best, evaluation is disciplined by our appraisals in company with our moral dispositions, such as they may be. They are not value neutral. They are value-seeking, value-enhancing, and value-preserving. Inevitably, we appraise with an existing fund of moral values. That is, the values that we bring to appraisal include distinctively moral concerns. Perhaps we habitually take the interests of others into account. We might be impartial and benevolent, too, and disposed to determine what is deserved or undeserved.

Both human traits and traits of the world constrain and direct our appraisals. The individual who is engaged in the process is not a mere blob of miscellaneous desires. He is experienced, more or less, in worldly conduct and is capable of learning in consequence of it. He also possesses some assortment of moral values and principles. Our evolution and experience have had the effect of producing beings who are capable of many distinctive responses and actions, a rather ill-defined set of which we have denominated *moral*. The moral denomination is, roughly, that which we have selected as having a peculiar value for the conduct of associated life. For many persons, these values have a high priority relative to other of our concerns. For others, the priority is not so high but not nonexistent, and our respect for moral conduct seems often to have the power to make us feel guilty when we betray it.[2] No occult powers or properties are being invoked. We are creatures who have distinctive interests to which we have given an epithet intended to be laudatory, namely, "moral."[3] Possession of such interests does not deliver us from ambiguity, uncertainty, or wickedness. Still, some of an individual's interests are moral in quality. In part, then, his responses will be of a moral nature, and they might be strong.

There are many virtues that are supreme human resources, but this is not yet the occasion to consider them. My concern at the moment is to point out that individuals caught up in the conditions of appraisal have, not surprisingly, some capacities and powers that are well suited for these demands. If we didn't have some prowess in deliberation and social conduct, we would not be survivors of the remorseless process of natural selection. Adults in general and parents in particular have a great interest in the moral training of the young, and we characteristically devote great energies to it. It is a necessity of life. All the same, success is limited. No candid thinker can deny the human capacities for greed, oppression, rage, and destruction, and the moral philosopher who neglects them is wasting our time.

To this point, the outline of the main components of evaluative activity—appraisal, as I have called it—is only begun. I have spoken of rudimentary qualities of the individual, and I will return to this issue. We must be equally attentive to the ways in which the world to be evaluated is populated. Consider some of the most conspicuous topics of inquiry that would be incorporated into appraisal. The subject matter includes many physical events, to be sure, but that's hardly a beginning. *Any form of being that anyhow enters into one's feelings, estimations, and actions—or that is even thought to do so or might do so—is subject to evaluation and is in some measure determinative of one's judgment.* In this inclusive class there are persons of all sorts to be considered: friends and enemies, parents, children, officials, rivals, colleagues, the virtuous and the vicious, the innocent and the guilty—arrayed in many configurations. For most people, the population to be studied is believed also to include supernatural beings of various potencies and biases. We are likewise concerned with laws, institutions, and practices as actual or potential ingredients of the environment. We also evaluate rules, principles, ideals, obligations, rights, and standards relevant to a variety of forms of conduct. They have massive bearing on our fate and hence on our thinking. The relations denominated by a moral vocabulary are not ethereal beings. They are modes of *practice*, interconnected with other practices. To carry out a putative obligation, for example, is at the same time to support or obstruct various expectations, plans, and possessions cherished in the conduct of life. Keeping a promise sustains loyalty and trust and social cooperation, but in a given instance it might be done at the price of excluding service to other values, such as charity or even the general welfare. Neither can we think effectively of justice unless we regard it as a body of practices embedded in the comprehensive landscape of human powers and activities.

The determination of the *priorities* of distinctive practices surely must be included in such appraisal. The option between the good and the wicked is rarely problematic, but the difference between good, better, and best is incalculably important to the erotic soul. Do you place popularity above integrity or the reverse? Why? The answer must lie in response to an honest vision of what a life can mean. Everywhere we are faced with the urgent demand to establish priorities in character and conduct. Few questions are more important in the formation of a good life. The alleged logic of deduction is impotent here, while philosophic appraisal is all-important: the determination of the interconnections of values in their mutual friendships and antagonisms.

The fateful task of making judgment relies on knowledge of many things. The existence, whereabouts, and activities of gods and other forces are a first priority. Knowledge of the order of natural events is necessary. Embarking on any venture, we make assumptions about how one event is or is not connected to another, and we make predictions about the consequences of actions and policies. These consequences are functions of complex and sometimes inscrutable natural processes. There can be no success in most such investigations without some knowledge of the natures of the individuals engaged in them. Policies, institutions, and our hopes go afoul if we misjudge the general tendencies of human nature. Likewise with forms of moral conduct: Does what is claimed for them in theory bear any resemblance to their practice? Are there fundamental characteristics of human nature, for example, that would turn an egalitarian scheme of justice into a tyranny?

Worldly students of human nature do not deploy their knowledge for the sake of deducing a moral principle from a value-neutral fact. They have more important matters to consider. They want knowledge of human nature for the same reason that one wants knowledge of any sort of thing that moves in the world. What does it do? What will it do? What can it do? How can it support or threaten our endeavors? What is congenial to it and what is dangerous? Wordly students *begin* their investigations of human nature with urgent values already in prominence: the fear of violence and upheaval, the need for social stability, the promotion of liberty, the fear of tyranny, the nurturing of civic responsibility, and the warding-off of corruption, to name just a few. It is *within* this vital context, and for services to it, that knowledge of human propensities is cherished. Given what we know of our characteristic yearnings and frailties, how are values to be secured? What conditions encourage industry and virtue? What institutions in what arrangements might be resistant to characteristic weaknesses? Which ones are apt to inspire allegiance and loyalty? How does the pursuit of any of these conditions promote or retard the others—or still other values not yet reckoned? What have we learned from observation and historical experience that suggests answers to these questions? Such is the role and virtue of knowledge. Further experience might show that our conclusions have been in error in some ways, so the inquiry is resumed. We find that many of the goods that we cherish are not compatible with others. Perhaps our institutions haven't performed as expected, or they have unanticipated effects. Perhaps some of our judgments about human nature have been misguided. We are forced to think again and perhaps to revise our priorities. We examine the whole of civic life to conceive of possible adjustments. The appraisal continues.

It has been implied in passing that *historical* knowledge contributes substantially to knowing better, and so it does. I would put it more daringly: every serious philosophy, for all the well-deserved acclamation for its new thinking, is still in large part a summation of a long and arduous history—the "highway of despair" that teaches wisdom. This is not to endorse the sophomoric view that there are no transhistorical or transcultural truths. It is to say that we do not learn everything all at once, and we do a lot of forgetting. There have been profound trials of life in the course of history, and the wise man is the inheritor of this legacy. He must know politics, religions, cultures, and customs as repositories of information about the resources and limits of the human venture—which is not to suggest that such repositories are easily accessible.

Self-knowledge, of course, is indispensable to many appraisals. One relies on beliefs about his own capabilities, weaknesses, and limits and about his deepest needs and most enduring goods. More subtly, he would be aware of the biases that insinuate prejudice into his inquiries and cause him to give special attention to some kinds of values and to neglect others. At least he would do so if he were to have any pretense at objectivity and impartiality. We would likewise make a conscientious attempt to learn what other persons have at stake in a given situation or in respect to a given policy or form of moral practice.

A further element of philosophic appraisal must be mentioned. This is a kind of discernment—discernment of the good, for example. Is it possible that good things are not easily seen? It is certain that they are not. Our experience is motley, preoccupied, distracted. We are obsessed with narrow and limited concerns, or we gyrate into sheer fantasy. But life has promises of order, renunciation, and meaning that are concealed from the distracted sort of mind. Our gratitude to the occasional sage or poet who has surveyed the world with scope and penetration and identifies some of these goods, giving them voice, and inspiring us to ideal values. The elaborated insights of a Plato, a Spinoza, a Nietzsche, or a Santayana are gifts of disciplined genius, not of skill in deduction. No conceivable is/ought logic accomplishes their work. Think, then, of the waste when generations of students are taught to read moral philosophy with one question uppermost: Are these evaluative conclusions certified by a morally neutral criterion? If not, they are discredited. Hence every invitation to an ennobling ideal is passed by. The student does not even look for them any more than does the teacher. But these are invitations to the eros already kindled within the human breast. Except in a figurative sense, they are not true or false but lovely or discordant. They are certified by their aptness for a given nature and by a reckoning of their real possibility within the frame of a whole life. Obsession with the logic of is and ought—or with other forms of spurious foundationalism—tragically fore-closes the opportunity of genuine philosophic appraisal.

Closely akin to this mode of discernment is another: the perception of the qualitative differences between one professed good and another. It is essential for us to know the relations between events, of course, but aware-ness of their intrinsic qualities is equally necessary. Otherwise, we are inca-pacitated to judge of the relative merits of competing goods. What is the dif-ference between pleasure and happiness, for example, or between lust and love? What are the variations in experience of hedonism as distinguished from the life of virtue? One's grasp of such differences is dependent upon experience, which we might have at first hand or which might be intimated to us by a parent or friend, or perhaps a poet or novelist. Awareness of qual-itative difference is patently indispensable to the moral life, yet the powers of the is/ought logician, as such, cannot even approach this subject.

There is another kind of knowledge that is part of appraisal, the most distinctively philosophical. It consists of beliefs about the generic character of the whole as it bears upon human destinies. Our aspirations are thereby given a certain chastening and definition. If we are Platonists, for example, we will believe that the cosmos is a harmonious whole determined by perfect and unchanging essences. There is a definite place and end for each nature within it. Each human being is fitted by nature for a well-specified role in society. In satisfying that nature, each person attains both his fulfillment and a sense of belonging to the whole. A lovely idea! But John Dewey, for one, challenged it fundamentally. He charged that it is, in effect, a scheme for retarding the great plurality of forms of activity that people are eager to undertake and capable of accomplishing. It is a formula for arresting human flourishing. Dewey, the pragmatist, insisted that there are no forms of finality in the universe. Rather, change and novelty are universal and irreducible traits of the whole. Accordingly, the good of life consists in learning how to act effectively with processes of change. Growth replaces a certain stasis as the generic nature of the good. The aims and possibilities of life are envi-sioned in very different forms by the pragmatist and the Platonist. For many an earnest seeker, such inquiries surpass all others for their bearing on the nature and meaning of human existence.

For love of the good, there is a profusion of concerns, both forbidding and exciting, that we must take into account. To do it well requires many virtues: discernment, courage, imagination, realism, and a gift for generalization—among others. Their exercise defines much of the philosophic enterprise. The completion of a philosophic appraisal, incorporating vast ranges of vital life, would consist of fairly definite proposals for the conduct of life, predicated on knowing better. That is the consummation of wisdom.

To be sure, most appraisals can safely be more limited than a philosophic tour de force. Those persons who have the experience and information pertinent to a given predicament are those who know better. A teenaged boy believes that the best life is one of unconstrained hedonism. His father knows that such a life would be a disaster. He knows that hedonistic practice precludes the recognition and husbanding of powers that will prove invaluable to his son over a lifetime and will sustain the greatest goods. He also knows that capitulation to self-indulgence surrenders the inner resistances to ever more reckless and irresponsible temptations. Father's aim is not to demonstrate that happiness is good and misery is bad; that question is settled. Nor is he of a mind to deduce a normative judgment from a descriptive. He is trying to help his son! He fears that the boy is pursuing a disastrous course. He would like to convince him of that, but if there is not immediate success in that venture, father will insist that son not follow the treacherous and self-destructive inclination. Son believes that a life consisting of instant gratifications would be marvelously happy. Father is wiser. He knows better. He tells son to clean up his room, get rid of the headphones, and apply himself to his homework.

Broader questions are treated in a like manner. In some influential circles, the traditional family has been observed to be a scene of patriarchal oppression, and a new world of happiness, equality, and fulfillment awaits its abolition. But opposing argument contends that males raised without strong fathers are disastrously prone to all manner of social pathologies. Adult men, moreover, who do not have the responsibilities of caring for a family are more apt to be given to crime, violence, emotional disturbance, failure in work, drug addiction, and alcoholism. Fewer men (the opposition continues) will choose marriage or stay in marriage if they have what they perceive to be a marginal or unappreciated role in it. Now, what is at issue in this controversy? Nobody is contending that oppression, addiction, pathology, emotional disability, and the like are desirable. Nobody is saying that love, security, responsibility, and emotional strength are undesirable. Truly at issue are questions of the following sort: What environment is most conducive to the socialization, maturation, and happiness of the young? What individuals have the dedication requisite to providing that environment? Are there differences in the upbringing appropriate to male and female? How does the presence or absence of children affect the lives of adults? What divisions of responsibility between husband and wife are most conducive to the welfare of all? What sorts of bonding between adult males and females prove to be most satisfying to both? If perfect harmony is impossible, what sorts of accommodation might be worked out that would tend to maintain the endurance and happiness of the bond? Appraisal and readjustment proceed. The answers to these questions might be uncertain and ambivalent, but the one who has them knows better, and we cherish his wisdom. The focal issue here is the status of the family. If and when the answers to these questions are unambiguously available, we will have rather little indecision regarding this vital matter—which is not to say that a generally desirable social form is best for each and every individual.

A similar analysis applies to the broadest and most urgent moral problems: the nature of justice, for example. Each proposal—whether it be that of Aristotle, Locke, Marx, Rawls, or whomever—anticipates that the social order founded on justice will (when suitable conditions exist) promote harmony, stability, high morale, and other good things. The author of each of these theories would renounce his brainchild if in fact it produced runaway strife, mayhem, poverty, and misery. The nature of the controversy—once again—centers very largely on beliefs concerning the results that will be achieved or could be achieved consequent upon a proposed social arrangement. Any system of justice has its peculiar advantages and disadvantages. Certain goods and evils are distinctive of each. Moral considerations stand in uneasy tension with other moral considerations. Accordingly, you will say, the controversy is not necessarily resolved by knowing better. I have already remarked that the method of appraisal does not preclude indecision and disagreement. No method does, but we might choose between alternative modes of deliberation by considering how each is answerable to the actual toils of life rather than to criteria of theoretical elegance and rather than catering to pristine intuitions. To observe, moreover, that different schemes of justice would both support and exclude different goods is not to bring the controversy to a standstill. Push the philosophic appraisal further: What is your appraisal, and how does it differ from mine? *What* goods are sacrificed or secured in the alternative cases? *How much* sacrifice occurs, and how much good is secured? These questions admit of answers. The evidence will show, in fact, that all schemes of justice are not equal.

Philosophic appraisal can be a long and complex process, with many opportunities for misjudgment and disagreement. This topic will reappear and be refined, especially in chapter 5. But for now let it be asserted that, in the company of candid experience, it is the only source of wisdom. Many philosophers, however, covet something quicker and more decisive, such as *The* form of the good, *The* word of God,[4] or a categorical imperative. These are mere artifices. I have elsewhere called such stratagems prejudicial simplifications of the moral condition.[5] They are prejudicial because they neglect crucial features of the moral life. Perhaps but a single consideration—if not produced of mere fancy—is isolated from out of a mass of mortally important concerns and is declared to be singularly decisive. An individual might believe, to be sure, that he has an absolute and unmistakable obligation to act in a certain way on the basis of a single principle. He might hold, with Locke, that reason obliges him "never to interfere in the life, health, liberty, and possessions of another." That might be a highly serviceable principle, but it is nei-ther omnicompetent nor unexceptionable in the tragic and varying contin-gencies of the moral life. And surely it is not drawn from reason alone, as Locke supposed. It is in effect the result of philosophic appraisal—of a sym-pathetic and experienced analysis of the possibilities and limitations of human conduct, which Locke himself mistook for the deliverance of a priori reason.

d. Foundations

One of the commonest errors among philosophers is to assume that we must commence normative deliberation already in possession of moral founda-tions. We must have an impregnable standard of human perfection, or a uni-versal principle, or a rock-bottom set of rights already in hand. Accordingly, they devote sweat and reputation to the production of such a foundation. The solution to specific questions then lies in the application of this won-derful device. The philosophers have the order of events exactly turned around. Universal principles, moral ideals, and foundational convictions—so far as they are deserving of credence—are *consequent* to long labors, experi-ence, and judgment—not antecedent to them. A lifetime of courageous and pertinent inquiry coupled with the lessons of worldly practice might lead to a deep confidence regarding the paramount goods that human existence can sustain. One has become confident that he knows better. He has finally *attained* a foundation. Such a foundation can be sure without being dogmatic. One should acknowledge that he has more to learn and should be capable of learning. To recognize these imperatives is not tantamount to flirting with relativism, however. I must be a fallibilist regarding even the law of gravity; I acknowledge that it is possible that our understanding of the phenomenon will undergo some refinement or limitation. Still, I am warranted in putting a huge measure of confidence in it. I might be equally confident in main-taining that it is better to maintain one's integrity than to grovel for the sake of popularity, and my confidence might be measured in my willingness to suffer ostracism for the principle. It is conceivable, nevertheless, that some hitherto unrecognized consideration might modify my conviction. Until the (unlikely) occasion that such a consideration actually comes before me, I will remain steadfast.

Once some wisdom has been attained, of course, it can be taught to others, and in historical fact, this is what happens. The wisdom of the fathers is passed to succeeding generations, and perhaps it is celebrated in song and story, as it ought to be. Unfortunately, such teachings become ritualistic, the wisdom behind them is lost, and they become resistant to further appraisal.

To possess such a foundation is not the same as to declare it universal. The extent to which certain norms and ends of conduct can be extended to indefinitely many and varied populations and circumstances is a matter to be discovered, not to be proclaimed a priori. It can hardly be a decisive objection against the foundation of knowing better that neither it nor the evaluations that emerge from it will enjoy universal assent. No body of ideas has ever accomplished such a marvel. Universal moral consensus is never to be had. I am confident, however, that no intellectual procedure could move us closer to consensus than this one of candid and searching philosophic appraisal. I am also confident of this: any mind in love with the good has no resource to compare with it.

Those who produce universal and certain principles antecedent to philosophic appraisal are doing little more than foisting their prejudices upon us. Others, who are skeptical of these traditional philosophic ambitions, assume that the failure to achieve them spells the termination of moral philosophy as a serious discipline. All the while, the notion of philosophic appraisal lies dormant and unknown—at least in academic circles. As I mentioned in the preface, however, I take what I subsequently named philosophic appraisal to be modeled after the wisdom of the Socratic school. A philosophy makes a genuine contribution to human good when it tells us more about the nature of man and the world than we knew before, and when it explains how we can appropriate this knowledge for the moral life. There have been several philosophers who have succeeded rather well in this, including in recent history Santayana and Dewey. Unlike the pallid exercises that have dominated the Anglo-American department of philosophy for the last half century, each of these two—each in his own way—articulated a synoptic vision of man and nature, where the determining principle of their reflections was the bearing of these investigations on human order and aspiration.

I intend that the succeeding chapters also provide some life-supporting wisdom. They will take up some of the questions that belong to moral philosophy in the Socratic mode. Chapter 2, "The Cosmic Landscape,"[6] will give an account of the attempts of several philosophers to know better from the most comprehensive standpoint. They investigate not only the nature of the whole; they also ask—to put it simply—what it is good for. How does the nature of things answer to our fears and aspirations, and how does it discipline them? What are its resources and limitations for human existence? (A suggestion of the import of this inquiry was just given by reference to Plato and Dewey.) One's conception of the whole of things both enlarges and chastens his thinking about the meanings of human life, and, as we shall see, several moral philosophies are given distinctive force and character by the nature of their encompassing worldview.

Chapter 3, "Worldly Metaphysics," is a continuation of "The Cosmic Landscape." It propounds a morally pertinent description of nature. It is largely a reconstruction of John Dewey's naturalistic metaphysics. Dewey's philosophy provides a splendid integration of moral thought with beliefs about the nature of nature. His is certainly the most thorough and discerning such effort in the past century, and it is a sterling model to follow; but it is flawed, sometimes seriously. It invigorates our power to know better, but in some instances it neglects crucial features of the nature of nature.

"By Nature," chapter 4, gives an account of what is meant by a moral philosophy according to nature, but it is not an attempt to resurrect theories of natural law. Nature has features that are decidedly normative in conduct and aspiration. It provides disciplines and direction for life, as we shall find. We cannot suppose, however, that it does so for beings who are not already invested with some assortment of moral concerns. It is for those who seek enlightenment about a just and happy life. *Within that context*, the appropriate study of man and nature provides wisdom for the conduct of life. The result is to know better, not to possess infallible principles. Pertinent distinctions between nature, custom, and convention are introduced. Custom is not an autonomous domain of moral values juxtaposed to nature nor is convention. The historicist critique of moral judgment is evaluated and rejected.

"The Moral Order" is chapter 5. Rather than thinking in terms of theoretically derived principles, morality is examined as forms of conduct necessary for the preservation and prosperity of associated life. The investigation of these forms is idle, futile, or pernicious if it is undertaken in ignorance of the nature of the forces of human nature for both destruction and accomplishment. An initial discussion of the moral nature of man is advanced, together with an analysis of the sorts of moral considerations that are pertinent to the formation of judgment. These are the considerations to which we are responsive *as moral beings*, and they are normative according to nature.

In chapter 6, "Justice and the Division of Moral Labor," an account is given of justice, duties, and rights as instruments for sustaining and enhancing a moral order—rather than as disembodied principles. The fundamental notion of the division of moral labor is introduced. It would relieve us of the needlessly burdensome assumption that our moral responsibilities extend indiscriminately to all persons.

The discussion of the life of eros begins in earnest with chapter 7, "Priorities." Our common and passionate tendencies to self-indulgence are taken as most subversive of a vigorous moral order and the achievement of ideal goods. Hedonism is contrasted with virtue, principally as characterized by Aristotle, and the classic equation of virtue and happiness is examined and, with reservations, defended. In accordance with the terms articulated in chapter 4, virtue is in accordance with nature—not least because it is the essential ingredient in sustaining our most fundamental goods. At the same time, hedonism is flatly rejected as a satisfying life. Despite its unwisdom, even so, it seems to be the plague of current thought and practice. In what sorts of social order is virtue apt to languish or to flourish? Which forms of social order might themselves be objects of love?

Chapter 8, "Custom and Morality," characterizes and defends morality according to custom. Custom is not essentially in contrast to either nature or intelligence. Wisdom according to nature, indeed, is potently embodied in custom but by no means in every custom. Moral education is most effectively undertaken as inseparable from custom.

In "Uncommon Goods," chapter 9, the nature of the erotic life is explored more fully, at first by means of a comparative analysis of Plato and Nietzsche, the two greatest exponents of eros. This is followed by a rendering of three ideal goods: the scientific ideal, integrity, and completions of nature. The ideal of individuality, properly construed, is incorporated into that of integrity. The costs, corruptions, and blessings of these goods are considered.

Some of the ways in which life can have meaning within the framework of nature are characterized in chapter 10, "Meanings." The first task is to distinguish morbid forms of the question "What is the meaning of life?" from constructive and fruitful forms. What are the meanings of life for a free and disillusioned spirit? They might in fact be plentiful. Death need not be dreadful, and it does not nullify the meanings of life. In full cognizance of human finitude, wisdom according to nature has much to affirm. It is consummated in a form of natural piety.

Notes

1. An extensive treatment of representative attempts to make ethics into a science is in chap. 3 of my *Rediscovering the Moral Life: Philosophy and Human Practice* (Amherst, NY: Prometheus Books, 1993).

2. My thinking on this topic has been especially helped by the work of James Q. Wilson, *The Moral Sense* (New York: The Free Press, 1993).

3. At this point, I don't want to be unduly fastidious about the meaning of "moral." Nothing so distinctive as an Aristotelian or Kantian conception of morality is suggested. The definition of the word has to be rather inclusive, or our thinking will exclude a range of worthy and effective human capacities that are unmistakably vital to the conduct of life.

4. Different gods have different words, and the word of just one god is subject to alternative interpretations. Still, if we did have a clear and certain word from an omnipotent and judging god, that word would no doubt be as decisive a moral consideration as could be imagined. In any case, the process remains an appraisal.

5. See *Rediscovering the Moral Life*, esp. chaps. 3 and 7.

6. I borrow this phrase from Santayana. It comes from the essay "The Elements and Function of Poetry," in *Interpretations of Poetry and Religion*, vol. 2 of *The Works of George Santayana*, Triton ed. (New York: Charles Scribner's Sons, 1936).

| 2 |

The Cosmic Landscape

Philosophy occasionally attains a kind of grandeur: a thinker produces a synoptic vision of the nature of things and with it a conception of the possibilities and limitations of human life. Such a philosophy answers to a common need. What reflective person has not pondered the nature of the encompassing whole and its pertinence to human destiny? For most persons, of course, an answer is given ready to hand in some existing religion, so the wonder is promptly laid to rest. Or, if religion seems unpalatable, one might hastily conclude that there is nothing to know about the order of nature that could have any bearing on how he conceives his own existence. The more inquisitive and harder to please, however, might study philosophy, and one might discover a deep affinity for an existing system of thought. Subsequently, what passes for philosophy is a tinkering within the details of the system, or perhaps a desperate defense of it, no matter what. Only the rarest thinker will be still harder to please. Rather than be caught up in ideas per se, he is bound to ask of any philosopher whether he really knows whereof he speaks. This questioner doggedly insists that what he knows of the world and what he experiences of it are not sufficiently accommodated by what a master has written. This is not an invitation to subjective and irresponsible theorizing. It is a demand to know the world better and more pertinently than it has been known before. The demand is extremely difficult to satisfy. Most attempts are failures, but the successes are the masterpieces of human speculation. For his part, such a philosopher creates an ideal good in his own right: his thinking elevates his life beyond normal animal consciousness. He has conceived and articulated human reality in the whole nature of things, and he thereby endows his self-knowledge with cosmic meaning.

The attempt to comprehend the whole of things, which is popularly, if loosely, called metaphysics, might be intended by its author to accomplish many goals. Not unusually, there is the hope of discovering some kind of being that gives unfailing assurance to claims of knowledge and moral good—the traditional foundational enterprise. This endeavor has been widely, but not universally, discredited. I am with those who think that this absolutist ambition is in vain, but I do not suppose in consequence that there is no way to determine that some knowledge claims are more reliable than others. Nor do I suppose that a synoptic vision is either impossible or of no practical consequence. Whatever else they might have had in mind, such thinkers as Aristotle, Lucretius, Augustine, Kant, and Hegel offered us comprehensive characterizations of the nature of the whole and of the human undertaking within it. Their value resides not in the success of their venture after infallible principles, but in the thoroughness and accuracy of their characterizations of what exists and in their ability to discriminate therein what is of real consequence to human eros. They seek to learn what the world is by its nature good for and what it isn't good for. It makes no small difference whether it is like Aristotle said it is, or whether Augustine had it right, or Hobbes. Remember the predicament of the traveler to foreign places recounted in the preceding chapter? He wasn't looking for a deductive system of ideas. He needed to *know better* about the conditions that would determine his life in his intended abode, and the person who could help him with that would be of immeasurable benefit. Philosophers might help us to know better in that highly beneficial way. They might tell us whether there are conditions in the very order of things that could discipline our aspiration and be congenial to our industry. Perhaps, as many have thought, the crucial requirement is a proper understanding of both man and nature and of the relation between them. Philosophers can also lead us astray. We make a fateful gambit, as I have suggested, in throwing in with Dewey rather than Plato, for example.

In part, the inquiries that have occupied all such thinkers have been properly delegated to scientists, and philosophers must be prepared to appropriate such knowledge where it is needed. The formation of a synoptic vision—and with moral relevance—is not a science, however, and is not reducible to science. In the form of metaphysics that I prefer, at any rate, what we seek is not causal explanation but discrimination, description and generalization, drawing from all of human experience. Such generalizations are selected, formulated, and ordered in a way to offer a view of the whole, one that gives scope and clarity to our understanding of the human condition. I will call this a *worldly* metaphysics.

Our prospective traveler has a choice of whether to go or not to go. Short of suicide, we don't have a choice of whether the universe will be our abode, but it is nonetheless difficult to know what it is good for—what it can and cannot hatch for us. Wisdom is scarce, and a good philosophy might provide much of it. It is commonly pointed out that the philosophers who produce these synoptic visions are prone, in their human frailty, to weave into the fabric of the universe characteristics that they deeply wish to be there, whether they are or not, and they are likewise apt to ignore or deny characteristics that they wish were otherwise. How human it is to deny unwelcome truths! Evil, for example, is sometimes declared to be somehow unreal. Perhaps, too, an epistemology is concocted that will allow us to affirm what we yearn for and to deny what is unwelcome. Yes, there are many obstacles in the way of wisdom, but this is not to say that the undertaking must be futile. Philosophers can strive to be courageous and honest and can succeed in some measure. There is, in fact, real wisdom embodied in many philosophies.

In the present chapter, I will survey some of them to see how each, by its distinctive teaching, would impart a particular form of wisdom about the conduct of life and its ideal values. The lessons are heterogeneous, so there is much at stake in thinking clearly about the alternatives. The selection is unsystematic and far from catholic, but the cases seem especially pertinent and influential. They focus on successes and failures in discerning morally pertinent features of the universe. They are presented as visions of the cosmic landscape, as Santayana called it, indicating what their authors took to be "the large facts" that determine the human estate. They are not elucidated in terms of the technicalities of their composition, and my portraits will not go beyond an elementary account of these philosophies. Scholars are sure to find my understanding problematical in this or that particular, but to be faultless about every detail is not essential to my intent. I am concerned to provide insight into the moral resources and meaning of these distinctive systems of thought. I wish to discern how each succeeds in knowing better— or worse, as the case may be—rather than in providing a geometric explanation of everything.

a. PHILOSOPHIES AS SOURCES OF WISDOM

Plato's thought is often taken as paradigmatic of what we would hope a philosophy to accomplish and as the benchmark for all subsequent efforts. It discloses an intelligible order of the universe, whose nature, if we could know it, would assure unfailing knowledge and evaluation. This nature, determined by the form of the Good, provides the pattern to which we must conform to attain wisdom and happiness. Indeed, the constituting principles of the cosmos include nothing imperfect or evil, so the defects of existence constitute a lesser domain of being.

Whatever else it does, Plato's theory of forms expresses the conviction that nature is teleological—it tends to characteristic perfections, and these characters define the really real. The forms must be changeless and eternal, else they would not be perfect, but everything that we experience undergoes mutation. Accordingly, there must be an order transcendent of the experienced world—that "heaven of ideas," so difficult to know but crucial to our well-being. In terms that presumably would be validated by the intelligible order, Plato discerns the nature of both human and political perfection. The highest human excellence is available only to those of the "golden" nature, which few possess. Those with the "silver" are greater in number, but most numerous are those of "brass" and "iron." All natures, however, are suited for definite occupations in the social order, so in a wisely ordered polis, everyone, presumably, would be doing what he does best. All are at home in the harmonious social and cosmic order.

Plato also provides a manual of the nature of typical hazards and failures in human endeavor. This might be the philosopher who disdains conditions that suffer change, but he displays an astonishing fund of worldly wisdom in discerning how societies and individuals go right and go wrong. The account of a permissive and egalitarian society in book 8 of *The Republic*, for example, is without equal. Finally, he assures us that the order of things is of a sort to constrain and discipline our stupidity and wickedness: the follies and corruptions of life are a consequence of failure to conform to the divine order, removed from which there is only confusion, discord, and suffering.

Such is the familiar outline of this philosophy. I cannot believe, however, that Plato regarded his own thinking to be nearly so tidy and assured. Often enigmatic and ironic, his writings offer innumerable clues that one ought to be imaginative and discerning in trying to grasp their import. *The Republic*, for example, contains abundant evidence that one of Plato's intentions is to ridicule the pretensions of utopian political thinking, not to defend it. It is crucial to consider what the meaning of Plato's philosophy might be if he himself would have us be skeptical about a literal reading of it. That is an issue to be confronted after taking a further look at some of his remarkable ideas.

What of *The Symposium?* Even a brief appreciation must give attention to this work of surpassing genius. The notion of the hierarchy of being, consummated by the eternal and unchanging, is once again conspicuous, but it is not clear that the ideas of greatest moment in this discourse are always to be taken as brute fact. Each of the genial guests at Agathon's banquet gives his account of the nature of love, of the god Eros. Finally, Socrates relates the teachings of Diotima, wise woman of Mantinea. Mortal man, she had told him, is driven by eros for what is immortal. Some people are pregnant in body only, Diotima continues, and they find their immortality in giving birth to children. Others are pregnant in the soul, and they yearn with a divine passion to give birth to the beauty within them. What are these things of beauty? Wisdom and virtue, she says, above all the wisdom of ordering states and families.[1] Hence we honor the wisdom of a Lycurgus or Solon. Homer and Hesiod are also among the immortals, for their poetry is immortal. Such persons beget what is "immortal," that is, creations of supreme beauty, and they are immortalized for doing so. All these parturitions are called instances of beauty (*to kalon*).[2] Beauty itself is one and divine, and we are driven by eros to contemplate it directly. In communion with this lustrous being, a man will bring forth true virtue.

That which comes into existence, undergoes change, and passes away, Diotima admonishes, is inferior to true being, *but it is nevertheless the fate of mortal life*. It is not to be escaped. So we bring forth into the changing world that which is ideal, and live by what is ideal, so far as we can. We give birth to what is immortal, or we contribute to its propagation, and we thereby have some participation in the highest. This is the teaching of Diotima. Just after her story has been told, Alcibiades bursts upon the scene, and he tells the company of the absolutely singular beauty of Socrates. Socrates is the greatest lover. The objects of his love are wisdom and beauty, and his eros has given birth to incomparable virtue.

The portrait of Socrates is among the invaluable legacies bequeathed to us by Plato, and generations of souls have meditated on its meaning and been inspired by it.[3] Plato's conception of the highest virtue is more immediately accessible in *The Republic*, where the presentation is less dramatic and more systematic. Wisdom, courage, temperance, and justice are given elaborate, sometimes idiosyncratic and sometimes controversial, definitions, and their interdependencies articulated. It is a heroic account of the ordering of the human soul in a manner to be equal to whatever contingencies will beset it, after the manner of Socrates himself, who went cheerfully to his death rather than act contrary to himself.

All virtues are given by nature: they are inherent aptitudes, but they are not equally distributed. Only the golden nature is capable of virtue in its fullest. For any person, however, his virtues require an appropriately educative polis for their realization. Hence there are two great engines of moral prosperity, nature and the polis. Nature alone is insufficient. Plato is acutely aware of how even the best of natures is susceptible to arrested development and corruption. The polis, too, is insufficient by itself, for it cannot create something out of nothing.[4]

The account of the unity of the virtues, accompanied by the portrait of Socrates, is one of the most stirring renderings of human excellence available in world literature. Of course there are many ways that we might question it, and there are competing ideals. If the questioning is undertaken candidly, the inquiry is one of the most wide-ranging, demanding, and fruitful challenges that can engage the human imagination. No doubt what Socrates calls justice in the soul is beyond the competence of any but the most unusual sort of person, and probably it comes principally as a gift of the gods.[5] Inspired by the Socratic ideal, eros can be rewarded with lesser achievements, but the ideal was not articulated to be a popular attraction.

I remarked earlier that it is difficult to think that Plato intended his own philosophy to be taken invariably at face value.[6] Philosophy, he held, is a spiritual discipline: it is a matter, in large part, of learning how to attain wisdom and virtue. The writing of philosophic dialogues, moreover, is meant to help others to attain these invaluable powers: a proper teacher always intends that his tutelage make his pupil a better man. The way to satisfy the Platonic discipline, according to orthodox readings, is to acquire knowledge of the forms, and virtue and happiness follow inevitably. But the acquisition of wisdom is subtler, more elusive, and wider-ranging than such readings suggest, and to help others in such a quest requires a varied arsenal of devices. It is pertinent, accordingly, to make some (hurried) observations about how it seems that Plato is a teacher of wisdom. Thus it might be that we become more capable of sharing it with him. He had more in mind than to set forth premises and conclusions in a complacent logic, for that alone will never lead us to the ideal. A serious teacher, after all, can also aim at being suggestive and provocative; he can use ironies, silence, and dramatic action to prompt his readers, and he might well regard complacency as a sign of deficient intellect. He can challenge human powers in addition to those of intelligence: wisdom also demands courage, independence, self-awareness, humility, insight, and imagination. Plato suggests that it also requires suffering.[7]

Wisdom is not just the possession of an object of knowledge. Its actuality requires a multitude of capacities and strategies. It will be revealing to ask of the nature of this eros that drives us to the ideal. According to Diotima, Eros is born of Need and Resource. He is "barefoot and homeless, sleeping on the naked earth, in doorways, or in the very streets beneath the stars of heaven, and always partaking of his mother's poverty. But, secondly, he brings his father's resourcefulness to his designs upon the beautiful and the good, for he is gallant, impetuous, and energetic, a mighty hunter, and a master of device and artifice—at once desirous and full of wisdom, a lifelong seeker after truth, an adept in sorcery, enchantment, and seduction" (*Symposium*, 203c–d). Addressing eros, obviously, is by no means a merely logical task. Plato knows what might beckon to the erotic soul and ignite it, what might turn it and capture it, and he incorporates his supreme gifts as poet and dramatist with those of thinker. This is not to say that he is willing to abide indefinitely with contradiction or to accept the unproved. He emphatically rejects misology. One does not have to be an analytical philosopher, however, in order to be a conscientious seeker of truth. When Diotima says we necessarily love the good and the beautiful, we could easily refute the claim; that is what the analyst does, and he lets it go at that. Plato, too, could refute the claim several times over, but he is here being evocative, not logical. How *can* one direct a youth toward becoming a better man? The natural history of knowledge and love of wisdom is not an altogether orderly affair.

Just to fathom Plato's beliefs regarding the nature and worth of our cognitive capacities is exceedingly difficult, and no interpreter can be cocksure about his own conclusions. It is remarkable to witness the extent to which the dialogues—most of all the middle ones—seem to accumulate contradictions. They gyrate, most notably, between lengthy expressions of dogmatism and then of unrelieved skepticism. Each stance, moreover, is at various points gently mocked.[8] Most scholars are determined to read such passages in a way to turn them into a rational system after all, but that betrays a mind somewhat less inquisitive and chastened than Plato's.

Why do we find such remarkable juxtapositions in his texts? It is helpful to remember that Plato is as much poet and dramatist as philosopher. Accordingly, he might be prompted on a given occasion to portray a manner of thinking and declaiming rather than to expound a doctrine of his own. If you were a wise and gifted dramatist, and you wrote dialogues on philosophic questions, you would not make every character but one a dunce, and you would make no character without blemish. Fragments of both brilliance and the wrongheaded would turn up everywhere, though not in equal proportions, and never in an entirely ordered and finished form.

Perhaps, in the larger context, Plato is suggesting that wisdom is neither complacency nor finality, nor is it despair for any serviceable knowledge. He urges (as Aristotle was to do) that the good life lies between the extremes of excess and defect, which are always to be shunned. Did Plato believe that dogmatism and wholesale skepticism are such extremes? Does he wish to evoke a vision of the pursuit of wisdom and virtue in a world where perfect certainty of its ultimate principles might escape us? Plato's is habitually taken as the paradigm of systematic philosophy, but we might reasonably propose quite the opposite: not only has he no system, but he gives little evidence that he is trying to produce one, as he moves in and out of a theory of forms and different renderings of the nature of knowledge. We would, nevertheless, be assured of at least one constant in his thought: the love of virtue and nobility in the soul.

While Plato is a more fugitive and demanding thinker than one might initially suppose, he undoubtedly believed that philosophy would be rewarded, wisdom would be rewarded. Surely he had great sympathy for the theory of forms, if not certainty about it. There is no reason to doubt that he believed that nature possesses an intelligible and beneficent order, but to be assured of its precise nature might be beyond human competence. Socrates speaks with this suggestion in several passages, especially in *The Apology*. His remark in *The Phaedo* that philosophy is a preparation for death should be taken in this vein. I take Socrates' declaration that he never in his life had the slightest fear of death to be forthright. To overcome fear of death was not his problem. On the other hand, it fulfills Socrates' divine calling to conduct his finite and limited existence by pursuing virtue through love of wisdom. The mortal soul, however, in the coils of the body, can never attain unalloyed knowledge and virtue. Philosophy, accordingly, strives for that which could only be perfected in a physically unencumbered soul.

Reservations about the literal meaning of Plato's writings, the critic will say, disembowel his philosophy. What good is it if it fails to deliver apodictic certainty? It delivers much, in fact. It is noteworthy that Plato's account of perfect virtue in *The Republic* is presented without any claim that the portrait is actually modeled after the forms. Socrates confesses to having no such knowledge, but he does make a superb case for the life of virtue on its merits. That is, justice in the soul is the condition of the highest happiness. The virtue of virtue lies both in its conduciveness to *eudaimonia* and its contribution to civic life, and the devoted lifelong pursuit of virtue gives our existence its highest meaning. Such ends are not deduced from the very idea of the good.[9] They are embraced by the aspiring soul who courageously searches the world's contingencies, hazards, and ideal possibilities. The great good of nobility of character is an idea that Plato never relinquishes, and that good is discovered and confirmed in experience. To aspire to justice in the soul in a world that cannot be confidently known in its ultimate characteristics requires much knowledge of man, nature, and politics, if not of the transcendent forms.[10] Plato is confident that he possesses much of this knowledge. He knows the typical traits of human nature, for example, its characteristic weaknesses and strengths and its possible excellence.

Speaking through Socrates, he is acutely conscious of the lures of corruption and of our great susceptibility to it, yet the constitution of things tends to be unforgiving of weakness: a slight departure from the path of virtue leads easily to vice. The achievement of the good life, according to Plato, permits little deviation from virtue and requires discipline and dedication. All this can be true without having to accept the theory of forms as such. Did Plato himself, moreover, literally believe that Homer and others had to have beheld the very form of Beauty itself in order to produce their immortal works? Did he likewise believe that the laws of Lycurgus were actually perfect and that memory of him will be literally everlasting? Plato uses metaphors like "divine" and "immortal" in reference to the works of mortal life to convey a notion of human ultimacy, which evokes the deepest feelings of awe and reverence. Neither is it juvenile hyperbole to speak of perfections. It is, once again, to use an expression that imparts a sense of the apex of extraordinary human accomplishment. I am not trying to rewrite Plato. It is very likely that he believed that there are ideas of such perfections and that these ideas are constitutive of being. The question is whether he would confidently assert that he knew them. Only a god could be sure, as Socrates likes to say. To *love* such a quest, nevertheless, is indispensable to wisdom.

Thus, Plato can be read without accepting the theory of forms as a precisely and finally determined doctrine—and with immense profit. Here a critic will ask, "If the theory is not essential to Plato's moral philosophy, why need we concern ourselves with cosmic geography?" The question is fatal if we assume that we are trying to formulate a deductive system, where Good is known absolutely, and we unerringly classify particular events as belonging to that form or not. But that is not what knowing better is about. We want to know what the encompassing whole might hold for us—for our chastening disappointment, perhaps, and for our wisdom. The belief that the essences of things—whatever they might be—are changeless is itself a fateful assumption. Surely nature is ordered with a certain severity: it is intolerant of vice and congenial to virtue. Something has to account for the observable order and its perfections, so we experiment with earnest conjectures on the subject. Without such reflections, in any event, thinking about the meaning, or meanings, of life in the cosmos would be sorrowfully limited and undisciplined.

Someone in whom Socratic yearnings cannot be aroused must be indifferent to these matters, but someone who is moved by them will seek to know whether or how the world might tend to such outcomes. He becomes engaged in philosophic appraisal. His inquiries might, to be sure, lead him to conclude that the possibilities of the world bear no resemblance to this classic account of them. On the other hand, he might come to believe that Socrates knew better, after all, and he would try to follow something like a Socratic way of life.

The cosmic picture according to Aristotle might be more suitable than Plato's in giving context to a Socratic life. They share the idea that eros is the primal force in the cosmos, and their views about the perfection of human nature are nearly identical (though Plato's are more nuanced and more compelling in their presentation). They likewise hold that nature is a hierarchically ordered system of ends—*final causes*, in Aristotelian parlance—where each nature has its proper place. While he shares with Plato the conviction that contemplation of the eternal and unchanging is a supreme good, Aristotle asserts that the grasp of these divine objects is impertinent to practical life. Hence he distinguishes theoretical from practical wisdom, the latter of which occupies itself with matters that admit of being other than they are. The ultimate goal of practice is still the completion of human nature. Particular decisions, however, are conditioned by so many situational contingencies that ethics, he insists, can never be a science. The man of practical wisdom has knowledge of the telos of human striving, so, in effect, he aims always at the act of virtue, but the determination of what that act might be in a given situation can be problematic. Accordingly, extensive knowledge of practical affairs is vital to human excellence. Aristotle himself exhibits this kind of wisdom in masterful fashion in his *Politics*.

For most of those who ponder the nature of the whole, the uppermost question is whether it contains or presupposes gods and of what sorts. Philosophies that take this primary focus often display insight into the human condition. Despite the interest of theological speculations, I pass them by, impatient to contend with the problems characteristic of modern metaphysics. Variants of the Platonic and/or Aristotelian philosophy, adapted to Christian thought, flourished through the Middle Ages and the Renaissance. They were given a fundamental shock by Descartes, who was locked in embrace with the newly emerging physical science. Nature, he explained, is nothing but matter in motion: dead, inert, matter and nothing more, propelled mechanically and meaninglessly through eternal night. The qualities formerly attributed to it (the so-called secondary qualities) took refuge in the self-enclosed sanctum of mind. Nature is no longer our home; it is indeed wholly other than anything human. It could no longer be conceived as holding a place for us in a moral order. The grief from this uncompromising alienation is aggravated by the concomitant conclusion that we have no experience of nature. The objects of direct consciousness—all things lovely and hateful, the rich manifold of immediate experience—have been expelled from nature and have taken up residence within the mind, and they have no ascertainable relationship to the external world. Henceforth, the problem of knowledge is to determine how an internal image can correspond to a (postulated) external object that cannot itself be experienced. Other persons, too, could be assumed to exist only in consequence of (a tortured) inference.

The great moral world has retreated within subjective mind. Philosophers henceforth occupy themselves by scouring the inner realm for norms of conduct. Lo and behold: they find moral laws contained within this circumscribed and autonomous domain! It could be radically liberating. No longer saddled with the idea of a natural hierarchy of stations, Locke, for example, was free to declare that all men are "free, equal, and independent," and between them "all the power and jurisdiction is reciprocal, no one having more than another." All men are endowed with equal rights, known to reason, which the civil and political orders are bound to respect.[11] The state does not exist by nature. It is an artifact of human reason, deriving its just powers exclusively therefrom and obliged to be its obedient servant. Neither can we speak of the good according to nature. Locke says that each man pursues his own good in his own way, so long as he does not transgress the rights of others. In keeping with the denial of natural hierarchies, he is also prompt to assert the equality of talents among men. Anyone may achieve much, so long as he is not oppressed by arbitrary power and providing he will apply himself.

In accordance with Cartesian thinking, Locke tended to regard the individual as a separate substance. Human nature is complete without benefit of social participation, and society is a sum of essentially separate beings. Fully actual individuals, each endowed with reason, rights, and a conception of his own good, convene to establish the body politic. This form of individualism proved an effective assumption in throwing off the weight of established institutions. Later thinkers who were not followers of Locke nevertheless found this conception both incorrect and repugnant, for it denied the social nature of man and the good of man in social union.

If we suppose that Descartes gave us the right picture of things, then we can proceed in no other way than to consult the inner beacon, the light of reason. In principle, no *worldly* discipline of reason is allowed or needed. But in fact, of course, this is not what was happening. Locke's reliance on reason gave him, in effect, free rein to articulate his liberal allegiances, drawn from his experience and from the ambitions of a class grown impatient with lordly prerogatives. These were largely humane allegiances—there is much to be said for "liberal" or "bourgeois" values—but the putative rationalistic derivation of them is not subject to criticism and modification. Rationalistic moral philosophy pretends to be unchastened by obdurate empirical fact and uninspired by the possibilities lurking in nature and experience.[12] The dualistic philosophy can learn no wisdom from nature, of course, and it struggles with the conception of a virtually impotent experience.

As suggested above, there is at least a certain convenient, albeit spurious, resource in Cartesian dualism, which affords the thinker the opportunity to cloak his hard-won experience in the mantle of infallible reason. Those cases, on the other hand, where the response to the new science took the form of sheer materialism seemed to be more threatening, for mind was reduced to the behavior of matter. In spite of well-reasoned philosophies and well-lived lives to the contrary, materialism is widely believed to be fatal to "spiritual" values. If there is no higher order of being, there can be no source of moral principle at all, so it is believed, and materialists and naturalists can only grovel in sensuality and other ignoble obsessions, while secretly abiding in nihilism. It is widely said that if you are a materialist or a naturalist, you are committed (perhaps unwittingly) to the idea that morality is a chimaera and that there are no ideal values. The philosophy of Locke's predecessor, Thomas Hobbes, would be taken as a case in point. Hobbes considered himself, in fact, to be a Christian and an upholder of Christian values, but he attempted to derive his moral principles exclusively from materialistic premises.

He believed that nature is nothing but matter in motion, and the motion is that discovered by Galileo: an object proceeds in a straight line at a constant force and speed until its motion is stopped or diverted by the force of some other object. Human beings are ruled by the same law, for they are nothing but conglomerates of matter, so a man will pursue his object of desire until forced aside by some other man. This being so, nothing is more important to man than power. Life is "a restless desire of power after power that ceaseth only in death." From the moral standpoint, the state of nature is utterly lawless. When Hobbes observes that in that condition every man has a right to all things, "right" has no moral connotation. It means that, except for sheer force, there is nothing in the state of nature that prohibits anyone from pursuing any object whatever. It is evident that the laws of motion will quickly make life, in the immortal words, "solitary, poor, nasty, brutish, and short." It would be rational, accordingly, for each man to give up his right to all things, provided everyone else does so as well and provided that there is a sovereign power to enforce the peace, which otherwise could not be self-sustaining.[13] With this account, Hobbes defines the dominant conception of the modern state: a mass of inherently unrelated individuals governed by indivisible sovereignty.

When and if some tolerable social order is established, human nature does not change; it acquires no virtue. Nothing in nature or morality can override self-interest. (The laws of motion are not suspended, after all.) The sovereign maintains an equilibrium of these forces by dint of overwhelming strength. This is not an edifying vista, but given his premises, and leaving aside some qualifications, Hobbes' argument is impeccable. Society hovers ever at the brink of anarchy, a condition that will not be wished away by sentimental argument. Little wonder that materialism is widely dreaded.

Of those few who tried to amalgamate the new science with a conception of a supreme good, Spinoza was the most audacious and disciplined. He denied that man, nature, and God are three separate substances. They are one, which may be called God or Nature—an eternal, infinite, and necessary being and without traits of personality.[14] God is not a person. Nature, then, is not providential and is devoid of final causes. The universe does us no favors and intends none. Spinoza is contemptuous of philosophies that rely on a personal god or that resort to teleology. Yet God or Nature possesses the inestimably valuable trait of perfect intelligibility, the nature of which Spinoza sets forth geometrically in the *Ethics.* With apodictic clarity, rational knowledge of God discloses that the mind is an inseparable function of the divine essence and necessity. Possession of this knowledge brings an unqualified acceptance of the necessity in all things. One who loves Spinoza's God is also in a state of perfect freedom—freedom from the anxieties and travails that accompany attachment to finite and mutable objects. Both hope and fear vanish, replaced by perfect peace and the "intellectual love of God." "A free man," Spinoza says, "thinks of nothing less than of death, and his wisdom is not a meditation upon death but upon life." Inconsistently, perhaps, Spinoza held that the embrace of necessity does not imply a withdrawal from diurnal enjoyments and duties. Though the good of the free man no longer rests on possession of finite things, he will join with others in the effort to bring about the conditions where each may effectively "persevere in the power of his own being."

It is a part of wisdom to know the way of the world and to be reconciled to it. Spinoza took such acceptance to its limit. It is made possible by the three traits of being: unity, necessity, and intelligibility.[15] (The predication of any further traits is an error, the consequence of "inadequate and confused" ideas.) Unreserved acceptance also requires a mind that is capable of coming to this knowledge and actually does so. "But all noble things are as difficult as they are rare," Spinoza observes. The garden variety determinist can never be reconciled to events after the manner of Spinoza, for he must also have adequate knowledge of God or Nature as the perfect object of love. Then and only then is one disabused of dependency on transient goods.

The nature of things proves to be supremely good for the rational intellect, and with his formidable mind, Spinoza won a blessed unity with the divine order. It must be admitted, however, that Spinoza's Nature is less than the sum of all things 'twixt heaven and earth. A reductive philosophy fails to accommodate salient sorts of realities, whether good or ill, discerned in candid experience. An earnest soul acknowledges many and varied goods, for example. Perhaps there *is* some sort of moral order, such as we find in the Greek metaphysics of nature, but which is lacking in a universe exhausted in pure intelligibility. To be sure, a soul that has consummated its intellectual love is unconditionally reconciled to necessity, whatever it brings, but a more commodious Nature might possess inherent moral qualities as well. Santayana, who held Spinoza in awe, was constrained to remark, "That the intellect might be perfectly happy in contemplating the truth of the universe, does not render the universe good to every other faculty; good to the heart, good to the flesh, good to the eye, good to the conscience or the sense of justice."[16] In a view of the cosmos without discount, all such goods are real and precious, and they must find their rightful place in a philosophic account of things. At the same time, there are real evils that would not be invisible to a candid philosopher.

Spinoza's reduction led him to a sublime wisdom, but it is significantly different from that of Socrates. A better account of nature insists on recognition of *limits* in the ways of the world, a view conspicuous in Greek thought. There, wisdom consists in large part of having respect for the inherent constraints within the order of things, leading one to have appropriate expectations about the plural and finite goods and evils that the world affords. Spinoza's absolute reconciliation, in contrast, sweeps away all finite attachments. What becomes of the imperative to know and to respect the limits of specific sorts of things? The chastening of our love for this or that particular good, in distinction from other goods, becomes inconsequential. In a crucial sense, Spinoza's love is indiscriminate.

There is precedent for Spinoza's achievement of love for the whole of Being as such, and it is attempted again in some idealists of the nineteenth century. But let us first consider a somewhat different sytem of thought, that of Kant. I have been pointing out that it makes a telling difference in our conception of human possibilities if one philosophy rather than another turns out to approximate to the truth. Just so, the cosmic landscape according to Kant depicts a remarkably distinctive human role in the order of things. He accepted the verdict that Newton's science expressed the whole truth about the physical universe. Accordingly, nature (once more) is nothing but matter in motion, and it is through and through a product of the necessity of physical law (in this case, laws having their origin in the human understanding). Such a universe, taken as such, is without God, freedom, and immortality. These, Kant was sure, are the paramount concerns of human beings. They are not to be denied, however, for the Newtonian world machine is not exhaustive of all that exists. Nature, including human nature, is mere *phenomenon*, or *appearance*, while things as they are in themselves, including rational nature, are *noumena*. While we cannot in the strict sense have knowledge of the noumenal realm, we have established the real *possibility* of the objects of our greatest hopes. We can, therefore, have a rational faith in God, freedom, and immortality. "I have therefore found it necessary to deny *knowledge*, in order to make room for *faith*."

Morality, as Kant conceived it, is incompatible with determinism, for moral responsibility implies unconditioned freedom of the will. That which is not free is subject to neither moral approval nor moral condemnation. Nature, accordingly—including human nature—is without moral worth or even moral pertinence. When Kant declares, "Now, I say, man and, in general, every rational being exists as an end in himself and not merely as a means to be arbitrarily used by this or that will,"[17] he means *rational nature alone* exists as an end in itself. He says so explicitly just a moment later: "The ground of this principle is: rational nature exists as an end in itself."[18] Rational nature is nonhistorical, noncultural, and universal—not a creature of nature in any sense, and it is an end in itself *because* it is rational in this way. Inseparable from its freedom, the moral worth of reason is predicated on its legislation of universal law to which it is also subject. In rapture about the a priori legislative character of rational nature, Kant asserts that the "purity" and "holiness" of the moral law are owing to its being unconditional, necessary, and universal,[19] and no empirical law can satisfy these requirements.

Rational law, then, is a priori and entirely formal; it takes no account of matters of experience. The categorical imperative specifies no particular act. It commands unconditional allegiance to the *form* of universality and necessity. To treat rational nature as an end in itself, therefore, is no more and no less than to conform to the idea of law as such—to observe the categorical imperative: act always on that maxim that you can will to be a universal law for all rational beings. The moral question is simply this: Can a maxim take the form of universality? It is a logical question, not an inquiry into the contingencies of human practice. If it can be universal, then it is your duty to follow it; otherwise, not. What is accomplished? Conformity to law as such. In a bold but consistent move, Kant divorces morality from happiness, for human nature is so determined that happiness must of necessity be its end, and this end, consequently, is without moral worth. Kant is not opposed to happiness; it simply lacks *moral* quality and cannot justify moral action. One may pursue it when duty does not call.[20]

Kant does not pretend to derive his moral thought from value-neutral facts. The moral law is fundamental in and of itself. Reason necessarily respects it, he says. The law "extorts" our respect. One may doubt, nevertheless, that "All so-called moral interest consists solely in respect for the law."[21] This is, in truth, an extremely limited moral universe. It is composed only of the a priori formal law and the exclusively rational nature that generates it. To be sure, Kant investigates the *foundation* of morals, which is noumenal freedom, but knowledge of the foundation is unnecessary for moral judgment and practice.[22]

The law is self-sufficing. There are no moral lessons to be learned elsewhere, and none are needed. We may heed neither the plurality of goods incipient in the contingencies of life, the possible consummations of human nature, nor the varying demands made on our loyalties by a multitude of associations. Neither doubt nor tragedy will cloud our thoughts. When our seeker after knowledge of uncertain climes goes to Kant for moral advice, he is advised, "Inexperienced in the course of the world, incapable of being prepared for all its contingencies, I ask myself only: Can I will that my maxim become universal law?"[23] (Notice that he merely asks *himself.* Neither worldly inquiry nor interpersonal consultation is relevant.) All this seemed perfectly rational to Kant, but if we were actually to try it—that is, actually to introduce no knowledge of "the course of the world," to undertake no philosophic appraisal—the result would necessarily be vacuity. There is no wisdom to be found in this philosophy; knowing better is categorically excluded.[24]

Kant has been attractive to many minds for various reasons. There is something grand in the idea of moral law applicable to all persons without exception and with no recourse to evasion or modification. He has a conception of perfect impartiality and disinterestedness that excites the moral dispositions of many readers; his conception of unconditional freedom and responsibility has likewise been widely embraced. His emphasis on the notion of duty is affective, too, for that is a crucial moral relation. But most of all, perhaps, his sometimes magisterial rhetoric prompts his admirers (and Kant himself, on occasion) to import content into his a priori principles that in fact is not and cannot be there. His determining assumptions forbid their entry. The zeal of his followers seems to blind them to this embarrassment. In spite of its admirers, Kant's formulation of moral principle is, as it stands, bankrupt of any powers of direction, and revisionist Kantians such as Rawls, fare little better, for they refuse to be disciplined by pertinent worldly knowledge.[25]

In a later chapter I will urge that a Kantian conception of impartiality is morally repugnant. For the moment, just a passing comment on the idea that without free will, responsibility must vanish: Kant's conviction on this score is not compelling—or so our worldly experience instructs. If human beings are capable of learning, then reward and punishment are not only permissible but massively important in the conduct of life, whether there be indeterminism in the world or not. Holding persons accountable for their actions is our principal manner of teaching them. Individuals thereby become more likely to perform the tasks expected of them; they become more reliable, more *responsible*. No Kantian moralist, on becoming (reluctantly) convinced that determinism is true, would thereupon cease to reward good and punish evil. He would not be so cruel to his children, for example, that he would no longer enforce certain standards of behavior. If he ceased to do so, he would find out very quickly what a Hobbesian state of nature really is. No one would acquiesce to such conditions when real evils are avoidable and real goods within reach. To do otherwise would be irresponsible!

Subsequently, the moral universe expands. For Hegel and his followers, the great adorned world (with some reservations) reappears as indispensable to wisdom. The whole is the self-realization of *Geist*, Spirit (or God or Reason or the Absolute), articulating itself in historical time, until that point where all that Spirit is in its essential potency becomes actual. The whole is not divided into distinct substances; Spirit alone is substance, and what we call matter has no existence independent of *Geist*, and it could have none. At all stages of time, at any juncture of history, the whole is constituted in its entirety by the thinking of the Absolute in its own self-development.

The temporal process of Spirit is not pretty. The upheavals and destructions that mark the course of history are not denied. ("Highway of despair" is Hegel's expression.) Powered by what he calls the "negative," history proceeds in a dialectical pattern. A series of "contradictions" or "opposites" is generated from within the historical process. A contradiction is not the annihilation of whatever has preceded it; it incorporates its antecedents in a higher unity. History marches on, each successive stage more inclusive than its predecessors. At any stage, everything that exists constitutes an organic whole: all things are interconnected. Each part has its distinctive function in determining the nature of the whole in its totality, and the nature of each part is exhausted in being an expression of the whole.

More and more of the Real is manifest as time goes by, and eventually Spirit is fully actual, and it is fully harmonious. All opposites are dissolved in the totality. That is, seen as part of the perfection of the whole, they are not really contradictions. Indeed, from the standpoint of the philosopher who comprehends this process, at any stage in history the conflicts as such are seen to be, in truth, *appearance*, for they are really necessary constituents of the self-realization of spirit, which is "rational." In distinction from appearance, the rational and the real are one: the real *is* the rational. The truth of cosmic teleology reconciles us to the torments of the damned. Hegel calls the final perfection of the Absolute its freedom.

Suppose the world has some resemblance to this portrait. What would it offer us in the way of wisdom and unwisdom? Recalling Plato's lovely account of a cosmic and social order with a place for everyone, Hegel's philosophy evidently restores us to a home in the universe and thereby fills a deep longing. In contrast to the dualisms stemming from Descartes, nature is no longer alien and inscrutable. We belong to a larger whole, and it to us. We not only fill a definite and necessary role in the divine order, but it is our just and proper role. Spinoza had offered salvation only in consequence of the most heroic and singular efforts. Hegel seemed to make it everyone's. The individual is not the isolated figure set in contradistinction to society, but his being and good are inseparable from it. Society, like the cosmos, is an organism, not a mere aggregate of self-complete persons. It constitutes the self of each individual, whose self-realization it is to recognize a real unity with the social organism—an instinctual awareness of oneness with the whole. The young Dewey was much attracted to Hegel on just this account, and the idealists' legitimation of a palpable sense of belonging was gratefully received by many thinkers who were alienated by the dualistic and atomistic conception of things that is conspicuous in modern philosophy.

Though they be a mere seeming, the evident conflicts in the unity beg for a moral accounting. From a philosophic standpoint, as we have seen, they can be recognized for what they are: appearance. The philosopher, moreover, is consoled by the recognition that the present historical condition, which is the inevitable form of Spirit's temporal development, expresses the limit of what is both possible and good in the current epoch. Nothing could be better than what is, for now, the real. For the illiterate and ignorant, consolation lies in the distinction between the real and the apparent will. When they are dissatisfied with the social order, or rebel against it, it is their *apparent* will that objects; their *real* will, on the other hand, is in accord with the whole and accepting of it. In the words of a later Hegelian, F. H. Bradley, their true freedom is to perform the duties of their station. The wisdom in this posture is to appreciate one's participation in the good of a communal unity and to be reconciled to the insuperable limits in earthly affairs. One recognizes the inherent irrationality of expecting institutions to satisfy the demands of a juvenile and impatient ego. For the philosopher and the common man alike, the good of life consists in achieving the appropriate consciousness of the whole.

Although absolute idealism was welcomed for purporting to negate the alienation of the individual from society and the universe, it differs in a decisive way from the earlier account of things that predominated in the ancient and medieval worlds. The difference is not just that Being is actualized in historical time. More important is the relation between the individual and the whole. Plato had told us that there is a divine order to which we might conform and thereby attain happiness, but he did not say that we inescapably *are* in harmony with that order. That is an unusual state, to be achieved by wisdom and discipline. According to the idealist, however, we are in harmony so long as we do not deviate from the existing state of things. It is hard *not* to be in harmony; the real will, presumably, is necessarily in unity with the whole. Within such a scheme, knowing better seems to demand nothing in the way of active appraisal, and the achievement of the good does not require wise and sustained initiative. One serenely accepts his experience just in the way that it occurs. Many ordinary people who have never heard of Hegel, as well as philosophers, yearn for this state of mind.

There surely is wisdom in being skeptical about the idea that existing structures are merely arbitrary and at the same time plastic to the touch of social engineers, but resistance to undertaking deliberate change is taken to its limit by the idealist, and the apparent will is left to suffer in futility. The thoroughgoing conservatism in this philosophy made an idealist like T. H. Green, for one, uneasy. He doubted that all persons equally enjoy their respective status in the Absolute. Although a liberal, he remained an idealist nonetheless, but Dewey, for this and other reasons, was moved to undertake a sytematic rethinking of this philosophy. For him, a form of naturalism comes to replace idealism, and he no longer regards the whole as a divine order. Accordingly, he is not constrained to say that everything that exists is "really" good. He despised apologetics. Goods are not to be achieved by attaining the correct consciousness of the whole but by overt conduct. It is more constructive to try to change the world than to change your mind about it regardless of what it does.

Dewey also insists on a form of pluralism: the universe of human existence is decidedly not one interconnected whole. Social oppression, separation, and conflict are not mere appearance, and for all practical purposes any given event in nature functions independently of most other events. The birth of a child in China occurs without influence from the bad weather in Georgia; my moral failings cannot be blamed on the corruptions of government in Cuba; variations in the rings of Saturn are without connection to the virtues of your latest book. In brief, we can address distinguishable problems short of moving the Absolute itself. Yet Dewey did not give up the idea of organic unities, of which an individual might feel an integral part and in which he might flourish, but such unities are *constructed*. They are formed in consequence of deliberate and intelligent effort. They are finite, plural, and liable to instability and corruption. There is no relationship to other human beings and the world that is final and unchanging. Dewey, nevertheless, believed that one can sustain a reverent piety toward the natural world, so long as it is discriminating.

Hegel's philosophy is in fact brilliant in many ways, within the confines of the absolutistic system outlined here. Dewey himself judged Hegel, after Plato, to be the philosopher most worth studying. It is the nature of the system itself that it must combine a total cosmic embrace with social apologetics. Such is the peril of demanding unqualified acceptance of the whole. One can, of course, support various objections to idealism without endorsing Dewey's philosophy in toto. A critical reconstruction of Dewey's metaphysics will be undertaken in the next chapter. The present discussion will conclude with some observations on the philosophy of George Santayana. He does not share the eminence of the foremost philosophers in history, yet he has a manner of philosophizing that must appeal to a candid mind that is also a lover of the good.

The "chief issue" of philosophy, according to Santayana, is "the relation of man and of his spirit to the universe."[26] He is not referring to the mind/body problem of Cartesian fame but to the more far-reaching, chastening, and instructive question of the whole situation of human powers and aspirations in the natural world. The philosopher is he who would survey this condition to arrive at conclusions about the nature of human goods and ideal values that nature makes possible, and he would know of the renunciations and forms of endeavor necessary to them. Santayana regarded philosophy as a discipline that might bring one to distinctive and comprehensive goods of the soul; he practiced it in that way, and he succeeded in it. Such has been the ambition of many a speculative mind—or so it seems. But most such undertakings have been, in Santayana's term, *shams*. Philosophers have been notoriously enthused to invest the universe with the traits that they wish to find there, making the order of things conform to a vain and tender psyche, rather than conforming the soul to whatever might truly be within the reach of nature. Santayana is particularly scornful of the German idealists, who had the colossal ego to suppose that the determining principles of the universe are those of the human mind—or more precisely, in effect, the mind of a given philosopher. Technically, of course, these traits were said to originate with the Absolute Mind (or Will), but this divine entity was in fact conceived after the *human* mind or will. A truly honest philosopher, by contrast, is a great rarity. He is "disillusioned" both in the sense of thinking without illusion and in reconciling himself to the truth. In Western thought, those few who qualify as disillusioned are the Greek naturalists and atomists, Lucretius, and Spinoza. The final question for a philosopher is, "What inmost allegiance, what ultimate religion, would be proper to a wholly free and disillusioned spirit?"[27]

For Santayana, that allegiance must be predicated on a materialism but not on the reductive versions that have flourished in modern philosophy. Rather early in his long life, in 1905–1906, he produced *The Life of Reason*, an extraordinary work, in five volumes, the like of which has not been seen since. He adumbrates an inclusive conception of nature such that mind is a function of physical processes, and qualities in all their glory are real properties of natural events, emergent with life and consciousness.[28] There is no attempt to conceal or to deny full reality to the ugly traits of existence, nor does he populate the cosmic landscape with reassuring beings of his own invention. His principal theme is moral. The aim of the life of reason is *harmony*, which, ideally conceived, is "an ultimate harmony within the soul and . . . an ultimate harmony between the soul and all the soul depends upon."[29] While contemplative experience—always favored by Santayana—is incorporated within this ideal, the life of reason is predominantly one of active converse with the world. Ideal fulfillments are not just imagined; they are actively produced.

He proceeds to discriminate where the life of reason has actually been approximated in society, religion, art, and science. (Ethical life is included within science, broadly conceived.) This is a project wherein almost any writer would make a fool of himself through pedantry, laborious prose, and provincial sympathies, but Santayana's articulation of goods and ideal values resident in the salient forms of experience is discerning, humane, and catholic. His study incorporates analyses of various philosophies, religions, and social orders that have more or less succeeded in conceiving the life of reason and practicing it, and notable failures are examined as well. How profoundly rewarding to engage in imaginative dialectic with the mind of Santayana!

The philosophic assumption at work throughout these volumes is what he calls the Aristotelian principle: everything ideal has a natural basis, and all natural processes are capable of ideal fulfillment.[30] In thoroughgoing opposition to modern dualisms and reductionisms, this is a principle of continuity, in accordance with which human nature, mind, art, religion, science, and their characteristic goods are neither orginal existences nor detached and self-sustaining beings. They are emergent of nature. Each has its natural history, which Santayana tries to distinguish and articulate. This is also a principle of realism and resource: insofar as we have knowledge of these processes, we are constrained to acknowledge what nature can and cannot do. Our ideal values will be conceived in terms of the real powers and constraints of nature; reason and imagination gain both discipline and efficacy. Ideal goods are completions of natural energies, ordered to the inherent potentialities of nature and significant of its best possibilities. "Ideals are not forces stealthily undermining the will; they are possible forms of being that would frankly express it. . . . [H]e who finds them divine and congenial and is able to embody them at least in part and for a season, has to that extent transfigured life, turning it from a fatal process into a liberal art."[31]

The Socratic school was most successful in *conceiving* the life of reason, but Santayana observes that its *practice* can be at best intermittent and only partially accomplished. The human being tends to be urgent in his demands, disordered, and unruly, and he does not easily become more rational and composed in consequence of education. More fundamentally, "the realm of matter" is barely tolerant of human aspiration. Instead of postulating static Being, Santayana refers to "the universal flux," which is fundamentally a chaos. When some order is established in the soul or in society, it is merely an "eddy" in the universal flux. The human capacity to establish and preserve stable conditions is not commonly equal to the demands made on it. This is historical fact. Conditions that succeed in some measure in sustaining a humane order are rare and precious. They have been products neither of abstract intellect nor deliberate social policy. Custom and tradition are typically to be respected, for they represent a sort of Darwinian success story that is beyond the capacity of "rational" planning. Naturally occurring accommodations are wiser than the enthusiasms of the social engineer. In the main, custom and tradition have been realistic adjustments to the persistent facts of nature. Religion, art, and culture have clothed these facts in symbol, myth, and ritual—often with remarkable imagination, insight, and beauty, and such instinctive lessons have far more efficacy than didactic pedagogy. This is not to say that Santayana was uniformly opposed to the critical application of intelligence to social problems. He was not, but he was typically skeptical about its powers and ambitions. Intelligence is often overmatched by the universal flux. Clearly, the life of reason is not modeled upon the disembodied rational nature postulated in modern philosophy. The attempt to discern and articulate ideal goods in accordance with the Aristotelian principle demands recognition and respect for the inherent ordering powers that nature sometimes displays.

Increasingly, as he aged, the life of reason seemed to Santayana to be an ideal increasingly out of practical reach. He formulated and practiced, instead, a form of spiritual life, as he called it, which in his parlance is a "post-rational" morality. It is a disengaged and contemplative life, where worldly appreciations and attachments are renounced in favor of loving things "only as ideas."[32] Santayana could in that way love the eros in all things without becoming embroiled and partisan in their actual loves, hatreds, and sufferings.

Many students are disappointed by this turn in Santayana's later thought.[33] Yet he by no means supposed that this version of spiritual life ought to be universal. Santayana was a pluralist. He did not believe that there is a unitary end in the nature of things for all creatures. Even the life of reason—not to mention postrational morality—admits of a plurality of forms. Life in the spirit, as Santayana rendered it, was his reconciliation to "omnificent power" and, in his way, mastery of it. All the same, there is a stunning omission in Santayana's analysis of the life of reason. Even in his discussion of classical Greek philosophy, he gives no prominence to the notion of virtue. True, Socrates sought harmony in the soul and with the cosmos but not *any* harmony. There are *perfections* of the soul, virtues; justice in the individual is their actualization and proper ordering. Admittedly, to come within reach of such excellence is prodigiously difficult and rare, the product of single-minded and protracted devotion—and the blessings of the gods. It is an ideal, an aristocratic ideal, but nonetheless in accordance with nature. A few mortals will come tolerably close to it, thereby giving testimony to the best possibilities of nature. The sobriety of Santayana has much warrant, after all, but it might be that he simply lacked the innate aggression, or toughness, to entertain these possibilities for exceptional moral prowess. So far as there are such possibilities for virtue, so far are there potent resources for the life of reason.

Reflections of the sort entertained by Santayana and by the others whom I have reviewed have engaged the imagination of aspiring souls for centuries. My selection is limited; many names might have been added to the list. (Nietzsche, I think, would be the most instructive, but I am reserving consideration of his philosophy for chapter 9.) In any event, there is evidently a deep need for such reflection and a yearning for its good issue. Sophisticates believe that the endeavor is bankrupt, while the paradigms and agendas that prevail in current academic thought have exiled these concerns from respectable philosophy—pending, presumably, a solution to the technical problems that absorb my colleagues. I have suggested that success in these artifices will leave them no better off, no better prepared to answer to the imperatives of eros and the moral life. These are issues to be pursued in due course. The immediate task is to articulate a morally pertinent conception of nature.

NOTES

1. Notice "families." In the presumed "ideal" state of *The Republic* (written at about the same time as *The Symposium*), Socrates would ban the family. The treatment of it in *The Republic* is one of many pieces of evidence that that work is in part a dramatization of philosophic hubris. Compare Aristophanes, *The Assembly of Women*.

2. The sense of this word is broader than *beauty*. It is used for *fair, fine, good,* and *noble* as well. It is a term of inclusive and highest praise.

3. Although the Platonic Socrates is unrivaled in wisdom and virtue, Plato did not portray a man without fault or failure, nor did he intend to. He was too wise for that.

4. Through the personage of Socrates, Plato remarks occasionally in this and other dialogues that there might be an exception to this rule, when someone's virtue can only be accounted a gift of the gods. He is thinking of Socrates, who presumably did not have an exceptional education, and he might be thinking as well that there is something freakish about the most extraordinary individualities.

5. A more definite meaning for this figurative expression will be offered in chap. 4, sect. d.

6. One of the obstacles to a less literalistic reading of Plato is the authority of Aristotle, who always seems to take him to be without nuance, irony, or playfulness, and he appears not to be at all interested in the character of Socrates. There are good reasons for not regarding Aristotle as infallible on these matters. There are times, in fact, when he seems to write in ignorance of key writings, as in his treatment of courage and death, and we cannot be sure that Aristotle worked with precisely the same texts as we possess today.

7. This is implied in the myth of Er (*Republic* book 10). Those souls that had come from heaven, Er relates, tended to make very unwise choices, and the general reason for their failure was that they were inexperienced in suffering (*ponos*). Those who had come up from earth fared better, for they had known suffering (619d).

8. Especially charming are the cases where Socrates holds forth with a grand and highly conjectural theory, his interlocutors taking it all in without a murmur, and then he himself confesses that only a god could know whether such an idea is really true! (See, e.g., *Phaedrus*, 246a, and *Republic*, 517b.) Equally engaging are discussions where his fellows are once again without demurral, and Socrates admonishes them that they are only telling stories for their own amusement (as in *Phaedrus*, 265c, or *Republic*, 536c).

9. The presumed ordering principle of the cosmos, by the way, would not be denominated *the Good* if that order were not beneficent for human happiness. *The Good* is not a morally neutral principle.

10. I urge the reader to contrast the education prescribed in the first nine books of *The Republic* to that which is adumbrated in book 10 in the myth of Er. I find this myth the most instructive in the corpus—and the most underappreciated.

I can't leave the question of the meaning of *The Republic* without noting the stunning declaration by Socrates at the conclusion of book 9 (592a–b). Long after the companions have solemnly affirmed that the ideal state cannot exist without the philosopher king, Socrates announces that a true philosopher would never lend himself to worldly politics of *any* sort. Without saying it explicitly, Plato has pronounced the ideal state an impossibility. Hence the face-value reading of *The Republic* as a work of political philosophy is likewise pronounced dead.

11. Locke refers to this condition as the state of nature, but this is not Aristotelian nature, which is long dead. Locke refers to a condition prior to or independent of civil or political jurisdiction.

12. Hume was to be wiser than Locke before him and Kant after him, for he did not mistake the lessons of common life for the deliverances of a priori reason.

13. When Hobbes says we renounce our right to all things, the emphasis is on *all*. We give up the right to *everything*, as such, but *particular* rights (e.g., to private property) might be retained by common consent. The right of self-preservation, he says, can never be sincerely renounced. We do not give up the very condition for which we enter into the social contract in the first place.

14. More precisely, mind and body are necessary *attributes*, as Spinoza calls them, of the divine unity.

15. Spinoza holds that the essence of God or Nature comprises infinite attributes, but to the human mind Nature is intelligible only in the attributes constituting mind and body.

16. Santayana, "Ultimate Religion," in *The Works of George Santayana*, Triton ed., vol. 10 (New York: Charles Scribner's Sons, 1937), p. 253.

17. Immanuel Kant, *Foundations of the Metaphysics of Morals*, trans. and intro. by Lewis White Beck (New York: The Liberal Arts Press, 1959), p. 46.

18. Ibid., p. 47.

19. "Unconditional" means the law is independent of any empirical consideration in both its origin and import. "Necessary" means absolutely exceptionless. "Universal" means applicable to any being of any sort that is possessed of rational nature.

20. One may pursue happiness from the moral standpoint if a maxim to do so is universalizable. The merit in the maxim is derived solely from its universalizability, not from a desire to give or receive happiness. Not surprisingly, Kant has nothing helpful to say about the nature of happiness.

21. Ibid., p. 18*n*.

22. He also argues that we must postulate immortality, as well as God to provide it: we are obliged to perfect our nature, which cannot be accomplished in this life, so there must be a future life in which to do it. Moreover, he argues inconsistently, there must be happiness in proportion to moral merit, and this does not happen in earthly life, so it has to be heavenly.

23. Ibid., p. 19.

24. For a fuller discussion, answering some typical objections (including the argument that Kant is not a mere formalist), see my *Rediscovering the Moral Life* (Amherst, NY: Prometheus Books, 1993), pp. 242–47. See also sect. a of chap. 6 of the present work.

25. See *Rediscovering the Moral Life*, pp. 203–204, 214–17, 247–68.

26. George Santayana, *Scepticism and Animal Faith*, Triton ed., vol. 13 (New York: Charles Scribner's Sons, 1936), p. 6.

27. "Ultimate Religion," p. 245. Written in homage to Spinoza.

28. The more detailed account of his philosophy of nature is given in *Realms of*

Being, in 4 vols., 1927–1940. *Scepticism and Animal Faith* (1923) he called an introduction to *Realms of Being*. Santayana's philosophy of experience is more ambiguous and incomplete than I have suggested in the summary comments above. Still, his intention was always to philosophize in a manner that is faithful to experience. Theory must be the servant of candid experience.

29. See George Santayana's *The Life of Reason*, vol. 3 (New York: Charles Scribner's Sons, 1936), and *Reason in Religion*, Triton ed., vol. 4 (New York: Charles Scribner's Sons, 1936), p. 7.

30. *The Life of Reason*, vol. 1, and *Reason in Common Sense*, Triton ed., vol. 3 (New York: Charles Scribner's Sons, 1936), p. 28.

31. *The Life of Reason*, vol. 5, and *Reason in Science*, Triton ed., vol. 5 (New York: Charles Scribner's Sons, 1936), p. 151.

32. *Dominations and Powers: Reflections on Liberty, Society, and Government* (New York: Charles Scribner's Sons, 1951), p. 57. This is the full quotation: "For spirit, it is only as ideas, as essences, that things can be seen or loved; and it is only as an essence, or as the truth about some fact, that existence can be possessed or retained by a free spirit."

33. I am one of them. See my "Ultimate Religion" in *Overheard in Seville: Journal of the Santayana Society*, no. 16 (fall 1998): 1–13.

| 3 |

Worldly Metaphysics

Like most areas of philosophic inquiry, metaphysics has taken widely differing forms and served different purposes. The inquiry into *highest* or
ultimate being has been the most conspicuous endeavor. In this form it is typically taken to be explanatory of the whole nature of things and perhaps
foundational, too, in the sense of purporting to give certification to cognition
and evaluation. In other versions, metaphysics has attempted to discern the
traits that are universal to all existences, of whatever kind: the traits of being
qua being. It has characteristically asked, also, what is substance? Is it material, spiritual, or something else? What is the nature of these several substances, and how is the world composed of them? Is one an idealist of some
form? Or a materialist, or perhaps a dualist? Metaphysics has also been the
investigation of the subjective conditions of all experience. A closely related
effort has been the attempt to discern the categories of all thought—or perhaps of all language, but I am not concerned here to multiply instances, of
which there are more.[1]

While each of these investigations has its peculiar interest and esoteric
qualities, metaphysics can also be conceived as seeking a form of intelligibility for the universe of *practice*. This would be a discernment of the general
characteristics of nature that are salient for our fortunes as living beings, and
there need be nothing esoteric about such investigations. The greatest metaphysicians of this sort were the Homeric bards. These were sages, who gave
divine embodiment to the distinctive forces of nature and rendered their
powers in unforgettable imagery. Ideal goods were celebrated in radiant

immortals, personifications of art, love, beauty, and wisdom. Fateful traits of human nature were dramatized in the struggles and destinies of the gods, and the adventures of mortal fools and heroes confirm the wisdom of these teachings. Not least remarkable about the Homeric philosophy is its realism: it neither denies evils nor promises extravagant goods; it is astonishingly true to the limits, depths, and ideal possibilities of the human condition. What has been accomplished by inspired poets is unwittingly imitated by lesser men. It is a familiar practice: a reflective person learns in time to recognize the threatening and the congenial features of existence, and he naturally organizes his experience in generalizations.

Dewey's metaphysics, as expounded in his great, if unwieldy, *Experience and Nature*, is of this sort. Dewey called it a naturalistic metaphysics, but it has been aptly called a metaphysics of practice.[2] It pertains to *all* forms of human practice, but I will be parasitic on Dewey's work to formulate something a bit more narrow: a metaphysics of moral practice, broadly conceived, which could also be called a *worldly* metaphysics. The subject matter is nevertheless highly inclusive: the entire context of the nature of things as it bears on aspiration, practice, and the meanings of life. Fundamental relevance to moral life constitutes the principle of selection and analysis, but it is a matter of inquiry and judgment to determine which traits of the encompassing whole satisfy that test. Insofar as moral practice is inseparable from other forms of practice—such as science and art—worldly metaphysics distinguishes general features of nature that are fateful for these other activities as well.

A metaphysics of practice draws our attention to crucial and pervasive features of the world that demand our study and respect and which we neglect at our peril. These generalizations have, then, a pedagogic function. They direct our reflections to distinctive sorts of events and caution us to be mindful of them: events crucial to our conduct and well-being and ultimately to our wisdom. To be neglectful of them in either moral theory or practice is an invitation to impotence and failure or, at best, irrelevance. The latter has been the fate of many philosophies.

A metaphysics of the moral life is a way of systematizing what one has learned about the generic features of the human condition. It is a discernment of traits that demand recognition in mortal existence and an exposition of the wisdom in taking deep cognizance of them. In light of the unconscionably reductive character of modern philosophy, Dewey's foremost task as a metaphysician was to restore the natural world to its experienced fullness. In the aftermath of the neglects and misadventures of modern thought, the ways in which our characteristic works and experience are significant of the potentialities of nature would be set forth. Otherwise, we are condemned to an impoverished analysis of the conditions and resources of the moral life. There already exists a substantial body of interpretation on the topic of

Dewey's metaphysics, but I will undertake what these studies do not. I find Dewey's metaphysics to be incomplete. I intend to explain what I take the shortcomings to be and how they might be remedied. As a sort of intermezzo between exposition and reconstruction, I will write briefly of the method and aims appropriate to this sort of inquiry.

This is not a foray into ethical theory as such. One might, for example, study ethical theory in isolation and consequently decide, say, to be a utilitarian. One could be a utilitarian and still be a moral idiot in the sense of being ignorant and unrealistic about the powers and limitations of the human condition. The onset of ineptitude occurs even before this, however. One would be profoundly unwise to formulate or to adopt an ethical theory that was not predicated on knowing better, and a worldly metaphysics presumes to direct our attention in a systematic way to the sorts of things that must be attended to if we are, in fact, to know better. The major moral philosophies have been—and must be—first of all studies of the generic human condition. Then one can make a just appraisal of the possibilities of our predicament, rather than blunder along with a miscellany of moral sentiments and half-baked intuitions.

a. DEWEY'S METAPHYSICS

Sharing the grave reservations of William James about the dilute and impotent character of modern thought, Dewey took it to be essential to characterize nature fully and accurately as a part of any philosophy that might clarify and fortify human effort. The reigning philosophies were reductive at best or simply false. Absolute idealists, for example, declared that the real nature of things is nothing but a rational order of ideas, constituted by the very essence of absolute mind. John Stuart Mill, by contrast, followed the stereotypical reading of Hume's philosophy in holding that reality consists of a mass of unrelated bits and pieces. A third form of recent metaphysics has defended the materialist reduction: nature is nothing but the mechanistic system of matter in motion. An assumption common to all three of these views is that experience is through and through subjective: it occurs only *within* mind. Its characteristic traits, accordingly, are radically other than those attributed to nature. According to this view, the entirety of our experience is ordered by inherent laws of mind, the nature of which owes nothing to whatever may be the constitution of the external world. So it is and must be that the putative world beyond the confines of mind is impenetrable to experience, and nothing of what the world is experienced to be can legitimately be predicated of it. Philosophers have presented us with this systematic dualism: on the one hand there is the world of ordinary life, untutored by philosophy, that discloses innumerable qualities and features inseparable from our plural forms of converse with it, and which decides our fate. On the other hand there is the world as described by a modern metaphysician: a complete cipher from the standpoint of experience.

Such views were repellent to both James and Dewey,[3] but unlike Dewey, James did not undertake a fully fledged account of the nature of nature. Dewey's accomplishment as a metaphysician consists of the formulation and defense of two fundamental positions. First, his establishment of the continuity of experience and nature permitted him to insist that nature has the traits it is experienced to have. That is, the traits that we experience are traits of *nature*, rather than traits of a realm of being essentially differentiated from it. Dewey had no intention to maintain that experience is *never* subjective. He is not denying such familiar events as fantasy, imagination, and reflection. His point is that our common experience of the world really is *of the world*, and what we experience there is true of the world. Second, his discernment and elaboration of the most important traits of experience—that is, of nature—gives us the most adequate account of the nature of nature to be found in modern philosophy.[4] I will review each of these positions. The first one—the continuity of experience and nature—I will not quarrel with. The second one—his characterization of the traits of nature—is what I find to be insufficiently developed, and I will try to improve on it.

The continuity of experience and nature

To put Dewey's conclusions in compendious form, we can say that he conceives organism and environment in organic unity, rather than in dualistic terms. Cartesian dualism and its inseparable companion, subjectivism, had attained axiomatic status in philosophy, but the axiom, Dewey urged, has no warrant in experience itself, nor in the cognitive function of experience known as scientific inquiry. The dualistic dogma was, indeed, the *product* of an unwarranted simplification of nature, rather than its cause. Without giving it a second thought, Descartes followed a philosophic tradition of great antiquity, dating to Parmenides and the Eleatic school: being as such—that which has complete reality—is changeless. A single stark assumption defines the tradition: that which has full objective reality does not change. That which changes is not fully real. Before us yawns the chasm between being and becoming—also denoted in such formulations as the dualism of appearance and reality, subjective and objective, experience and nature. This unfortunate heritage Dewey called the classic tradition in philosophy. It was his achievement to overturn it and radically to reconstruct our conception of nature.

According to the classic tradition, being is or possesses changeless essence, and essence is exhaustive of the nature of true being. That which changes, then, does not share in being. To use the technical term, an essentially invariant entity is *substance*. It is fully actual, perfectly complete within itself, and its nature (once more) never changes. The changing properties that might be predicated of it do not really belong to its nature; such features are erroneously predicated of substance. Natures are inherent. Essence (or *form*, to use another equivalent term) is internal to substance; cognition of it provides no information regarding the relationship of one event to another.

Supposing this much, one must also suppose a radical discontinuity between reason and experience. There is no object of experience that does not undergo change, so that which is changeless—essence—must be the object of a different faculty, reason. Descartes dutifully took it for granted that the nature of the really real is disclosed exclusively and entirely in the object of rational knowledge as such. Notoriously, he observes the wax candle, the properties of which undergo change as causal conditions vary. Its shape, color, temperature, hardness, aroma, and so on all suffer variation. Only one property is constant: extension per se. Accordingly, Descartes finds, the essence of the candle and of any material object is to be extended, no more and no less. By a similar logic, Descartes is incapable of doubting that mind is, in essence, a thinking thing, so it can be nothing else. Mind, then, is utterly other than body and body than mind. It is inconceivable, by this logic, that any kind of body can be a thinking thing. Existence is divided into two mutually exclusive substances; never the twain shall meet.[5]

The idea of extension per se is not an object of experience. We have the experience of this or that extended object but never extension in essence. The very idea of extension is a purely rational object. Essence is the object of rational knowledge, not of experience. None of the other properties displayed by the candle, or by any object, are of its essence, so, Descartes concludes, they cannot be real properties of the object at all. Things that change do not possess objective reality.

Embracing the ancient assumptions about static being, Descartes must expel all other traits from nature. Things that change are not literally annihilated, nevertheless. They are, after all, experienced. They have to have an existence somehow and somewhere. Where will that be? Descartes had no choice but to hustle all experienced properties out of nature and into the sanctuary of mind. There they must abide in complete privacy, apart from nature. Now we must insist, retroactively, that to speak of experiencing external objects is a misnomer. The objects of experience huddle within the mind. Accordingly, the object of experience is experience.

One who affirms this argument finds nature radically depleted. Imagine him sitting in a garden with his grandson on a warm summer day. He delights in the sweetness of the boy, and he is sensuously conscious of the aroma of flowers carried on soft winds. He contemplates a red robin against a blue sky and relishes his cheerful song. He is sensitive to nuances of change in the qualities surrounding him. But he must concede to the truth: none of these things has the qualities that he experiences. There is no real distinction between daylight and nighttime; his grandson has no sweetness; the air has neither warmth nor chill; the breeze is neither soft nor aromatic; neither the robin nor the sky has any color; and the bird has no song. Nature, says our subjectivist, is nothing but extension, and everything of which he is ever conscious is imprisoned within his escape-proof mind.

Subjectivism is regnant. Thus modern philosophy is born, bequeathing the radical dualism of experience and nature and taxing the ingenuity of philosophers ever since. There seem to be insuperable problems in holding that the qualities of experience are true of the external object. These are qualities that come and go; they are impermanent and could not be predicated of substance. At the same time, there is great reluctance to accept the total alienation from nature. Our experience is insulted, and our seeming home is really nothing but matter in motion in universal darkness.

It was characteristic of Dewey's treatment of any philosophic conundrum to ask why the problem exists at all, and he typically found that an impasse had been created due to spurious assumptions that define the problem. The fruitful approach, then, is not to struggle with such a riddle in its own terms but to eliminate or completely recast it by a critique of the assumptions that have brought it down on us. Dewey was incomparably brilliant in these analyses, and the present instance is no exception. He made no attempt to "solve" the problem of the dualism of experience and nature. The confounding philosophy of Descartes was, Dewey judged, owing to the prejudice that the really real is changeless. Rid of that idea, we might commence a helpful investigation of experience and nature.

If we were to think of the matter in candor, Dewey believed, we would not presuppose that being is changeless, and neither would we suppose that whatever undergoes generation and corruption is somehow less than fully real. Objects are not substances and neither is the human subject. The classic doctrine of being is not proven, much less self-evident. It is in fact mere prejudice, given protection by the philosophers' longing for the eternal and unchanging. Then there is nothing inherently problematic in accepting the only evidence that we have. We observe that natural processes combine and reorder themselves in innumerable ways and in doing so produce multifarious outcomes, populating the universe with an astonishing array of phenomena. Throughout, these are processes of *change*. There is process, not substance. Anything is subject to change. *Natures change*. What had been regarded in the classic tradition as a contradiction in terms turns out to be a fundamental truth! The cognitive object, according to Dewey's analysis, is not inherent essence but the correlations between processes of change.

These swarming outcomes exhibit nature's potentialities. Experience is one such outcome. It is one of nature's potentialities brought to fruition. According to Cartesian understanding, by contrast, the object is an antecedently complete substance, and so is the subject. If so, we must confess that neither substance either gains or loses properties. According to Dewey's thinking, on the other hand, that is a gratuitous (and ruinous) assumption. Nature is polymorphic; her means and ends are not substances. They *change*. They gain and lose properties in profusion. A wax candle, for example, might gain the property of being soft or sweet or yellow or hot, and it can also lose them. In any case, properties of that ensemble of events that we call *the candle* are gained or lost.

The wondrous displays of experience are the outcome of an inclusive field incorporating processes of both organism and environment. (We can call this a *field* theory of experience, but Dewey himself does not use this expression.) Each display is a product of an entire field of interacting processes, which Dewey calls a *situation*. Each such outcome will undergo change as the constituents of the situation vary, but there is no longer any warrant to rip these changing properties away from nature and stuff them into mind. Dewey liked to observe that the *situation* is fearful, lovely, threatening, confused, and the like. Granted, a situation would not have all the same features and just these features if a human creature were not a constituent element of it. The qualities of a situation are attributable to many powers, but they do not become less real because their preconditions include specifiable human capacities. Properties do not disappear into their antecedents. We may—with relief and thanksgiving, I would suppose—restore normal credit to experience: it discloses the full and variegated adornments of the real world. When we have disposed of the assumptions that land us in subjectivism, moreover, the problem of knowledge ceases to be that of speculating how a private subjective image might resemble a putative external object. The problem becomes simply that of determining how properties of a given observable event undergo change in relation to variations in other such events. The whole process is open and above-board.

Nature is marvelously different from that spare and skeletal being of the classic tradition. Dewey's critique of classical metaphysics restores nature to itself. Nature is what it is experienced to be. When you see robin redbreast and listen to his song, what you really see is a bird with a red breast and what you really hear is his song. In that particular field of relations, these qualities truly exist; in a different complex of relations, they would not. So it must be with all things that exist, but that does not make them unreal.

We should honor Dewey's achievement. More than anyone else, he deserves credit for the fall of Cartesianism, and this was an epochal event. Descartes had isolated mind so radically that it had to become a universe of its own. Accordingly, all the behavior, knowledge, norms, and rules of life fall wholly within it. There is in principle neither chastening experience nor disciplined aspiration to be gained from the world itself, which must remain for the subjectivist a nonentity. In truth, however, wisdom can be gained nowhere else. When that principle is abandoned, it becomes a fully intelligible venture to investigate the possibilities of knowing better, as I have called it.

In any case, worldly wisdom is not a topic that technically trained philosophers have much concern with. The contrast between academic philosophy and serious philosophy is evident in their respective intents. Academic philosophers who happen to be puzzled by the status of qualitative properties speak only of colors, sounds, and feels, as such—never mind which ones. Their questions are a prelude to nothing else. Dewey, on the other hand, was concerned to identify and characterize the properties of nature that have a decisive bearing on our fate and on our conception of the meaning of our existence. His resultant analyses and generalizations constitute his naturalistic metaphysics. He synthesized his observations of nature into five generic traits: the precarious, the stable, qualities, histories, and ends. He did not characterize these traits as fully as he should have, and he did not make enough distinctions. As we shall see, his remarkable and often brilliant moral philosophy, articulated in so many different works, would have been better if he had had a better metaphysics.

The traits of nature

The *precarious* includes all situations in which there are obstacles, alarms, confusions, disruptions, disorder, and the like. These are situations, obviously, that we encounter repeatedly; they are pervasive in human experience. From famine, flood, and terrorist attacks to lost keys, spilled milk, and unexpected visitors, we are incessantly confronted by the problematic in forms both great and small. It is essential to recognize these conditions as properties of situations, not of subjective mind. They happen; the terrorists are real; we must contend with them, and an honest metaphysics cannot fail to give them full standing. If they are not accorded full reality, then such philosophizing is condemned to being an impotent, if pleasant, apologetic—like absolute idealism, for example.

The *stable* refers to that in situations that is ordered in some way, having both a structure and an endurance of sorts. The stable, too, is generic to all situations, though it may be barely discernible. Rarely is a situation totally confused, and we may seize upon what is stable in it to help get our bearings and to proceed in our activities in some constructive manner. The stable has a very rough correspondence to what in classical metaphysics is regarded as true being. I say "very rough" because Dewey's conception of order and of cognitive objects differs momentously from those of the tradition. The traditionally conceived object of rational knowledge, as we have seen, is not derivative of experience, and it is not indicative of the relations between experienced objects. It possesses an essential and unchanging nature, and no properties that are subject to change can rightly be attributed to it. Not only did Dewey explode the idea that changing things must be exclusively subjective, but he showed that the object of knowledge is not essence but the correlations between processes of change. The scientist asks how variations in one sort of event are correlated with variations in another. Once that correlation is determined, he can predict what the effects will be of introducing a specifiable change in the process. The law of gravity, for example, states that the variation in the attraction between two objects is a function of their mass and the square of the distance between them. Mass changes and distance changes, but the correlation is constant.[6] Accordingly, we can predict the change in gravitational attraction consequent upon a determinate change in mass or distance.

Constancy of correlation is what Dewey mostly has in mind in *Experience and Nature* when he speaks of the stable. The stable is neither substance nor transcendant form but inherent correlation. It does not exist apart from change but permits us to predict it. In contrast to the merely contemplative objects of the classic tradition, this is an eminently useful notion. Experimentally, we learn the conditions upon which experienced events depend, and this is to learn how variations in these conditions result in variations in their outcomes. The determination of these relations increases our power to predict and control them. We can learn, for example, the conditions upon which plentiful yields of grain depend: variations in the genetic constitution of seed will bring variations in yield per acre, so we can deliberately introduce the conditions that will bring us the richer harvest. Or, if students are dull and listless, we might find out what variations in educational conditions would make them alert, curious, and persistent.

Dewey's account of the stable focuses almost exclusively on two paramount issues. One of them concerns the nature of the principles of order that are investigated in science. They express the correlations between natural events. The other is to consider the relation between the stable and the precarious. In classical metaphysics, precarious phenomena are not accorded full being. They are, at best, becoming, mere appearance, merely subjective. There is an ontological dualism of the stable and precarious. Dewey wished to discredit this dualism and relegate *it* to nonbeing. Precarious events occur as inseparable parts of processes of change. They are integral to an order of events, but we are unaware or ignorant of that order or powerless to contend with it. Our task is to determine how precarious events occur so that we might bring them under some control and direct them to welcome ends, if possible. The true Being of the classic tradition, by contrast, is powerless to direct processes of change to anticipated outcomes. Dewey's most fundamental charge against the tradition was that it is inherently incompetent to contend with change. Platonic forms and Cartesian essences are impervious to the hurly-burly of relations constituting the experienced world.

Dewey also wished to restore qualitative immediacy—*qualities*—to full membership in nature. The qualitative is not just the hackneyed examples of smells, colors, tastes, sounds, and touch but also such complex, engrossing, and dangerous qualities as the amiable and the hateful, fearful and alluring, tragic and triumphant. Persons will often disagree regarding what events are deserving of such epithets, but Dewey's point is that the qualities that elicit such judgments and arouse controversy are constituent of nature. The traits denoted by moral and aesthetic expressions are likewise objective. However debatable or uncertain our ascriptions in a given case, what we refer to by the good, the bad, and the beautiful are qualities of natural existence. In an obvious sense, these ascriptions ought to be debatable, for if we are seeking wisdom, we must regard them as provisional and withhold our commitment until we have made an appropriate investigation of our situation. These objects of regard and disregard could not be treated as worldly, however, on the assumption of the dualism of experience and nature.

A crucially important characteristic of nature is what Dewey calls *histories*. These are processes of qualitative change. Inasmuch as the most sweeping revisions in a naturalistic worldview occur in consequence of rejecting the notion of static being and bringing change to the forefront, Dewey's notion of histories is the most fundamental in his philosophy. Remember that these are processes of *qualitative* change—as when an acorn, with all its properties, mixes with other conditions and becomes an oak, with all its properties. In the Cartesian heritage, such a process is unintelligible: all beings are fully actual; matter is what it is forever and always, and so is mind. Neither ever becomes essentially different. Apparent qualitative differences are all in the mind, and our splendid oak has dissolved into a meaningless swarm of atoms. There is no oak tree, as such.

Dewey's notion of a history recalls us to Aristotle, for whom the notion of change from potentiality to actuality was central, but there are consequential differences. Aristotle, of course, had maintained that complete being is eternal and unchanging, and he believed that potentialities and actualities are changeless essences inherent in a given sort of event. Dewey, by contrast, argued that the potentialities of nature are a function of variations in the turmoil of causal conditions. The possible changes that an acorn can undergo, for example, are not inherent to itself alone but depend on the indefinite number of variations with which it might combine. The nature of the acorn itself is determined by a multitude of conditions and is itself subject to change. Accordingly, the possible ends—actualities—achievable in nature are neither changeless nor determinate in number. Nature, Dewey insists, is capable of indefinite variety.

Merely to recognize histories is just the beginning.[7] Inasmuch as the constituents of these processes admit of variation, nature produces remarkable diversities and novelties. These variations are not just rearrangements of brute matter. They produce those qualitative realities that are rubbed out in reductive philosophies. The notion is used to great effect. Mind, for example, rather than being regarded as a separate, immaterial, and original substance, is analyzed as the outcome of a complex history, and Dewey writes at length on what he takes to be the main factors that evidently compose it. Deeply respecting the notion of a history, he refuses to call himself either a materialist or an idealist but a naturalist. Merely physical conditions are necessary to mind, but this is not sheer materialism, for mind is not matter per se. It is one of the qualitatively distinctive functions of complex material events. Under certain conditions—including, Dewey held, social interaction—nature produces mind. Mind is one of the potentialities of nature, but to hold this position is not to be an idealist either. Rejecting physical conditions, idealism, too, takes no recognition of histories.

Human nature itself is the outcome of a history uniting organism and environment. Experience is likewise the product of a natural history, and so is knowledge. It is significant to regard such events as the outcomes of processes of change. Human nature is not a fixed essence; it is dependent upon innumerable variables—most of them, Dewey believed, in the social environment. The individual, then, is not destined to a fate determined by an antecedently established nature. It is equally important to regard knowledge as the outcome of a history. In the classic tradition, knowledge was thought to be sheer rational cognition—what Dewey aptly called the spectator theory of knowledge. Our knowledge, however, is in fact the outcome of a process of overt activity. The inquirer deliberately manipulates the events of nature to observe what they do under specified conditions. He is a participant in nature, not its passive spectator. The difference between the two conceptions of knowledge is not to be lightly passed by. The experimental techniques upon which Dewey's theory is modeled are responsible for the astounding and accelerating advances in knowledge in recent history.

The ultimate significance of experimental method, in Dewey's view, is moral. The good is the *constructed* outcome of a history, and the means are expressly scientific. The deliberate direction of the course of nature requires knowledge of the correlations between its constituent parts. In pursuit of the good, we neither adhere to an antecedently given form nor create something ex nihilo by sheer will. We construct the good out of the problematic conditions resident in a unique situation. There are suggestions in it of joy and satisfaction and omens of hurt and failure, too. What is one to do with such portents? He devises a plan of action, perhaps in collaboration with others, to reorder the situation in a manner to create a harmonious whole, if it can be done, by deliberate action. Thus a good is constructed.

The composition is by no means normless. We seek happiness and satisfaction, to be sure, and we are attentive to a medley of moral considerations. For an individual of strong moral dispositions, indeed, personal satisfaction cannot be purchased at the expense of what he takes to be the legitimate claims of others. But what satisfactions are available in this particular situation? What instrumentalities and obstacles are peculiar to it? What are the expectations of others in these more or less singular circumstances? How much should they be credited? There are no a priori answers. More than any philosopher in history, Dewey urged that the formation of values be carried out in a deliberately consultative and collaborative manner. This procedure he called social intelligence, or democracy as a way of life.[8] It presupposes, among other things, a moral regard for others and the conviction that cooperative behavior is apt to be both effective and fulfilling. Still, such norms do not typically lead to certain and unequivocal plans of action. Absolutist philosophers to the contrary, nature rarely provides such assurances.

Dewey's most repeated and detailed attention to histories is in regard to goods or ends. As a matter of fact, in order to give them conspicuous attention, he treated *ends* as a distinctive trait in its own right. This is the last feature in his metaphysics to be sketched. In light of the analysis of histories, it is already evident that ends are characteristic of nature, and merely to establish this much is in defiance of modern philosophy. Nature does not possess ends in the manner conceived by Aristotle, however, with every existent having an intrinsic defining purpose, but ends are not subjective either. Dewey's point of emphasis is that by means of intelligent participation with nature, we can bring welcome consummations into existence, each one more or less unique to the character of a given situation, but in any case exhibiting the coalescence of real potentialities of nature.

Dewey thought this orientation a vast improvement over the classic tradition, according to which one simply conforms to an alleged moral absolute. The logic of the classic tradition is, in effect, deductive: one cognizes the eternal forms, classifies a moral problem as belonging to one of them, and acts accordingly. "This is an instance in the world of becoming that falls under the form of Justice," one supposes. "Therefore, this is just." The supposed absolutes, however, are but the prejudices of a cultural or political elite, Dewey insists, and conformity to them is an imposition on the potential forms of flourishing available to human action. He can only celebrate the demise of moral absolutism.

Although there are consummations to particular situations, there is no permanent or ultimate end. A life should not have a trajectory aimed at a static condition of some description; nature will allow no such arrangement. We must learn to live with change, with all its contingencies. Dewey, consequently, repeatedly condemns a dualism of means and ends, where the alleged end is both static in form and discontinuous with the potentialities of nature exhibited in real situations. He urges that we seek the good in the *process* of life, rather than in the attainment of a "fixed end." He characterized this process with remarkable insight and consistency, noting its rhythms and resources, and sometimes specifying its distinctive rewards with eloquence. This process he denominates *growth*, and "Growth itself is the only moral 'end,'" he writes, in full coherence with his conception of nature. The paramount good within the processes of growth is what Dewey called shared experience—sustained human companionship and community.

Dewey's best writings on growth occur in his discussions of art—art as experience and practice. Art (or growth) is a continuing assessment and appropriation of natural forces to create consummations with whatever contingencies arise in the course of experience. It is at the same time a refinement, enhancement, and expression of human powers. Such activities construct particular unifications with nature. Further incidents of a precarious sort will upset the ongoing unity, so we attempt to create a new unification. The construction of goods demands a medley of intellectual and practical talents, among which would be counted the habits especially distinguished as virtues. When Dewey gives his attention to virtue, he writes of characteristics that are effective in participating with the ongoing rush of things, marked by novelty and variation. He urges open-mindedness, flexibility, adaptability, creativity, and—above all—experimental and collaborative intelligence.

It is especially noteworthy that his analysis of histories and ends places a premium on creative and experimental intelligence. This conception of active intelligence is in radical contrast to that of the classic tradition, in accordance with which the good or some other principal of conduct enjoys a complete and changeless form antecedent to action, where our obligation is simply to conform to it. His position constitutes the thoroughgoing substitution of experimental reasoning for deductive. It is the substitution of "arts of control" for "arts of acceptance." He thought of this conclusion as the principal import of his metaphysics. Thus he consummates his thoroughgoing reconstruction of the classic tradition, and he was confident that its implementation would bring a liberation and happiness to be cherished above any precedent condition. There might be great wisdom in Dewey's conclusions. The good of life would not be dependent upon expectations of El Dorado but in the daily vitality of activity, with its innumerable finite satisfactions, its continuing growth in powers of thought and action, bathed in the light of shared experience.

b. Purpose and Method in the Metaphysics of Morals

So much for a summary review of Dewey's metaphysics. Its fundamental pertinence to wisdom in the moral life is evident. I will shortly state my judgment
regarding some notable deficiencies in it. That analysis will benefit from a discussion of the method and aims of this sort of inquiry. The "method," if I may
call it that, is to be observant of the full range of human experience, wherever
and however it comes within our ken, and to be discerning of its conspicuous
and eventful features. There are ways in which scientific knowledge is indispensable to our queries, but that is not the only source of information. We
learn from our own experience, if we are willing to discipline it. Poets,
prophets, and historians are the allies of philosophy. They are abundant in
suggestion and depiction of the climactic traits of existence. The poet limns
teeming cities, skies, lands, waters, gods, and impersonal forces, and he gives
voice to the characteristic energies, loves, and torments of life. The philosopher takes the same subject matter and tries to systematize it: What pertinent
generalizations can we make from all these particulars—generalizations that
somehow incorporate all of them, one hopes?

There is a distinct element of choice in formulating these conceptions.
They do not refer to separate and distinct realms of being; they are selective
of traits from the entire commingled range and tumult of experience. We
distinguish what seems distinctive, important, and pervasive, and no doubt
there is overlap and redundancy in our formulations. Dewey, for example,
might have decided to keep his treatment of ends wholly within that of histories, and there would have been no error of fact in doing so. Yet, obviously,
he wished to make the subject of ends as prominent as possible—as well he
might, inasmuch as the discernment and characterization of ends has been
both a vexed issue in philosophy and a matter of intense human attention.
Although choice is an ineliminable feature of such analysis, the results are
neither unreal nor arbitrary. These are actual features of natural existence
that are discriminated and characterized, and their selection and analysis are
valuable insofar as they present distinctions pertinent to the common anxieties and ambitions of human life.

One might formulate a metaphysics with rather few traits, as Dewey did,
and give each of them a complex analysis, or one could go to the other
extreme, making many distinctions and presenting a large number of traits.
There is considerable advantage, I think, in tending to relatively few and
more inclusive categories, for the result is a philosophic vision more readily
available to our imaginative grasp and more affective in our subsequent
reflections and practice. However one might decide to discriminate traits of
nature, it is essential to think of them as functions of the common matrix that
is nature itself, rather than as inhabitants of impermeably separate places. As

a case in point, we have seen how Dewey delineated the precarious and the stable and the continuities between them.

A metaphysics of morals would distinguish germane features of natural existence and enlighten us regarding their import for the conduct of life. The varieties of experience thereby conveyed are meant to teach us about nature in a manner that will enlighten our conduct and aspiration. Consider the massive reorientation, for example, in the rejection of static being and the development of the idea of histories or in the meaning of the stable, the precarious, and ends. Such a metaphysics might also put the fear of god—and some thanksgiving, too—in the heart of anyone who would be wise. This is not cosmology. It is an inquiry into the nature of nature as we find it exhibited within the ambit of experience, articulated in terms of the traits there disclosed. It is a work of both art and science. It is nothing so grimly methodic as a sort of check-off list of matters to attend to. Its aim is at once panoramic and profound. In its way, it provides an integrated vision of the whole; it articulates the primal moral functions of nature; and it alerts us to our persistent tendency to dishonest simplifications. A mind that ponders such a metaphysics might attain a certain gravity and a disposition to realism, while furnishing the imagination with a sense of the richness and power of nature's possibilities. Dewey's moral thinking was not formulated by doggedly following the suggestions of his philosophy of nature; rather, the two inquiries were complementary: each body of ideas continued to develop in response to growth in the other. The analyses in the present chapter illustrate the reciprocally invigorating relations between metaphysics and value theory. Moral experience is drawn upon to contribute to the elaboration of a naturalistic metaphysics, and recognition of vital traits of nature gives scope and efficacy to consideration of the moral life.

As a final anticipation of building upon Dewey's metaphysics, there should be a word about the meaning of the phrase used above, "integrated vision of the whole." What is that? Such a philosophy, as Dewey intended it, should be both *inclusive* and *synoptic*. He did not use these expressions himself, but we may ask how *Experience and Nature* exhibits these characteristics. The study is *inclusive* in the sense that it incorporates within nature what had hitherto been unjustly excluded or orphaned—such as immediate qualities, the precarious, and histories. The restoration of nature was preceded by a defense of the propriety of treating such traits as characteristic of nature at all. Dewey's project of inclusion undertook still more, most notably an account of mind, knowledge, and human values as emergent of natural processes. That is, he not only distinguishes histories as a trait of nature, but he also undertakes to give a reckoning of some of the most important of them. He denied himself the luxury, for example, of just postulating mind as an original entity. Such an accounting has to be scientific, so Dewey's more or less pregnant suggestions should be regarded as hypotheses, not finalities. The immediate point is that his philosophy of nature amounts to more than "the detection and description of the generic traits of nature," as he put it. It is supplemented and enriched by showing how mortally important phenomena are intelligibly and plausibly conceived as functions of nature.

Dewey's metaphysics would be *synoptic* in the sense that there would be no morally significant phase or feature of nature that is left outside the orbit of attention. The issue is not whether these traits belong to nature at all. The question is whether Dewey has succeeded in discriminating all the traits that demand attention, and, for that matter, whether the traits that he has discriminated have been appropriately elaborated. I judge that Dewey was successful in being inclusive, but he failed to be synoptic.

c. Some Limitations in Dewey's Metaphysics

Four of the traits defined in Dewey's metaphysics demand qualification and elaboration: the stable, the precarious, ends, and histories. In addition, a metaphysics of the moral life must attend to conflict, the toilsome, power, the negative, and limit.

The stable refers to a kind of order, and *order*, in fact, is a better term, for it is more generic to the pertinent range of phenomena. The correlations disclosed by scientific inquiry identify an order in events, to be sure, but there are uncounted additional sorts as well. Any kind of systematic interdependency is an order. A biological creature is an order that comprises suborders. The creature and its environment is a still more inclusive order. The human personality is an order; a social grouping is an order; and so is an institution, such as a court of law. There are political, economic, and religious orders. There are moral orders of many sorts, constituted by varying conditions, objectives, and relations of precedence. There are artistic orders, formal orders, and astronomical orders. The list could go on. It is important to recognize that orders vary in their ability to endure or in their susceptibility to collapse, and our evaluations of them have much to do with these tendencies.

Dewey was aware of the multiplicity of orders, and he analyzed and evaluated many of them. Oddly, his metaphysical analyses, as such, are largely confined to the standing in nature of the causal orders investigated in natural science, and his work here is groundbreaking. But he does not otherwise make this class of beings—orders—a focal concern in his reflections on the nature of nature. This narrowed field of attention is objectionable because any adequate vision of the nature of the whole ought to make the notion of order more inclusive and prominent. A compelling assessment of human striving, indeed, would be to characterize it as the attempt to establish and

maintain orders against the incessant forces of dissolution. This idea is mem-
orably suggested by Santayana's phrase "eddies in the universal flux." That
expression could be used to denote the entirety of human accomplishment.

Consider next the precarious. Dewey thinks of it in terms of obstacles
and perplexities—perhaps great obstacles, but in any case he regards it as
demanding inquiry and action to set it right. This notion does not do justice
to many of the contingencies of experience. Repeatedly, we find that events
are volcanic, convulsive, and overwhelming. We find that human nature itself
can be this way in its depths of irrationality and passion. It is all very well to
take such conditions as invitations to intelligent action, but that course is
often not open to us. It might be inconsistent with the realities in which we
are engulfed. It is wise to recognize that nature is not always waiting
patiently to be reconstructed. Situations may be irresolvable, tragic, not
amenable to any happy remedy, or not docile to experimental intelligence.
Dewey had some sense of this occasionally, but his characterization of the
precarious is undoubtedly biased in favor of his Baconian obsession to bring
nature under control for human benefit. And we can do this sometimes, but
at other times we might have little recourse but to a response of a more emotional nature, or we might flee, or stoically accept defeat and even destruction, or perhaps conclude that further attempts at reconstruction would do
more harm than good. A metaphysics of morals is bound to acknowledge that
things are often of such a nature, and it dictates the formation of virtues that
are not commonly honored in Dewey's philosophy. What he dismissively
referred to as arts of acceptance will always have a fundamental importance
in our existence.

Dewey's analysis of ends is breathtaking. He completely overhauls the
classic tradition and articulates, in its place, a metaphysics of change. Not just
in theory, but in reference to life experience itself, he discredits the notion of
fixed forms of perfection. Then, aggressively and triumphantly, he proceeds
to articulate and celebrate the goods of process. These discussions have enormous merit. They urge that life should be ordered in such a way to make the
process inherently fulfilling, and they constitute one of the most powerful revolutions in the history of philosophy. But, in his enthusiasm, Dewey took the
revolution to excess and neglected some profound goods.

Technically, the critique of moral absolutes is impeccable, but the notion
of growth tends to be needlessly indiscriminate. His remarks are couched too
much in terms of the consummations of particular histories and not enough
in terms of an ordering principle or principles for the process throughout a
lifetime. A life must have thematic unity; otherwise it threatens to descend
into a sort of dismemberment, the life of a dilettante, with no unity and no
sustained direction. Die-hard defenders of Dewey will howl that he *does*
speak of ideals, and he cautions that in any situation we must ask not just how

to contend with the immediate problem but also to consider what kind of a person we are becoming in virtue of choosing one way or another.

There is a measure of justice in this rejoinder—but *only* a measure, for Dewey has little to say on this topic. When he refers to ideals, he merely waves at them and speaks in abstractions. Ideals of participation in art and science are mentioned without elaboration, or "shared experience" and "democratic community" are extolled; the ideal of democratic personality is mentioned now and then but never articulated systematically. Dewey seems actually to be impatient with such topics; he is in too great a hurry to pause to present a full and moving portrait of human possibilities. This appears to be more than oversight. Unlike Santayana, Dewey was not absorbed in the discernment and clarification of specific ideal goods.

Without falling into a discontinuity of means and ends, it is still possible to speak of the completion of a system of energies; it is possible to articulate a notion of the distinctive wholeness and excellence of a life. Dewey seemed to have little regard for an end so removed from the present that it organizes and directs an entire life—a protracted, distant, disciplined, daunting, luminous ideal for eros, such as the attainment of virtue, for example, or knowledge, beauty, or wisdom. In truth, he never seems to have conceived much of an idea of human excellence, confining his reflections, such as they were, to the democratic nature. As I will suggest in a few moments, Dewey's problem in this regard is not incidental; it is characteristic of the romantic's disdain for limits. But all ideal orders, however, imply limits, and they can be defined without recourse to changeless being. All goods, nevertheless, are transient, but the *meanings* of goods, as we shall find, are enduring.

Dewey's lack of attention to ideal goods also detracts from his discussions of the construction of good, which is always characterized as the attempt to solve and consummate a problematic situation. This way of putting it gives short shrift to the demands of eros. It does not adequately describe the poet, painter, or composer, for example, to say that he is trying to resolve a problematic situation. He is contending with such a situation, to be sure, but *he is trying to create a perfection*; he aims at what is most beautiful in the materials at his disposal. And so it might be with a variety of aspiring souls: they seek what is surpassing and what is best. One could reply that Dewey is appreciative of such efforts, so the difference between his view and that of the lover is merely verbal, but I doubt that the rejoinder is true. Dewey was decidedly uncomfortable speaking in terms of superlatives and perfections: such things are suggestive of the dreaded Platonism, with its hierarchies and fixities. The erotic dimension of life does not receive its full due in his writings, so his analysis of ends is insofar wanting.

The fourth trait of nature that calls for fuller analysis is that of histories. Brilliant as are many of Dewey's treatments of various histories, his bias is in favor of considering those that eventuate in some welcome manner. But nature brings not only positive outcomes. It also undergoes degradation and corruption; it produces failures and evils as well as successes, frequently with enthusiastic human complicity. Once again, in other words, Dewey's view of nature is insufficiently realistic, or—in Santayana's term—disillusioned. Of course Dewey must acknowledge, in principle, corruption as well as genera-tion, but he seldom does so, and many students of his thought—both admirers and critics—have thought that his view of human nature, for example, is far too charitable in assuming that our deep failings require no more than better education. Failure to be sufficiently cognizant of funda-mental traits of nature augurs insufficiency of wisdom.

One might proceed further in the analysis of Dewey's metaphysical dis-tinctions, but I see no pressing need to do so. Instead, I propose five traits that were slighted by Dewey but which belong to a genuinely synoptic description of nature. The first of these is *conflict*. Dewey's Hegelian soul would never rest content with taking conflict as final and irreducible; in his mind, it is always something to be overcome and transcended. He didn't have enough Schopenhauer in him. In much of our experience, conflict is just that—*conflict*, not a prelude to a greater harmony. Many philosophers have rightly seen it as part of wisdom to recognize that the impersonal forces of nature are indifferent to human aspiration and frequently crush it. Likewise, human beings crush each other. Many conscientiously entertained moral values, moreover, are in opposition to each other and promise no reconcili-ation. Contrary to utopian hopes, for example, egalitarian ideals and the love of freedom can never be in happy communion, nor can the ideal of equality of opportunity be perfected in the company of family life. Within the same breast, indeed, there are incompatible yearnings and moral commitments. Failure to give sufficient acknowledgment to such conditions mars Dewey's ethics and social philosophy, which occasionally flirt with superficiality.

Exemplary of this not fully resolute contemplation of experience is his treatment of the relation between individual and society. Uncounted tirades against the dualistic analysis fill his pages. He especially targets classical British liberalism, according to which the individual is regarded as a com-plete entity within itself, standing in radical juxtaposition to society. Against that position Dewey promotes the view (descended mainly from Hegel in modern times) that goes a long way toward concluding that the individual is constituted by the sum of his social relations. Admittedly, Dewey's analysis is that human nature is a product of the *inter*action of the organism and the environment, but it is clear, in fact, that he did not regard biological condi-tions as a potent determinant of what is significant in human nature and con-duct. With his thoroughly socialized conception of human nature, he leapt to the conclusion that there can be no inherent opposition between individual and society, and he seems to have thought that the possibilities for harmonious community are virtually unlimited, once we get the hang of education. Individuality, on this theory, must be understood as a distinctive form of irreducibly social behavior.

There is an obvious sense, however, in which the British view is closer to experience. The *theory* of atomistic individualism, I would agree, is untenable. That just means we have a poor theory to explain the facts of experience. Conflicts between individuals and groups are manifestly plentiful. Even if we disregard the murderous oppositions that characterize the relations between hostile groups and violent individuals, we must recognize that even friendly associations endure many forms of discord. Conflicts occur and persist between persons of good will who love each other. They are within every family and every form of association.

There are different respectable theories about the formation of human nature, but even if we take the view that each of us is socially constituted, we are still constituted quite differently. We are all misfits, more or less, and I would wonder what sort of individuality a person possesses if he is not something of a misfit. To be an outsider, indeed, is often the only honorable course. Dewey for his part was no friend to the congenitally alienated and ill-adjusted individual, as such: the unreconciled and reclusive sorts are simply a challenge to better methods of socialization. The philosophy is utopian and dangerous that conceives the aim of moral and social policy to be the creation of seamless communities. The policy must be intolerant and oppressive at best, totalitarian at worst—destinations utterly abhorrent to Dewey himself. I by no means suggest that we let every conflict bloom. I am saying that any realistic philosophy must take conflict more seriously than Dewey did.

The next trait I propose in a reconstructed worldly metaphysics is that of *the toilsome*. In saying this, I intend the reminder that in our transactions with nature, including those with each other, the achievement of aims frequently exacts much expenditure of blood and effort, and the value of the results is not necessarily proportionate to the costs we have endured. We often meet with disappointment. Nevertheless, the effort must usually be made: we must eat, we must survive, we must try to satisfy our obligations, we must tolerate people and conditions that are nearly insufferable. But suffer we do, and we must renounce many hopes. There are forces in impersonal events and in human beings that resist the will. They require toil. They are toilsome. We regard individuals as immature and even emotionally retarded who do not reckon such things; yet, in contemporary society, this adolescent cast of mind is like a plague. Any impediment to the fulfillment of desire is taken as proof that corrupt and benighted powers are exploiting us, while a perfectly harmonious order lies just beyond the tissue of present events.

Of course there are corrupt and benighted powers, and we have every reason to resist them, but our remedies are punier than we might suppose, and the hard work that is necessary under even the best conditions is not to be underestimated. Here, too, Dewey's philosophy fails us. He typically gives little recognition to the simply toilsome or even fails to acknowledge it. Everywhere we find him teaching that nature can be turned to good account; means can be as fulfilling as ends, and ends can fructify indefinitely. My judgment is that things are not so plastic to the discerning touch of creative intelligence. We will do all that we can to better our lot, but a genuine realism will spare us from Panglossian expectations.

The notion of *power* could be incorporated into the account of every trait examined in this discussion, but it is wise to present it as a worldly feature in its own right. *Power* is the third such character that I add to Dewey's analyses. In doing so I follow Santayana, who repeatedly speaks with pertinence of "omnificent power." In any situation, one could hardly imagine a condition more deserving of attention: What are the agencies with which we contend, and how much force do they command? Which of them are beneficent or hostile, insidious or blatant, malleable or unyielding, impersonal or personal, in self or other? These are obvious questions, of course, but that makes them no less important. A worldly metaphysics ought not confine itself to the abstruse. Its aim is to be synoptic in regard to the characteristics of nature that are especially consequential for the moral life. Moreover, though the questions be obvious, that does not mean that they are asked or that a sufficient inquiry is made. It is dismaying to see how often philosophers or "opinion leaders" are neglectful of the question. They are naive or complacent about making an unsentimental assessment of the forces at play in any circumstance. Hence power is deserving of its own place in a metaphysics of morals.

My critique suggests that Dewey, propelled by his desire to see how we can make things better, is guilty of his own sort of selective emphasis. But, as I have also remarked, things often don't get better. Accordingly, a worldly metaphysics must make prominent what I will call *the negative*. This is not a negative that powers the dialectic onward and upward; it is not an evil on its way to becoming good; and its reality is not to be veiled by naming it a privation of being. Sometimes—indeed, commonly—the world is simply grotesque and crushing in the fates it deals to its hapless occupants. There is unredeemed destruction, wickedness, and suffering. Sometimes we are resolved by our witness of catastrophe and random misery to resist such horrors, but that does not make them any the less horrors, and it does not bring such things to an end. Nature is often overwhelming, unforgiving, and remorseless.

The negative has a distinctively moral component. There is so little justice in the world, and the enormities of injustice occasion fathomless pain and bitterness. It is exceedingly difficult to accept and endure the fact that nature brings such torment, so the imagination contrives pathetic and fanciful schemes to afford a belief that there is, finally, no injustice and all will be set right in the end. In moral honesty, nonetheless, one can never be reconciled either to undeserved miseries, to the triumphs of pettiness, vanity, and pretense or to outright vice and evil. He simply carries on, somehow, if he can.

In a metaphysics that would contribute to wisdom, the negative must be admitted without discount. What can wisdom teach in the face of such obdurate truths? At least it says that one must form his expectations of the world realistically, and it counsels us to distinguish, seek, and celebrate those goods to which nature seems relatively well disposed. These we may love and cherish, scarce as they might be, without the assumption that there is guarantee against their failure or eclipse. This is a difficult but necessary wisdom.

The final trait of nature lacking in Dewey's metaphysics is that of *limit*. It is the greatest lack. Its absence encapsulates the fundamental difference between a romantic and classical worldview. I do not renege on my support of Dewey's surpassing critique of the classic tradition, but to deny the notion of changeless being is not to deny that nature has limits. Dewey made no such denial, of course, but he did not recognize their nature and towering importance in the conduct of life.

Provisionally, I define limit in the obvious sense of obstacles both within and without ourselves that preclude continuance in a given activity or aspiration. For everyone, there are limitations of strength, talent, patience, time, and much else, just as there are features of the environment that will not be moved, and no one can attain an enduring satisfaction with his life without knowing his limits and being reconciled to them. But there is a subtler and equally powerful sense that I also wish to convey: the continuation of an endeavor past a point where the quality of the activity undergoes radical and unwanted change. There are occasions when we exceed our capacity or that of worldly resources, or we exceed the capacity of others to share in or tolerate what we are doing. Limits, in other words, can also be thresholds that divide a good and admirable activity from destructive excess. We unduly press the limits of work, friendship, ambition, desire, and hope and thereupon sour the very conditions that sustain and reward our efforts. We easily go too far, and when we do, we are apt to ruin what has already been achieved. To be a friend is invaluable, but it is not license to make unlimited demands on the resources and patience of the beloved. When the limits are transgressed, the friendship is threatened. To be courageous is fine; to be foolhardy is destructive. Aristotle's doctrine of the mean, of course, reverberates in these reflections, and Aristotle's philosophy expresses the accumulated wisdom of ancient Greece.

As Aristotle observed, the mean lies between excess and defect, "but *in regard to goodness and excellence* it is an extreme." His teaching, which I have taken the liberty to italicize, implies that limit is frequently determined on a moral basis. We should not, accordingly, assume that limits are always of a negative nature. Nature, to be sure, often displays its absolute vetoes, but we also institute prohibitions of our own. We rightly limit many forms of behavior. Without doing so, we would fall into deadly chaos. We raise our children with limits, without which they will turn into monsters, and we cultivate internal limits, or constraints, that control wayward impulse and liberate constructive energies. Limits, accordingly, often make things better. The Greeks knew that human excellences are at the same time boundaries. To the man of virtue, these boundaries are not onerous; to know and respect them is requisite to optimal human conduct and feeling, to *eudaimonia*. Very often, of course, we are ignorant of limits, or we overestimate or underestimate them. Undue caution brings insufficiency of enterprise and failed opportunities, while *hubris* calls forth the vengeance of the gods. Knowing better is all-important. He who would be wise must search out limits in nature, society, and the individual.

It would be unfair to say that Dewey simply dismissed the ancient learning. He should not be identified with the idiot-level romantic, who wants to be free of limitations of any sort. Still, he does not give this fundamental notion a place in his metaphysics, and this is unwise. Obsessed with the confining characteristics of moral absolutes and excited by the idea that nature is a scene of change and variety, he thought almost exclusively in terms of liberation. Filled with zeal for human flourishing in plural and novel directions, his enthusiasm allowed him to skate past some of the most obvious requirements of life.

To neglect limits is not only to invite calamity, it is also to be unprepared to contend with limits *as limits*. Dewey's focus as a moralist is always to explain how we can prosecute histories from their precarious initiation to their consummatory end. This is a fine thing to do, and Dewey explicated the process superbly. But for many reasons we can't always proceed in this happy fashion. Life is not one unending project of creative intelligence. Instead, we encounter folly, wickedness, depravity, weakness, incapacity, deprivation, and heartbreak. Dewey does not speak to the conditions for which intelligent remedies fail or are inadequate, yet we must somehow learn to contend with such limits, even to become reconciled to them, if possible. Dewey, however, becomes angry when he refers to moralists who emphasize the formation of dispositions suitable to the inevitable vicissitudes of life. When the cultivation of deep-seated attitudes becomes our focus, he complains, such a preoccupation draws our attention away from the imperative of reforming social conditions.

> All the theories which put conversion "of the eye of the soul" in the place of conversion of natural and social objects that modifies goods actually experienced, are a retreat and escape from existence. . . .
> It is not in the least implied that change in personal attitudes, in the

disposition of the "subject," is not of great importance. Such change, on the contrary, is involved in any attempt to modify the conditions of the environment. But there is a radical difference between a change in the self that is cultivated and valued as an end, and one that is a means to alteration, through action, of objective conditions.[9]

If we were to take these statements at face value, we would have to suppose that such things as loss, adversity, humiliation, disaster, failure, and death never occur. Even disregarding this unfortunate myopia, however, Dewey's treatment of virtue is inadequate. As remarked earlier, his attention to the virtues is largely confined to those that are effective in constructing processes of change: openness, adaptability, experimental intelligence, and the like. This analysis neglects the fact that most change should be resisted. The unruly and insistent demands of the young, for example, should not be indulged; one's own tendency to self-indulgence must be corralled. Corruption and wickedness must be opposed; numberless forms of foolishness and stupidity must be discouraged or stopped, and we must enforce a resolute refusal to tolerate bullies, terrorists, and oppressors. It takes large measures of wisdom, strength, courage, and constancy.

It is the greatest weakness of Dewey's moral philosophy that it has no effective principles of moral authority. So transfixed is he with emancipation that the need for limits on conduct seems never to have been urgent for him, but this issue deserves investigation fully as much as the notion of growth. With an appropriate respect for limits, we realize that life cannot be a movement from one intelligent project to the next. Its most profound problems demand a different response, and here Dewey fails us. It is a failure to deal with limits.[10]

For one whose mind is not fixated on technicalities, vital questions to be pressed upon a metaphysician are these: "This nature of which you speak: *is it congenial to man?* What is it good for? To what human cravings is it responsive, and where will it disappoint?" To such pleadings Dewey has hopeful replies. Nature is more eventful and procreative, and more fluid, than had been supposed within the classic tradition. While it is, accordingly, more ambiguous and uncertain regarding human fate, and provides neither final assurance nor ultimate compensation, it is more answerable to human imagination, creative powers, and readiness for experimental ventures. When nature also calls forth realism and courage, initiative and intelligence are more apt to be rewarded. Once emancipated from the ossifications of the tradition, we are capable of more plentiful and varied consummations and an enriched experience, because now we work in collaboration with the prolific energies of nature. While life has typically been a burden to be endured, as Dewey saw it, nature—properly understood and cultivated—can secure goods in plenty. To be congenial, then, is a *potentiality* of nature, pending the appropriate use of intelligence.

One wonders whether nature is apt to be so responsive and so ample, and whether there is not more wisdom in the classic tradition than Dewey supposed. These are themes to be resumed. Let it be said for now that a worldly metaphysics, if it is to serve as an adequate heuristic for our moral labors and aspirations, must show regard for qualitative immediacy, order, the precarious, ends, and histories, and it must also be mindful of conflict, the toilsome, power, the negative, and limits. The poetic imagination, nonetheless, craves a single image for the whole. Although none is adequate for that purpose, perhaps the most befitting is a union of histories and ends, suggesting the central vision of ancient and medieval metaphysics: nature as *erotic*. Here nature is conceived foremost as *living*—the abundance of life forms exuberantly straining to achieve the fulfillment of their being and often succeeding! Mankind celebrates nature's opulence, witnessing the profusion of growing things completing their nature in beauty and order. It is no wonder that the ideal of self-realization has been so conspicuous and attractive.

Lovely and inspiring though the image be, it is inadequate. There is not an inherent harmony of natures; they are neither ordered by a supreme principle nor directed to one. This metaphysical vision also neglects characteristics of the world that are alien to the idea of cosmic perfection; our conception of the erotic must be chastened. The recognition of the precarious, the negative, and limit is chastening. This correction also finds expression in Santayana's matchless image, eddies in the universal flux. Likewise sobering is the Zoroastrian or the Manichaean teaching that good and evil are coeval principles of being. Even then, the conception of the erotic will retain its primal force and truth. It will gain vitality and allure precisely when it is recognized to be so much at hazard.

The formulation of a metaphysics of morals is in any event controversial, and the determination of nature's resources and limits is frequently problematic. Although parts of Dewey's work can be faulted, it is fitting to be reminded of the magnitude of his achievement. More effectively than anyone else, he rescued philosophy from the autism inherited from Descartes and restored the natural world to its rightful status as the source of wisdom and value, and he himself provided much wisdom. The thoroughgoing alienation of experience from nature is at an end, and nature—for all its risks and limitations—now seems a more familiar and homey place than it used to, and it could even be celebrated for the ideal goods that might be wooed from its bosom.

A worldly metaphysics aims to provide an inclusive and synoptic representation of the whole, yet in some ways it is a comparatively modest undertaking. It has no ambitions for the systematic ordering of being suggested by Plato's philosophy; it discourages the rationalistic pretensions of a Spinoza;

and it falls well short of the absolute knowing promised by Hegel. Nor does it divulge the meaning of life. Nevertheless, it furnishes a vision of the features of nature that are fateful for mortal life, and it will not attempt to costume the world in anything but the garments of truth, regardless of what we might prefer to believe. It thereby provides an invaluable context, giving vision and discipline to the moralist, that his inquiries be neither impertinent nor truncated. In fact, it *will* in due course help us to think effectively about the meanings of life. The immediate task is to think productively about the ways in which nature is normative.[11]

NOTES

1. For example, the problem of free will is sometimes called metaphysical and so is the question regarding the nature of causality, and that of the nature and existence of universals. Needless to say, metaphysical inquiries are prone to distortion due to prior commitments, such as the desire to make the world intelligible in religious terms or to support an antecedently given ideology.

2. By Robert Neville in his *Recovery of the Measure* (Albany: State University of New York Press, 1989), p. 93.

3. They were repellent to some others as well, including Santayana, as we have seen.

4. Some scholars would argue that Whitehead is more deserving of that distinction. Dewey and Whitehead had remarkably comparable diagnoses of the crippling tendencies of modern philosophy, and both insisted that any adequate account of nature could not divest it of the qualities found in experience, but there the similarities end.

5. Descartes believed that God is a third substance, so all existence is divided into three parts.

6. The correlation might not be *exactly* invariant, but it will be nearly so.

7. The idea of histories has much in common with Santayana's so-called Aristotelian principle, but Dewey examines the idea more thoroughly, and he typically analyzes particular histories in more detail.

8. For a fuller analysis of social intelligence, see my *Excellence in Public Discourse: John Stuart Mill, John Dewey, and Social Intelligence* (New York: Teachers College Press, 1986), esp. chap. 5.

9. Dewey, *The Quest for Certainty*, in *John Dewey: The Later Works*, vol. 4, ed. Jo Ann Boydston (Carbondale and Edwardsville: Southern Illinois University Press, 1988), pp. 219–20.

10. This being said, it is pertinent to remark that moral philosophers of today are hardly cognizant of such matters. A notable exception is John Kekes, *Facing Evil* (Princeton, NJ: Princeton University Press, 1990).

11. An earlier version of "Worldly Metaphysics" was presented at Rutgers University as the inaugural of the Emmanuel G. Mesthene Lecture series, spring term of 1994. My paper was dedicated to the memory of my friend Manny Mesthene.

| 4 |

By Nature

The universe has no moral order, but nature has established local and temporal orders that provide guidance and power in the conduct of life. The family is such a moral order, and so is the condition of justice as characterized by Aristotle. Such orders do not derive their moral qualities from transcendent forms. They are derivative of the specific conditions of human life in a characteristically demanding and unforgiving environment. We shall see that they have their own imperative quality in consequence of the fact that nature is inhospitable to alternative arrangements. They are not mere conventions.

The moral life gains an invigorating intelligibility when approached as part of an order, or several orders, constituted by nature. Then it makes perfectly good sense to speak of morality according to nature, and the study of that subject will be rewarding. Such themes will be considered throughout the balance of this book. Nature is decidedly normative, but the sense in which I understand this to be true has never been articulated. The principal theme of the present chapter is to elucidate the idea of "by nature" and the inquiries pertinent to using it to clarify and enrich the moral life.

The expressions "by nature" and "according to nature" have a long and varied history, with mixed results—sometimes illuminating, sometimes obfuscating, depending in large part on how "nature" is construed. Almost all philosophers have been agreed, nevertheless, that a thoroughly positivistic conception will support no notion of morality. The Cartesian system, the most conspicuous case in point, eradicates all possibility of appealing to outward nature as a guide to moral aims and behavior. When nature is thought to be without moral import (and when the notion of laws of reason lacks credibility), a further distinction is typically introduced: morality by convention. The ethical life is thereby judged to be a human contrivance, without constraint or direction from nature, and depending, apparently, on whatever happen to be the preferences of a given population. In fact, however, the distinction between nature and convention is more elusive than might be supposed, as we shall find.

In reflections on the possibility of morality according to nature, the standard assumption has been that if nature determines moral principle and practice, it must itself be invested with an inherent normative order. The order might be constituted by Platonic forms, derivative of the supreme form of the Good. A similar conception is that of Aristotle, who held that nature is ordered with intrinsic ends for human action and for all beings. Or nature might be essentially informed with divine law or laws, as the Stoics, Christians, and others have believed. Perhaps some power within the greater scope of things is endowed with an incontrovertible moral nature—as Kant believed of reason. In all such cases, either reason or revelation discloses the fixed patterns of conduct, and it remains to mortal flesh to abide by them. At the same time, deviation from the perfect order means calamity of one sort or another. If the principles of the universe are indifferent to human cry, on the other hand, they can have no *moral* significance. With a wholly impersonal constitution of being, all things are equally by nature: catastrophe and bounty, hatefulness as well as generosity, villainy and heroism, good fortune and bad. "By nature" implies no moral discrimination. It is a prescription for nihilism.

Many have thought that this conclusion is compelling, if not self-evident, but it is not. Indeed, the view that amoral nature can have no moral lessons is not only mistaken but heedless of experience. One of our most noteworthy adaptations, as I remarked in chapter 1, is to have developed a disposition for what has been denominated *moral* evaluation and action: we have a moral nature. That is, we possess at least minimal capacities and aptitudes for the conduct of associated life. Human life has evolved within nature and persists because of its adaptability to the myriad and daunting challenges of the surrounding order. Nature, in effect, has provided us with the means to contend with her, including the provision of at least a rudimentary moral nature. To be sure, we have evolved murderous and treacherous traits as well, and we are decidedly inconstant in the observance of what we take to be moral requirements. Those of the race who are even modestly attentive have recognized how perilous these violent and lawless tendencies are for the continuation of a thriving community. In recognition of this very fact, they teach with all the urgency at their command that it is essential that we do all that is possible to support the moral tendencies and discourage or redirect the destructive ones. Were it not for our self-serving and belligerent inclinations, morality would be an easy matter, and it would not be such an obsession of socially responsible individuals. They are sufficiently aware of the facts, however, to recognize that moral conduct is absolutely necessary for social life. The nature of nature is such, that is, that moral qualities are an essential part of our existence. There are prohibitions that must be established and enforced. There are, in addition, duties that must be done; there must be willingness to sacrifice for the group; the members must tend to be honest, trustworthy, and loyal. Without these and similar conditions, the order will fall into quarrel and anarchy and become defenseless. Our survival and well-being are massively dependent upon forms of conduct that will sustain a moral body, and most persons recognize and respect that dependency. We give moral concerns high priority because they deserve it; they demand it, for our very lives.

It is from this point of view—that of an intelligent moral being in the midst of life—that the study of nature's ways in constituting the moral life is not only a legitimate study but of the most vital importance. Widely varying patterns of conduct and aspiration are open to us, proffered by all manner of authorities, but they are by no means equally sustainable or equally satisfying; many are vicious and destructive. *Why* are they not equally sustainable or satisfying? Nature, we have found, has much to say in answer to this question. To protect ourselves from folly and destruction and to secure some happiness and security, we would heed her voice, and we would make every attempt to ensure that we have heard her clearly.

We mortals strive for many things, including peace, order, beauty, security, community, fulfillment, freedom, and even fair play. Such tendencies germinate in nature; they express nature's possibilities, and they are supported and defeated by the course of natural events. Given such facts, we evidently have much to gain from knowing and appreciating nature's ways. As lovers of good, and knowing mayhem, insecurity, and failure, we search the nature of things to learn of its constraints, hazards, opportunities, and supports, such as they might turn out to be. How is nature accomplice in our several ambitions or resistant to them? Would some of our practices and aspirations be modified by better knowledge of nature's chastening effects? There are ideal goods that we crave and that might impart a finer meaning to life; then we might be richly rewarded with pertinent knowledge of nature. From our standpoint as moral beings inhabiting the natural world, we court such knowledge, which would surely benefit us and make us wiser. A morality according to nature need not presuppose that the universe is ordered by an inherent moral principle. It need only proceed on the assumption that there is wisdom in learning how nature limits or supports our striving and even yields meaning for such intelligent and reflective beings as ourselves.

There is legitimate controversy, to be sure, regarding the extent to which the moral life might be tempered or enriched by pertinent knowledge of nature. The flux of things might be highly permissive, after all, permitting wide latitude in conduct without injury—or even with great benefit. This was Dewey's view, as we have seen, and today legions are far more insistent than he that the requirements of conduct admit of indefinite variety. In its extremes, this is a sentimental and self-serving revery. Nature plays a strong hand in determining what we can and cannot do to sustain an acceptable and even thriving life.

Now, from the point of view of a being who is literally without moral experience and dispositions, there could be no moral lessons to be gleaned from the nature of things, even if such lessons are available to those not so bereft. The lessons are for *us*, those already possessed of moral concerns or having some susceptibility to moral considerations. I have no doubt, indeed, that all philosophies of morality according to nature have precisely this origin and would not otherwise exist. Whatever the literal truth of these philosophies, their adherents share the conviction that the workings of nature leave little room for effective maneuver; there is an objective order in accordance with which we might live decently and well, but apart from which there is discord and failure. Such a view is obviously true for action in immediate converse with nature, where many events blatantly resist the will or forward it. The fisherman, hunter, farmer, and builder are instructed and called to account by the unsentimental course of events. But are there comparable lessons for the moral life?

It would be mad to refuse this study from our standpoint as moral beings, and, to tell the truth, the traditional inquiries have themselves originated from just this perspective. All of them, however, took a dubious turn, for they failed to investigate nature in a manner that would truly serve their aims. They endowed nature with moral ends and laws and regarded this investiture as the conclusion and triumph of their philosophy. They did not determine whether there are more or less abiding structures intrinsic to natural processes that limit or support our ambitions to sustain a happy moral order. They did not guess, apparently, that our moral values have a distinctive character and worth precisely because they have proven themselves to be singularly precious forms of conduct in just the sort of world that we inhabit. As Dewey repeatedly complained, they unwittingly transformed functions of experience into a transcendent order, while neglecting to determine the true origin and nature of these functions.

There is a lack of realism and discipline in these traditional authors, for they contrive a fictitious nature to give warrant to their dearest moral convictions. As Dewey and many others have observed, metaphysicians are prone to design the cosmos after their moral biases. In effect, what would be the determination of the good according to nature turns out to be the determination of nature according to the good! The bias comes first: a philosopher finds something precious in experience, and then he characterizes the way of things to give this good a special status and warrant. He begins with a moral allegiance and then reads it back into the heavens. Then he supposes that the heavens provide the mandate for this good. On top of this (unwitting) misrepresentation, he has found it repugnant to give full status to the objectionable and hideous features of existence, so his philosophy, though comforting, is less than honest. He has purchased a singularly moral universe at the expense of a kind of dissembling or, at least, a kind of self-deception. However edifying, ignorance of unwelcome facts is an invitation to impotence and calamity.

In its way, nevertheless, it might be an effective step to conceive nature according to the good: the discriminated value is given a conspicuous status and probably a fearsome authority. In another way, however, the philosopher has been a slacker: he has not only neglected to be realistic; he has also failed to engage in the hard work to determine the real sources of this good, its harmonies and dissonances with other goods, and the conditions necessary to sustain its being. Presumably, the favored conduct is of real worth, perhaps of great worth, but it does not possess it by mere fiat, and it is perilous to absolutize it. It deserves recognition, praise, and defense due to its part in the economy of the life of troubled and passionate beings in a difficult environment. If this is its status, it is indeed a good by nature.

A prophet, on the other hand, will simply declare that divine law commands, for example, the keeping of faith with others, and he can let it go at that, but a responsible philosopher would be observant of the indispensable role of promising in social action and in human bonding and loyalty, themselves of surpassing worth. He might judge that we have a disposition by nature to cherish loyalty and bonding, and likewise, perhaps, the propensity to be true to one's word is in some part inherent or satisfies a native demand of the psyche. In brief, the lover of wisdom, striving to know better, undertakes a searching philosophic appraisal: he wants to learn the true conditions of the moral life. He could conclude that the real warrant for keeping faith is the many goods that the practice sustains, including, we suspect, the satisfaction of inborn demands of one's nature, while the sanctions for faithlessness are the penalties that must be exacted of the betrayer, lest such betrayals become epidemic. In most cases, these warrants and sanctions are sufficient to regulate conduct, but they must be learned and remembered by our infirm nature. The meaning of fidelity to one's trust would be dramatized in arts and memorialized in public observances and religious devotions, where they would be endowed with gravity and authority.

What is displayed indisputably in the philosopher's ventures is that there are values in life that men will seek with ardor and possess with joy. These values prompt the question of the status of their existence in the larger frame of things. We are led into theory, which takes many forms and assumes many functions, most of them ersatz. The urgency of the inquiry is not to satisfy theoretical speculation, but that we may secure, enhance, and teach these goods. Surprisingly, perhaps, the encompassing theory in itself achieves an importance in the minds of some that exceeds that of the goods themselves, and furious theoreticians cogitate in their chambers in ignorance of the real vicissitudes of life.

The attention to theory would be legitimate, however, if it held, let us say, that the existence of precious goods depends upon discernible natural orders. Then we revere the order as the precondition of that which we love. If the theory turns out to be mistaken, we would redirect our inquiries and eventually our piety to those conditions that in fact secure our good. It is a far more dubious use of theory to suppose that it somehow *justifies* our love. Our attachments often do require justification, of course. They would be justified, so far as they could be, by the process of philosophic appraisal, but the theory-stricken mind persists in the endeavor to measure the value of a good by reference to something that is different in kind from a value—something value neutral, presumably. Evidently, the security and complacency attained by such a device is craved by human beings of every description. Even today, in our supposedly sophisticated age, philosophers and others still wish for an authorizing principle that is of a different nature than the values that are truly vital in a given affair. An arcane theory of abstract right, for example, is invoked in defense of treasured conditions of experience, but it is not the *theory* that makes them precious and worthy of devotion. It is essential to recognize that a good or a rule of conduct does not perish with its counterfeit credentials. If a philosopher produces a rationale for virtue, say, or for the keeping of one's word, and the rationale is later exposed as bogus, we are hardly compelled to despair for nobility of character and for elementary honesty. We do not succumb to nihilism; we simply reopen our investigation of *why* these values have earned such preeminence in the conduct of life. We must distinguish between theoretical contrivance and the manifest goods of experience, but the distinction is rarely made.

I will return to this theme, but here it is appropriate to elaborate the meaning of "according to nature" and to enumerate and clarify the sorts of inquiry that would help us to become wise through this study.

a. Investigating Nature with Moral Intent

Although there have been elements of misunderstanding and imposture in ancient models of morality according to nature, the idea of investigating nature with moral intent is not invalidated but clarified. There is more than a remnant of virtue in the ancient conviction that there is an order of things that we neglect at our peril. In the classic paradigms, "by nature" meant in accord with a law or an archetype; a definite pattern of conduct is prescribed, or a definite end is depicted as the inherent perfection of nature. According to a model that is more faithful to the realities of our existence, stated now without any qualifications, I submit the following: *For a moral being, "by nature," in its moral signification, refers to dispositions, ends, or patterns of conduct that are well suited to human endurance and flourishing, and significant deviations from these conditions tend to meet with frustration, failure, and even disaster.* It is essential to confine the definition to conditions that do not admit of much variation in the determination of the desired result; we are speaking of those cases in which nature requires a certain regimen of us. The purpose of saying that an event is by nature is not simply a matter of convenient classification. The point is that there are constancies and limits in nature that impose a discipline and direction on our ambitions and actions, regardless of what our ill-informed hopes or adolescent fantasies might be.

Adherence to these natural orders is not commanded by a superhuman authority. Where nature is not equally hospitable to all forms of behavior, human experience comes to recognize which forms are congenial and which are not. We practice and teach the one, while resisting or fleeing the other and warning of its inadequacies and dangers. We try to identify the particular conditions, both within us and without us, that give facility to our efforts or hinder them, and these, too, are transmitted to others. We likewise come to learn—usually painfully—that there are great benefits to be had by establishing and observing certain priorities and enduring certain renunciations in our lives, and they become part of our education and lore. Such, in germ and in brevity, is the natural history of the moral life, and whatever resources we might possess for criticizing and expanding it must develop from such knowledge and experience.

There is here no model of an is/ought logic, which has turned out to be a fool's errand. We are not starting out from a value-neutral posture. Rather, with our swarm of necessities and interests, we learn from continuing experience, appraisals, and practice, and we modify our assessments and conduct accordingly, so far as possible. The "logic," such as it is, is the same as that of the practical arts mentioned earlier. The arts of the hunter, farmer, and builder are learned from ongoing experiments with nature. The learning begins with the needs to eat and to build and sometimes to engage in sport, and the needs themselves are products of nature. To be sure, there are several forms of effective hunting, farming, and building, but all forms are not equally productive and satisfying, and there is not an indefinite number of them. Most of the possible ways of doing these things are ineffectual and even dangerous. There are good and better ways of hunting, determined by how well attuned to nature the practice has become, and there are individuals whose endowments make them good hunters and those for whom such capacities are scarce.

Like the arts of the woodsman or seafarer, how much do our obligations, our goods, and our justice admit of some determination by nature? Such vital practices as keeping our word and telling the truth are obviously in this pattern. They are not conventions. They are functionally indispensable in human association; it is in the nature of shared conduct in a precarious and resistant world that these norms be upheld and enforced. *Here is a lesson for the moral relativist:* It is not a potent reply to observe that it is sometimes preferable, say, to fail to honor a promise or that it is sometimes harmless to do so. Standing by one's word is a *norm* in two inseparable senses: it is a requirement, a principle, to be sure, and it is also the *usual*, the *expected*, conduct in the sense that it is normally required. It is normally rewarded, and deviations from it are normally punished. To be the norm in this sense is not the same as to be an utterly unexceptionable rule.[1] It is a form of integrity maintained as a matter of very high priority relative to most possible contingencies. It is a benchmark of moral conduct against which deviations are judged, sometimes favorably, but the burden of proof is on he who would make the exception. It is taught, exercised, and rewarded in this status as an essential norm or rule for the conduct of life. No society could flourish or even survive if it were not that keeping promises be regarded as a practice of high priority, as being the norm. Hence it is according to nature. This is a first example of uniformity in the moral life from one culture to another.

In a preliminary sense, "by nature" now has a serviceable meaning, and inquiry into goods according to nature is an enticing—possibly urgent— venture. The question remains as to what further examples might be adduced and how finely our moral conduct is formed, directed, and constrained by recognition of nature's demands and rewards. We must also ask whether there are not other sources of value and norms that are different in kind.

Many observers, once more, are confident that such persistent natural orders do not exist; they are mere conventions—altogether the consequence of socialization and subject to limitless variation. To speak of a form of justice, for example, as an arrangement in accordance with nature is to be subject to ridicule. Likewise, the denial of human universals has been the mainstay of most social science in the past half century. The "nature" of any particular individual is determined by the process of socialization, it is said. Change the conditions of learning, and you change the individual to his very core. Such is the hope of any utopian: give me control of education, and I give you the individual and the social order. But if there are such universals, their existence suggests certain constancies of human dispositions and aims that would be resistant to the social engineer. Hierarchical social structures, perhaps, are universal; the preference for local customs and authorities might be the same. There are further candidates, but this is not the place to enumerate them. This is a controversy that can be settled only with forthright inquiry, but it is supremely attractive to ideologues to believe they can inscribe their own law on the human heart. It happens that the consensus among social scientists is under dire threat. Wherein nature is especially potent and wherein it is not is on the agenda of responsible scientists, who are developing the resources to measure these proportions with some accuracy.[2] In any case, it is beyond intelligent denial that these are vital questions to the moralist, whose reckoning of the moral life is highly dependent upon his assessment of the forces of both nature and culture in their continuities and conflicts.

Such controversies should be taken seriously. For the present, I must speak more fully about what sorts of inquiry a morality according to nature might encompass. We can distinguish at least three different directions of investigation. One of them is metaphysical. A candid inquiry into the nature of nature informs us of the fateful traits of the human circumstance, and our study would give us practical direction insofar as it is realistic about the traits of nature with which we must contend. A number of examples were given in "The Cosmic Landscape," where we found that a decisive cast is given to moral philosophies by their assumptions about the nature of reality. Those assumptions were sometimes profound but more often misleading. Those who labor in the vineyards of nature find there innumerable conditions that are *concealed* by Cartesian metaphysics, for example; yet there are real orders and contingencies in the nature of things of the greatest consequence for a living being, but they must be discerned and analyzed. Dewey in particular, I have urged, has given not just legitimacy but vigor to this undertaking. His metaphysics gives an intelligibility to moral experience that could not be provided in the terms of modern philosophy, which had chopped up, bleached, and mislocated everything of importance in the moral life. My own view was grafted upon his in "Worldly Metaphysics," where the moral import of many traits of nature was delineated.

Dewey incorporated many and various issues into his metaphysics, but they can be responsibly attended to apart from his explicit terms, and they have been. These are questions of such import that most philosophers have treated them as matters of fundamental consequence. What, for example, is the status of values in nature? Are they merely subjective? Are they free-standing objective phenomena? Are they functions of natural processes inclusive of self and world? Are there distinct levels of being, where value belongs to one rather than another? Are there values characteristic of the different levels? What is the nature of these levels and of their resident goods? Are there changeless perfections, or are all things in flux? Of what orders does flux permit? How would one live in a world without moral absolutes? What is the origin and function of morality in the nature of things? What is the status of mind in—or in opposition to—nature, and what moral powers and disabilities does it possess? All such questions are of first importance in the determination of a moral philosophy that would be adequate to the real conditions of human existence.

A morality according to nature need not presuppose independent normative principles governing the course of the universe, but that is not to say that it makes no difference what the nature of nature is. Whatever the order of things, for our very life and happiness it behooves us to seek pertinent knowledge of it and thereupon to contend with it and to become allied with its powers in discriminating ways. Perhaps inquiry will disclose that there are supernatural beings inhabiting the cosmos who intervene in terrestrial life. If so, it would be highly important to know their nature and what their interest in us might be.

A second investigation, to which I have already made reference, is into *human* nature. There are multiple ways in which knowledge of human nature can be appropriated in service to the moral life. Most fundamental is the issue of whether it is an autonomous substance possessed of its own laws, altogether separate from nature's ways. This question, I am confident, has been settled. Human nature is not a separate substance. It is a product of a larger order, and most features of our constitution attest to the work of the inclusive order in natural selection. To say this much puts us on the threshold of several more specific inquiries.

The first of them is to determine whether human beings are endowed with inherent dispositions of a fairly well established sort. If there are such endowments, the range of voluntary human action is confined within more or less settled limits, confounding the cultural engineers and many philosophers. To have dispositions that tend to be unswerving means that we possess confirmed motivations and evaluations. Many of our moral capacities might be defined in this way. It is possible, as some think, that nature might have been more liberal with us than we know: the race might have native potentialities that have hitherto been smothered by the stupidities and corruptions of existing regimes, and a new flourishing of human powers awaits their liberation.

Such questions are critical. Depending on your assessment of human nature, you might formulate a philosophy that makes very high demands on individuals, assuming them capable of conduct not heretofore witnessed on any scale. You might believe, following Godwin and others, that every individual is capable of shedding every bias in his nature and with them the exclusive attachments or obligations that we form. The fact that one is father or mother, for example, or husband, wife, or friend, would then have no *moral*

implication. A properly moral woman could and would lavish as much attention and resources upon total strangers as upon her own children, if not more.
Continuing in the utopian vein, we might produce perfect egalitarians, who
would relinquish their hard-won goods to raise others to their own level,
regardless of how it happened that the inequality occurred in the first place.

The philosophy of the Socratic school makes high moral demands of a
different sort: it holds out the prospect of perfecting one's nature, where the
standard of perfection is dazzlingly high—but bears little resemblance to a
Godwinian being. To achieve "justice in the soul" is the devoted project of a
lifetime, driven by eros. This philosophy assumes, however, that the project is
suitable for only a few, those who possess the potentiality for such excellence.
If your thinking is like that of Hobbes, by contrast, your demands on the
behavior of individuals will be at the barest minimum: you expect them to be
able to comprehend the nature of their condition in the state of nature and
the only means for remedying it, and you expect them to be sufficiently intimidated by the power of the sovereign. If, to suggest a further case, you hold
that human nature is potent, uniform, and relatively constant, you must
assume that any existing order, whatever its particular problems, is a fair representation of moral nature, and you will be severely critical of any philosophy
that requires a radical makeover. Such was the view of Hume, who found that
custom credibly displays the universal powers and values of our species.

Evaluations and actions that are largely determined by innate characteristics are rightly said to be by nature. Likewise, goods—that is, ends—that
are not simply adventitious but occur as a completion of some inherent appetition, exist by nature. Perhaps, indeed, we are by nature idealists. Passionate
energies and attachments issuing from our genetic inheritance promise their
own ennobling fulfillments, cherished by the aspiring soul. We yearn for a
wholeness and connectedness. We seem to be creatures who dislike fragmen-
tation and discontinuity in ourselves and in the world. A mind in love with
the good wants to locate its beloved object in a larger and encompassing
whole—not in mere whim, nor in convention, nor coherently arranged intuitions, but as part of an inclusive and sustaining order. The lover recoils from
the idea of life as a mere aggregate of feelings and actions. He seeks a life that
will approach unity and completion—at best an integrated whole in continuity with a larger order of goods. A philosopher with knowledge of human
nature in its extended continuities might identify real possibilities of such
fulfillments, scarce and difficult though they be. They would be goods
immensely satisfying to our nature.

Yet the suggestion of innate disposition is apt to conjure up the image of
perfectly fixed judgments and behavior, turning us into automatons. That
would be a misconception. It will be helpful to elaborate the idea of "by
nature" when it pertains to human motivation. It is entirely possible to

observe conduct that is at once highly adaptable and attributable in large measure to established nature. "According to nature," as I use it in this context, denotes both the *origin* and the *priority* of the responses that individuals characteristically make to typical features of their environment. According to nature, one is natively susceptible to certain kinds of stimuli in distinction from others, and response to them in particular has high precedence relative to other promptings. The response, while relatively strong and constant in general aim, might well result in a plurality of different actions. In such a case, the diverse particulars of conduct belong to a single class, determined by the nature of the fundamental instinct. A mother will typically and persistently act in a way that is protective and nurturing of her child, through good fortune and bad, though the particulars of her conduct will vary with circumstances. Other conditions will also appeal to her, and she will frequently be moved to action by them, but not ordinarily in a manner that threatens the welfare of her young. Massive variations in the environment will not move her to abandon her devotion.

Even where nature is especially demanding, education can qualify the response, perhaps significantly, but the fundamental motivation does not admit of wide variation. The response is not ex nihilo but ex naturam, which is often of great potency. When a disposition is strong and enduring, its possessor will make every effort to modify the environment to satisfy the need rather than be acquiescent or indefinitely accommodating. Here, variation is in the environment and the ways of utilizing it, not in the fundamental motivations of the agent.

Although these elemental dispositions are not inflexible, they constitute powerful and enduring structures in the moral life. The incautious observer easily concludes that diverse forms of conduct imply diversity and plasticity in motivation. If that observer is also a zealous reformer, he has little compunction about calling for radical institutional change. Remarking wide variations in, say, family life, he announces, "There is no inherent necessity in the role of the mother or father, so we shall abolish the family in favor of a less exclusive form of socialization." Given the fact that a deep disposition can lead to marked variations in action, however, the eager reformer evidently makes a colossal mistake. The powerful appetition must be satisfied, and where it is forbidden, conflict and failure will follow, while the alternative institutions will lack the requisite love and fortitude.

The judgment of what occurs by nature is not to be determined a priori or to suit one's ideological preferences. Still, a candid observer would be right to suppose that when forms of behavior are fairly uniform across significant environmental differences—even in defiance of the attempt to teach alternative behavior—then the conduct is almost surely according to nature. Likewise, when we find that individuals display great dissimilarities even when they are in similar environments, the chances are that differences in nature are at work. Plato had the right question:

> Was this the basis of your distinction between the man naturally gifted for anything and the one not so gifted—that the one learned easily, the other with difficulty, that the one with slight instruction could discover much for himself in the matter studied, but the other, after much instruction and drill, could not even remember what he had learned, and that the bodily faculties of the one adequately served his mind, while, for the other, the body was a hindrance?[3]

Both the *direction* that learning takes and the *aptitude* for it betoken native differences. One student shows musical gifts at once, for example, while another, in spite of all the time and effort devoted by himself and his teachers, remains an incompetent. But the incompetent does not typically care that much for music anyway. He loves architecture and building, let us suppose, so he is apt to turn in that direction.

Nature does not invariably speak with a uniform voice. She has, in fact, many voices loud and soft; they might be cacaphonous. There are innate conditions of anyone's talents, cognitive powers, preferences, temperament, and moral dispositions. In a given individual, some of these innate capacities and biases of personality will be very strong, others weak. The strong will not easily be turned aside by environmental enticements, but the weak ones would be more malleable. Some of these tendencies will be admirable and some dysfunctional and hurtful. The clamor of native propensities, moreover, might be ill suited to converge to a harmonious whole; an individual might be deeply ambivalent and conflicted by nature.

Even with the best of education, sometimes, not much can be done to develop a talented and virtuous human being. Nature has made some persons impervious to such instruction. A discerning and potent education, nevertheless, is indispensable to the development of native aptitudes and leanings, when it can happen at all; and education must also try to discourage the undesirable or dysfunctional traits or to channel them to good purpose—as innate tendencies to aggression might be directed to combat enemies of peace and security. The formation of character is rarely, if ever, a matter of introducing materials that are indifferent to the nature of the learner. It happens more typically that we appeal to some of his tendencies in order to contend with others. Some instinctive dispositions are turned against others within the same breast—perhaps in the service of some good that is also instinctually based. This is what happens in the socialization of males, who are natively disposed to live the life of a playboy, propagating their genes at any and every opportunity and in the process being irresponsible to the various mothers and children left in their wake. At the same time, however, a male has a disposition to protect appropriate females, to establish enduring bonds of loyalty and affection, and to protect his children, so he is also moved to care for a permanent family of his own making. The impulse to family is also supported by other natural tendencies. A female discriminates among males in large part on the basis of their perceived willingness to devote their attention exclusively to her and her expected offspring, so she is less apt to make herself available to a man she cannot trust. A given society, too, has a vital interest in the flourishing of families, which provide an indispensable civilizing function, while a large mass of unconnected males is extremely threatening to its internal peacefulness and coherence. A husband and father tends to be both a better citizen and a harder worker. He "gets married and settles down," as the saying goes. Hence we celebrate marriages as communal events, in part because they help to sustain the invaluable condition of a more adult and reliable social order and in which the young are apt to be responsibly nurtured. Much in the way of public pressure is therefore directed at the male to encourage him to respect marriage and to be a good family man. Due to an innate need to be accepted by the group, the male is normally receptive to this pressure. And (to repeat) he is also genetically equipped to derive (sometimes matchless) satisfactions from family life. Thus, out of a seeming chaos of instincts, the male propensity to spread their seed without limit and to neglect responsibility for the mothers and their children is sharply restrained; in many cases the lust for promiscuity is moderated; and a man might find the greatest goods of his life within the confines of his family.

Not uncommonly, individuals are unaware of their natural needs. It is notorious, for example, that individuals can suffer anxiety and demoralization due to the absence of a natural good, but they do not know that their condition is due to such a deprivation. An individual who does not experience social order and support suffers from anomie, with its attendant ills, but he does not know that this is the cause of his suffering. Perhaps he is not explicitly aware that he has a powerful natural need for trustworthy and lasting social bonds. At the same time, it is wise to remember that there is also danger in the idea of latent unmet needs. Everyone is delighted to tell us what we "really" need, but these alleged needs might be nothing more than the fantasies of a deranged moralist.

The upshot, in brief, is that to approach morality according to nature is exacting and perilous. Our theories and intuitions about human nature and its moral capacities can be disastrously mistaken. As a final caution, we should also consider the possibility that behaviors of various sorts are deeply influenced by genetic conditions, but those conditions themselves might vary so much from individual to individual or group to group that there is little uniformity of conduct according to nature. That is, if there are no human universals, there could not be much in the way of common wisdom about the conduct of life. Such caution is especially pertinent in regard to the determination of the ideal goods that might beckon any particular individual. Here, happily, we seem to find plentiful variations. All the same, we will find, I suspect, that there are sufficiently universal properties of natural life to support a decidedly finite range of virtues from which to define human excellence.

A third sort of investigation of the possibilities of conduct according to nature is to distinguish desirable conditions that can be achieved in only one or a few ways. If the means to the end are quite limited and definite, rather than proliferating in lovely variety, then the end would be appropriately designated as occurring by nature. Nature, once again heedless of our sentiments, imposes its own regimen. As previously remarked, the case of sticking to one's promise is a forceful example. One of the necessary conditions of a satisfactory social order is that individuals abide by their obligations to one another. The only alternative is a kind of totalitarianism, where everyone's life is regulated by central authority, so we fervently prefer that the virtues of fidelity be taught and enforced. We need not insist that our allegiance to the social order is by nature or that we have a natural affection for the teaching of obligations. Even if there were no innate condition that attaches us to our duties, and even if our idea of a congenial society were wholly a product of learning, we would still be faced with the necessities presented by the two alternatives: tyranny or moral development. Perhaps there is not a native drive either to build or to have buildings, but if buildings become a crucial part of our existence, our work immediately becomes subordinate to severe constraints from nature. If by means of responsible appraisal we distinguish an end and the means to it are determinate, then we have no good choice but to adopt them. Then we have a rule of life, a principle: something one must do to carry on in a manner that is supportive of cherished values—such as that of fulfilling common responsibilities. The Socratics had a sweeping rule of this sort: there is no enduring good to be attained without the possession of virtue.

The question of the nature of justice also belongs in the category of necessary means to ends. Any society requires well-established and respected rules for the allocation of scarce resources and for the distribution of rewards and punishments. Without commonly accepted norms of this sort, social disruption and violence are inevitable. No one will deny that. But which norms suffice to accomplish the desired functions? If there are several equally effective alternatives, then the only necessity is that one of them—whichever one—be established.

If you are going to bake a cake or become a medical doctor, the sequence of preparatory events is rather clearly prescribed. There may be little prompting, of course, to do either of these things, and for many outcomes there are several alternative means, so nature imposes less structure on our energies. For an inventive mind, still more options might be conceived. Still, it is essential for anyone to know that nature is not utterly permissive; it is often demanding. Anyone's life is largely governed by forms of necessity— the imperatives that must be endured if we are to sustain the daily forms of action on which life depends. Of course the demands vary, and the determination of who should satisfy them varies, but it is part of the nature of life that there will be required and often toilsome performances of many kinds. From taking out the garbage and washing the dishes to providing for one's family, preserving the environment, and protecting the community, life inevitably imposes disciplines that we might wish were otherwise but must satisfy nonetheless. This entire class of activities exists according to nature. We are not only bearers of duties; we are also seekers of the good, but we too readily formulate ideals without reference to the needful powers and disciplines or to the limits that distinguish eros from folly.

In some noteworthy cases, happily, the optimal means to the end are well defined and at the same time in accordance with our nature. The traditional family—an intact unit headed by father and mother—proves to be the best means for the rearing of children into tolerably competent adults. This structure is by nature in that there is no competitive alternative to it, and it is in the nature of its constituent members that this arrangement should prevail. It is by nature that a man and a woman desire a stable and continuing companionship of trust, support, and affection, and by nature they desire to reproduce and sustain their heritage into further generations.[4] The children desire above all that this unity be sustained. With sufficient knowledge of nature, we might discern additional forms of association that likewise serve invaluable ends while also satisfying conspicuous demands of human nature.

A like observance of nature is called for when we consider the relations that various putative goods sustain to one another. Personal initiative and responsibility, private property, freedom, material security, and social solidarity are all treasured, but the ways in which they might be interdependent or mutually repugnant must be determined, and they do not appear to be endlessly manipulable. What is the connection between lively personal responsibility and unconditional welfare entitlements, for example? Can freedom persist without virtue? Without private property? Could a culture survive, much less prosper, if it were governed by Rawls's principles of justice? How well, if at all, can social unity exist with multiculturalism? There are scores of vital questions of this sort. They are inquiries into the constraints on what can be accomplished in the ordering of human institutions, and these constraints are often severe. We cannot, accordingly, have everything that we want, and we must learn renunciation. Perhaps it seems platitudinous to recite such issues, but how many lives and societies are ruined by those who are ignorant of nature or impatient with its labors? Nature will work its ways, so knowledge of it and respect for it over a lifetime are invaluable.

b. Nature and Nurture

The disciplines of nature cannot be the only source of wisdom. We must also recognize other origins, measures, and sanctions of moral experience—such as socialization, custom, tradition, culture, and convention. For now, all these conditions can be lumped together as *environment*, where environment is understood as a source of learning—or *nurture*, in the popular terminology. As we shall see in a moment, the distinction is less clear than one might at first suppose.

Although there has been great variation in belief about the nature and conditions of learning, all philosophers who have believed in nature have also believed that our native potencies require a definite form of learning in order for them to develop and become actual. Human beings vary widely in their capabilities to learn, whether it be the learning of moral virtues, mathematics, or literary composition. This is not to say that one's capacities to learn have some sort of unitary direction. There seem to be ambivalent and contrary possibilities in every individual. A good education aims at discerning those that would be productive and admirable, devoting a lifetime to their cultivation. If the discernment has been true and the cultivation effective, the possessor of these qualities might enjoy the greatest satisfactions of which he is capable.

The distinction between native powers and the environment can be made in a way that does more to obscure than to clarify. We should not think of the environment as being *nature* neutral, an instrument made of cultural whole cloth interacting with the individual, as if wholly by convention, where nature is nowhere to be found. Nurture itself is deeply invested with nature. Those who learn the arts of hunting, farming, and building can tell us that. They learn from interacting with their respective environments, which themselves function according to nature. The hunter seeks game, and he seeks every distinctive sign in the terrain left by the potential kill. At the same time, his quarry has its characteristic means of evasion, attack, and defense, which the hunter must learn, and he must equip himself with weapons appropriate to fell the animal. The distinctively human surrounding is often driven by nature. Parents are the most important part of the child's environment, and the parents are typically dedicated by nature to care for the child and tend to his prosperous upbringing. When boy meets girl, each is part of the other's environment, and each is largely motivated according to nature. Another instance: the exercise of social stigma is a cultural phenomenon inseparable from nature. The fact that stigma is effective presupposes that people are naturally averse to the disapproval of their own social group. That, moreover, to which a society directs its stigma might well be according to nature—as in stigmatizing irresponsible fathers and mothers.[5] In general, in our social converse we are always alert to the characteristics of others: their generosity, jealousy, envy, aggression, courage, trusworthiness, inconstancy, and so forth, and we are aware of the conditions under which the reactions are apt to occur. In such cases, that is to say, we are responsive to environmental behavior in which natural human tendencies are prominent. Effective learning and behavior are continuous with natural powers of both the learner and his environment. Nature's characteristic powers permeate the dialectic of individual and environment as a unified process.

The learning environment has a profound effect on the individual, but the individual's nature also has an effect on how the environment will retard or nurture him. What the environment will be and what it will teach depend in significant part on the nature of the learner. A child with a bold and adventurous temperament will seek out different conditions with which to develop than will his more cautious sibling. An individual with strong and consistent dispositions will be moved to reconstruct his environment in a manner that will suit the demands of his nature. In such cases, the heritable characteristic is a more powerful and persistent component of the inclusive learning environment.

Some impulses may be initially so undefined that they can be formed in highly diverse and novel ways. Nurture brings differing measures of innovation, focus, and direction to the motives and evaluations of diverse individuals, and these socialized values might be highly affective. Even if the nurturing springs from a native disposition, the learned behaviour itself might be novel. Thus it may happen, perhaps, that a person and even a community can acquire some traits that owe relatively little to nature. These traits might be corrupt, of course, but they can also be an improvment—increased gentleness and sensitivity, according to some, and even the extinction of, say, competitive and hierarchical habits. The reality of this phenomenon is widely supposed and counted upon in the transformation of human nature and society. These ambitions will founder, however, if there are urgent dispositions that will not give ground to the new way of life. Determined socialization runs headlong into nature. For seventy years, the officials of the Soviet Union strived to create a new being, socialist man. They failed completely, but they did not fail to destroy millions of lives in the attempt.

For so-called social thinkers—to consider another typical case—it seems the inevitable response to human savagery is to wring their hands and pronounce that we must learn to rid the human race of its barbaric habits. Although moderation of propensities to aggression and brutality is possible in many cases, there is no evidence that they can be eradicated or drastically reduced on a wide scale, and there is surely no immediate prospect of it when someone is breaking into your house. One who is more respectful of nature would observe that even the most shameless killers calculate their odds of success. They restrain their depredations if they are convinced—sometimes it takes overwhelming force to do so—that they can't succeed in their hostilities and will be severely punished for them.

I have been saying that the expressions "by nature" and "by nurture" suggest a spurious dichotomy. Perhaps it is a better beginning simply to ask how people learn, distinguishing whatever variables there are and determining their respective potencies, relations, and conflicts. The variations in the institutions and practices that we refer to as custom, tradition, and education would correlate in many different ways with variations in genetic and other biological conditions, but this is not to say that the native powers would not be formidable. In many instances, they might be the most potent and consistent variable. In any case, custom, tradition, culture, and socialization are extremely important, but it is improbable, to say the least, that they are wholly self-determining. Surely, indeed, the endurance of custom and tradition in human life owes much to an innate need and affection for them. We have affection for established order and continuity in culture. One is rooted in a distinctive legacy that is to be cherished, preserved, and carried on. Perhaps the value of this sort of rootedness is owing to a natural need for belonging to a personalized and accepting whole.

Although there may be many universal qualities of human nature that are potent in the moral life, it would be obtuse to deny significant variations in the sources and character of moral qualities, even within a given culture, and a seeker of wisdom should hope to know and appreciate them and to understand their functions in the determination of variations in moral life. But let us consider the view that all distinctive forms of life owe virtually nothing to nature: they are, in the strictest sense, *conventions*. Hence morality, too, would be only conventional.

c. By Nature and by Convention

The question is whether the conventions of culture have an autonomous existence, not attributable to nature in any significant degree. If a convention were sui generis and at the same time a repository of its own irreducible values, then it would indeed be a competitor to nature and perhaps a great improvement on it. Suppose we follow the radical feminists and dismiss the differences between male and female as "only a convention, only a social construct." Then, presumably, we would be in a position to eradicate all forms of male/female relations that are predicated on the assumption of natural difference and establish an alternative order, one of perfect equality and concord in all things.

But not so fast! Are the values at stake in this scenario merely conventional? What of the status of equality and concord, the norms that convention would promote and satisfy? Are *they* conventional, too? If so, what gives them some sort of warrant for moral superiority? What is the basis of their appeal? If they are not conventional, the radical seems to have sacrificed the claim that culture is free-standing: he is invoking values deeply rooted in the nature of things, perhaps, neither to be supplanted at will nor to be manipulated into any configuration. If he refuses to make that sacrifice, he must be prepared to make the case that his conventions are superior to others. Why are conventions considered better or worse? If one speaks, for example, of the evils of oppression and the blessings of liberty, he seems hardly to have brought up anything fundamentally conventional. Or maybe he appeals only to happiness, yearning to extend it. There is nothing conventional in the desire for happiness, either. The issue must revert to a primal question: Can human nature and institutions be modified indefinitely to attain certain ends, such as the eradication of oppression and the unlimited expansion of freedom? Can happiness be attained in innumerably different ways? Are there natural *moral* constraints regarding the quality and distribution of happiness? Convention might not be nearly so free and accommodating as the feminist has supposed.

If conventions were truly self-determining and self-sufficing, then their values would not (according to the conventionalist) be appropriately judged by reference to standards that arise from the disciplines of nature. That would deprive convention of its autonomy. If a convention could be justified only conventionally, how would the moral precedence between nature and convention be established? The preferred response to this embarrassment is brilliant in its simplicity: There is no nature; there is only convention. "Well then," one might feel compelled to ask, "how can we compare the relative merits of different conventions?" The historicist, who is in effect a thoroughgoing conventionalist, says—triumphantly—that there are no criteria for doing so.[6] When we claim to judge the relative merits of two different conventions by reference to a principle that purports to transcend them both, what we are actually up to, he declares, is simply to invoke a third convention. When we judge parochial convention A in comparison to parochial convention B, we do no more than appeal to parochial convention C. Most persons are horrified by such a doctrine. It is relativism gone all the way to nihilism. To condemn the Holocaust is no more than to juxtapose different conventions and leave it at that. All moral standards are equal. To be accurate, really, we should not say *equal.* All we can say is *different.* The final import of millennia spent in search of wisdom is this: "All moralities are different."

We are right to be horrified. This is one more instance of the insular character of philosophy, easily lured on by the herd instinct, ideology, and love of celebrity. It is false to say that there are no moral standards by nature, and it is false to say that no moral standards transcend cultural differences. Abundant empirical evidence contradicts the historicist.[7] I have already submitted the cases of telling the truth and keeping promises—practices that are universally necessary for any tolerable form of community life, and several further examples are yet to be offered. Suppose, moreover, that it were established that a given standard of judgment, in contrast to others, was (a) predicated on knowing better and (b) more humane. Will the conventionalist reply that "knowing better" is meaningless or irrelevant, and will he say the same of "humane"? If so, he speaks the language of the sociopath. Those members of the human race who are not sociopathic, or who are not devoted at all costs to the trendy, can continue in their moral labors without the anxiety that they are deluded.

This is not to say that there is one incontestable and invariant criterion for judgment, but to acknowledge some indeterminacy is not to give ground to the historicist. There is more than one possible moral standpoint, but they are alike in being *moral*, and the meaning of "moral" is neither utterly plastic nor conventional, as we shall find soon enough. The claim that convention is irreducible to nature will not survive scrutiny. I am not using "nature" as we find it in Plato, Aquinas, or Locke. I make no claim that the various workings of nature that constitute the moral life cause no strife, tragedy, and uncertainty; but neither am I supposing that worldly wisdom won't amount to much, after all.

Nor do I say that nothing in human experience is exclusively conventional. Just as I held that we don't know how to make a radical distinction between nature and nurture, neither do we know how to make a similar distinction between nature and convention. Just as with the nature/nurture problem, it would be helpful to avoid the assumption that nature and convention are separated by a watertight bulkhead. Would it not be more productive—to say it again—simply to determine the multiplicity of factors in life, whatever they be, that we could appreciate in order to learn how to live well and to foster vigorous moral orders?[8]

Having confessed that the nature/nurture and nature/convention distinctions are indeterminate, do I not also confess that the project of wisdom according to nature is misconceived? Not at all. This is a crucial principle of my discourse: There are indeed stable and persistent orders of nature, many of them products of natural selection, and knowledge of them is indispensable to wisdom, to knowing better. They discipline and enlighten the moral life. Many of them function congruously with variations in cultural conditions, but at the same time, there are innumerable norms and proposals for moral action that are incompatible with these orders and will be brought to grief by them. Convention may be wholly plastic, but nature is more stubborn. Perhaps there are few such orders, or perhaps many, but whenever any such order can be ascertained, an increment in wisdom has been achieved. Folly might be diminished, and life might be happier and stronger.

Before putting this theme aside, let us consider the possible meanings of variations in moral conduct, whether within a given culture or between one culture and another. Facile theorists are prone to draw the wrong conclusions from them. It is critical to ask *why* these variations have occurred. There are several possible explanations, and they could occur in combination. Do variations take place as an adjustment to distinctive circumstances? When hunter-gatherer tribes cease a nomadic life, for example, and become prosperous due to agriculture, they evidently become concerned about the distribution of property in a way that they were not in their previous life. Or might variations be a consequence of different beliefs about the nature of crucial constituents of the moral condition? The founders of utopian communities, as a case in point, believe that the natures of their citizens will undergo drastic and appropriate changes in the new social order. It could also happen that variations occur due to neglect of natural conditions: a society ceases to attend to the need for moral education, let us suppose. And perhaps there are differences in moral conviction and behavior due to there being real differences in human nature. Some groups might be inherently more warlike; others more pacific. Many changes in moral conditions, moreover, have occurred due to deliberate effort: a tyrannical regime is overthrown by a dedicated and courageous rebellion, and it might even be replaced in time by a free society.

Surely each of these sorts of factor has some role in accounting for the varieties of moral life. In our quest for wisdom according to nature, what are we to make of them? The historicist would like to think that each of the diverse forms of life is irreducibly singular, but the diversity might well be attributable to normal and predictable functioning of human nature in rather different environments. Another breed of putative conventionalist, on the other hand, would have us believe that variations in moral life are due to the limitless plasticity of human nature, which they will obligingly reconstruct for us.

We might agree with the conventionalist in acknowledging the diversity of customs throughout human association, but we might well ask, in addition, whether this diversity betokens fundamental *moral* differences. The Chinaman displays all manner of culturally distinctive practices, but he seems not to display the moral qualities required by the utopian. He displays those that are despised and denied by the would-be moral designer. It is a matter of consummate importance to know whether and how moral nature is subject to overhaul.

Before making further comment on these themes, let us take up a familiar objection to any attempt to make generalizations about human nature. Any claim of a typical form of conduct is sure to be brought low, so it would seem, by a counterexample. The highly aggressive and violent female is counterposed to the stereotype of sweet femininity, just as the retiring and ever-so-compliant male is held in evidence against the stereotype of the macho man. Generalizations *are* often simple-minded, and a well-conceived example to the contrary is their ruin. On the other hand, the claim of a putatively falsifying instance can be equally simple-minded. To understand the basic principles of the way nature distributes her variations will illuminate morality according to nature. More than this, an appreciation of these principles affords genuine wisdom regarding human fate. I have in mind one principle in particular. It is one of nature's originals—not a derivative of natural selection.

d. Inegalitarian Nature

> Don't you feel that it is reprehensible? Isn't it obvious that such a person is trying to form human relationships without any critical understanding of human nature? Otherwise he would surely recognize the truth—that there are not many very good or very bad people, but the great majority are something between the two.
>
> How do you know that, I asked?
>
> On the analogy of very large or small objects, he said. Can you think of anything more unusual than coming across a very large or small man, or dog, or any other creature? Or one which is very swift or slow, ugly or beautiful, white or black? Have you never realized that extreme instances are few and rare, while intermediate ones are many and plentiful?—Plato, *Phaedo*

Nature is extravagant. She disposes turbulent and variable powers, and she typically produces even a single event with a multitude of different causes. What swarms of forces come together to produce each one of the fauna and flora that inhabits the earth? How many conditions conspire to produce a man? And what variations, great and small, have produced this particular man? One of the consequences of nature's inestimable fertility is that she sorts the occurrences of particular phenomena into a perfectly definite pattern. This is the arrangement referred to by Plato in the *Phaedo*. It is one of his several references to the fact that variations in the frequency of phenomena are not equally distributed. There are few at the extremes and many at the mean, and this seemed a very important fact. Plato identified what came to be known centuries later as the bell-shaped curve, and he was right about its importance.

Any type of phenomenon that depends for its occurrence on a plurality of independent causes will, with sufficiently repeated instances, turn out in the so-called normal distribution. In some instances, the normal curve would be produced by as few as five or six separate causes—a paltry number for intemperate nature. Whether it be human intelligence, the height of oak trees, or moral virtue, nature will draw the same curve; the temperatures of a thousand stars will be distributed in the exactly replicated pattern. Variations in each of these phenomena will have a definite distribution of the frequency with which they occur. There will be a continuum from the smartest to the dullest man with many in between, and from the tallest to the shortest oak with many in between. At the extremes there will be very few, and at the mean there will be many. Remarkably, this distribution can be given exact measurement. Slightly more than two-thirds of occurrences (68.27 percent, to be precise) will fall within one standard deviation below the mean and one standard deviation above it, while the conceivable physical limits at the extremes will occur at only the rarest intervals. The frequency at each point on the continuum is predictable: the astrophysicist can tell us how many of the thousand stars will fall into position in each determinate range of celestial temperatures. Plotting this distribution gives us the bell-shaped curve (also called the *Gaussian* curve, named for the discoverer of its mathematical properties, Carl Friedrich Gauss).

To say that a cause is independent means that its occurrence is not conditional upon whatever other causes are concomitantly determining the phenomenon at issue. However much the several causal agents might interact to affect the same object, each starts out for its own reasons, as it were. Independent causes commonly have effects on each other, to be sure. Still, the occurrence of these causes is not dependent on the same antecedent conditions. Genetic processes, soil conditions, disease, crowding from other vegetation, sunshine, air temperature, humidity, nutrients, rainfall, and accidents of fortune are among the factors determining the growth of an oak, and they will have effects on each other, but they are not functions of the same antecedents. Rainfall and soil nutrients are determined by different conditions, but both have an effect on the growth of a tree. Hence they are called *independent* causes. (Notice that I have listed *classes* of causes. A class might have any number of instances. Each instance of rainfall, for example, is a separate cause. The number of independent causes multiplies, though the number of classes might be limited.)

Another requirement is that there be a sufficient number of the products in question. If we knew the height of only two oaks out of a thousand, we would have no idea what the height of trees would be at various stations on the curve. In addition, the sample must be representative of the entire population. If you determine the distribution of only those oaks above average height, you will not find a bell curve. The "law of large numbers" applies throughout: the more independent causes and the more representatives of the population under examination, the more closely will the distribution correspond to the mathematical curve.

Typically, it is the scientist who studies the variations in natural events and employs the laws of probability to calculate the chances that an event of a specific character will occur. We will have a weak grasp of the *moral* life, however, if we fail to recognize that its characteristic features are also subject to the same laws. Virtue and vice, wisdom and folly, goods and evils—all are functions of nature's swings between poverty and superfluity. Paradoxically, it seems, she is *quantitatively* niggardly when she is at her *qualitative* best—and worst. No one can be wise who does not acknowledge, somehow, that all facets of human endeavor converge on the mean, and whatever is most precious must also be rare. These are lessons to be considered in due course. But a philosopher must wonder what it is about nature that she disburses her bounty with such mathematical indifference. It seems miraculous that it should be so.

The laws of probability are mathematically impeccable, but why must nature confirm them? Why is she so obliging of Dr. Gauss? It is because nature abounds with powers—copious, varying, driven into numberless arrangements? A profusion of random causes, themselves undergoing variation and combining and recombining in astonishing diversity, will produce a great array of distinguishable outcomes. The variations in outcome will not occur with equal probability, because some are easy for nature to produce and others very difficult. A Mozart is an extreme, an exquisite rarity, but it is easy to produce average musicians, who therefore occur in abundance.

To think of the nature of distribution abstractly, suppose a continuum of variations that are the product of multiple causes; but it doesn't matter what particular sort of phenomenon we are considering. (Maybe it is the range of differences between musical genius and total musical incompetence or between the tallest and the shortest adult oak tree.) For convenience, divide the outcomes into seven classes, numbered from one to seven. This is the crucial point: Given the complex and varying causal processes, some of these outcomes can be reached in many different ways; others can be reached in perhaps only one way. That is, there are some results that can be attained by means of a high number of different combinations of causes, and there are other results that can be produced by only one or a few combinations. Outcome number four is reached by the greatest number of combinations; three and five are reached with a plurality of different causal sequences, but fewer than number four. In these cases, nature displays a sort of redundancy in her operations. Destinations one and seven, on the other hand, are each attained in a very few ways or perhaps only one each. There is little if any redundancy here; nature exhibits parsimony. There will, accordingly, be a high probability for the incidence of some outcomes and a low probability for others.

The more the preconditions cited above are present, the more will the distribution take the bell-shaped form.

The distribution at the midpoint of the continuum is not only the most plentiful in number but is also *average* in its characteristics relative to the extremes. The midpoint is designated the mean *because* it is an average, but why must the central zone be populated by average natures? Why are there so few tiny oaks and huge oaks and so many of middling size? Why so few idiots and geniuses and so many of modest intelligence? Why not a multitude of geniuses compared to those of average intelligence? The answer once again lies in nature's prodigality. At any intersection of many independent causes, there are polar limits toward which the combined causes can tend. The incidence of differences in any sort of outcome will be ranged along the span between the limits. Depending on the composition of a particular causal nexus, the tendency will be toward one limit or the other or to the middle. Some causes will tend one way, some others will tend in the other, but they are transiently united in a nexus, so their combined efficacies will tend to neutralize the polar tendencies. The composite effect of these tendencies, that is, will tend toward the intermediate. That is the compromise destination, so to speak. Accordingly, the midpoint is also the average of whatever occurs at the extremes.

There are conditions that are conducive to making oak trees big and conditions that retard or prevent their growth. In a juncture of such conditions, some tend in one way and some tend in the other, and their combined effect is to produce a middle-of-the-road tree. At each distinguishable causal nexus—for example, the ratio between rainfall and the extent of the root system during a given interval—the tendency could be either toward vitality and growth or toward weakening and disease. Through the entire period of the growth of the tree, there will be innumerable and varying causal conditions, and when there are these quantities, the tendencies to great height and to arrested development will moderate each other, so the result will be an average oak. To produce a towering oak, by contrast, almost every contingency must tend in the same way, toward growth, unimpeded by opposing tendencies—a most uncommon happenstance amid nature's fecundity. The same improbability governs the production of a wee oak.[9] So nature's events tend to the intermediate in two inseparable ways: the closer to the middle of the continuum, the greater the numbers and the closer the convergence on the commonplace.

By the gods of probability, there are bound to be many more mediocre than exceptional people, and many more so-so days in your life than either great days or terrible. Knowledge of these gods helps us to appreciate much in life: a good day, a perfect day, a perfect day for two people together, a good marriage, a good man, a good book, a good society. All such events depend on countless contingencies. Thus we aptly say of many goods that they are in the hands of the fates or exist by the grace of god. So many contingencies cannot all turn out for the better, yet sometimes they do! Then, one can only say he is blessed. He happens to be one of the exceptional beneficiaries of the laws of probability.

Excellent conditions are necessarily rare. The *combination* of excellent traits is rarer still—vastly so. In possessing high intelligence, a man is one person in ten. One person in ten will have exceptional moral character, and one in ten enjoys unusual physical vigor. One person in a thousand will possess these traits together. The confluence of such traits must be rare, and their persistence is always in jeopardy from all manner of threats and deficiencies. The same prodigal gods toss events into varying combinations, in which the presence or absence of but a single power might throw the entirety into disorder. We are always threatened by decay, which might already have begun. The incomparably wise Greek poets had a sense of the fateful importance of needful human qualities existing together. The lack of one—an invulnerable heel, let us say—brings ruin to the whole, or the presence of one weakness in an otherwise healthy soul, such as arrogance, causes a life to founder. Oedipus was felled due to a lack for which he was not responsible: ignorance of his mother's identity. Such are the stunning contingencies of human fate—and a fact of life that one cannot ponder too well.

There is a note of fatalism in this analysis, and surely there is wisdom in acknowledging that circumstances are often beyond our recognition, much less our control. Experience teaches, however, that deliberate change is possible. Any individual, as he develops or neglects his powers, might move forward or backward on the curve, especially when he identifies the principal causes of his change. Causes are not of the same productivity. The presence or absence of a given condition might be dependent upon thousands of causes, but there might be one or two of them that are especially potent, and we might be able to do something about them. Intellectual achievement, for example, ranges from astonishing to abysmal. It depends on many factors, but some are more effective than others, and we might have some control over them. Education is the most obvious, and that is something that we can deliberately extend and improve. The position of an individual in the distribution of intellectual achievements will in any case improve over a lifetime; and if he has the appropriate educational opportunities and exploits them, he might achieve much. This is not to deny that there are many other factors at work—motivation, native intelligence, health, available time and resources, emotional maturity, encouragement, discipline, and others, just as there are any number of conditions that discourage achievement. All of these would have to be propitious for the most exceptional attainments to occur. Everything must fall into place, as the saying goes.

All contingencies are not equal. Wealth, power, and position, for example, can compensate for many deficiencies. On the whole, *good character* is most important of all. Of the numberless contingencies making for a good life or bad, character usually matters more than anything else. The multitude of causes indifferent to our fate or hostile to it lose much of their potency in the company of moral virtue.

When many persons in a population are afforded improved education, or somehow acquire superior character, the normal curve does not disappear; the entire curve shifts to a higher mean. The only way to eliminate the curve would be to identify and take control of enough of the variables to reduce the number of independent causes to a very few. We would have to possess near-perfect knowledge of the functioning of the environment, virtually complete control of it (including its human occupants), and a mastery of genetic engineering. (Some madman will seize this idea as a rationale to get started on the project at once.)

A less grand but still valuable application of the laws of probability is in regard to the appearance of seeming counterexamples to human universals. Do the existence of the masculine female and the feminine male constitute a disproof of claims regarding the differences between males and females? Hardly. When we observe a masculine female, we should not say, "If one woman can be masculine, so can any woman." True, in the normal distribution, a few females will be quite masculine, and a few males will have markedly feminine traits, but the *average* male has ten times the testosterone level (for one thing) than that of the average female, and in many individual cases the difference is much greater. Accordingly, the distribution of characteristics of males by no means coincides with that of females. We must compare the distribution of traits across an entire population. Then we say that, in general or on average, males are more aggressive than females—and usually far more aggressive. Ignorance of the ways in which nature distributes variations is evident in the assertion that if one person possesses certain qualities, then any person can possess them: one thinks, "If one individual is brilliant and caring, anyone can be brilliant and caring," but that is simply false.

Claims that take the form of asserting that all members of a population possess exactly the same property are obviously vulnerable to contradiction by a single exception. When more sophisticated generalizations are made, a seeming counterexample is genuinely telling only if it can be shown that it is not just a position in the normal distribution of characteristic traits or behavior. In our ideologically desperate environment, it is not surprising to find scholars using the seeming exception in support of the theory of the "radical plasticity" of human nature.[10] Their point is to show the feasibility—given the appropriate social engineering, of course—of producing the required moral type: socialist man, democratic man, genderless man, altruistic man, sensitive man, rational man, utilitarian man—take your pick. It would take a juggernaut of evidence, however, to overwhelm the palpable teachings of experience—not to mention the tide of recent scientific work. Through the centuries, observers of human nature have attested to and recounted our distinguishing passions, follies, and strengths. Poets, philosophers, travelers, and historians from different times and places find a variety of customs but a familiar human nature.

Contrary to ideologically facile interpretations, we find much that is universal in human conduct: male dominance, tendency to aggression, hierarchical behavior, sexual dimorphism, religion, family, tribalism, preference for kin, preference for local attachments—to name a few, and there are concomitantly universal objects of pride, ambition, love, fear, defense, and enmity. These tendencies find expression in a striking array of customs. Nature, to be sure, is sufficiently profuse in her agencies and distributions to ensure that each phenotype is always distinctive. No two of us are ever precisely alike.[11] To acknowledge this (largely) welcome fact is not to deny that nature has also equipped us, for better or worse, with common capabilities and attachments that go far to establish the parameters and the crude ore of the moral life. That ore sometimes produces precious metals, even gold, but the moral utopian is trying to practice alchemy.

Against the first-hand evidence, there is a formidable burden of proof on the defender of the plasticity thesis, who should not be allowed to get by with no more than a theory tailor-made to satisfy utopian sentiments. The burden of proof requires much more than reference to the conduct that occurs at the tails of the bell curve. Individuals habituated to thinking in terms of ideologically fashionable theories are neglectful of public evidence, to be sure, and they are also inattentive to what Dewey calls primary experience, lived experience. Such life is saturated with instinctive responses and intentions, but they pass unheeded. One cannot then be instructed by acknowledging them and their stubborn refusal to go away. His own self-knowledge, indeed, is impoverished and dishonest. He does not, for example, recognize how much the content of his thought is dependent upon his love of reputation and standing—his eagerness to win the favorable attention of certain well-placed individuals.

Still, given the fact that many human characteristics are distributed on the Gaussian curve, isn't it a misnomer to speak in such cases of human universals? Doesn't "universal" imply identity throughout all instances? Such an important topic should not be left to the dictionary. We should say, for example, that certain traits, distributed normally, occur in all known populations. The lust for status is one such characteristic. It occurs everywhere, and it is highly potent in a wide variety of behavior, though there are always some individuals who are happy to stay out of the competition and others who are obsessed with it to the point of madness. For practical purposes, the important fact in speaking of the universality of any trait is that it is sure to turn up everywhere, in all manner of environments. When we discern such phenomena, it is a good bet that they exist by nature. Moral theory or practice that would neglect them or try to eradicate them invites confusion, failure, and the tyranny of re-education camps.

e. Nature and Good Judgment

Nature works her ways in the soul whether we like it or not or whether we know it or not, but so far as we have knowledge of these ways, we are less apt to undertake fatuous moral crusades and more apt to pursue ideals that will gain nature's support. To determine what might be accomplished in the domain of morality is not an a priori intuition. In any case, the resolution of moral perplexity will rarely be one of perfect confidence, and it will never be one of perfect agreement. No disillusioned thinker can entertain these goals; they are for theorists who only nominally inhabit the planet. In contrast to those who suppose that there is nothing to be gained in the moral life from knowledge of nature, there are those who believe that nature somehow prescribes explicit and invariant principles of conduct. I share neither of these views. My thesis is this: *Pertinent knowledge of nature is indispensable for knowing better*—knowing better about morals and politcs and their corruptions and about ideal goods. Such knowledge is plentiful. Knowing better can support or establish the presumption in favor of many norms of conduct, but it cannot lead inexorably and invariably to good decision, inflexible principle, or moral unanimity. Nevertheless, it makes us wiser—more apt to make wise judgments. A canny sense of what the world will afford relieves us of much folly and frustration, and it lights the ways to moral vigor and achievement.

We wish to exercise good judgment regarding the moral *life*—real human practice. It is a daunting mission, and most philosophers have not been good at it. They characteristically look for wisdom in the wrong places, if they look at all. Consider the moral condition: seemingly numberless and diverse values are generated, refined, cherished, and defeated within the moral life. Including our presumed foundational principles, they are a product of innumerable conditions and considerations. They are not all of equal importance by any means, but is there a foolproof criterion of inclusion and exclusion or to establish unequivocal priorities? Moral experience is complex, crowded with values, often disordered, conflicted, tragic, and inscrutable, and it admits of variation in how it can be conducted. Yet in anyone's life, it pleads for order and direction. How do we criticize or evaluate these sundry constituents of a morality?

Philosophers come upon this scene and appropriate it for their own pleasure. They have proven to be highly inventive, for many of their answers are irrelevancies and even fabrications. Consider G. E. Moore, a sacred cow in philosophic circles. He provides not the merest intimation of why his one, simple, nonnatural property is deserving of the appellation "good." It does not dawn on him even to raise the question. In failing to say one word as to why we should invest this perfectly vacuous property with value, he contributes nothing to an understanding of the moral life, much less to an enhancement of it. He is not atypical. One of the most widely practiced philosophic strategies is to isolate (or invent) one feature of the moral world and make it alone decisive. As Dewey often observed, selective emphasis is the greatest philosophic vice. In their love of simplicity and authority, philosophers substitute a cut-off, artificial, or attenuated part of the relevant whole for the whole itself; and the champion of one isolated segment duels with another, neither of them shedding light on the moral condition.[12] The preferred fragment of reality could be the will, or reason; it could be ordinary language; it could be power, love, sympathy, or inclusive fitness. According to Levinas, the source of moral obligation is *the look*—as if ten thousand social relations, demands, and rewards have nothing to do with it! Those who resort to the putative transcendental conditions of communication would have us suppose that the mere existence of discourse mandates sweeping (and radical) moral obligations.[13] John Rawls systematizes intuitions—out of all worldly context—and they turn out to have a stunning resemblance to those of late twentieth-century left-liberals. Utilitarians are so ignorant of the moral life that they leave out of account some of the most profound values that human beings possess. One could go on.[14]

We are all devoted theorizers, to be sure, but theory can be responsible to reality. I am not foolish enough to believe that a dedication to such responsibility will sweep before it all argument—even one's own. Still, somewhere an erotic soul might actually be helped to know better; he might attain a meaningful comprehension and good. On a broad scale, informed with a sufficiently full and realistic conception of the human condition, one could ask which virtues are both possible and appropriate to our circumstance and which human inklings to aspiration are worthy of devoted cultivation. Given a just inventory of human powers, resistances, and variations, one could ask whether there are forms of social order that would be particularly congenial to our nature or natures—rather than to our sentimental intuitions. Such speculations, in which I will indulge in due order, are anything but novel, but there are resourceful ways of entertaining them, just as there are futile ways. In fact, we find direction in the limits and resources sheltered in the orders and instrumentalities of the whole of life. It is there that we must turn if we would bring some kind of realism and priority into moral practice. Of course, our venture will not be crowned with either unanimity or finality, but wisdom should despise such ambitions. The failure would not be the fault of philosophy, however, but of nature's own lack of completion and harmony. Ambiguity, change, conflict, limit, and destruction are real. Still, we sometimes manage to achieve and sustain a measure of good order.

f. Why Believe in Nature?

In succeeding chapters, my appraisals will frequently be dependent upon assumptions about the nature of man. I have nothing esoteric to contribute to the subject, I depend upon common observation of human behavior. Observation has often been denied or explained away by theorists, but theory unverified by experience is unworthy. On the other hand, new theories, highly dependent upon biological and neurological science, have recently been in rapid development; and they tend to explain and confirm our common experience.

Why give credence to biological psychology? The following are a few general considerations, none of which is here presented with any qualifications or reservations. The new sciences of human nature accord far more respect to the idea of innate predispositions and abilities than have the social sciences that reigned until lately. The new sciences are confirming what has been observed in the world for as long as there have been students of human nature. Men, for example, struggle for dominance, and women prefer dominant males. Man is in the thrall of a powerful herd instinct, and the herd takes the form of a hierarchy under the dominant males. The fundamental social unit is the family, and the heads of families will work, sacrifice, and die for the sake of their offspring. Man is neither egalitarian nor particularly rational. He is swept by violent passions that cannot be attributed merely to bad education; they are native to his being: covetousness, vengefulness, jealousy, hatred, selfishness, callousness, and the lust for status, for example. A man's "rationality" is spent largely in trying to satisfy such powers and to contend with them in others. The ability to moderate these demands and to postpone gratification is hard won but by no means impossible. Indeed, some people are innately more capable of resisting impulse than others. Moral qualities, too, have potent biological constituents, and as with other traits, there are variations in moral capabilities.

Observers of human nature have always identified great differences from one individual to the next. In spite of titanic educational efforts and the best of will on the part of the learner, some individuals can memorize, write, paint, compose, calculate, comprehend, reason, sing, dance, or be courageous and steadfast, and others cannot. I am not supposing that the scientists have gotten all the way to the bottom of these phenomena or have even attended to all of them or that they would uniformly endorse my generalizations. Neither do they enjoy unanimity among themselves. Still, their inquiries add weighty support to the archaic belief that man has a more or less original nature.

Utopian theorists have long dreamed of making man more rational and sensible. With sufficient command of education, we can be made to desire only what is orderly and good, and a society can be established that will be perfectly harmonious, happy, and rid of vice. This is the Crystal Palace abominated by Dostoevsky and dismissed with derision by Nietzsche. There has been no success in these ventures to confirm the hopes of the theorists. But ignore the ambition to create a marvelous new social order. Consider only the hope to educate individual persons who will be rid of weakness, neurosis, and folly. This experiment has been undertaken repeatedly—sometimes by experts in psychology, devoted to their project. All parents want this for their children, but they don't get it. Think about it: If we were as malleable as the theorists suppose, we would have learned long ago to rid ourselves of incapacity, conflict, suffering from ourselves, and stupidity, and most of us would be models of virtue, order, and happiness.

Today, instead of explaining away the obdurate tendencies of man, as sociologists have attempted to do, the behavioral geneticists, for example, are determining how human differences vary with variations in genetic similarity. The most compelling evidence comes from the study of identical twins, especially those separated at birth and reared in different environments. They are astonishingly alike, eerily alike. Although ideologically committed critics deny it (and villify it), there is also definitive evidence supporting the heritability of IQ and the correlation of intelligence with success and failure in a great span of further activities. The heritability of many other traits is under study. The advantages that these inquiries have over conventional social science are at least three: first, they are able to correlate variations in behavior with genetic variations. Second, they study adopted children (best of all when they are adopted into a distinctly different environment than that of their biological parents), and they observe that the capacities and characteristics of these children resemble those of their biological parents and siblings more closely than those of their adoptive parents and siblings. Third, they utilize biological and medical research. Increasingly, biologists are able to identify a direct correlation between specified genetic conditions and behavioral traits. The medical profession and neuroscientists find that there are many mental afflictions, such as depression, that are effectively treated with chemicals, where attention to such disorders had once been the monopoly of psychoanalysis. I do not for a moment suppose that social and environmental factors are irrelevant. They are often extremely important, but they are not deployed on the mythical tabula rasa. They function with sometimes obdurately innate characteristics.

It is worth noting that the investigators who explore these topics are extremely unpopular in politically correct circles. They are virtually forced into an underground science. In this environment, they are less likely to make unsupported or reckless claims. The fact that they will pursue their inquiries in spite of the real punishments dealt them by their adversaries is evidence of candor and integrity.

I also find it compelling that the behavior of our nearest primate relatives, the chimps, is so like our own in many ways. The chimpanzee is incapable of our astounding intellectual and artistic achievements, and he has far, far less in the way of ideal goods (including that of lifetime bonding), but his social behavior has much in common with ours. Is it plausible that his behavior is instinctive while ours is irreducibly cultural? Would the similarities be mere coincidence? All other animals, in fact, not just primates, have inherent inhibitory responses, for example, that reduce their tendencies to perpetrate mayhem on each other. If other animals, our evolutionary forebears, possess inherent capacities for definite forms of social behavior, why wouldn't we?[15]

NOTES

1. The colloquial expression "as a rule," captures the intended sense. To say we behave in a certain way as a rule implies that observance of the practice has high priority, but it is not without exception. "As a rule, we treat people as being worthy of respect."

2. See the final section of this chapter for the general case for the evolutionary approach and reference to some representative works. Except in a few cases throughout the following, I will make no specific attempt to appropriate such literature for the sake of supporting a claim about inherent characteristics of human nature, but I will frequently appeal to common human experience. I accept the great plausibility of the idea of inherent propensities and talents, which has long been sustained by universal human observation and now increasingly by scientific inquiry. Let the candid reader be judge.

3. Plato, *Republic*, 455c, trans. Shorey.

4. *Life Without Father*, by David Popenoe (New York: The Free Press, 1996), is one of many recent works reporting the carnage done to the children of fatherless families. In *The Case for Marriage* (New York: Doubleday, 2000), Linda J. Waite and Maggie Gallagher summarize and contribute to the accumulating evidence that most persons are distinctly better off married—including having a better sex life. James Q. Wilson has also contributed substantially to these discussions with his *The Marriage Problem: How Our Culture Has Weakened Families* (New York: HarperCollins, 2002). His work brings greater historical perspective to the functions of marriage and family than the others cited, and he has a most suggestive analysis of the origins of the degradation of these vital institutions. (I will comment on his views in a later chapter.) Two of the most respected recent works on the innate differences between men and women are *The Evolution of Desire* by David M. Buss (New York: Basic Books, 1994)

and *The Red Queen* by Matt Ridley (London: Penguin Books, 1993). On the latter topic, one might also peruse *The Inevitability of Patriarchy* by Steven Goldberg (New York: William Morrow, 1973).

5. The vanishing of stigma receives prominent attention in Wilson, *The Marriage Problem*. To be nonjudgmental about unmarried females having babies is to endanger the principal foundation of society.

6. Is the will to be triumphant also no more than a convention?

7. The historicist typically defends his philosophy by claiming that every culture is incommensurable with every other, and mind is without remainder a precipitate of culture. These are doubtful claims, and I have never seen a rigorous defense of them. One of the main props of contemporary historicism is a particular philosophy of *language*, as in the case of Richard Rorty. If, on the other hand, we suspend our thoughts about language and consider the *behavior* of people in cultures other than our own, we will notice huge commonalities. Take for instance Aristotle's *Politics*, which characterizes inexhaustibly the political conduct of persons throughout the polities of the ancient world. Many varieties of ambition, brutality, treachery, stupidity, vengeance, wisdom, virtue, and statesmanship are on display, but never does the reader find anything *foreign* in these accounts. Rather, one nods in recognition, thinking, "Now that's familiar!" Given the incommensurability thesis, however, one would have to confess to having no insight into the behavior observed by Aristotle.

8. Many social scientists examine the distinction between morality and convention. Three of them, in a recent helpful study, find that ideas of proper moral conduct show remarkable similarity between cultures, but they use a conception of morality that makes it something rather limited and almost esoteric, almost Kantian. Their confined notion of morality is accompanied by an expanded notion of convention. Two of their examples of convention are shaking hands and showing respect for authority. It is astounding to suppose that respect for authority is conventional, but the matter of shaking hands is more subtle. Its function as a form of greeting is to display amity and respect, a readiness to participate willingly and honorably. The same function might be accomplished by other means, of course: by a certain form of address, for example, or by bowing or some other sign of courtesy and good intentions, but in a wary and dangerous world, where we always seek the trustworthy, the function is precious, indispensable, and, in fact, universal. There is no good reason to think of it as a convention. See Elliot Turiel, Melanie Killen, and Charles C. Helwig, "Morality: Its Structure, Functions, and Vagaries," in *The Emergence of Morality in Young Children*, eds. Jerome Kagan and Sharon Lamb (Chicago and London: The University of Chicago Press, 1987), pp. 155–243.

9. Mathematically, such odds are comparable to those of flipping a coin twenty times and having it come up "heads" every time—or some stunningly high percentage of times. Given the normal causal conditions in flipping a coin, the more tries there are, the more they will divide evenly between heads and tails. It is extremely unlikely to get a wildly disproportionate number of one or the other in any set of twenty; but if you spent all your life flipping a coin, these improbable results would occur, but at very rare intervals.

10. "Radical plasticity" is the admiring phrase of Owen Flanagan, *Varieties of Moral Personality* (Cambridge and London: Harvard University Press, 1991), p. 335.

It is remarkable, given his subject matter, that Flanagan makes no reference anywhere in his purportedly definitive text to any of the treatments of moral personality provided by evolutionary and biological psychologists.

11. In cases of identical twins, idiosyncratic differences are astonishingly minimal. Many human differences are determined by very few causes (eye color would be an example), and hence they are not distributed normally. Possibly there are character traits in this category. If so, it is a virtual certainty that they are of biological origin; the environment is too multifarious to produce invariant results.

12. Although Dewey was unaware of it, Hume made a very similar and compelling critique of the corruptions of philosophy. See Donald Livingston, *Philosophical Melancholy and Delirium: Hume's Pathology of Philosophy* (Chicago and London: University of Chicago Press, 1998).

13. This is the view promulgated by Karl-Otto Apel and Jürgen Habermas, among others. The mere *existence* of communication, they say, implies socialism! How's that for magic? See *Rediscovering the Moral Life*, pp. 268–77.

14. Utilitarians and Kantians will be discussed in chapter 6.

15. There are many sorts of evidence for the existence of more or less definite forms of behavior, and many of these forms constitute both constraints and authoritative advice for the moral life. Some of the footnotes in this chapter, for example, note 4, have cited pertinent studies, and there will be several more such references in chapters to come. In addition to these, I list below a small selection of recent sources that, in various ways, have contributed to the study of the innate characteristics of the species:

Thomas J. Bouchard is director of the studies of identical twins at the University of Minnesota, from which a number of seminal papers have emerged. See, for example, T. J. Bouchard, "Do Environmental Similarities Explain the Similarity of Identical Twins Reared Apart?" *Intelligence* 7 (1983): 175–84, and T. J. Bouchard, D. T. Lykken, M. McGue, N. L. Segal, and A. Tellegen, "Sources of Human Psychological Differences: The Minnesota Study of Twins Reared Apart," *Science* 250 (1990): 223–28. Remarkably, no one has yet put together an anthology of essays on twin studies.

David B. Cohen, *Stranger in the Nest* (New York: John Wiley & Sons, 1999). The author's intent is to distinguish wherein a child's personality, intelligence, and character are determined by genetic factors. His hope is to relieve parents of the burden of supposing that the problems in their child's dispositions are mostly owing to failures in upbringing. He considers in detail a broad range of current scientific studies, so the text is a valuable introduction to state-of-the-art research on the nature/nurture debate.

Michael Levin, *Why Race Matters* (Westport, CT, and London: Praeger, 1997). A highly sophisticated analysis and summary of relevant issues and inquiries. Particularly valuable study of the arguments made by those who insist that all differences between individuals are attributable to variations in the environment. Equally valuable is a careful critique of the arguments made against those who defend genetic inheritance of behavioral traits.

Steven Pinker, *How the Mind Works* (New York and London: W. W. Norton, 1997). A tour de force in regard to the rapidly developing school of psychology that holds that the mind is composed of more or less discrete functional modules, each of which attends to specific intellectual and practical tasks—rather than being an ever-ready all-purpose problem-solving machine, poised as a whole to tackle whatever comes along. In effect, Pinker's view is an amalgam of Kant and Dewey. It is Kantian in holding that we are endowed with innate forms of cognizing, reacting, and evaluating, but (in Deweyan fashion) these forms are not a priori but the consequence of our evolutionary history: They are derivative of the intercourse of the species with brute reality throughout the eons.

Steven Pinker also is the author of *The Blank Slate: The Modern Denial of Human Nature* (New York: Viking Penguin, 2002). This is a devastating critique of the many ways, scientific and otherwise, that modern thinkers have attempted to deny that man has an intrinsic nature. He insists, moreover, on exposing shoddy science and shoddy scientists, regardless of their reputation or the cachet of their ideas among the cultural elites. He demolishes, for example, the pretensions of the historicists and postmodernists. His characteristic acumen seems to be suspended on occasion. I find this true in his comments about justice, free will, and parenting, among other issues.

J. Philippe Rushton, *Race, Evolution, and Behavior*, 2d ed. (New Brunswick, NJ: Transaction Publishers, 1997). Rushton advances a broad theory of how natural selection has brought about typical differences between the distinctive races of man. He presents extensive evidence displaying certain definite tendencies in behavior regardless of divergences in culture. The existence of these tendencies is significant in its own right, apart from their bearing on Rushton's theoretical inquiry.

E. O. Wilson, *Consilience* (New York: Alfred A. Knopf, 1998). This work, by the founder of sociobiology and the author of many significant works about human nature, undertakes to propose what form a synthesis of human knowledge would take. Ethics is the crucial component of the proposed unification. "In the course of all of it we are learning the fundamental principle that ethics is everything. Human social existence . . . is based on the genetic propensity to form long-term contracts that evolve by culture into moral precepts and law. The rules of contract formation were not given to humanity from above, nor did they emerge randomly in the mechanics of the brain. They evolved over tens or hundreds of millennia . . ." (p. 297). *Consilience* is also valuable for its account of the remarkably sophisticated methods of inquiry used in contemporary biology.

Richard Wrangham and Dale Peterson, *Demonic Males: Apes and the Origins of Human Violence* (Boston and New York: Houghton Mifflin, 1996). Acknowledging both the masculine propensity to violence and the remarkable parallels between chimpanzee and human behavior, the authors explore the evolutionary continuities between ape and man. "We have seen that chimpanzees and humans share, with each other but with no other species, a uniquely violent pattern of lethal intergroup aggression visited by males on neighboring communities. . ." (p. 26). Uncommonly well written.

| 5 |

The Moral Order

The Greek philosophers loved order in nature and believed it to be definitive of the whole, yet at the same time, in their wisdom, they were always aware of the nearness of corruption and chaos. The most stable institutions are vulnerable to collapse; the happiest circumstance gives way to failure and misery. The ancient perception was sound. Under most conditions, maintaining a tolerable order of life is our first priority and our greatest challenge, and individuals are willing to go to almost any length to preserve security, possessions, and family and to maintain their independence from alien powers. The dangers and obstacles are enormous: competitors and enemies, scarcity of resources, and vulnerability to the hostile forces of nature. War, death, disease, and civil disintegration seem always at hand. Not least, by any means, the hostile forces include the innumerable lusts and failings of human nature—not only in our adversaries, but in our allies, and in ourselves, too. Callousness, treachery, and cruelty are everywhere conspicuous; cowardice and incapacity are no less familiar. Men are typically endowed with love of conquest and control, and they are susceptible to murderous rage and insatiable hatreds.

Our conduct is so irrational that it is difficult to see how natural selection should not have been rid of us long since. We are also amazingly intelligent, however. Just as we have learned to cope with all manner of impersonal forces, we have learned much about how to cope with the natural forces of human nature. We develop arts for hunting, fishing, farming, and building, and we likewise develop the genius to recognize and contend with our neighbor's avarice and ambition. At the same time, our own cupidity is often checked by a reckoning of forces arrayed against it. Intelligence does not abolish lusts and weaknesses; it acquires appropriate expectations about human passions and learns somewhat about strategies that might be equal to them. The desires for survival and increase are thereby served. We behave in this way routinely, and we do it well enough to have made it this far.

As it stands, this tableau is one-sided, for there are also virtuous and gentle souls among us, and the dove, as Hume said, is intermingled with the serpent in our frame. Appetites are moderated as well as exacerbated. There are safe and halcyon times, and everyone has some capacity to live with insecurity. Challenge and uncertainty, indeed, inspire initiative and strength. My point, however, is to stress the incessant *liability* to corruption and defeat—a liability relentlessly confirmed in human affairs. An entire population needn't be debased, moreover, in order to be felled; a few ruthless and powerful individuals can lead the many to catastrophe—especially when the many are weak. The foolish, complacent, and self-absorbed refuse to recognize either the inherent hazards to social order or the great efforts that are required to maintain it. Indeed, they praise forms of life that are unsustainable. Fortunately, there are others who are well aware of the precarious nature of every existence. To them, the threat is vivid and everpresent. The wise have always known how difficult it is to establish and preserve a good society, and some of them acknowledge at the same time that there are natural demands and aptitudes that might be ordered in a way to enhance our existence and sometimes to give it ideal meaning.

The present chapter will initiate an analysis of some of the vital constituents of a moral order, showing how they function as parts of a more inclusive environment, thronging with all manner of hazards and opportunities. Such orders comprise innumerable conditions, some of them conducive to the endurance and vitality of the association and others that undermine it. No philosopher is worth reading who would not advance his theories about good and evil with a view to their purported functions as part of a working whole. I offer an appraisal of modes of thinking about this very context, their presuppositions and efficacies. The next chapter will discuss distinctively moral forms within a social order and suggest their genesis in the attempt to establish decent, perhaps thriving, conditions of associated life.

a. THE HUMAN INVESTMENT IN GOOD CONDUCT

If we speculate about the minimal conditions requisite to the endurance of a social order in primitve environments, we are apt to think of practices something less than moral: unsentimental exercise of power, unquestioning obedience, brutal discipline, and ferocious treatment of rivals.[1] But surely the situation of our forebears would not always be so simple, just as it is not for ourselves. Today or yesterday, the success of an association depends heavily on moral factors, which are not the arcane product of some intuitive or speculative power. The perilous nature of life and the tendency to personal irresponsibility testify to the urgent need for moral qualities in associated life. Steadfast loyalty to comrades, readiness to subordinate one's interests to a greater good, willing fulfillment of obligations, honesty in mutual relations, courage, and respect for the status and possessions of others immeasurably improve the durability of a group and contribute to its prosperity. These are not conditions that typically exist in abundance or in unalloyed form. Such traits, nevertheless, are widely recognized as life-sustaining. Any moderately perceptive and experienced individual knows that they are precious to the existence of a society, just as he knows that his own good is dependent upon a social order—though perhaps not the one that he happens to inhabit.

Of course there are many who are gifted at being parasitical on the work of others and adroit at excusing their own antisocial conduct. This is to be expected. Still, those who have any sense of the contingencies of associated life will recognize that *virtue*, in some rudimentary form, is a great asset, and they will have high admiration for it and will honor it. This is one of the first lessons of knowing better: *Human life has a profound investment in morality—* in elementary good conduct. Long before philosophers formulate esoteric theories of the nature of morality and the reasons for observing it, the insecurity of life and our susceptibility to corruption teach the value of good behavior. Virtue is equated with just such elementary ways of acting.

There are exceptions to the expedience of morality. A blindly obedient mob, driven only by hatred, might win the day, but this cannot be a mob for all seasons—for all demands and opportunities of associated life over time. Some theorists will say, too, that what appears to be virtue is really nothing but self-interest. Even if the theory is true, it implicitly acknowledges that self-interest can take various forms, some of which are more beneficial for shared life than others. It is usual, of course, for members of a group to show great partiality toward their own and usually for good reason, so morality begins with narrow focus. The virtues would be those dispositions that maintain the vitality of the group, tending to protect and preserve its fundamental goods.

When we speak of an investment in *morality* or *virtue*, there should be no uncertainty in the meanings of the terms. Especially in recent inquiry and commentary, *morality* tends to be equated with *altruism*, and that is a frivolous and even perilous equation. I do not wish to engage in a dispute about how to use words correctly; the fundamental issue concerns dispositions to judge and act in specifiable ways. *Altruism*, as we find it in recent literature, tends to refer to traits like compassion, sensitivity, and caring—the traits that are conspicuously advocated in politically correct morality. These are dispositions to sympathize with, promote, and care for the alleged victims of the dominant cuture. This is taken to be the core of morality, and superficial people believe that they have discharged their moral obligations in being sensitive and nonjudgmental (or feigning it). It is a "morality" that has above all produced hypocrisy, cynicism, and moral breakdown. In contrast, the dispositions to be honest, responsible, courageous, just, and willing to postpone or relinquish gratification are decidedly on the wane. Good conduct is hardly acknowledged, let alone honored, but its role is not marginal; it is not an indulgence at the periphery of civilization. It is central. Our "caring" civilization, in contrast, plays with internal collapse. To be sure, altruism in the form of self-sacrifice or the undertaking of great risk for others is sometimes a great and admirable virtue, and a disposition to be helpful and cooperative is invaluable. At this point I merely wish to avoid the trendy identification of morality and compassion.

This is a teaching according to nature: No life-sustaining association, no culture, no civilization can survive if it does not reward virtue and punish vice. So it will be taught, and when it is learned, moral education, however clumsy and intolerant, becomes a major and interminable task. Such is the human investment in morality. Good conduct is such a paramount resource, indeed, that it seems certain that through numberless generations and genetic variations, innate aptitudes for it would occur and would be selected. That is, in some significant degree, the occurrence of virtue in individuals would be according to nature.

Before thinking about the possibility of a latter-day Aristotelianism,[2] I will undertake a more modest venture. Let us consider the existence of a *minimally* moral being—whether it be the product of evolution or not. Put the question this way: What are the minimal conditions that enable a human being to be merely *susceptible* to influence by moral considerations? The nature of such considerations will be analyzed in the following section, but we needn't be delayed in asserting that the fundamental requirement for the minimal agent is to be responsive to the perceived needs and obligations of associated life. He must have at least enough cognitive power to recognize—perhaps only instinctively—that there are concerns at stake other than his own, which his actions might promote or retard. More often than not, of course, the bearers of those concerns will forcefully let them be known. The prototypical moral situation is not the isolated soul in soliloquy but the tumult of real-life exigencies, where good behavior is at a premium.

We should also endow our minimally moral person with enough imagination to envision possibilities and alternatives. He must have a memory, too, and be capable of learning. Equally indispensable would be a measure of sympathy. By this I do not mean grieving for those who suffer. I intend merely that a distinctively moral individual would be aware that other persons are each bearers of their own consciousness. He would, in addition, have some felt sense in a given case what the nature of the consciousness in the other persons is: their respective anxieties, consternations, attachments, hopes, and so forth. Finally, if he is capable of sympathy, he has some ability to know what it feels like to be those individuals: he must be able to share their feelings to some extent.

With all these capacities we must also endow our man with discernible moral dispositions. These are affective states, implying at least a trace of positive responsiveness to the perceived conditions of a situation, including the state of mind of its participants: a willingness to contribute, perhaps, or a propensity to help—some kind of concern that would prompt recognition that there are shared duties or emergencies that have to be met. There may be as well at least a grudging concession that the other person has claims to be considered too, along with one's own, and perhaps in competition with one's own. It is not simply an acknowledgment that there are exigencies that demand our participation or that other claims exist; one is also moved to take such conditions into account even if they are not fully compatible with one's own immediate interests. This recognition of other claims, moreover, must be sufficiently affective to modify the conduct of our minimal agent, on at least some occasions, in a manner that is somehow accommodating of them. One's awareness of moral demands might be initiated by the commands and entreaties of others, but there must also be an accompanying susceptibility to them. The intention of this moral creature would not have to be regarded as a form of hard-core selflessness; he is simply a being whose feelings are capable of being modified in a manner that is favorable to the concerns of some others.

This condition must be distinguished from simply adjusting one's behavior in recognition of the fact that the actions of others will promote or retard one's own ambitions just as they stand. A minimally moral agent would sometimes undergo *an adjustment in his priorities* because of a responsiveness to the perceived predicaments of others. His awareness of another need is *affective*, so his present interests, just as they have occurred, are qualified.[3] He now thinks, "I must drop what I have been up to and come to the aid of my comrade"—or possibly to the aid of a stranger. An individual is susceptible to moral suasion if, through direct experience, imagination, or by means of communication, he can be moved in at least a modest degree. One might give great weight to such considerations, as many people do, but to have a moral disposition in the minimal sense, one would at least feel some inner prompting to accord some regard for the other or for the fate of one's group. I do not insist that this regard be strong enough to move the individual invariably. It need be strong enough only to make him *susceptible* to influences of a sort that might on some occasion stir his soul into a modification of his priorities and finally his actions.

This is not asking for much, but without this minimal nature, no one could think, comprehend, or act morally. An exclusively *cognitive* consciousness, if it could exist, could not be a *moral* consciousness, nor could a being without any sort of cognitive powers be a moral being. Regardless of what Kant thought, to make a moral appeal to anyone exclusively on the basis of sheer reason is impossible, nor could any mere cognition of facts (i.e., without affective response) elicit a moral answer.

Although theorists are prone to discern a singular human feeling at the root of all moral propensities, it is hazardous to assert that a thriving moral sensibility is reducible to a single definite impulse. It is plausible that a medley of feelings is at work (probably not all of them at once): loyalty to the group, willingness to reciprocate, sympathy, friendliness, benevolence, wanting to help, courage, love of glory, protectiveness, desire for acceptance, desire to conform, and others will converge in the development of moral nature. The affections and rigors of associated life give shape and direction to such inclinations. The results are by no means uniform: due to variations in genetic and environmental conditions, the moral dispositions will vary widely from one individual to the next.

There is great significance in the fact that we have a moral nature. It is important in the first instance because, for any individual, his moral nature largely determines his moral capabilities: what he might or might not be able to accomplish in his conduct. It is also important because it gives intelligibility to the fact that moral conduct, as such, can be intrinsically rewarding. If moral behavior is not reducible to political or economic conduct or to simple prudence, then it can be satisfying in its own right. We feel immediate enjoyment in all manner of activities: plunging into the surf, dining, making love, listening to music, learning, conversing, and so on. In each instance, specific capacities of the individual are gratified. Just so, there can be intrinsic pleasure in acts of service, duty, justice, courage, and forebearance, when they issue from our nature. In virtue of our moral self, we can be joyful in the accomplishments of moral action and exult in history's moral successes. Accordingly, as the Greeks believed, a moral life might be happy just because it is moral, if our moral dispositions are deeply entrenched and well developed.

There is no good reason to deny that we possess such moral propensities. Let us not be deceived by the intense and universal displays of both petty and horrifying human motivations. The moral dispositions, too, are real.[4] When we are not blinded by allegiance to what seems a fetching theory to the contrary, we notice them in ourselves a thousand times a day, as we respond sympathetically, for example, to the numberless woes of others that bombard our attention. In recent years, a number of inquirers from varying disciplines have been investigating our moral nature. Much of this literature was surveyed and evaluated by James Q. Wilson in his book of 1993, *The Moral Sense*, in which he develops his own theses about moral nature, its sources, and development.[5] He affirms that we possess a moral nature, attributable primarily to our instinctive need for affiliative behavior, which prospers in varying ways or languishes, depending mostly on variations in upbringing. Our sympathetic nature, he concludes, is owing to the need for affiliation. Wilson judges that we likewise develop a capacity to be impartial, including the capacity to judge our *own* conduct from a disinterested point of view. Accordingly, he observes, we can and do condemn our own motives and behavior from a moral standpoint. (In common parlance, we possess conscience.) Functionally, this capacity amounts to an ability to accord higher priority to moral conduct than to other concerns. This ability is not always exercised, obviously, but it testifies to a genuine human respect for morality, to our regard for it, even when we are incapable of practicing it. It testifies, in my terms, to a susceptibility—sometimes remarkably potent—to moral considerations.

It seems bizarre to relate these findings as if they are esoteric facts and contrary to common life. Virtually any ordinary person acknowledges the occasional occurrence of such experiences as sympathy for the suffering of others or joy in their happiness, abhorrence of deliberately hurtful conduct, willingness to contribute to the welfare of the group, or a desire to unite with comrades to resist a common danger or to achieve a common good. In consequence of such experiences, moreover, we undergo alterations in our behavior, and we also acknowledge feelings of remorse when our own conduct is morally disappointing. *Theory*, however, often says something else. For their comparatively crude predictions, for example, social scientists believe it is proper to suppose that the intention of every individual is always to maximize his own utilities without inherent regard for the utilities of others. Or, for their part, many of those influenced by the biological sciences have subscribed to the so-called selfish gene theory. The justly distinguished zoologist Richard Dawkins argues that the gene is the unit of natural selection, and the function of genes is self-replication. (Genes that contribute to no such interest would become extinct.)[6] Accordingly, a gene is preserved when its presence in a population promotes the survival of that population, even if a particular individual in the group is put at risk by it. If there is a gene that causes a small animal to make a distinctive cry in the presence of a bird of prey, and if recognition of the cry excites his fellows to run and hide, many genes will survive, but the sentinel itself may well perish to the predator. The sentinel seems to have engaged in altruistic behavior, but in truth his genes have made him a sacrificial lamb for the benefit of the duplicates of that gene inhabiting his population—all without deliberate plan or intent. When this theory, or something like it, is applied to human action, it seems to entail that altruistic behavior is undertaken only for the sake of kin. The closer the kin, the more genes there are in common, and the greater the likelihood of altruism.[7]

The utility maximization theory has been put at risk by Richard Herrnstein.[8] More pertinent to the present controversy is a book by Robert H. Frank, *Passions Within Reason*.[9] Frank points out morally heroic actions not undertaken for kin, yet he does not conclude that they are inherently anomalous. He argues that there are many sorts of moral behavior that might well be selected and at the same time would typically work for the benefit of their possessor. An individual possessing the appropriate qualities earns the trust and support of others, while he discourages those who might try to take advantage of him. A man who will not accept a business proposition that he judges to be unfair, even if it is more profitable than nothing, gains a reputation that encourages others to trust him and participate with him in common ventures, and potential exploiters are less apt to make him their target. Such traits are highly eligible to be selected for reproduction. Still, the man's motivation is not confined to the anticipation of such advantages; he wants justice to be done. Another individual—farmer Brown, let us say—is so insistent on defending his property that he will sue when a neighbor allows his cattle to graze on Brown's fields, even when the costs of the lawsuit would exceed the costs of illicit grazing. Brown's conduct is not self-defeating, however, for he is widely perceived to be a man to be reckoned with, so his neighbors are not tempted to try his patience.[10] For such behavior to be successful, of course, human beings have to be good judges of character. Natural selection has seen to it that most of us are tolerably competent to divine the inner promptings of another man's behavior.

Frank makes the telling point that the models of conduct utilized by theorists are typically unrealistic: they have assumed anonymous individuals who carry on but a single and unrepeated transaction with each other, but such models are contrary to experience. Human judgment and aptitudes have evolved in conditions wherein individuals must live with each other over long stretches of time. In such circumstances, individuals who succeed in one-time predations are not apt to succeed again, and those who are capable of making good predictions about the conduct of given characters will tend to identify the unworthy and unreliable and will try to exclude them.

The same sort of argument has been made by Steven Pinker, who summarizes the case in this way: "The first mutants who felt sympathy and gratitude may have prospered not by their own calculation but because the feelings made it worth their neighbors' while to cooperate with them."[11]

There is no need to be arcane in seeking out sources of morality. The first of them is the perceived necessity of such conduct, but we must also have the desire and aptitude for it, and these seem to have several points of genesis. Any practiced student of human affairs observes, for example, that the human animal is profoundly invested with the herd instinct, a stubborn unthinking insistence on conforming to the demands of the tribe, and with it a pathetic desire to be accepted. That is, our propensity to act doggedly in conformity with what is expected of us gives the lie to the notion that there is something unnatural about the typical willing adoption of social norms. The herd instinct is contemptible only some of the time. Along with certain other dispositions, indeed, it is essential to the formation of nobility of character and to acts of great heroism. It is clear that it tends to serve our species as well as it does others, so it surely is a product of evolution. The disposition to loyalty and commitment must be selected in the life of tribal bands, struggling to stay alive and to prosper. I would suppose, indeed, that we would invoke these tendencies as part of the explanation for our willingness to accord moral conduct high priority relative to other attractions. We recognize its consummate worth for simple survival.

The practiced observer even witnesses the prevalent *excesses* of moral sentiment. Inform a mass of college students of any putative injustice, for example, and they go into paroxysms of sensitivity and caring, demanding the immediate mobilization of all available energies to right the wrong. Much of that reaction is pretense, to be sure, as well as mindless, but it does not belie the fact there is in many persons a reservoir of genuine concern, often ready to overflow. This, too, is desirable for the group, so long as it is disciplined. In brief, the raw material of our moral propensities is not to be wondered at—and they are not all derivative of the herd instinct.

The ideas in Frank's researches are hardly a revelation for those acquainted with Socratic philosophy. The Greeks were surely correct in the belief that virtues are at once invaluable to both their possessor and to the community. Accordingly, it would be astounding if their existence owes nothing to natural selection. Of course, a virtuous individual will often put himself at risk in a manner that others will not, but this is hardly to deny that virtues are among the most precious possessions of an individual.

There is much to add to this discussion of moral nature, which will eventually tell us much about the powers of the moral life. There is wisdom in recognizing our vital dependency on good conduct. That dependency has surely played a part in the gene-culture interaction that is congenial to the development of moral nature; it clearly displays itself in the imperative to educate for virtue. The moral order is thereby conducive to the formation of a moral order *in the self* and even, sometimes, to an ideal fulfillment of self. I have been speaking of susceptibility to moral suasion. This trait can be identified as a responsiveness to moral considerations. Continued study of moral order requires examination of the idea of moral considerations.

b. Moral Considerations

Perhaps it is question-begging to refer to *moral* considerations. We shall see. The distinction between the moral, the immoral, and the nonmoral cannot always be made with great precision. Still, the distinctions are not arbitrary, but analysis is required to bring some clarity to the subject. The general context for the inquiry is the scene of our exertions to sustain a tolerable life by means of associated action—even a prosperous and meaningful life. My concern right now is to distinguish the sorts of considerations that are pertinently introduced in the attempt to distinguish a morally good action or to provide moral justification for actions or policies.

A word of caution: "moral" is also appropriately used to denote what is taken to be the *best* or *most virtuous* action; it is a term that would distinguish the most superior from everything else. That is not the meaning I am explicating here. I distinguish moral *considerations* from the judgment at which one might arrive in consequence of weighing them in a moral appraisal. I mean to suggest a broad class of phenomena that are *introduced* in the process of trying to determine a preferred action, or to try to settle a moral problem, or to justify existing or proposed practices. Rarely is a single moral consideration decisive in itself. By itself, it does not constitute a moral *conclusion*. It is but one of many considerations that is pertinently taken into account in moral deliberation.

In the analysis of appraisal in chapter 1, I said that any sort of existence that somehow enters into one's feelings, estimations, and actions—or that is just thought to do so or might do so—is in some degree determinative of one's evaluation. Moral considerations belong to this general class of beings. They are not mere ideas. They are real events and possibilities (or are believed to be so), the awareness of which is moving to us. These events may be features of our own character and personality or phenomena of our environment. They arouse indignation, scorn, condemnation, admiration, affection, respect, loyalty, and so on.

Not all evaluative considerations are distinctively moral. "This is a good dinner" is not a moral judgment, but the preparation of the dinner might well be a moral act. It might be the fulfillment of a duty, or it might be an attempt to feed the hungry. As a first approximation, one's purpose, action, or attained outcome is denominated *moral* or *immoral* when he entertains the intention or undertakes action with the idea, at least in part, to confer benefit or harm on another. That is, the agent means not just to accomplish some action per se but also deliberately to benefit or harm others in the process. "Benefit" and "harm" refer not only to bodily and psychological conditions. They have reference to any state of affairs that is valued, including those that are valued on moral grounds. An individual who is loyal to justice, for example, is harmed when justice is betrayed.

Instances of deliberate benefit or harm by no means constitute the entirety of moral considerations. The *motives* and *sensibilities* of an individual are also taken into account, and they redound to his credit or shame. Does a man *intend* to do well by another, or is he dissembling? Our moral approvals and disapprovals are largely contingent upon our assumptions about the nature of an individual's subjective state. Is he of a mind to be helpful or hurtful? Is he kindly or callous, courageous, or calculating? In other words, is he apt deliberately to contribute benefit or harm to human endeavor? Character matters. Knowledge of it is invaluable in deciding whether and how another individual is to be counted upon.

Always conspicuous, moreover, is the question of how an individual comes into possession of benefits and harms: Are they *deserved?* He may be justly harmed and unjustly benefited. Benefit and harm are judged in a context of such additional moral considerations. Material riches might be a benefit, but a man who attains them through theft is condemned and thought to have no title to them. Mention of desert suggests an even broader notion of entitlement: we ask about the respective *rights* of contending parties. Reference to rights invites seemingly interminable harangue and obfuscation. For the moment, nonetheless, it is sufficient to observe that there are various protections enjoyed and respected in the moral life, such as freedom of expression and the privacy of the home, where individuals act according to their own discretion, free from unwanted intrusion. While it is controversial to itemize and define such conditions, the idea that there should be secure and autonomous domains of activity in the moral life is fundamental in our experience, and the idea is vital to our moral considerations: What are the rights at issue? What warrants them? Who claims them? Have they been violated? What would justify their abridgement?[12]

A still further consideration is to determine the *responsibilities* of the individuals in a moral situation. It is indispensable to know who caused what to happen, but it is likewise crucial to determine who *ought* to be looking after things. Specified individuals may be designated or expected to perform certain actions, others not, and all individuals might be held to be responsible to exercise caution and foresight. In emergencies, virtually everyone might be thought to be obliged to help. In any event, the determination of moral judgment is in part contingent upon the assignment of responsibilities. Who fulfilled them and who betrayed them? These questions are essential in determining the fundamentally important distinction between guilt and innocence.

A final sort of moral distinction to be mentioned is the difference between judgments that attempt to be *impartial* and those that are inspired by prejudice and party interest. Again, this is a distinction that is sometimes difficult to identify in practice, and it is not always clear what it means to be impartial. Still, we recognize a difference between someone who tries in some sense to be objective and disinterested and one who is nothing more than a partisan for his favorites. It is testimony to our moral powers that those who are judged to be impartial are trusted and respected, while those who pursue a private agenda under cover of objectivity are regarded as scoundrels. We know that duplicity attacks the vigor and trustworthiness of the moral order.

This rather schematic outline of moral considerations is not isomorphic with actual experience, where moral considerations are more numerous, complex, and meaningful. We honor truthfulness, for example *as* truthfulness, and we condemn dishonesty as such. Perhaps these responses are a consequence of having learned that truthfulness is highly beneficial and dishonesty is harmful. Perhaps we also have some innate preference for the one and dislike for the other. At any rate, for the experienced moral person, there is revulsion at lying, and to be told that someone is a liar is by itself a moral rebuke. Hence moral considerations compound and multiply, but I trust I have not neglected an essential and irreducible variety.

These are at least some of the sorts of considerations that determine moral judgment. Incidents of this sort occur in various forms and arrangements whenever we contemplate the rectitude of an action. They are responses, elementary or refined, often of an urgent nature, to events of varying consequence to us. They engage and challenge the constituents of our moral nature, as well as other dispositions. There is a clear sense in which we live in a pervasively moral world. We are incessantly reacting to events as good or bad, morally laudable or offensive. Moral considerations elicit numberless forms of sympathy, acceptance, support, admiration, disapproval, loathing, and opposition. I am not supposing that moral decisions are easily made. Appraisals that terminate in confident synthesis might be highly taxing. I am trying to point out the sorts of considerations that are pertinent to making them.

While unambiguous judgments are sometimes difficult, moral considerations do not lead just anywhere. They are not value neutral, and we are not morally neutral in entertaining them. A benefit as such is not regarded with cool neutrality in comparison to a harm; the contrast between joy and suffering is not morally indifferent to us, pending some elaborate philosophic deduction. A benefit per se is approved; a harm per se condemned. Likewise, benevolence is admired and cruelty censured. Neither is the difference between the deserved and undeserved indifferent to our moral nature: there is a moral bias in favor of that which is merited. These are normal and natural human reactions. Similarly, as an evaluative term, "responsible" is an expression of praise, "irresponsible" of blame, and an impartial judge is an object of moral respect; a pretender is not, and he is not trusted. Such approbations and disapprobations, as Hume liked to say it, are expressions of our moral nature and typical of it. They frequently succumb to other of our impulses, to be sure, but the elementary distinction between the moral and immoral is not thereby abolished. Operationally, for anyone to acknowledge that a given property of events has moral quality is to testify that he ought to be moved by it—though in fact he might not be.

The moral quality of an action, *taken in isolation and as such*, is a good per se or a bad per se, and we regard it as such and teach it as such, with appropriate rewards and punishments. This is the unqualified nature of moral considerations. In the flux of nature, however, these considerations do not occur in unqualified form. They occur in varying, uncertain, and ambiguous congress with other events. Accordingly, my claims about our moral predilections is not to say that our judgments are unerring and that their objects are good without qualification. It hardly needs to be acknowledged that there are benefits that lead to greater harms, that exclude superior alternatives, or that are attained due to vicious behavior, and in our moral deliberations we take such differences deeply into account. Still, apart from qualifications, a benefit is taken to be a good, a harm an evil. To determine what is deserved and undeserved is often problematic and controversial, but that is not to deny that the one is regarded as morally good and the other morally questionable. Leaving all such provisos implicit, let it be said by way of summary that *the distinction between moral and immoral considerations is that between what is supportive of well-meaning human endeavor and that which is harmful to it*. There are other delimitations of the moral that are peculiarly dependent upon an antecedent theory, such as that of Kant, but I have no wish to contest theories at this point. I am concerned to identify certain classes of experience in distinction from others.

We are almost incessantly occupied with moral considerations. Might it be thought, then, that a given mass of them must be judged according to some autonomous principle that does not itself rely on moral considerations or is not reducible to them? When we think and speak with such conceptions as *justice*, *rights*, or *principle*, are we introducing considerations that are different in kind from the preceding? Are these the irreducible and authentic moral considerations that override all others and pass final judgment on them?

Here we are flirting with obscurantism. *When one speaks of justice, rights, duty, principle, and the like, his speech is impertinent and even unintelligible unless he regards these terms as referring to specifiable existential conditions.* "Justice" cannot have a meaning spun out of pure thought, that is, out of thin air. It is used to refer to a particular state of affairs, such as rewarding and punishing individuals according to their merit, or the preferred state of affairs might be equality of result, or each man contributing according to his ability and receiving according to his need, or distributing rewards in a manner that will benefit the least advantaged, and so on. In each case, a distinctive arrangement of human affairs is proffered and advocated. Each arrangement, each specified state of affairs, will conduce to our weal and woe in its own way, and the ways differ widely, sometimes massively. *This* is where our fate is at issue, not with an abstract concept, as such. So we ask of a proposed arrangement how it will work: What would be gained and what would be sacrificed by each set of relations in turn? In surveying these promised results, we are surveying moral considerations, each of which will have its appeal or repugnance to us. Such considerations are apt to be highly complex, and the promised results might not really be apt to occur. We must try to find out, to know better. We also judge that the expected consequences might be more or less uncongenial to human nature or perhaps highly acceptable. Thus our appraisal proceeds.

Specified conditions, relations, procedures, or practices are denominated with a moral expression, but our evaluation is not of the concept per se but of that which it denominates—those self-same conditions, relations, procedures, and practices. *They* are what we consider. If someone asserts, say, a *right* to due process of law, he is advocating that certain conditions be established and maintained: there will be certain procedures accorded to accused parties, specifiable individuals will be responsible for assuring that these procedures are observed, and failure to observe them will be subject to penalty. One advocates these conditions because he has a horror of innocent persons being convicted and of officials who decide all by themselves how guilt and innocence shall be determined. A *duty* is a specified practice on which a form of life is so dependent that it must be done, whether the bearer of the duty likes it or not. Failure to perform the duty makes one liable to serious penalty, and one who does his duty is honored. In the determination of a duty, in any case, the subject matter to be examined and weighed is the *practice* at issue. A *principle* is a prescription for a certain kind of conduct that shall typically be observed through great variations in circumstance—such as telling the truth and standing by one's commitments. That such forms of conduct are distinguished in this manner means that they are regarded as holding a high priority relative to most possible alternatives; and a man of principle is he who will not waver under threat of fear, seductions, distractions, and even death. The form of conduct prescribed by the principle is what is valued, as well as the character of the man whose conduct it is.

In all such cases, the conditions named by the moral terms are of great consequence, and it is this consequence that we consider in evaluative appraisal. When moral considerations are supplanted by edifying rhetoric, we are being merely sentimental, and we are not serving the best of the moral life. Terms like "justice" and "duty" are highly serviceable, for they distinguish and classify momentous forms of conduct. It would be inconvenient, to say the least, to try to do without them, but we must be mindful of what they stand for.

I have been speaking of moral considerations. I venture now a bald, grand, and seemingly outlandish proposition: *It is a universal characteristic of human judgment that the distinction between moral and immoral considerations is that between what is supportive of well-meaning human endeavor and that which is harmful to it.* The proposition is *bald* because unqualified and without nuance, yet qualification and nuance are necessary. I mentioned previously, for example, that there are considerations relevant to a determination of the rightness of benefits and harms; we don't simply accept them at face value. It is a *grand* hypothesis because it claims universality. Yet I would exempt sociopaths from the generalization, and I must also exempt any other sort of person that does not satisfy my definition of a minimally moral agent. I suppose, too, that any biologically humanoid creature who had never led a social life would be likewise incapacitated. Neither do I assert that any individual has this distinction between the moral and the immoral always on his mind. I say that *whenever* one is prompted to offer or demand a moral justification, these are the sorts of considerations he entertains. Finally, the hypothesis is *outlandish* because it seems so implausible.

I certainly make no claim here about human *behavior*. I am saying that virtually all individuals attempt to *defend* and *justify* their advocacies and actions by *claiming* that they had to be done on moral grounds, that is, on grounds that individuals are benefitted or rewarded by the proposed policies or actions, or they are deserving of them—even when the policies in a given instance are *in fact* motivated by hatred and cruelty. Every murdering tyrant claims that he is taking the necessary steps to usher in a golden age, and he must eliminate the parasites and exploiters in order to do so. The greater good—and it is a *greater* good, he insists—requires that some heads must roll. The "greater good" that he *in fact* seeks is the satisfaction of his own lusts, but that is not what he *says*. He might attempt to justify his savagery by claiming that his people are under assault from within or without by evil predators. When Hitler sets out to exterminate the Jews, for example, he attributes to them every conceivable vile characteristic: they are destroyers of all that is fine and good in civilization. Hitler is wrong and he is a liar, and he is infinitely wicked, but that's not the point. He presents (unfounded) moral considerations in his justification. Or the petty thug says his victim (somehow) had it coming—deserved it, or he says that he himself is a victim and is seeking his just compensation—and suchlike. Or he might even confess that what he did was wrong, but he couldn't help himself. In all such cases, the wrongdoer either appeals to what I have called moral considerations in order to justify or excuse his actions, or he gives up his lies and rationalizations and admits that what he did was not morally justifiable.[13]

There are exceptions to rules—as when we might willfully deceive in some circumstance, but such occasions give no solace to one who would argue that there is no generic distinction between the moral and the immoral. Being honest and being capricious with the truth are not acknowledged to be morally on a par. The man who coldly considers whether he will lie or be candid, having no preference for either until he has surveyed their respective advantages to himself, is a moral terror. Engaging in deliberate deception is never regarded prima facie as morally acceptable. It is injurious to well-meaning human endeavor. Immediately, we respond to the lie as an immoral act, but a deception could be undertaken for the sake of preventing a great evil or achieving a great good not otherwise available, and it would be justified only on some such account. That there are exceptions to rules presupposes that the *exception* must be justified; the rules are assumed to be on solid footing. They are the *norm*, as I have phrased it. Nor is there solace to the skeptic in the fact of moral conflict, which might be taken to suggest that one party must be advancing moral considerations and the other one is not. In the familiar case of moral disagreement, however, we do not find that it is constituted by one side defending itself on grounds of merciless cruelty and the other on gentle benevolence. All disputants use moral considerations, yet disagreement persists nonetheless. I have repeatedly adverted to differing conceptions of justice, as a pertinent case, and some of them are radically differing, but none is advanced because it will increase resentment and suffering.

A more fetching objection to the claim that we all resort to moral considerations might be to appeal to the familiar hypothesis that we know moral properties intuitively, but they are indescribable—as in the case of Moore's "good." A dubious epistemology and theory of meaning underlie these assertions. If their defenders could not explain how these elusive moral properties are contributory to human well-being and good order, one must wonder why they are deserving of their crucial standing.[14] Why should we care about them? Would their defenders be willing to say that the satisfaction of these properties could be *harmful* to well-meaning human endeavor? If not, why not? After all, if these attributes of reality are wholly autonomous in their authority, then their moral status could not be dependent upon the presence or absence of other properties. If they were dependent upon moral considerations, however, then their peculiar function has been negated. As I mentioned a moment ago, this is playing with obscurity. True, there are those who believe this theory, so they also believe that they do not consult moral considerations as I have characterized them. One must wonder whether this is their actual moral *practice*. If there are a few cases where this is really so, then my universality thesis would require qualification.

A more enlightening line of thought about the moral condition is this: Though we all appeal to moral considerations, we are not always led by them to the same conclusion. Why not? It should be no mystery. The conditions that determine any individual's moral principles and decisions are both numerous and diverse, and they will vary more or less from one person to the next. Specifically, five points deserve attention: first, it is part of wisdom to recognize that nature is not a perfectly harmonious order. All the events that we take into account in moral appraisal are not necessarily in friendship with one another. They often conflict; one will exclude another, and in any case there must be renunciations and sacrifices, but what should they be and who will suffer them? There are alternative possibilities for policy and conduct, each of which offers its distinctive benefits.

Second, it must be remembered that the individuals who entertain moral considerations do not possess identical moral natures, so they are apt to differ, more or less, in what they regard as most important. There are reasonable and understandable differerences about the respective priorities of values, and there are likewise reasonable differences in operative standards. We have admiration for people who observe heroic levels of conduct, for example, but we do not suppose that their behavior constitutes an appropriate norm of expectation for everyone. The third point concerns cognitive considerations, which can legitimately be shrouded with uncertainty and disagreement. For many individuals, the most decisive of such consideration is what God commands, while many others regard such appeals as groundless. We also disagree about the facts and possibilities of human nature, and we typically have to rely upon problematic predictions about the consequences that any proposed mode of behavior is likely to bring. Much simpler problems are common: pertinent considerations are overlooked, forgotten, unknown, or misunderstood.

The fourth point is that individuals do not engage in moral reflection with equal ability or conscientiousness. A few show extraordinary acumen in the discernment, analysis, and deployment of moral considerations, and these are the people most worthy of admiration for their judgment and sagacity. Most men are only seldom in a justifying mood, however, or they are too lazy or complacent to undertake serious appraisal, or they are dogmatic. They are easily influenced by peers, celebrities, politicians, and charismatic personalities. Maybe thay take the first value that comes to mind as being supreme: maybe they think that being nonjudgmental is the paramount virtue. Perhaps they are simply too ignorant or unintelligent to comprehend a complex analysis. In any event, nevertheless, such individuals are not willing defenders of a distinction between the moral and the immoral that contradicts the one summarized here.

Most important, no doubt, is number five: there is great variation among individuals in what has been learned in moral experience. Some persons have been very attentive to life's teachings and have learned much from them, while most others have not been close students of the moral life, or they have been taught very little about it. That is, some people know better than others. All individuals are not equally capable of such learning, as Aristotle observes. In fact, it takes virtue to learn and to accept the truths of the moral life, and most persons are more inclined to be dogmatists or sentimentalists. These are truths about the disciplines, sacrifices, and hard-won ideals that constitute a good life but do not offer effortless gratification. Are individuals with comparable experience and virtue more likely than others to tend to moral convergence? If they don't, must we not confess that virtue, knowledge, and experience have little bearing on moral judgment?

Moral convergence is one thing, moral unanimity another. The latter is impossible. Even totalitarian mind control does not succeed. The wish to bring all moral thought perfectly into line is either naive or tyrannical, and the attempt to insist upon it is one of our worst temptations. In contrast to the confections of philosophers, actual human beings—including those of incontestable virtue—have never displayed anything like a perfect uniformity of judgment among themselves, and they never will, though they all conscientiously profess in terms of moral considerations. It is most improbable, accordingly, that two individuals—no matter how conscientious—will find that their moral positions exactly coincide. Some combination of the causes of moral disagreement that I reviewed above will always exist. Happily, such unfailing invariability is not necessary for a just and enduring moral order, for we are wise enough to know that some moral disagreements must be tolerated in the interest of a greater good. Moral divergence occurs in every form of human association, but in the interest of perpetuating the union, we often accommodate ourselves to moral decisions we wish had been otherwise. This is not capitulation to evil. It is to recognize that not all goods are compatible, and sometimes we must sacrifice one good for the sake of another.

I do not mean to suggest that most *actual* controversy is reducible to the sorts of disagreements itemized above. The parties to an actual dispute will appeal to moral considerations, to be sure, but not uncommonly some or all of the disputants will in fact be behaving immorally: greed, lust for power, jealousy, pettiness, fear, and other such passions drive them to conceal, distort, and dissemble; they try to pursue a secret agenda that would not bear public exposure. Or they might be deceiving *themselves* or rationalizing, cloaking venality and ambition in moral rhetoric or contorting their hatred for an individual, perhaps, into a belief thay they are doing what is best for him. How typical it is, too, for pompous declarations of forbearance and patience to be a cover for cowardice. The moral code advertised by an individual or a group might in fact shelter all manner of vice and weakness—deliberately or by self-deception. With good warrant, Nietzsche found slave moralities suffused with resentment and cruelty. Moralities might be riddled with envy, greed, prejudice, and the will to dominate. Yet cruelty, envy, greed, prejudice, oppression, deception, cowardice, and the like are not defended *as such* with moral considerations.

Maybe there is a case somewhere of an individual who is not insane who sincerely claims to defend his conduct on explicitly moral grounds by saying—why not?—that he simply enjoys torturing children. Even a hard-core historicist or relativist would find the likelihood of such a case extremely implausible, and he would also have to surpass all records for convoluted theorizing to claim that the action of the torturer is no more subject to condemnation than that of a loving protector of the innocent and defenseless.

Perhaps my hypothesis *is* mistaken. It might at least be overdrawn. I am considering the resources of moral order. Perhaps there is less resource than I suppose, and perhaps in any case the resource now under examination is nothing but puny. That remains to be considered. In any case, a moral being need not be seriously detained if this is not a literally universal phenomenon. No one is willing to give up his allegiance to moral considerations even when there are others who rely upon criteria that are categorically different.

My view might seem outlandish because we do not immediately distinguish the actual character and conduct of individuals from the sorts of consideration to which they appeal in the attempt to give their works moral justification.[15] It is indeed a very remarkable fact, if it is a fact, that all human beings share the same general sense of what counts as a distinctively moral consideration, but it need not be regarded as miraculous. It might even be rather simple, in germ. *With the exception of rights, regard for every sort of moral consideration that I have distinguished is necessary for the survival of a human community.* They sustain and enhance common life. These are considerations that must be held in high respect and given priority in conduct, else life becomes (again) solitary, poor, nasty, brutish, and short. Ask, per contra, what would befall an association where harms were not morally distinguished from benefits or were even given priority. What would become of us if we did not distinguish and support motives that are intended to be constructive rather than destructive? Appropriating the opposite of moral considerations, let the rule—the norm—be to injure our associates and comrades, and be it proclaimed that those who do so will be honored, and those who do not will be thrown in the dungeon. A likely scenario! Moral considerations do not produce the invariant rule or abolish controversy, but they are precious and indispensable all the same; they cannot be cast aside as the determining conditions of normative judgment.

I have no wish to say that the attempt to support well-meaning human effort will never go awry or be tragically indiscriminate. I am asking what would befall any community that taught its members that the will to sustain common endeavors is bad in itself and will be punished. Or suppose "merited" as such were to mean "stolen," "attained by deceit," or "taken by force." Suppose also that there are no trustworthy sources of judgment and adjudication: What then becomes of trust, solidarity, and cooperation? What would be the fate of any association where there were no assignable and enforceable responsibilities? Where guilt and innocence had no connection to the determination of responsibility? No community that is heedless of these considerations will endure. I'm not here referring to the familiar fact of bad behavior: we all acknowledge the prevalence of every form of conduct from petty underhandedness to remorseless brutality. But we also fear and condemn them, recognizing that they must be checked if the community is to endure. Occasion can arise where to be underhanded or brutal might be a necessary evil, but it is acknowledged to be an evil, yet necessary for an indispensable good. I am asking whether life could endure if underhandedness per se, brutality per se, irresponsibility, and the like were taught and enforced as required norms—if people were praised and rewarded for these practices, as such, and were punished for neglecting or resisting them.

Of course, the members of a given community are apt to take an adversarial stance to other communities. They will be competitors and enemies, and all manner of carnage will happen, each side describing the other in the worst of terms. Here, once again, the issue is not that of *conduct*. It is a matter of what sorts of considerations are introduced. If the rival and adversary intends unmerited harm, then he is rightly called wicked. If the supposed enemy can be shown, however, to be innocent of predatory intent, he is no longer called wicked—unless, of course, the leaders of our tribe want to destroy him anyway. My point is that the lustful and evil behavior that is commonly witnessed does not disprove my claim that moral considerations must be of the sort that I have described for any community that would subsist. Indeed, if we were not so prone to irresponsible, greedy, and destructive behavior, the establishment of regard for moral considerations would not be a paramount need, but given the ease with which we indulge in treachery and wanton violence, it would be perfect madness to inculcate the idea that irresponsibility, dishonesty, and destruction are, as such, the objects of our blessings.

As participants in communicative and intelligent associations, we are repeatedly required to provide justifications for our conduct, and we demand them of others. In actual social life—in the family, say—we cannot get by with accounts of our conduct that appeal to behavior that is needlessly hurtful to others in the group or neglectful of their interests, including their moral interests. Children are taught moral considerations before they are taught principles: "You're hurting your sister!" "That toy belongs to Harold." "Tell me the truth." "Help mother clean up the kitchen," and so forth. In a real-life environment, one also learns very quickly of such indispensable notions as guilt, innocence, responsibility, reward, and punishment. Then, "to justify" *means* to make acceptable or desirable. Man becomes the justifying animal. By all manner of evasions, of course, we try to get around the requirement, especially beyond the circle of associations to which we are accustomed, but the requirement to justify with moral considerations has been established. It would be actively supported by our moral nature, and it almost surely originates in part with innate moral capacities and in turn contributes to their satisfaction.

The argument is presented, then, that *moral considerations exist according to nature*. They are not conventions. They are indispensable to shared life. Coupled with wisdom and courage, moreover, they might be ordered in a manner to constitute a good life. *Rules* are subject to evolution, revision, and exception. They are the norm in the sense explicated: they are observed "as a rule," in the colloquial expression, but moral considerations are *always* required in justifications, and they are appealed to when an established rule is questioned in a given dilemma. I speak of less than the lofty claims of old: of universal laws and absolute goods according to nature. Uncertainty and conflict are not abolished. At this point I say that (a) there are distinguishable classes of phenomena that universally go into the making and defending of moral principles, (b) they are universally vital to human life, and accordingly (c) they occur according to nature. That is, there is no getting around their observance without assuring the destruction of the moral order.

Such a conclusion seems to suggest that any morality conceived from moral considerations is bound to be according to nature, but that would be a hopelessly indiscriminate idea. Attention to moral considerations is the common *beginning* of moral judgment and action, but the *outcomes* of these appraisals admit of great variety. There are decidedly better and worse decisions that might be made. It is important to remember that not all moral considerations are equal nor are the reactions to them. A man of weakness and fear will not judge and select them in the same manner as a man of virtue. A man of wisdom, moreover, will be chastened and directed by a knowledge of nature of which others might be ignorant.

It might at first seem anomalous that individuals have this elementary sense of the difference between moral and immoral and so frequently ignore it, but this sort of phenomenon is familiar. There is nothing unusual in a swarm of passions and rationalizations that move an individual to do what he himself thinks he should not. Consider smoking, overeating, drinking too much, impulse buying, procrastination, sexual adventures, cutting moral corners, and so on and on. We are beings of intense appetites that are frequently at odds with the requirements of moral propriety, and we have many ways of trying to satisfy ourselves that we needn't heed them in a given case. Moralists have long made the distinction between the better and worse self, and the worse self can be remarkably ingenious and evasive, even when admitting and disparaging its weaknesses. Many persons are frequently conscience-stricken, but there are also many more who manage to avoid that state almost entirely. Even then, if they should happen to tender a justification for their actions, they will present it decked out in the vocabulary of justice and virtue.

If there is something less than perfect correlation between one's professed criteria and his actual conduct, what resources reside in the fact that there is uniformity in our judgment of what we take to be moral considerations? This is a serious issue, and I will contend with it soon. Whether and how this uniformity can be turned to good account is a matter for responsible inquiry. I am of no mind to invent illusory powers or to depend upon the fabrications of dreamers. This is a question about the real strengths and limitations of the moral condition. For now, the existence of this consensus furnishes a reply to the question of whether my account of moral considerations does not beg the question of the meaning of the adjective "moral." (Remember: I have distinguished between a moral *consideration* and a moral *conclusion*.) It turns out that I am using the word in roughly the same sense that the rest of the human race depends upon. Or, more precisely, I am supposing that there is close to a universal consensus regarding what sorts of considerations are pertinently introduced in order to defend or to condemn human motives and actions. This appears to be the moral consensus of mankind, and it clearly is not a convention. While it thereby survives the carping of the historicist, it is not a consensus about what is best. Call it a working consensus, or ground rules of a sort, or a consensus about the limits of the acceptable. Not anything goes, by any means. No position will be countenanced on moral grounds that is not defensible in terms of well-meaning human endeavor or at least is not guilty of needless harm. Hence moral dispute, however sloppy and indeterminate, falls *within* this domain of evidence. A nervous critic might ask what is so special about *human* criteria. Well, they are vital to *human* life; they are inseparable from it—from *our* lives. It is like asking why we should use criteria of human taste, nutrition, and health when we judge what we ought to eat.

This is neither an analysis of mere convention nor a discussion of the meanings of ordinary language. *It is about those real states of affairs that human beings will approve or disapprove when they deliberate in a manner that they themselves consider justifiable.* If we take no heed of moral considerations, or contradict them, then we will self-destruct. There is, therefore, a virtual unanimity regarding the general classes of events that we take to be pertinent to distinguishing the moral from the immoral, and every individual will acknowledge that he *should* be moved by these sorts of considerations. Present a moral being with a consideration of which he has been ignorant—some hitherto unrecognized pain or deprivation, some unnoticed claim to entitlement, some great good removed from obscurity—and his appraisal will suffer discernible if not decisive modification.

The moral absolutist will never concede that my response to the historicist and relativist is adequate. Nothing short of incontrovertible certitude will do! I will have to do without the support of the absolutist. Our inquiry can dispense with such grand philosophic assertions. The urgent question is to assess our resources for contending with moral differences and priorities in some common terms, short of simply deploying brute force and counterforce. The historicist and relativist deny that any such resources exist. In this they are wrong, and—without the support of the absolutist—the many great evils of human history may be confidently denounced for what they are, and the great goods may be unapologetically celebrated.

It is a further question whether the common coin of moral considerations counts for much in the search for moral concord. Even so, an individual can attain some confidence in his own moral convictions in distinction from those of others. Indeed, he would not make moral concord his first priority. He will not accept agreement at any price: it all depends on what he is asked to agree to. All manner of foolishness, sentimentality, and mediocrity find wide acceptance, after all. In the terms elaborated here, a wise moral judgment is one that records the result of a conscientious moral appraisal. In the end, such a result is determined by one's own resolution of all the considerations that fall within the ken of his appraisal. Until evidence shows up that indicates to the contrary, he knows better; he is wiser.

c. Can the Center Hold?

Yeats voiced profound misgivings about whether the "centre" can hold.[16] Such misgivings are warranted. Who knows if our civilization will survive? An indefinite plurality of conditions is necessary to sustain a good life, and we are not always sure what they are. We can be fatally mistaken about them or too weak to demand them. Many persons suppose that some form of absolutist ethics—their *own* form, to be sure—is one of the necessities. When the universal flux renders all life fragile and uncertain, changeless moral principles that are proof against every qualification and objection seem to provide the security we crave. There must be a truth in the very nature of things, we plead to heaven, that will hold things together.

Against this demand, the fact that we have a consensus about moral considerations seems a paltry matter—anything but a mainstay. We are uncomfortable with ambiguity and uncertainty, unhappy with discord, and fearful of disorder and defeat. Relativism threatens to make such dreaded conditions more likely to occur. We must have bulwarks against them, and we easily assume they lie in unchallengeable objectivity and universality. These are the treasures, we think, that we must possess. Many a reflective person urgently wants an objective morality, where "objective" means something on the order of "determined by a fixed and supreme feature of nature or of human nature." Then such a morality is not subject to the waywardness of whim, passion, and vice. We need only appeal, say, to a law whose luminous authority transcends such vagaries and dangers. If such a law (or perhaps a good) is objective in this manner, then it is also universal—surpassing opinion, custom, and history.

Very reassuring!—and surely we need reassurance, but we must not be hasty regarding the forms in which it might be achieved. Notice that the supposed worth of objectivity and universality lies not in themselves but in what they make possible: such conditions as security, vitality, harmony, and virtue. The supreme principle gives assurance to values that are *already* precious. This is the center that we would hold. Without these antecedent goods, the function of the principle becomes vacuous. Perhaps, however, as Dewey was fond of observing, the price for these assurances might include an oppression of sorts, and much the same assurances might be found in other means. It is worth remarking, too, that the love of objectivity and universality is not always above reproach. In many cases, certainly, it is motivated by a dogmatic and tyrannical nature. There is a powerful wish to make others obedient to our will, where the wish is disguised—sometimes even to its possessor—as pious allegiance to principle. To reduce every mind to one requires the thought police. The General Will is a tyrant, and a man of integrity and courage must resist it.

Both moral tyranny and moral anarchy are terrifying, but what can we do about them? The absolutist seems to be sure of the answers, but waywardness and wickedness, after all, occur very easily in the company of allegedly apodictic moral principles. For his part, the relativist has laid it down that we have no valid moral discriminations with which to undertake a project of invigoration. We might side with him only so far as to observe that it is not self-evident what causes a moral order to hold and to thrive. We hunger for wisdom and trustworthy authority. What resistance to either tyranny or relativism could there be in the consensus regarding the nature of moral considerations? On the face of it, this implicit accord would seem to offer little nourishment to such a hunger: our need is for stalwart principles and ideal goods.

It is needful to sort out the resources at our disposal to establish and preserve a vigorous moral order. Surely it is true that a substantial measure of moral concord is essential to the maintenance of any culture. A culture cannot accommodate all differences. It loses its distinguishing ethos, integrity, and morale, and it cannot endure. Respected and authoritative moral norms *are* essential, but it is not certain that the requirement demands a theoretical absolutism. There *are* bulwarks against relativism and the anarchy that threatens to accompany it. Remember that we do not seek absolutes for their own sake; rather, we need wisdom regarding the best constituents of moral order. Where is such wisdom to be found? Taken just in itself, I agree, the consensus of moral considerations offers nothing definite and assured, but we must think further about the powers it might generate in league with the further resources of man and nature. We may begin with further thought about moral appraisal.

As we have seen, such appraisal is a sometimes far-reaching and discriminating assessment of moral considerations. Moral beings do not begin their appraisal from a morally indifferent posture; they are cognizant of the fatefulness of their undertaking for the formation and preservation of a decent and stable life. A pertinent knowledge of nature is a vital and sometimes decisive resource in these appraisals. Certainly a fundamental theme in them is to investigate the means of social concord and vigor, and we might, in consequence, come to know better regarding these matters. Knowing better, then, would be our wisdom and intellectual authority. That is where we take our stand.

What assurance is there that you and I will take the same stand? We might have firm but divergent convictions, and perhaps that seems to amount to a kind of relativism. Still, the fact that we share the same generic sense of what is pertinently introduced in moral justification carries its own opportunities. The fact that most individuals are susceptible to moral suasion and that they recognize common moral considerations creates the very possibility of meaningful and effective moral discourse. Unanimity about the nature of moral considerations is the assumed background, the unarticulated context, of all distinctively moral deliberation. Deliberation, accordingly, does not start out indiscriminately, where any manner of proposal or justification will be taken seriously, much less respected. It denies justification to unprovoked hurt, for example, and whenever justifications are called for, the burden of proof rests with departures from elementary standards of conduct. Whoever would lie, break a promise, or seize someone else's property must give an account of his behavior that is compelling in the marshaling of moral considerations.

Knowing better incorporates its own form of objectivity in that it is predicated upon a conscientious analysis of the actual conditions of life. There are many objective constraints, limitations, and opportunities in the world that confound our dreams and our perversity, but these conditions are not fully determinative of moral judgment. Nevertheless, they tend toward the condition that I call *pluralism*, as distinguished from both relativism and absolutism. Apart from philosophic niceties, relativism means there is no good reason to prefer one moral judgment over another; there are no constraints on the moral judgment of a given individual that need have any standing in the judgments of anyone else. Absolutism means that there is one and only one right answer for every moral question. Pluralism, on the other hand, is the sometimes indeterminate state of affairs I described above in reference to discourse within the shared context of moral considerations, where disagreements inevitably arise. The indeterminacy of this condition can and does veer in the direction of anger, conflict, and chaos, but there are

resources—such as experience in concourse with the disciplines of nature—
that move it in the opposite direction.

Pluralism is not at a midpoint between absolutism and relativism. It is
much akin to absolutism in the sense that it believes in the possibility of discriminating and formulating powerful norms and principles that can be confidently defended against juvenile reveries, but it also insists on the elements
of fallibility, tragedy, and the possibility of learning better. At the same time,
it judges that the credentials of absolutism have been overrated. The absolutist might consider the distinction between an incontestable, unconditional, exceptionless, and universal principle on the one hand and, on the
other, a rule of life that has very high priority and is taught and enforced with
urgency. Philosophic appraisal abjures the unconditional, but it nevertheless
eventuates in prescriptions that win our profound devotion and loyalty.
Moral absolutes are not the only battlement against relativism, and the
resources of our common grasp of moral relevance are not impotent.

When we judge the powers of honest moral appraisal, informed with
wisdom, against those of the relativists, we will at the same time observe their
efficacy in comparison to the demands for moral absolutes. In this age, the
cultural illuminati require us to be nonjudgmental. This is no more than an
attempt to contrive moral cover for egalitarian ideology and/or unbridled
self-indulgence, but combined with mere sentimentality and the profundities
of historicism, their position has had some endurance. It has been a plague
on moral discernment and the willingness to distinguish good and evil. If we
turn to moral considerations, however, cultural relativism loses its cachet.
Systematic oppression, exploitation, and cruelty cannot be excused in terms
of such considerations. The differences between a free people and an
enslaved one are not to be dismissed as "just cultural." The regimes in
Bosnia, Rwanda, Iraq, and China must be unapologetically declared to be
barbaric. Liars and robbers have no moral place to hide. Denial of rule of law
cannot be morally comparable to vigilant protection of due process.
Courage, justice, and self-command are praised as moral virtues; weakness
and irresponsibility stand condemned—all this without recourse to moral
absolutes. Indeed, such elementary distinctions can be confidently made with
ordinary decency and practical awareness. Candid and reflective experience
is already deeply vested with knowledge of nature. Such is the wisdom that
one normally acquires in the observation of human behavior. Nature's teachings are not always esoteric, and they need not be invariably attributed to
philosophic speculation.

Unprovoked harm or harm that is not for an obviously greater good has
no evident defense in moral terms. A major principle is suggested, a workable
version of Locke's principle of forbearance is supported: do not interfere in
the life, health, liberty, and possessions of another without his consent. There

is likewise a sturdy presumption in favor of such rough but serviceable rules as "be impartial," "spare the innocent," "be responsible," "tell the truth," "keep your promises," and "give each person his due." Granted, such rules are neither exhaustive nor exceptionless; they do not identify our particular duties to assist others; and they do not tell us where wise paternalism might impose upon the principle of forbearance. Nevertheless, it is difficult to see how such norms could be contravened with other than moral considerations.

One becomes impatient with appeals to cultural variations as proof of moral incommensurability. Such appeals are question-begging: in contradiction to all common sense and experience, they presuppose that it is impossible to judge one culture to be better or worse than another. To come back to reality, however, we must acknowledge that some cultures are dreadful and cruel for *anyone* to live in—except, sometimes, for their ruling elites, while there are some for which peoples throughout the world will risk life itself for the opportunity to come to them—the discourses of Stanley Fish notwithstanding. Cross-cultural studies, moreover, give less solace to the moral multiculturalist than is usually supposed.[17]

I am persuaded of the truth of the position articulated by Kekes in several of his writings. He specifies and defends the minimal requirements of *any* morally good society. They are "civility, equality [in legal and political status], freedom, healthy environment, justice, order, peace, prosperity, rights, security, toleration, and welfare."[18] The ways in which these terms can be construed admit of controversy, of course, and the desired conditions will not always be fully compatible with each other. How these requirements might be actualized in a given society, moreover, depends on many historical variables, and there are plenty of moral problems that do not fall within the scope of these conditions. Nevertheless, the discussion of the minimal moral requirements of a good society is confined *within* these parameters, none of which, taken by itself, is morally problematic. All are enviable in terms of moral considerations. Kekes's analysis is a stake in the heart of the historicist vampire.

The teachings of our relativistic sophisticates sap moral vitality and resolve. Of course there are hard questions about the determination of responsibilities, exceptions, priorities, and desert. Nevertheless, there is a limited range of acceptable practices. Within this range there is room for an abundance of moral disagreements, but they are *moral* disagreements.[19] Though they are often momentous, they are usually benign in comparison to the miseries perpetrated by indisputably *immoral* conduct. We have an obligation to denounce and limit *wickedness:* the killers, exploiters, thieves, cheaters, liars, and parasites, among others. It does not take a moral absolutist to know that such behavior must be forbidden.

If we honored moral considerations in practice as much as we profess them, our moral difficulties would be greatly abated. The problem in helping the center to hold is less a struggle between moral theories than a resistance to human weakness and vice. Still, the mere acknowledgment of moral considerations without the exercise of wisdom will never lead us to moral excellence. With perseverence and knowledge of nature's prohibitions and promises, one might indeed distinguish "stalwart principles and ideal goods."

Knowledge of practical affairs is inseparable from wise normative judgment. It is a matter of appraisal to identify the real conditions of good conduct and cherished values. What are the norms of culture, society, and institutional life that will bring vigor and stability? What practices of moral education are well suited to such ends? I have been occupied with the merits of relativism and absolutism in that inquiry. Relativism (proudly) declares bankruptcy, but absolutism regards itself as the sine qua non of any decent society. I don't know what the evidence is—in case anyone has thought to present it—that belief in moral absolutes improves moral judgment and behavior. It seems to be an article of faith. I know many individuals of outstanding character who do not believe in them and a number of morally appalling individuals who do. I do believe, however—as one practical measure—that prevalent *moral standards* are mightily important in raising or lowering the quality of conduct. A standard as such is not a rule of action or a principle; it is a level of expectation, tolerance, and sanction. When we are brimming with understanding and forgiveness for children who lie or cheat, when we are indulgently accommodating of excuses, when we put up with rudeness, incivility, and abusiveness, or when we excuse irresponsibility, corruption, and cowardice or let them off with a trifling punishment, we are operating with very low standards. When we are weak and foolish in this way, we can be sure that the detestable conduct will continue and intensify. High standards tend in the opposite way. The case for high standards rests on moral considerations within the reach of almost anyone.

There is a functional equivalent to moral absolutes—in fact, an improvement on them: in a family, let us suppose, where it is clear that there are high moral standards, where there is an ambience of common decency and respect for others, and where good conduct regarding matters great and small is always expected, the father need not claim that it is always wrong to tell a lie or that God forbids the lie. He can simply tell his son, "If I hear of you lying to your mother another time, you won't be allowed to go to summer camp again" (or whatever). This authority is especially potent in a loving and consistent family. If he is a normal person in such an environment, the young man is not apt to lie, and he will hold truthfulness in esteem. It is to such practices at all levels of society that we must look in order to improve our morals.

The investigation of the multiple and interwoven causes of moral and cultural health is of the highest importance. Analysis of the varieties of moral practice and aspiration is essential to such investigations: misconceived moral ambitions are an assault on something much deeper than convention. What we know of the conditions that support and vitalize a moral order has come of long experience and reflection, and we have more to learn. By his nature, the absolutist contributes nothing to such inquiry. He just lays down his moral laws and pronounces *finis*! Social analysis would be confined to determining how to make societies conform to the antecedently given absolutes. It is worth remarking, to tell the truth, that these allegedly perfect principles are not really *given*, for they proliferate, and the prescriptions of one absolutistic system are sometimes in disaccord with those of another. When absolutists are arrayed against *each other*, there is stalemate. If they are truly absolutists, they have no ground to give; they can only thump on the table and shake their fists.

Most assuredly, just the same, there is often wisdom resident in moral absolutes. Their progenitors have drawn upon the hard-won lessons of the race, but they have transformed them into moral concrete. They have read such instruction back into the cosmos as transcendent and unalterable forms of being. Their concerns are genuine: they seek an upright, harmonious, and prospering society. But here lies their evident confusion: The vitally important inquiry into the nature and conditions of such a society is foreclosed, in effect, by their intransigence. For his part, the absolutist will say that my analysis is question-begging: it goes nowhere without presupposing a moral framework. I *am* presupposing a moral framework, but it is by no means absolutistic. To say it again, the appropriation of morality according to nature is undertaken by beings with a compelling investment in good conduct. Acutely aware of the many hazards of life, they are determined to contend with them as well as they can, but learning how to contend is sometimes a matter that admits of alternatives and variations. They will be—and they are—aided in their searches by the appropriate knowledge of nature. This knowledge is not of a sort, however, to bring an end to all uncertainty, ambivalence, conflict, and change, and it is still, to be sure, in process, and its claims are not infallible. I'm not following the stereotypical paradigm: no deductions of "ought" from "is" are forthcoming.

Because it is predicated on realistic analyses and is devoted to learning the conditions of a thriving moral life, the wisdom of knowing better is superior to that of absolutism. It is a wisdom that would be consummated by surviving the stern tests of practice. Nature, as I have said, has provided us with some resources to contend with her; wisdom, decency, and steadfastness are possible in some degree. Our experience is nurtured and invigorated with less desperate means than those of the absolutist; conscientious reflection has already taught us much. Although there are no guarantees of concord and rectitude, for example, all forms of morality are not equally self-sustaining and invigorating. Egalitarian moralities have proved a failure, and when compassion and permissiveness become the omnicompetent virtues, we court moral disintegration. Those who fulfill their normal responsibilities do the necessary work of the world. They ought to be the norm for everyone and they ought to be honored. But somehow they are ignored, perhaps unappreciated, and sometimes scorned, while others who are not contributing are the focus of moral display. This is not the way to encourage responsibility.

The main constituents in holding the center, or—in my terminology—maintaining the stability and vigor of a moral order, are good character and good conduct. It is by no means established that moral absolutism is a necessary condition for these happy outcomes. It is certain, however, that some forms of social arrangement are distinctly more conducive to the cultivation of moral character than others. This topic awaits fuller treatment. The idea of good character, too, requires amplification.

At this point, a final word on the efficacies of discourse: Practically, we come to a point when further talk is fruitless. One should not despair at this. In addition to the fact that there are sometimes perfectly respectable reasons for disagreement, there are fanatics, dogmatists, ignoramuses, fools, charlatans, cowards, and sentimentalists enough to disabuse you of any such ambition. When you are unconvinced by someone and you hold your ground, it is more than anything else because you believe you know better. Whatever uncertainty you might have, you are still at a vast distance from the swamps of relativism. You don't believe that all "experiments in living," as Mill called them, are equally good. Most of them are catastrophes. You know better than the hedonist, the utopian, and the zealot. In any event, you speak your piece, appealing to the moral dispositions of your audience, who might or might not be moved by the considerations that you bring to their attention. If that fails, so be it.

So be it, that is, pending further experience. Howevermuch invested with wisdom, discourse in itself is not the final resource. Nothing teaches like experience. It disabuses of folly as nothing else. Much of the knowledge of those who know better has been learned in this way.

Notes

1. It is politically correct to hold that prehistoric man was far less violent than our "civilized" version. The falsehood of this idea has been established by Lawrence H. Keeley in *War Before Civilization* (New York: Oxford University Press, 1996). Keeley, an anthropologist, exposes "the myth of the peaceful savage." The scale of wanton slaughter in primitive societies greatly exceeded that of later times. (Keeley also reports that his first two attempts to attain funding for his research were rejected. Later, when he disguised the hypothesis of precivilized violence, his application was approved. The tyranny of the herd instinct knows no limits.)

2. Chap. 7 will be the principal locus of this analysis.

3. Some philosophers hold that a moral act must be a product of free will. The position is ill advised. As I have remarked before, this is an argument maintained for the sake of preserving a theory, not for the sake of the moral life. See *Rediscovering the Moral Life*, pp. 204–208, and p. 54, above, and sect. a of chap. 6.

4. If you declare a human propensity to be horrifying, rather than merely frightening, you have exhibited moral feeling.

5. James Q. Wilson, *The Moral Sense* (New York: The Free Press, 1993). It is noteworthy that Wilson's book received scanty attention from professional philosophers, while notable representatives of other intellectual fields have heaped attention and much praise upon it. I take this phenomenon to represent the insular and effete state of academic philosophy.

6. See Richard Dawkins, *The Selfish Gene* (New York and Oxford: Oxford University Press, 1976) and *The Extended Phenotype* (New York and Oxford: Oxford University Press, 1982). The views of Dawkins are by no means undisputed. There have been arguments in addition to his to hold that by its very nature the process of evolution can only select selfishness and must reject altruism. They have been carefully analyzed and rejected by Elliott Sober and David Sloan Wilson in *Unto Others: The Evolution and Psychology of Unselfish Behavior* (Cambridge, MA: Harvard University Press, 1998).

7. Dawkins himself does not go this far but only at the expense of postulating a virtual dualism of nature and culture. To put it oversimply: Genes run nature, while culture is run by "units of cultural transmission"—or *memes*, as he calls them, such as "tunes, ideas, catch-phrases, clothes fashions, ways of making pots or of building arches" (p. 192 of the new ed. of *The Selfish Gene*). This dualism is ill defended and highly implausible; and so far as I have been able to determine, Dawkins does not consider whether the acceptance or rejection of memes might be largely determined by genes. See chap. 11 of *The Selfish Gene* and chap. 6 of *The Extended Phenotype*, with their respective notes.

8. Herrnstein's essays have been collected in *The Matching Law*, ed. Howard Rachlin and David Laibson (Cambridge, MA, and London: Harvard University Press, 1997).

9. Robert H. Frank, *Passions Within Reason* (New York and London: W. W. Norton & Company, 1988).

10. It can be rewarding to be virtuous and painful to be used, so the costs of farmer Brown's transaction are in fact reduced for him. This shows that acting on principle can be intrinsically satisfying, as I mentioned earlier in this section.

11. Steven Pinker, *How the Mind Works*, p. 406. He adds, trenchantly, "Of course, the genes are metaphorically selfish in endowing people with beneficent emotions, but who cares about the moral worth of deoxyribonucleic acid?" (Ibid.)

12. Rights as moral considerations could be reduced to specifiable benefits and harms, but I choose to make the pertinence of rights to moral appraisal explicit.

13. Voltaire was exactly right: "Hypocrisy is the compliment that vice pays to virtue."

14. See "How to Make Our Moral Ideas Clear" in *Rediscovering the Moral Life*, pp. 105–21.

15. The development of my thinking on this topic has been helped by that of Wilson in *The Moral Sense*. Wilson contends that virtually every individual, given a

truly dispassionate moment, will condemn his own bad motives and behavior and will suffer remorse for them. If it is true that everyone is capable of that sort of impartiality, then his conclusion follows inevitably; but I have not been convinced that everyone does possess it. I make a lesser claim: virtually everyone has the same generic sense of what counts as a moral consideration.

16. Things fall apart; the centre cannot hold;
Mere anarchy is loosed upon the world,
The blood-dimmed tide is loosed, and everywhere
The ceremony of innocence is drowned;
The best lack all conviction, while the worst
Are full of passionate intensity.
—from William Butler Yeats,
"The Second Coming"

17. See "Morality: Its Structure, Functions, and Vagaries," by Turiel, Killen, and Helwig, in *The Emergence of Morality in Young Children*, eds. Kagan and Lambs (Chicago and London: University of Chicago Press, 1987). Seemingly drastic moral variations often turn out to be the consequence of radical differences in cognitive beliefs—from tenets about the conduct of the spirit world to the alleged lethality of menstrual discharge.

18. John Kekes, *A Case for Conservatism* (Ithaca, NY, and London: Cornell University Press, 1998), p. 43.

19. Even the rancorous disputants in the pro-choice/antiabortion conflict attempt to argue by reference to moral considerations.

| 6 |

Justice and the Division of Moral Labor

The idea of minimal moral nature includes a susceptibility to be moved by moral considerations. I have discussed the nature and role of these considerations and spoken of their efficacies in the larger context of the forces of the moral life. It is time to make some further distinctions. A moral order is not a miscellaneous assortment of actions. There are definitive moral functions that emerge in the effort to establish and maintain it. These functions are means of coping with and utilizing the natural forces of human nature in an environment with both forbidding and friendly powers. I am thinking primarily of duties, justice, and rights. The fact that these are, or have come to be, paramount distinctions, is no accident. They did not fall out of the sky. They have developed in response to the perceived requirements, problems, and goods of associated life. To analyze them in that capacity, rather than as abstract principles, is indispensable to appreciating them—and defending them to those who are cavalier about the imperatives of common life.

In each of the three instances, the moral relations are answerable to distinguishable sorts of needs. Not surprisingly, the notion of *duty* is indispensable: there are many tasks that must be undertaken and fulfilled if life will persist. *Justice*, too, plays its own distinctive role. Where there is distribution of shares and rewards in common effort, and where there is competition for scarce resources and prizes, there must be widely acceptable principles in accordance with which such competitions and distributions can be conducted. Otherwise, we return to conflict and chaos. Then there are *rights*—significant domains of activity protected from unwelcome intervention from others. One of the reasons for loving rights is that they allow us to pursue and enjoy a multiplicity of goods without authorization from the state or our neighbor. In this, they seem parasitic upon the moral order, rather than supportive of it, for they do not oblige us to work for the good of the whole, but leave us to our own devices. They might seem a sort of luxury, perhaps foolishness, even madness. Plato and Aristotle believed that the personal activities of most individuals should be governed by the authority of the few, who would typically be magistrates of the law. Socialists and others (including fascists) have insisted that individual rights encourage selfishness, greed, and exploitation, while normal and decent persons would give themselves unreservedly to participation with the social whole. In respect to this issue, the historical record has been kind neither to the Greeks nor the socialists. Yes, the opportunities provided by rights can be decidedly ill used, and often they are. There are kinds of moral order in which rights can be disastrous, but there are others in which they are a wondrous blessing. I will proceed from justice to duties to rights, with a crucial interlude to introduce the idea of the division of moral labor.

a. Justice

With some reason, justice is sometimes conflated with impartiality. Both suggest an invariant moral baseline of some sort: whatever you judge good or bad, right or wrong, must be somehow applicable to any similar case without prejudice. Perhaps there is a common idea of fairness organic to justice and impartiality alike. There *is* some merit in the tendency to conflate the two, but only if they are properly understood. The most helpful analysis of justice, I think, begins with impartiality.

It is one of the most prominent characteristics of morality. It means something to the effect that we treat all claimants as being somehow on a par with one another: they are *moral* equals, however they might otherwise be alike or unlike. It is a distinction of consequence. Impartiality is inseparable from the meaning of all other moral properties in the sense that the latter are betrayed if they are not even-handedly extended to our treatment of all persons. Justice that is not applied impartially is a contradiction in terms. Still, the meaning of impartiality is elusive. We seek some sense of moral equality that is efficacious in our judgments and conduct, making them consistent, and is at the same time distinguishable from other forms of equality; yet moral theories have distinctly different renderings of it. It is possible for these theories to go dangerously wrong, and—no surprise!—they do.[1] Their error is to neglect firm and fundamental characteristics of nature. For more than a century, the dominant renderings of impartiality have been rooted in

Kant or Bentham. Dewey's pragmatism cannot be reduced to either of these philosophies, but he enthusiastically endorsed what he took to be, in effect, their conception of moral equality.

Kant, as I observed in chapter 2, was the inheritor of Cartesian subjectivism, which he took to its limit, finding that all our experience and knowledge is structured by antecedently existing a priori forms, which exist wholly within mind. Any a priori law is unconditioned by experience, by the particularities of circumstance, or by the vagaries of human nature. Rather than adapt to these contingencies, law legislates *to* them, however they might be configured. Moral law is no exception. It is legislated a priori by rational nature, and it is universal to rational nature. Kant is emphatic that a precept determined by the peculiarities of *human* nature in its varying circumstances is neither universal nor unconditional. A priori law, in contrast, is by definition necessary and without qualification. It legislates to all the variations in the moral life, whatever they be. No empirical contingency threatens its absoluteness or casts a shadow on its adamantly obligatory character. Otherwise, we have what might be called a practical rule but never *law*. Hence the omnicompetent imperative: Act always on that maxim that you can will to be a universal law for all rational beings. There is something magisterial in this idea. Think of it: one law, applicable to all, forbidding any evasion or modification to meet transient contingencies, yet a law respecting all rational natures equally.

To be impartial according to this law means that in our moral inquiries we heed rational nature only. Rational nature *is* moral nature. Morally, we consider others as rational beings and not otherwise, and our only motivation as moral beings is respect for rational nature. This motive is at one with respect for law. We do not consider others in their contingent nature, including their contingent motives. Only the will of rational nature matters. It is contrary to duty to discriminate between individuals on the basis of their distinguishing characteristics—the properties they possess as phenomena, appearance. On the face of it, this looks like the very soul of impartiality: morally, we do not think of individuals as rich or poor, old or young, black or white, Muslim or Jew, talented or dull, male or female. There is the same law for all, regardless of such distinctions.

Appearances to the contrary notwithstanding, an immediate problem with Kant's thinking is his idea that all rational natures, as such, are identical. That is sheer myth. All rational beings, so-called, will neither will the categorical imperative nor universalize the same maxims. Some, indeed, will find the norm of universalization suspect. Yet if universality for rational nature is the only test, where do we turn from that point to determine the law? We can't appeal to the contingencies of human nature and its varying circumstances. A related problem is the dualism of rational nature and human nature, where human nature has no moral worth.[2] This dualism exists only in virtue of Kant's philosophy, which dictates the dualism of the intelligible world and the natural world. Supposing, however, that we harken to the needs and imperatives of human nature. How do we accommodate them without losing our universality, necessity, and unconditionality? In such a case, Kantian universality and impartiality recede still further from our ken.

Perhaps they ought to recede. Consider this familiar case.[3] A murderer approaches you and asks the whereabouts of his innocent victim. What do you do? There might be various responses, depending on the circumstances. If you are personally able, you might subdue the killer right there. Or, if you are clever, you might mislead him and send him, say, into the arms of the police. If you are a convincing speaker, you might persuade him to change his ways, or you might risk crying for help, if there seems to be some within earshot. When some "rational beings" are capable of subduing, others of diverting, and others have great powers of persuasion, or when help might be near at hand or not, which of these actions can be a universal law for all rational beings without distinction? Such a law, drawn strictly from Kant's assumptions, must pay no heed to the differences in these rational beings or to their circumstances. So much for the concrete goods and evils of life! (Kant teaches specifically that in such a case we not be diverted by any consideration of consequences. Our duty is clear: tell the truth to the predator about the location of his prey.) Consider also that one of the most distinctive properties of the stalker is that he is *guilty* of evil intent, while his intended victim is *innocent*. These facts are consummately important, but they are contingent facts about these particular individuals—not facts about rational nature.

For Kant, there is no moral merit in any maxim unless it can be universalized. Now, the die-hard Kantian might say that the maxim, as distinguished from universality as such, can and does legitimately take account of empirical contingencies. This defense must fail. First, because the test is for universality for *all* rational beings—even those who live on another planet or in heaven, Kant insists. How could rational beings, otherwise so different, come to any conclusion—indeed, the *same* conclusion—with such a test? Only by making universality per se the all-sufficing criterion. Accordingly, all we need know of the maxim regarding a specific problem in the natural world is whether it can be universalized without self-contradiction. Second, the empirical conditions taken into account in the formation of a maxim must exclude *moral* contingencies, for the determination of what is moral is exclusively the *product* of universalization.

Apart from the fact that to insist on universality here is to forego the most effective action in a life-and-death situation, it is clear that the determination of the maxim itself is in fact consequent upon *antecedent* moral considerations: the guilt and innocence of the parties, the imperative to save a life and prevent murder, the judgment of how much one ought to risk one's own life in these circumstances, the assessment of the resources at hand. All these considerations are morally pertinent even before we think about formulating a maxim that can be universalized, but Kant says they have no moral standing until universalized. On pain of sacrificing life to theory, however, we must make moral discriminations *anterior* to such formalities, and they have decisive merit without even asking whether they can or should be universal law. In fact, they might be of a sort to *resist* universalization on moral grounds.

To be impartial in Kant's sense, we consider individuals only as rational beings and ignore everything else about them. This is not enough information to make a number of crucial moral distinctions. Unless one's first priority is to preserve theory for its own sake, we always take account of the particulars of any situation, including its inhabitants; we take account of the (perhaps dismaying) array of moral considerations presented to us. Kant was wrong: impartiality does not mean that we do not discriminate between individuals. The fact is that we must discriminate—between the deserving and the undeserving, for example, or the responsible and the irresponsible, as well as in other ways. Does it ever make a difference whether a man is a stranger or is my brother? Whether he has wronged me in the past or done me a good turn? Whether I have made a promise to him? Whether he is bent on inflicting harm? All such contingent considerations are morally and urgently pertinent. What further differences are morally pertinent and which ones not? Race is typically impertinent; gender often is so as well, while the condition of being guilty or innocent is almost never immaterial. Which are the morally correct discriminations? There is no responsible way to evade these questions, but they must be declined in Kant's philosophy, where rational nature is determined only by the idea of law as as such. For the sake of preservation of theory, one might argue that these contingent moral considerations would have to be justified by universalization. To do so, however, is precisely—once more—to take them out of their living and distinctive context.

A seemingly attractive feature of Kantian philosophy is that moral law dictates to contingencies, rather than adapt to them. This idea can be taken to represent the moral stance of the man of principle: he will not bend to the blandishments of temptation; he will not be swayed. This *is* a most admirable stance, but there is a massive difference between the determination of moral law and the resolve to obey it. It is in the former demand that Kant fails. Neither has he anything helpful to say about the cultivation of virtues that are necessary for principled moral practice. Once again, we are better schooled by the Greeks. Aristotle would say that a moral individual would determine the most virtuous course of action that *he* could take with the homicidal stalker, and such a man would display his virtue by not succumbing at the last minute to a weak or cowardly impulse.

Kantianism is the Platonic Form of moral philosophy conceived without reference to the functions of morality in sustaining life in a moral order. Kant's successors have proved no more pertinent than he. Kant demanded a universal and necessary law. The demand is not only mistaken but dangerous. Whose "universal" law must we obey? Who speaks for the General Will? The most illustrious of recent Kantians, John Rawls, has not sufficiently considered the perils of such uniformity. He, too, wants utterly "impartial" and immovable law, but we know that natural beings—the real agents of life and history—do not provide the requisite unanimity and invariability. So how are the desired qualities of law to be established? To attain his principles in this pluralistic and uncertain world, Rawls must concoct a "free and equal rational being," whose moral nature is universal and constant. Its definitive judgment will not be swayed by contingencies and variations.[4] But why must the judgment of this phantom be definitive? Why not some other phantom, or better, none at all? In any event, the social and political beings with whom we live every day, many of them morally admirable, are *displaced* by this theory. Following the lead of Kant, Rawls declares explicitly that respect for persons (i.e., being impartial) applies to actual individuals only insofar as they share the convictions of free and equal rational beings behind the veil of ignorance. Other convictions are not worthy of respect. In effect, Rawls respects only those individuals who subscribe to his philosophy. There is no reason to suppose that the displaced persons will accept the morality designed by their surrogates.

The problem with this entire strategy is that this moral creature is sheer invention; it resembles nothing real. In fact, it has been artfully designed to produce the antecedently desired result. This agreement would not be shared, however, by the huge majority of actual persons, who would bridle under this regime of justice.[5] (I believe, actually, that no one could live in the prescribed manner, not even John Rawls.) The regime would end in ruins. All social contract theories are flawed in this manner. They attain a specious consensus by presupposing sufficiently similar agents in the contracting circumstance, while actual persons are more variable.

We must look for a decent notion of moral equality outside the tradition of Kant. What about the utilitarians? Their view seems to be impartiality itself: everyone seeks pleasure and is averse to pain. In any situation, we will decide what is the morally right alternative by totting up in each instance the sum of pleasures, subtracting the sum of pains, and thus discriminating the greatest net gain in pleasure. We are impartial because in our sums we count each person as one and no more than one: the pleasures and pains of no individual are given special weight or precedence. What could be more even-handed than arithmetic?

Then, when we calculate the moral value of the works of a Jeffrey

Dahmer, for example, we must consider the pain of his scores of victims and their families, but we must also count against that figure all of the pleasure Jeffrey himself got from his efforts. (We might also make a guess as to how much pleasure various sadists have derived from hearing of these exploits.) The pain greatly dwarfs the pleasure, of course, so his slaughters are wrong. Otherwise, they wouldn't be. When we contemplate his punishment, neither must we forget the suffering that he himself will incur from it; such pains enter the calculation in moral opposition to his punishment. We can go ahead with it because his pains are judged to be a necessary sacrifice to future utilities.

The scenario is appalling. Dahmer does not *deserve* pleasure. He *deserves* punishment. He slaughtered innocent people. These moral considerations are decisive. We might be tempted to say that his pleasures don't matter, that he will be counted as less than one: we will exclude his pleasures from our sums. We should resist the temptation. We *do* take his pleasures into account; we do judge them. His pleasures are abominable and are utterly condemned; they count against him, not for him.

A simple arithmetical determination of pleasure does not settle what is good. Pleasures are not morally indifferent phenomena just waiting to be added up. They are not taken as morally neutral or morally equal until the outcome of the calculus is declared. Rather, we make moral judgments that distinguish good pleasures from bad. We might in fact judge that an entire population are corrupt, and we would have contempt for their greatest happiness. Such judgments issue from an existing moral disposition that has not been determined by utilitarian theory. The utilitarian, however, proceeds with the assumption that moral propensities and convictions antecedent to the calculus are morally irrelevant, and they might well be negated in consequence of the summing of future utilities. The impartial consideration of human beings consists in nothing more than regarding them as bearers of pleasure and pain. That's it. Then nothing remains but to measure and count. Just as for Kant to be impartial means to respect rational nature alone, impartiality for the utilitarian is to treat individuals as nothing else but possessors of pleasure and pain. Both reductions are propagated in innocence of moral experience and at its expense.

Scholars will be shocked by my stereotyping of the meaning of utilitarianism; they will hurry to point out that it has undergone many changes since the time of Bentham. Indeed it has—even to the point of making it sometimes unrecognizable. Though Mill, as a first instance, was unaware that he had done so, he eradicated the calculus by insisting on irreducibly qualitative differences in pleasures. Inconsistently, he continued to insist on the formulaic "each person to count as one and no more than one." Those who defend the distinction between *rule* and *act* utilitarianism also introduce extra-utilitarian moral criteria. One of the most problematic issues in this family of ethical theories is the determination of what is to count as a utility and how it is to be measured in intersubjective comparisons. Perhaps the most respected and influential in this school in recent decades, R. M. Hare says that we are obliged to be completely impartial between preferences when they are prudent and weighted according to their intensity. On the other hand, the most notorious of current utilitarians, Peter Singer, has stayed with the original Benthamite formulation. He propounds "the basic principle of [moral] equality: the principle of equal consideration of interests."[6] He promptly adds, "The principle of equal consideration of interests prohibits making our readiness to consider the interests of others depend on their abilities or other characteristics, apart from the characteristic of having interests."[7] The interests of *others*, he insists, means those of *other sentient beings*, of whatever species. The interests of all sentient beings must be counted equally *as interests*. "Of course, [sentient creature] X's pain might be more undesirable than [sentient creature] Y's pain because it is more painful, and then the principle of equal consideration would give greater weight to the relief of X's pain."[8]

What is common among all the variants seems to be this: Utilities, however they are measured, are the one and only moral test of all conduct. Their measurement takes no account of *whose* utilities they are or whether they are *deserved*. The utilitarian has two fundamental moral requirements: to calculate pleasures and pains without antecedent moral judgment of them and to count each person (or creature) as one and no more than one. These are no more than postulated requirements. They are anything but self-evident axioms; there has been no moral appraisal to justify them; and there is no evident reason to exempt them from it. How do they accord or conflict with our abundance of moral values? We are far from being a clean slate upon which utilities are registered. Our obligations, our loyalties, our sense of justice are older and deeper by far than thoughts of the utilities of individuals conceived without any moral differentiations.

We humans have innumerable and diverse native responses, which might be moral in nature or largely determinative of our moral judgments: feelings of tenderness, solicitude, fairness, responsibility, obligation, bonding, loyalty, gratitude, recoprocity, and so on in all their varied intensities and combinations. They are linked to a swarm of cognitive beliefs about the whole moving, changing composite to which they belong. Of such stuff are moral convictions and actions made. We cannot merge all such feelings into pleasures and pains indifferently and just add them up. They each and all have *moral* weight in our experience independently of being aggregated into quantities of utility. The utilitarians—and the moral rationalists in general—would deny the instinctive attachments and ambitions that make morality possible at all. Instead of counting each person as no less and no more than one, we might count them as more or as less than one, as moral experience dictates. We *do* show preference for individuals under certain circumstances, but it can be of a morally legitimate form.

Let us juxtapose a contrived theory to experience and nature, as disclosed in moral appraisal. When a utilitarian makes a solemn promise—a marriage vow, let us say—there is always a tacit proviso: "I will do as I have pledged unless and until such time as I determine that the greatest happiness of the greatest number warrants otherwise. Be assured that I will be perfectly impartial. I will count you as one and no more than one, just as I will for any and all anonymous and unknown persons of any description whose pleasures and pains might fall within the orbit of any actions that I might take." For anyone else, making a promise means something rather different, something on this order: "From now on, you shall count with me as more than one. I hold your good to be superior to that of others to whom I have given no comparable oath. You can count on me through good times and bad." The tacit proviso in this promise might run like this: "I will make exceptions in cases of emergencies, where a calamity can be mitigated by letting my promise lapse for a short time," or "If our bond should become an unredeemable disaster for both of us and for our children, then let us be done with it." But there is in any case a heavy burden of proof to be sustained by whomever would break the pledge. The general utility is not a conspicuous consideration in such decisions, if at all. The good of those intimately involved is paramount.

Human trust and solidarity depend on such commitments. "He has pledged his sacred honor," we hear, and "A man is no better than his word," says another. We admire and respect individuals of such integrity. Utilitarian calculators, on the other hand, will never make a community; they will not bond; they will not be friends. A military unit of utilitarians could not muster the solidarity to make them effective warriors; something more powerful and precious than calculation would be wanting. When my long-standing and trusted comrade is being defrauded of his home and reputation, should I leap to his defense, or should I undertake research into other cases, now unknown to me, locate one where the utilities are greater, remain indifferent to other moral considerations, and devote myself to diminishing the newly discovered pains? (I can explain to my faithful friend that I am a utilitarian. Or might I suppose that the other utilities are someone else's responsibility?)

Another obvious case where we show legitimate preference for distinguishable individuals is within the family. I have an obligation to care for and nurture my own children that exceeds any obligation to care for my neighbor's children, much less the children of persons unknown to me. This is an obligation recognized and respected by everyone. Accordingly, the fact that the family is by nature an inegalitarian institution does not arouse the judgment that it is inherently unjust. We expect persons to be responsible first to their own children, and when they are not, we reproach them. When children are neglected, we try, more or less, to help, but we suppose the principle remedy is for the parents themselves to be more responsible. To have a child, indeed, is to make a massive and unconditional commitment, rather than to assume that you will treat your child as no more and no less than any other being in the world. You have promised your life to that child! Is not much of the current debasement of the family—and the culture—owing to the fact that parents are less and less inclined to make such a commitment?

This promise is perfectly natural because of the love that parents have for their children, if for no other reason, and because children require so much in the way of parental resources. Natural selection has been at work. Genes that do not find a way to replicate themselves will perish; those that do find a way will continue. Accordingly, like other reproducers, human beings are genetically biased in favor of their own offspring. Sexual selection is part of this equation. A female seeks a mate who will, among other things, provide her with the most vigorous offspring and who will protect them and help them to flourish, in preference to others. Females will try to reject males who do not seem promising in this regard. The number of females who are looking for a mate who is apt to give preference to the young from outside the gene pool will diminish and eventually disappear.

It is highly probable that natural selection also accounts for our penchant for deliberate and sustained commitment. Such a predisposition may well be a dimension of the herd instinct, reinforced and ennobled in myth, poetry, and education. Tribes and other groups in which this propensity is strong will, other things being equal, have greater fitness than populations in which it is weak. The likelihood is slim, on the other hand, that our propensity for loyalties to special groups is merely conventional. The capacity for that sort of bonding can't be taught. (Inasmuch as group solidarity is a huge asset in the competition for scarce resources, such loyalty would be according to nature even if it were wholly a product of learning.)

The utilitarian was first doubted because of his refusal to count Dahmer's pleasures against him and because he did not take account of desert in judging the distribution of pleasures and pains. The victims were innocent and Dahmer was guilty. That settles the matter. They did not deserve to be killed and Dahmer deserved to be hanged. Are these judgments merely conventional? I certainly hope not! I hope that we have a natural aversion to the sorts of atrocities for which the cannibalistic serial killer was convicted, and I hope that we have a natural aversion to the pleasures in which he indulged. The literature indicates that such immediate reactions are largely innate.[9]

I have made several references to desert. Is reward according to desert a convention? An exploration of this idea will help us to think wisely about impartiality and justice. It might be regarded as a mere truism to say that each person should get what he deserves. What else should he get? But the idea is problematic in at least two ways: first, the very notion of being deserving can be questioned, as Rawls has done, leaving the question of the distribution of reward and punishment to compassionate philosophers and social planners, who disdain to take account of desert. (They disdain to take account of any values inconsistent with those of a "free and equal rational being.") Second, and more seriously, it can be asked what characteristics make a person deserving and what sort of reward is deserved. Following an already ancient tradition, Aristotle stated that each man should receive his due.[10] This arrangement implies, to paraphrase the original, that likes must be treated as likes, not as unlikes. Unlikes should not be treated as likes. According to this formulation, people who are unequally deserving should not be equally rewarded. Rather, there is a proportion between the extent to which one is deserving and the level of reward. If I am twice as deserving as you, I should get twice the reward. Aristotle acknowledges that there are legitimate controversies in regard to what makes one deserving, but it is not controversial, he thinks, that reward should be proportional to desert.[11] He defends this view by observing that departures from the principle cause the eruption of resentment, hostility, and civil discord. Justice is what holds the polis together, he says. If these claims are true, then the theoretical alternatives to Aristotle's position cannot be successfully defended with moral considerations.

Typically, we suppose that to attain a just reward one must qualify for it, earn it. Such expressions imply that some form of competence, contribution, achievement, or special status must be demonstrated, some standard of excellence or merit must be met or exceeded. (Likewise, we deserve some form of punishment when we fail to meet certain requirements or when we violate them.) The standard would be pertinent to a specified endeavor. If you contribute well to the advancement of business, learning, literature, athletics, statesmanship, or science, then you deserve a level of recognition comparable to the level of achievement in that undertaking. Recognition could be in the form of money, status, trophies, honors, power, and so on, or some combination thereof. *This is a discriminatory process*: there is a conscientious attempt to distinguish those who satisfy or surpass the standards. If justice is being served, the process rejects discriminations that are impertinent to the standards at issue. Hence skin color, sex, or religion would not be taken into account in determining excellence in mathematics, law, music, and personnel management, for example.

Although not found in Aristotle, the notion of justice is typically extended to the condition of deserving *help*—aid or assistance of some kind. Some individuals *deserve* help. Perhaps they have been deprived, injured, or impeded due to no fault of their own—perhaps in spite of their own diligence. It is evidence of our moral discrimination that these are people we wish to aid or see to it that they are aided, while the parasitical, feckless, or lazy elicit no such response. Our admiration for responsible conduct and our disapproval of negligence would seem to lie behind this distinction.

There is a substantial and growing body of literature pertaining to the topic of what people take to be just and unjust and how their conduct varies with variations in the observed forms of justice.[12] The populations examined include cross-cultural and historical samplings. Remarkably, old Aristotle seems to have been vindicated—often by inquirers who know nothing of him. That is, Aristotle's view is almost universally shared, and his admonitions about civil hostility and disruption have been borne out. There are very few associations that have succeeded in enduring for long without adherence to proportionate desert. Utopian societies and egalitarian communes, for example, either perish or become Aristotelian. Studies reported by Thomas Sowell indicate that individuals are willing to transfer resources to help disadvantaged people to compete for rewards, but they are unwilling to accord them preferential standards of merit in the actual conduct of the competition.

The few exceptions to these principles of justice are religious orders, such as monasteries, the members of which presumably have no interest in earthly reward. But even here, admissions to the order are carefully monitored; stern authority, indoctrination and discipline are required; and expulsion for failure is routine. That is, their particular form of justice requires powerful enforcement to keep it going. Tyrannies, too, might endure for more than a season.

The terms of justice are not entirely precise. There are reasonable arguments about standards of desert and about who satisfies them, and there are legitimate questions about when they apply. Sometimes simple equality might seem fairer, or some other method of distribution will seem best. Market mechanisms, for example, will not always result in a just distribution by Aristotelian criteria, but that does not mean that we should scrap these mechanisms in favor of bureaucratic regulation. Classical liberals tend to equate justice with whatever is agreed to in the process of bargaining. A fault with this conception is that bargaining power is often unequal. Still, it is commonly true that the actual process of bargaining is implicitly guided by Aristotelian assumptions: the parties seek what they believe they deserve. "A fair day's pay for a fair day's work" is a familiar watchword.

The free market also works on the assumption that the discoverer and/or developer of scarce resources is entitled to their ownership and the benefits thereof. If you find oil, gold, lands, ideas, or technologies, you might come into great riches in consequence. We might say you *deserve* the reward, and in many instances that would be an appropriate judgment. In other cases, men happen upon great resources even with little effort, and it doesn't seem quite Aristotelian to say that they are deserved. We have learned, just the same, that when the state takes custody of the fruits of private discovery and development, the rate of risking such initiatives drops off precipitously, and we are more apt to suffer poverty than prosperity. We also bridle at the loss of freedom. Accordingly, it is wise to let the market have its way in such cases. Efforts to make a wholesale substitution of another system of justice, on the other hand, where unlikes are treated as likes or likes are treated as unlikes, prove to be tyrannical.

Why does the Aristotelian relation tend to work well? Why do others fail? Certainly the simple matter of incentive is important, offering greater reward for greater achievement. Where people receive equal shares for unequal work, those who do more work gradually reduce their output. It is educationally effective, moreover, to reward and punish individuals in proportion to the extent of their good behavior and bad. It is difficult to imagine a child who would be responsive to Rawls's difference principle, in accordance with which the fruits of achievement must be funneled off to the least advantaged. To be a Rawlsian, he would have to be sent to a re-education camp.

However important the function of incentives, the appeal of justice is more than that. We *admire* distinction and excellence, and we wish to recognize and honor them. There is still more: it seems to be in our nature to be hurt and resentful when we are not treated equally with someone else who seems no more deserving than ourselves. It need not be a matter of feeling short-changed in terms of financial reward; it's a matter of simple recognition for our achievement. We also protest when persons other than ourselves are not rewarded in proportion to their desert or whose reward is not comparable to that of individuals who are no more deserving. There is research that shows that persons who believe they have been *overrewarded* tend to feel uneasy on that account. In addition, we do not feel cheated when someone of greater merit than ourselves is accorded greater recognition. We might envy him, doubtless, but there is no claim of injustice. This is a finding of great consequence. Men do not seek equality of reward, but justice. Only intellectuals profess egalitarianism—for others, of course.

The fact that this sense of justice is so common suggests that it occurs by nature. That suggestion gains support when the attempt is made to educate people to adopt a different scheme of justice, and the attempt fails. Seventy years of socialist indoctrination failed miserably, and the actual behavior of Communist Party elites never showed a trace of sympathy with egalitarianism. We can speculate about the conditions that would select for a disposition to embrace proportionate equality. It is plausible that the inclination is derivative of our marked propensity to reciprocate, or possibly it is one with it. This propensity saturates our judgments and conduct. We count it as a moral obligation to exercise it. "One good turn deserves another" is always a conspicuous reminder. Failure to observe it is condemned and abhorred, and we prefer to exclude from our company those who do not return services or favors.

Continuing research on this topic moves more and more in the direction of concluding that we are instinctive reciprocators.[13] It is an invaluable trait for social beings, but it must be coupled with the knack for detecting likely betrayers of a proposed cooperation; and most of us become rather good at that. We learn to engage in cooperative activity in the expectation that our contribution will be rewarded in turn. At the same time, we come to place great store by reputation. One with a good reputation is sought out for collaborative activities; one without is left to fend for himself. The genetic conditions that are conducive to the formation of good reciprocators and good judges of character would be selected.

Reciprocation is the exchange of value for value. If greater value is given, greater value is expected in return. This is the germ of the behavior that Aristotle outlines in his discussion of justice. A demand for the proportionality of contribution and compensation develops in the practices of reciprocity. At the same time, there is demoralization of reciprocators who have not been returned value for value, and they distrust and exclude those who do not exhibit a willingness to honor proportionate return. In any event, it would be no surprise if those who happen to have the gifts for effective reciprocation turn out to be fitter for survival than their rivals. Accordingly, it would also be no surprise if there is widespread susceptibility to affirm and embrace this form of justice.

I have neither known nor heard of a person who actually behaved as a Kantian, utilitarian, Rawlsian, or egalitarian. Though I am not past all possibility of persuasion, I do not believe that anyone—or certainly *very few* persons—could be educated to perform in compliance with these doctrines. (And how somber and burdensome their lives would be!) Returning to the notion of impartiality, then, it seems that *the way to treat persons impartially is to treat them justly.* By nature, the foremost way to display impartiality is to be just in the manner transmitted to us by Aristotle: give each man what he deserves, and what he deserves is proportionate equality.[14] Nature gives us no small instruction here. We have a convincing notion of moral equality and justice. We might reasonably hope that a society that practices justice in this manner would tend to an appreciable measure of order, prosperity, and absence of rancor.

Without contradicting the Aristotelian position, we could say that there is a still more elementary form of impartiality: insisting that all persons receive a candid hearing to determine what they deserve. We have this sense in mind when we speak of an impartial judge. The enriched version of this procedure is the practice of approaching individuals with a genuine willingness to hear their case, without presuming the worst about them—even with the expectation that they will have something worth hearing and taking seriously.

Even apart from the fact that the terms of justice are inexact, the idea admits of exceptions. Sometimes we believe we should not treat a person according to what he deserves. We might show kindness or mercy instead, but only if we thought it would improve that person and not hurt others. These qualifying conditions occur with much less frequency than the casual moralist supposes. No one should get the idea that justice is easily set aside.

A culture depends on more than justice, nevertheless, and there are moral practices and judgments that are not predicated on desert—such as considerations of duties and rights. To have rights, indeed, is another (and not wholly compatible!) form of moral equality. Something must be said about them in distinguishing the sorts of norms generated in the struggle to sustain a moral order and to give it life, but I will hold off that discussion long enough to speak of duty and to introduce a concept implicit in the preceding discussions. It is the idea of *the division of moral labor*: it is about the ways in which we distribute the moral work of the world—the division of moral responsibility, if you like.

b. THE DIVISION OF MORAL LABOR

There is a distribution of moral responsibility implied in the nature of justice, duties, and rights. Justice is a norm for the exchange of values and for the distribution of scarce resources. Rights establish (among other things) domains of autonomous activity, within which one is protected from unwanted interference; duties constitute required kinds of conduct for the preservation of the community or some smaller group. Individuals have their own duties; they are not allocated indifferently to everyone without distinction. Each of these three sorts of activity incorporates distinctive requirements. Justice requires an apportioning of contribution and its rewards according to a definite form. There is a ratio of reward to performance. The determinations of what is to be contributed, what is due, to whom it is due, and from whom it is due are judged and decided apart from taking into account the general welfare or our duties to the human race. What I deserve as, say, an engineer working on projects for my employer is determined without reference to such broad and abstract considerations. In the context of determining what I deserve in that capacity, these other matters are extraneous. There is a certain moral autonomy in just transactions. The nature of such exchanges suggests that a moral order incorporates rather definite divisions of moral responsibility, the necessity and legitimacy of which are dependent on nothing so barren of moral discrimination as the theory of the general utility.

Like justice, duty is a prime form of dividing the labor of the moral order.

We shall see that the relevant moral considerations in the assignment of duties are reducible neither to the provision of what is deserved nor to the general happiness. In chapter 8, we shall also see that rights are judged by varying criteria. Rights, too, when they exist, constitute a moral arrangement that releases their possessors from taking the welfare of the whole into account. One may mind his own business, as it were, and see to his own problems.

Perhaps these appear to be commonplace observations, but the idea of the division of moral labor has powerful and far-reaching implications. Consider the matter of the distribution of responsibility more broadly. The fundamental thought is that we are not equally responsible for everyone and everything. Rather, in most cases, responsibility is possessed by distinguishable individuals, groups, and institutions; it is exercised for the benefit of specific individuals and groups. What might seem a normal and natural arrangement, however, gives the horrors to some moralists. They cannot abide the very thought of a moral division of labor. Somehow, they suppose, we are remiss in our moral duty if we do not take *everyone's* good into account whenever we make a moral decision, and they likewise suppose that our duty extends equally to everyone's welfare. We may study the matter more fully by moving on to the idea of duty.

c. Duty

Typically, duties are distinguished when there is important and sometimes indispensable work to be done, even when no particular individual is eager to do it. Nevertheless, the work is not to be evaded, and failure to do it cannot be tolerated. What a man deserves might or might not coincide with his duties; he might have to sacrifice what he deserves in order to defend his city, for example. We especially honor the one who sets aside his personal projects in order to do what is needful. We also speak of duties when we refer to forms of conduct that are not optional. We voluntarily accept them, perhaps, but once accepted, there is no turning aside. Such are the duties of work and family, for example.

We come by our duties in many ways, invoking a variety of moral considerations. As we have seen, the making of a promise establishes a profound and specific obligation: I am pledged to you in a manner that I am to none other. The promised services belong to none other. While not all obligations are incurred by promising, the acceptance of a responsibility is the functional equivalent of a promise: "I will do my duty," you have said. Other duties are incurred in customary and informal ways, such as those belonging to friendship, family life, and some of the professions, and, as we have seen, some may simply be imposed on us. Not infrequently, duties are undertaken for remuneration: when you accept a post in the firm, you accept definite responsibilities. In any event, when a duty has been determined, a specific division of labor has been established. Parents, teachers, scoutmasters, cooks, engineers, employees, and lawmakers: in assuming their respective stations, they assume specific obligations. Not all of their duties will be welcome—certainly not all of the time—but that does not excuse failure to fulfill them.

There are demands that must be met if the work of the community is to be sustained, and it is a matter of high priority that they be met as well as possible. Accordingly, the assignment of duties is a matter of consequence. We want the best man for the job. Duties, accordingly, often fall to the persons or institutions who are best qualified to fulfill them, but qualification is wisely determined not only by judgments of aptitude and competence but also by singling out individuals who have the strongest motivation to be responsible in the expected manner. Give the job to the man who sees its necessity and embraces it as such! In contrast, responsibilities should not be defined in a manner to allow their bearers to escape the consequences of foolishness and malpractice. Although it is mad to assign duties without accountability, it happens with regularity. Bureaucrats, for example, are wont to impose regulations that might well be disastrous, but they suffer no ill for their arrogance. Teachers, too, will use their students as guinea pigs in experiments that turn out to be harmful, but the teachers suffer nothing for it.

We are fitted for many responsibilities by aptitude and training, and these characteristics typically reflect native capacities. Expertise and a gift for leadership, for example, owe much to nature, and the motivation to undertake and fulfill certain duties is often a product of innate propensities. In many instances, the duties are so demanding that the proper motivation is both rare and essential. The requirements of being a parent are preeminently of this nature. Most parents, to be sure, are well motivated, but they are driven to care for their *own* children. Surrogate parenting is more apt to incline to irresponsibility. Parenting is emphatically a division of moral responsibility according to nature.

We would be shallow to suppose that duties are exclusively burdensome. There are persons who are so devoted to their paramount duties that they hold them to be superior to themselves, to their own lives. We call them sacred. Such persons live for something greater than themselves, in the familiar expression. Sometimes these duties are joyful, and they typically give direction and structure to a life and sometimes meaning. One rightly takes pride in having done what is expected of him, of discharging his duties with skill and dedication. Without them, most individuals lead a rather aimless and meaningless existence, wondering why their hedonistic successes come to so little, after all.

There are, to be sure, moral duties that apply to virtually everyone and whose benefits are not confined to singular individuals and groups. Telling the truth comes to mind, as well as a general disposition to honesty. Obeying the law could be added and the prohibition of doing harm. Certainly one of the most indispensable moral functions is the prohibition of the many forms of destructive, hurtful, or otherwise antisocial conduct, as in "Thou shalt not kill." Such observances are expected as an essential part of almost any form of human relationship. They become a matter of honor to anyone who would be a contributor to the human enterprise rather than a parasite upon it. To recognize such obligations is not at the same time to negate the idea that we are not equally beholden to everybody. In specific instances, our moral tasks are more exactly delimited. Keeping one's promise might be universally a duty, but when you have made a promise to a particular individual, you are obliged to *him* in that case.

There are also duties to be helpful and charitable to those in need. That is, anyone of even a modestly developed moral nature would feel such a prompting and would feel some inclination to do something about it, as the occasion seems to require. In many sorts of circumstance, it is only humane to affirm a duty to be charitable; to fail to render aid is often the worst of abominations. Charity, nonetheless, is a practice that can be done effectively or foolishly, wisely, or indiscriminately, whether undertaken by individuals, institutions, or the state. Experience has taught that there is an apt division of moral responsibility in the provision of charity. Families, churches, local communities, and established groups do a better job at it, by and large, than bureacrats and professional dispensers of other people's resources.[15]

In any case, charity is not the foundation of duty or of the moral order. Humane offices are responses to failures in the order or to its mishaps and calamities. There are higher priorities: fulfilling those tasks that preserve the life of the whole and its many parts, and even enhance them, whether in daily practice or in moments of exceptional demand. When those who sustain these duties are not honored, the civilization is on its way to collapse. It is clear, moreover, that there are limits to the charitable impulse. Though we are willing to help out in emergencies, we will not sell the family farm in order to aid the improvident or make major sacrifices in our own family in order to put the neighbor's kids through college. Such cases represent natural and appropriate divisions of moral responsibility.

The failure to recognize such priorities pervades the thought of many a theorist, whose agenda is uninstructed by nature. Consider once more John Rawls, who reflects the sentimentality of contemporary liberalism. With Rawls, and with slave morality in general, the status of the least advantaged is the very lodestone of justice: any and all inequalities are justified only insofar as they improve the lot of the least advantaged. Nobody is otherwise entitled to any improvement in his condition, no matter what he contributes. For their part, the least advantaged are not required to do anything to justify their entitlement; they have no duties to fulfill. Save that of remaining disadvantaged, there are no conditions that they must satisfy to retain their benefits. They needn't work or try to find work. They needn't be responsible in any way. One hardly knows whether to laugh or cry at the prospect. This is a mad theory, a prescription for creating an ever-enlarging mass of permanently disabled men; a prescription also for discouraging marginal workers from exerting themselves, for they will believe it is to their advantage to slip a rung into the ranks of the least advantaged. It is a prescription for raising the most intense hostility to the least advantaged from everyone else. In effect, charity has become folly.

The Greeks had a better sense of priorities. With a tincture of justice—but only a tincture—they have been criticized for neglecting the role of charity in the moral life. It was the stated mission of Socrates to help his fellow citizens to become virtuous, and he was essentially right in that ambition. Virtue is needful above all else. Except for episodic misfortune, the virtuous will neither require charity nor want it, and we have learned that "welfare" has no enduring good unless it leads to the virtues of personal responsibility. There are crises, disasters, and overwhelming adversity, of course, and in response to them we often take a broader view of our duties, for the duration of the exigent situation, hoping to put stricken people back on their feet, able to discharge their customary obligations. There are also devoted individuals and agencies who take responsibility for those who have no prospect of recovering from their condition. Admire them as we will, we should not be diverted from the fact that Socrates had a wiser sense of the priorities of a moral order.

Duties constitute an apt division of moral labor. The idea of such a division is actually a commonplace of experience. There is an idea in general intellectual currency, just the same, that to be moral means to be concerned for everyone and without preference, and that will be our criterion for moral decency. Utilitarians, socialists, and egalitarians are especially drawn to this notion. Hence, they insist, we are dragged away from morality by our allegiances to specific individuals and groups.[16] Such allegiances can be dangerous, certainly, but the very idea of the distribution of moral responsibility survives this belief about morality and the universal welfare. Apart from worried theorists, everyone recognizes and acknowledges that specified distributions are just. I do not think of myself as responsible for someone in central Asia, and the Asian doesn't expect it of me. I'm not even responsible for the welfare of my next-door neighbor, for that matter. In my office as policeman, fireman, or legislator, however, I have explicit duties to definable individuals, among whom my neighbor would be included. It is a commonly accepted division of moral labor that each man pull his own weight—to use a familiar phrase—and it is a good principle on the whole. People must be expected to be responsible, and we are by nature inhospitable to the deliberate parasite.

I do not intend these comments as a denial that there are public goods that are best supported by shared duties and collective action or that taxation to finance various causes must be illegitimate. I mean to suggest the familiar and natural values that divide the labor of a moral order. Though they are not utterly inflexible, they are also limits, and it is fatal to debase the finite responsibilities that arise within them.

By and large, the general welfare will take care of itself when everybody does his particular duty, but that is no routine achievement. It is a signal fact of human nature that our duties are not always borne willingly. For anybody, there is often a divergence, a gap, between what he would like to do and what he is obliged to do. That gap easily becomes a chasm, and it occurs with regularity. We are naturally unhappy and reluctant when we are obliged to fulfill certain offices, especially when we would much rather be doing something else, as often happens. So we look for an excuse—almost any will do—to shift our tasks to someone else. Accordingly, any sustainable moral order gives high priority to inculcating a sense of responsibility. There are serious penalties for failing to live up to acknowledged imperatives, and those persons who are unusually dutiful are treated with proportionate respect and honor. When social policies mitigate or pardon irresponsibility, on the other hand, we tend to become only too willing to shirk our duties. When functionaries, for example, take over the obligations of private individuals, the substitutes have less motivation—perhaps none—to fulfill such tasks, and at the same time the private individual has a diminished sense of responsibility. He readily becomes less resourceful and reliable in the life of the group. Men become less responsible to women and to their own children when law and custom no longer insist upon dutiful conduct. No-fault divorce, easy abortion, and state subsidized illegitimacy have allowed men to live out their most juvenile fantasies—to everyone's detriment.

We should never think lightly about this demand of the moral order. When you know it is *your* duty, and when others know it is your duty and expect it of you and will not do it for you, and when you are rewarded for fulfilling your duties and scorned for failing in them, then you are more apt to be responsible. A civilization should do all that it can to encourage this happy condition. Concern for the general welfare is praiseworthy, but it should not be an indiscriminate and wholesale concern; its possessor would foolishly regard himself as responsible for the general happiness. He would be wiser to discern the appropriate divisions of moral labor and encourage the discharge of their respective duties. There is no way, of course, to satisfy the soul who recognizes that the division of moral labor will leave some people better off than others and who insists that each individual has an obligation to try to maximize everyone's happiness indifferently. Such a person declaims in ignorance of nature.

d. RIGHTS

Justice is widely respected and coveted. Duty is likewise honored. Duties are sometimes onerous, but we acknowledge that they must be done in order to sustain and invigorate the moral life. A distinctively different division of activity is denoted by the idea of rights. It is inspired! When the state and our fellow citizens have so little compunction about appropriating our property, keeping us silent, demanding that we conform to their beliefs, or otherwise managing our lives, it is paradise to wring a concession from them to keep out of our business. Not only are we free from hated interference in vitally important concerns, but we are apt to prosecute these concerns with greater vigor and accomplishment, benefitting ourselves and others. In brief, the division of moral life we know as rights are domains of activity that may be enjoyed by individuals and associations without external authority; what people do within their rights is their own affair. Rights open up a world of opportunity and excitement that is otherwise unavailable, or it is at any rate muted. Our forefathers called these the blessings of liberty.[17] But are we not flirting with disaster so long as we are diverted from concern for our social duties? And might not justice itself be threatened by private right?

These are critical questions, and I won't desert them. For the moment, I wish to point out some remarkable peculiarities of this division of moral activity and its uneasy relations with justice and duty. In most cases, individuals are possessors of rights simply in virtue of citizenship in a certain political jurisdiction.[18] Rights are not earned by someone because he has passed some sort of test or displayed unusual achievement. Unlike our just deserts, they are not accorded to particular individuals who have been discriminated from others. Due process of law, freedom of association, freedom of speech, and freedom of worship belong to all citizens indiscriminately.[19] We do not have to compete with one another for them. Of course, they might be earned in the sense that they initially had to be fought for, and succeeding generations would deserve them in the sense that they continue to defend and preserve them. Nevertheless, they are still possessed by the entire citizenry without distinction and just in virtue of being citizens.

The indiscriminate possession of rights is a form of impartiality or moral equality, but it is unlike that of treating individuals according to what they deserve. To accord and to respect rights is not a way to judge one man in distinction from another. In a context where discrimination is called for, considerations of justice become pertinent, but historical experience has taught that there are contexts where such discriminations are impertinent, unwelcome, and injurious.

What is the wisdom that lies behind this distinction between rights and proportionate justice—and behind the volumes of moral rhetoric? The behavior that is protected by rights is often the most cherished. Once survival and domestic stability are secured for a time, the autonomy of home, family, work, possessions, religion, friendships, voluntary association, and various forms of expression becomes the highest priority. Justice is sacred; duty is essential; but rights give the best opportunity to attain and preserve, we believe, all manner of priceless goods. (They do not perform expressly in this way in every instance. They might secure protection from arbitrary authority, as in the right to due process, or they might afford the possibility of political empowerment, as in the right to vote.)

There is typically much struggle and competition for goods. This fact is widely recognized and accepted. In the contention for scarce values, we prefer—in the interest of peaceful order—that the struggle be governed by rules. Here the demand for justice becomes conspicuous. It does not occur only to give acceptable order to competitive relations; any voluntary collaborative undertaking requires reciprocity, the proportionate exchange of value for value. But the *right* to pursue goods is not proportionately allocated. Rights are not awarded according to desert, nor do we compete with our fellow citizens for their possession. In a crucial sense, they should not be regarded as a scarce resource, where demand necessarily exceeds supply and we must contend with each other for their ownership.

Wisely conceived, rights are a condition that can be held by everyone. Invaluable as they are, if they were apportioned only by a competition, the struggle would be unthinkably fierce, and the sense of justice would be overcome. Rights are a prime facilitator of the *pursuit* of happiness. Only a fool supposes that the *possession* of happiness is a right. To attempt to assure such "rights" is the insidious but certain route to tyranny. Regimentation must replace freedom, and the notion of desert must be negated.

As with any moral arrangement, the institution of rights is not without its serious—even fatal—corruptions. Coveted though they be, to have rights is no guarantee of wisdom and virtue. Insofar as one's conduct is protected by right, he may pursue all manner of folly and excess, and he will often do so. Moral education is one of the prime duties of civilized life. When it succeeds, individuals would be less apt to exercise their rights ineffectually or foolishly. When this duty is displaced or dissipated, however, rights become treacherous and vulnerable. Experience suggests that they are more subject to abuse in their exercise than other distinctive constituents of moral life. Moreover, they are by no means the primary instrument of social solidarity. There are other forms of life within the moral order that encourage cohesion and loyalty.

Even in the best of cases, the exercise of these freedoms can be problematic. The way in which other persons utilize their protected forms of behavior, for instance, might well irritate or offend us. The offense could be deliberate. Just as we must accommodate to all manner of natural necessity, we likewise accommodate to many of the ways in which others exercise their rights, but the possession of rights is also a resource. Consider freedom of speech. It is an invaluable instrument of inquiry and learning and a great asset in exposing corruption and oppression. It is often exploited for ill use, to be sure. We might have to endure propaganda or verbal assaults on our dignity, for example. But a culture loses its intellectual honesty and moral manliness when it accords a higher priority to sensitivity than to freedom. The virulent spread of political correctness shows us how readily ideological mania turns to systematic mind control—in the name of sensitivity in the present instance. It is far better to tolerate the excesses of freedom of speech than to place your mind in the keeping of the Ministry of Truth. We might instead employ the self-same powers of free speech to contest lies and to confront insult and accusation. Free speech, rather than legal prohibition and regulation, becomes an instrument of justice. Who will mount the responsibility to use it in this way? If too few seize the initiative, we take a fatal stride into moral passivity and thought control.[20] A certain virtue is required if we are truly to respect the rights of others and to utilize our rights effectively. Otherwise, the singular morale and vitality that rights contribute to the moral order will diminish or disappear. We will inhabit an order of moral monotony and regimentation. Lawmakers salivate with anticipation.[21]

An analysis of rights must be cognizant of further problems, at least as troublesome as those surrounding their occasional offense to others. We must judge of rights in the context of the inclusive moral order, where notorious perplexities arise. All rights are not fully compatible with each other: within the confines of my home, for example, my right to private property might be invoked to forbid your right to free speech; freedom of association, likewise, can run head-on into the right to equal protection of the law. Rights do not constitute a harmonious whole, nor do rights, duties, and justice. The moral life affords no such ease. Rights take their place in the social order in the company of duties, and the two are not invariably in concord with one another. Wherever a right is categorically established, duties may not squander it. You may suppose that I have a moral duty to refrain from using insulting language or a duty to help the poor, but insofar as I have a right to free speech or to the disposition of my own property, no one may coerce me into performing either of these duties. On the other hand, I might have a right to life, liberty, and the pursuit of happiness, but I also have a duty to serve my country, to obey the law, to keep my promises, and to make necessary contributions to a plurality of shared activities. Normally, I have no right to evade these duties, even if they threaten my life, liberty, and well-being. Here, rights withdraw in the presence of duties.

Where I have a right without qualification, accordingly, I have no duty that contradicts it (nor, for that matter, do I have another right that does so), and where I have an absolute duty, I have no right that permits me to compromise it. It is a familiar tension: many moral values conflict with freedom, and freedoms encroach on each other. Duties, commitments, and loyalties prohibit certain behavior in which we would otherwise indulge, and some regimes will so extend our duties that there is no room left for freedom. A great expansion of rights diminishes the scope of duty, and as duties are multiplied, rights disappear. It is a momentous dialectic, and it has no certain and final resolution. Such are the inevitable consternations of the moral life.

The injudicious proliferation of rights makes people neglectful and even contemptuous of their duties. Rights, after all, are not burdensome; they can become a form of indulgence, but duties are often hard and thankless work, so we want more rights and fewer duties. It is also wise to be judicious in the distribution of duties. Keep them to a few and make them count, and make them obviously pertinent to vital life. The assumption of duties is far more palatable, too, when they are undertaken voluntarily, as in the family, and a strong sense of responsibility makes them less apt to be onerous. Leave men to their responsibilities and do not micromanage their affairs. Regulative bureaucracies, to the contrary, love to proliferate duties. This is one of the ways they make life a hell.

There is a noteworthy tension between justice and rights, of troubling consequence. Within a sphere of moral activity constituted as a right, individuals might well engage in injustice and legitimately so! They do not exceed their rights. By right of private property, for example, the owner of a commercial enterprise might make his son its president, though the son doesn't deserve it and might bring the business to ruin. A private university might exclude Jews, blacks, atheists, Catholics, and males from its faculty and student body, regardless of how deserving they are in virtue of their intellectual achievement and scholarly promise. Groups of friends, private clubs, and owners of restaurants can be as tribal as they please. Within private associations protected by right, moreover, there may be denial of rights otherwise assured. A business may limit the freedom of speech of its employees. Universities, of all places, have come to limit this freedom routinely—and smugly.

The will to overcome these perceived injustices is usually well meant, but it is dangerous. There *is* an opposition of norms, not necessarily of a transient nature, but the knee-jerk compulsion is to suppose there is a quick and easy remedy in extending government authority over what had previously been protected by right. The relish of officials and bureaucrats is to regulate and control, which they do with a deadening hand. They gleefully erode our beloved autonomy, the very freedom that helps us to do our work with intelligence and zest. Regulators kill morale and vitality and vitiate the development of personal responsibility. Life becomes strangely solemn. Yet there are powerful alternatives to the expansion of the state: the free market, for example, will chasten the doting businessman. A plurality of alternative institutions, as there might be in education and in private associations, is apt to have similar effects. The competition between them will cause some institutions to be more welcoming: they put considerations of merit above gender, for example. Insofar as they do not, the availability of a diversity of private associations increases the possibility for an individual to locate somewhere more to his liking. Conditions of this sort tend to diminish racial conflicts and exclusions, rather than intensify them, while preserving the spirit and energy attendant to private rights.[22] All such forms of influence are especially potent when coupled with publicity and social mobility. Under such conditions, individuals have the opportunity to avail themselves of the services of competing associations.

Moral suasion is sometimes effective, too, which is not to say that it is always wise. More fundamentally, the exercise of rights is most productive when accompanied by moral and intellectual virtue. Corruption can undermine any form of practice, to be sure, and the abuse of rights is especially likely. Consequently—whatever the perplexities that arise in the moral order—any society is in grave jeopardy where alert and diligent moral qualities are lacking in the populace, and likewise any form of association is blessed when such qualities are plentiful. There will still be uncertainty, tragedy, conflict, and failure, but the resources for contending with them most effectively will be present.

Another word about the tension between individual rights and social solidarity: rights will not necessarily undermine the strength, unity, and vitality of the moral order. Everyone in the order possesses them, and there can be widespread thanksgiving to inhabit a society in which such treasures exist. One is grateful to live in a free country. For that reason, allegiance to the order might be intensified, and when the need for common action arose, there might be greater willingness to contribute. Such gratitude alone will never suffice, however. It must be inseparable from great objects of loyalty held in common within the inclusive social fabric, and—once more—there must be deeply affective dispositions to satisfy fundamental duties. Such virtue is not self-incarnating. *In a free society, there must be institutions that foster allegiance to justice, encourage a firm sense of duty, and impart a vital sense of individual responsibility.* Without them, rights will succumb to all manner of vice and weakness, and any feeling of social solidarity will wither, while the state expands.

I do not offer these observations as solutions to life's tragedies but as a cautionary note. They help us to recognize vital constituents of a vigorous and happy moral order while acknowledging that they have no perfect union. At the same time, we recognize the perils inherent in the ways these forms of life might combine—or fail to combine. Thus we might have the wisdom to undertake difficult and dangerous choices.

The remaining chapters will offer further commentary on these themes, but we must also start to give attention to life's best possibilities.

Notes

1. See Gouinlock, *Rediscovering the Moral Life* (Amherst, NY: Prometheus Books, 1993), pp. 161–67.

2. All motives of human nature are what Kant calls inclinations. He says, "The inclinations themselves as the sources of needs . . . are so lacking in absolute worth that the universal wish of every rational being must be indeed to free himself completely from them." (*Foundations of the Metaphysics of Morals*, trans. and intro. Lewis White Beck [New York: The Liberal Arts Press, 1959], p. 46).

3. This example is closely modeled on one of Kant's own. See "On the Supposed Right to Lie from Altruistic Motives," in *The Critique of Practical Reason and Other Writings in Moral Philosophy*, ed. and trans. Lewis White Beck (Chicago: University of Chicago Press, 1949), pp. 346–50.

4. Actually, this is the (alleged) moral nature of individuals inhabiting liberal democracies—fewer than the world population. Rawls offers no empirical evidence to substantiate this claim about the moral nature of denizens of liberal democracies. He doesn't even attempt to do so.

5. See *Rediscovering the Moral Life*, pp. 214–17, 247–68. The most conspicuous denial of fundamental human values is the rejection of any notion of desert. Rawls does not scruple to "educate" real-world citizens by all "rational" means to endorse his principles of justice. This policy would work no better than did the moral indoctrination in the Soviet Union from 1917 to 1989.

6. Peter Singer, *Practical Ethics*, 2d ed. (Cambridge: Cambridge University Press, 1993), p. 21.

7. Ibid., p. 22.

8. Ibid., p. 21. Singer has become notorious because he takes his utilitarian theory to its logical conclusions, which many have found repugnant. A human infant, for example, is entitled to no consideration from his parents (or others) just on account of the fact that he is human.

9. Once again, the most compendious source of information on this topic is Wilson's *The Moral Sense*. The fact that some individuals do not have these sympathetic responses is not proof against their innate origin. Remember the lessons of the bell-shaped curve.

10. Aristotle, *Nicomachean Ethics*, trans., intro., and notes, Martin Ostwald (Indianapolis and New York: Bobbs-Merrill Company, Inc., 1962), book 5.

11. His example of controversy about desert is the question of political power. Is it deserved due to free birth, wealth, or excellence? In the *Politics* he urges that each of the three has a legitimate claim on a share in ruling (but not an equal share). The demand of any group for exclusive rule is disastrous to the stability and morale of the polis.

12. See *Rediscovering the Moral Life*, pp. 175–84 for a fuller analysis of some of these issues, and see Wilson, *The Moral Sense*, pp. 60–65, which supports the same

theses. An impressive range of research into actual social experience has given great credibility to the Aristotelian position. Here are some of the main sources:

Charles J. Erasmus, *In Search of the Common Good* (Glencoe, IL: The Free Press, 1977). An anthropologist, Erasmus examined widely varying communities around the world and throughout history, and he found that all of them evolve toward a form of justice as reward according to desert. This form can be successfully set aside only with the most severe discipline, usually in strict religious orders.

Jerald Greenberg and Ronald L. Cohen, eds., *Equity and Justice in Social Behavior* (New York: Academic Press, 1982). A large selection of articles in the field of inquiry launched by Homans: equity studies. Cross-cultural research displays a variety of forms of justice, but in regard to distributive justice, the Aristotelian paradigm is the most widely found and respected.

George C. Homans, *Sentiments and Activities* (Glencoe, IL: The Free Press, 1962), pp. 61–75, 91–103, and *Social Behavior: Its Elementary Forms*, rev. ed. (New York: Harcourt Brace Jovanovich, 1974), pp. 241–69. A distinguished sociologist examines forms of justice in social behavior, finding that the distinctly preferred form of practice is that which had been specified by Aristotle.

Melvin J. Lerner, *The Belief in a Just World: A Fundamental Delusion* (New York and London: Plenum Press, 1980). Lerner's empirical research and experiments reveal two salient points: (1) Individuals desperately want to believe that the world is somehow essentially just; (2) Justice is invariably construed as each person getting what he deserves.

Thomas Sowell, *Preferential Policies: An International Perspective* (New York: Morrow, 1990). Sowell's research confirms what Aristotle had reported: when equals are treated as unequals or unequals are treated as equals, society erupts in hostility, conflict, and violence. For a more compendious account, see his "Affirmative Action: A Worldwide Disaster," *Commentary* 88, no. 6 (December 1989): 21–41. Sowell is unusually gifted at taking a philosophic abstraction (such as justice) and determining how the fateful idea can be evaluated by reference to testable hypotheses.

13. An excellent survey and analysis of this issue and others is found in Matt Ridley, *The Origins of Virtue: Human Instincts and the Evolution of Cooperation* (New York, Viking Press, 1997). Ridley does not apply the results of his research to the topic of justice.

14. Justice, Aristotle implies, also depends on special status. There can be no doubt that he would say that it is just and obligatory to give preference to the care of one's own children. He observes that the gravity of an unjust act is greater if the relationship is a close one. People who are close owe *more* to each other (1160a). Yet it would be contrived to say that our children deserve our care in the sense that they have earned it. Surely, nevertheless, we are *obliged* to give them our care, for we have produced them, and surely *my* children and *your* children are not likes in the relevant sense. In addition to the fact of my affection for my child, she deserves my attention due to her status as *my* child. Aristotle says that his discussion of friendship (*Nicomachean Ethics*, books 8 and 9) is an extension of his analysis of justice. In friendship, for example, what one party owes to another is dependent upon the status of each. Young and old, child and parent, teacher and student have duties to each other defined by the respective position of each. There is also a sort of friendship between

fellow citizens, he says, just because they are fellow citizens. He evidently refers to a kind of bonding or loyalty that characterizes members of a community, even when they are not friendly with each other in the usual sense of that term. They have, consequently, obligations to each other that they do not have to noncitizens.

15. See, for example, *The Tragedy of American Compassion*, by Marvin Olasky (Washington, D.C.: Regnery Gateway, 1992) or Myron Magnet, *The Dream and the Nightmare: The Sixties' Legacy to the Underclass* (New York: Morrow, 1993).

16. Rawls, as we have just seen, belongs in the egalitarian camp. In *A Theory of Justice* he expresses deep reservations about the legitimacy of the family, because it threatens the impartiality that his version of justice requires.

17. Many societies enjoy more or less delimited spheres of activity where individuals are free to make their own lives according to their own judgment, but these spheres are not declared to be rights, and they are not protected by law.

18. Enthusiasts for rights are apt to say that individuals have rights whether they occupy a certain jurisdiction or not. They cry that human rights are universal. There is great emotive force in such declarations, but in philosophic analysis it is wise that they be tempered. There are seemingly countless questions pertinent to the definition, enumeration, and assertion of rights. We must always be willing to make an appraisal of any proposed right. Many such proposals will be endorsed with great confidence, but many others will be denied. For zealots and ideologues, however, anything coveted with great passion is declared a right. It is wholesome and pertinent, therefore, to argue that there *ought* to be a particular right rather than to say there *is* one. Then the right that is advocated can be subjected to appraisal.

19. In truth, not all rights are indiscriminate, such as the right to vote. With some justice, John Stuart Mill asserted that the right to freedom of speech and to "pursue our own good in our own way" should be reserved to those "in the maturity of their faculties." I overlook such distinctions in the present context.

20. I do not defend the position that any and all speech should be protected, but here I wish to stress that infringements on speech should be entertained with the greatest caution, and we must look to other ways of addressing degraded (or allegedly degraded) exercises of this liberty. I will not attempt to specify the legitimate forms of restraint on speech.

21. In politically correct analysis (i.e., virtually all contemporary analysis), being tolerant of the behavior of others is equated with being nonjudgmental, where "nonjudgmental" means "accepting without differentiation." According to this equation, we must not simply put up with much that we regard as foolish or misguided; we must actually approve of it! The consequences of this confusion are disastrous: sensitivity training to indoctrinate us to accept views or conduct that we find unacceptable. Big Brother is elated. His view has been thoroughly examined and forcefully shredded by Robert Weissberg in his *Political Tolerance* (Thousand Oaks, CA; London; and New Delhi: Sage Publications, 1998).

22. This has been a conspicuous theme in the writings of Thomas Sowell. See, for example, *The Economics and Politics of Race* (New York: William Morrow and Company, Inc., 1983) and *Ethnic America* (New York: Basic Books, 1981). Sowell's emphasis has been on economic freedoms.

| 7 |

Priorities

.

Plato traces the degradation of human nature from its best to its worst. The decline is presented in almost fatalistic tones: a horde of clamorous impulses is resident in the soul, and once we begin to lose control of them, they become progressively more shameless and imperious, submerging any nobler tendencies we might have. One of the foremost occupations of *The Republic*, accordingly, is to argue that the various forms of the life of self-indulgence are ill-conceived and disastrous. That Plato makes this theme so prominent testifies to his conviction that human beings are intensely prone to pursue such a path, and they tend to be ignorant of any superior alternative. Right from the start, Thrasymachus embodies the philosophy of unlimited self-assertion, and the power of Gyges (in the myth recounted early in the dialogue) would seem to be the envy of anyone: he can be unjust at will, while always appearing to be just. Glaucon is uneasy with these arguments, but he is not equal to refuting them. Before turning in desperation to Socrates, he relates the evidently universal opinions that justice is another man's good and that it is only due to our powerlessness that we are obedient to the law.

One of the book's most vivid images is that in which human nature is represented as a many-headed and insatiable monster, against which the counterpoised forces of reason and courage seem pitifully inadequate. It is an enormous achievement for them to succeed, but the benefits of success are reported to be unsurpassed. Whatever the obsessions of academic philosophy, it is clear that Plato regarded our powerful tendencies to immediate gratification with both fear and contempt, and no good life is possible that cannot turn these powers to good account, so far as possible. For some, at any rate, there can be significant success in this venture.

There are several stages in the degeneration of a well-ordered soul, and at each one the ability to control ourselves and to resist further deterioration is diminished, until at last the soul falls impotently to the command of the foulest passions. What we could call hedonism is but one of these stages, the democratic character, for which there is no priority among desires: all are equal and equally worthy. The democratic man

> lives along day by day, gratifying the desire that occurs to him, at one time drinking and listening to the flute, at another downing water and reducing; now practicing gymnastic, and again idling and neglecting everything; and sometimes spending his time as though he were occupied with philosophy. Often he engages in politics and, jumping up, says and does whatever chances to come to him; and if he ever admires any soldiers, he turns in that direction; and if it's money-makers, in that one. And there is neither order nor necessity in his life, but calling this life sweet, free, and blessed he follows it throughout.[1]

As the final lines suggest, such a life is commonly regarded as the best. "Isn't such a way of passing the time divinely sweet for the moment?"[2]

Hedonism, then, seems the most attractive of all forms of life. The corresponding political order is one in which any constraint is increasingly resented and any claim to superior authority in the conduct of life is derided and thrust aside. Adults pander to the demands of the young. This is also the regime, Plato believed, that is the most fertile culture for the emergence and flourishing of vice—for the dominance of the tyrannical character.

Plato's characterization bears an ominous resemblance to American culture as recently depicted by Robert Bork in *Slouching Towards Gomorrah*.[3] Our egalitarianism and permissiveness, Bork observes, have brought a precipitous decline in standards of conduct, thought, and achievement. I am strongly inclined to agree with Bork in many respects; in some, I would be even more pessimistic than he. Let it be said, in any event, that one of the most powerful and natural threats to a vigorous moral order is the great temptation to hedonism. Most persons wish they could pursue such a life, but they are impeded by the necessities of survival. "Let me gratify my every desire" sounds like paradise itself, and—unlike vice—it seems harmless enough. The passions of hatred, violence, and ruthlessness are unmistakably dangerous to any moral order, while mere self-indulgence seems rather innocent. Nobody but a pleasure-hating prude could be opposed to it. From the standpoint of wisdom, nevertheless, hedonism is also one of the stupidest and most unworthy temptations. It makes us defenseless against vice, whether in ourselves or in others, and it squanders our noblest and most gratifying potentialities. In itself, it is not as threatening as outright wickedness, but Plato is surely correct in his conviction that it cannot provide effective resistance to the spread of evil character and conduct. In truth, the importance of his conviction cannot be overemphasized, and to be forgetful of his warnings is disastrous—as our experience repeatedly confirms.

I will comment on hedonism as a strategy for getting through life. The discussion will incorporate many issues of first consequence, for the strategy must be compared to some alternatives. Following that analysis, I will turn to the question of the institutions in the moral order that seem to be effective for resisting corruption and for supporting a good life.

a. HEDONISM, HAPPINESS, AND THE VIRTUES OF VIRTUE

The dream of the perfect hedonist is to live without inhibition or postponement of gratification, and in his mindless way he even supposes that the presumed necessities of work, discipline, and sacrifice are but lies issued by the ruling elites to perpetuate the servitude of everyone else. According to this philosophy, one attributes his unhappiness to the fact that much that he wants is denied him. He suffers from having his pleasure withheld, and he believes that the suffering is wholly gratuitous. When he generalizes this experience, he concludes that more freedom is the answer to all his suffering. More freedom: more happiness. The hedonist dreams of a world where he may always seize his object, which will never betray him. The rigors of virtue are unnecessary, and life without puritanism and vested interests is effortless. He says that all constraints and duties are no more than emotional hang-ups, and the only purpose of authority is to protect the wealth and power of oppressors. It is wise to believe that nothing is sacred—save one's own self-indulgence. Some people really believe this. It is articulated, for example, in the one-time best-seller and bible of the youth movement, *The Greening of America*.[4]

Remarkable how such a juvenile fantasy can be believed! The beginning of wisdom is to recognize that life is hard, there are no easy ways out, the goods of life are typically hard-won, and social order is always at risk of corruption and even collapse. Some goods are not as hard as others, of course. The seemingly easy ways—such as to come effortlessly into possession of wealth—are apt to turn out to be the deadliest traps. The ring of Gyges is a curse, not a blessing. Nature is jealous of the conditions that sustain a good life; she gives them up to rather few, and they are achieved with difficulty. Most of our struggles rely on the complicity of others, and they—just as ourselves—are prone to weakness, malice, lust for power, avarice, and treachery. The unfailing human susceptibility to vice makes the moral order continuously vulnerable and all our ventures perilous. The fact that life is hard is not to be wholly lamented. The rigors of existence have called forth strength, courage, integrity, and wisdom, and perhaps the love of beauty and order as well. Otherwise, we would have never left a mindless existence. In any event, we have developed seemingly innumerable approaches to getting through life, with widely varying success. My concern is with the hedonist.

The pleasure-seeker who has outgrown adolescent fantasy is well aware that he must somehow acquire the powers suitable to command his environment effectively, so that he may reap its delights. One must work hard to acquire the wherewithal to have all the sex, possessions, and other indulgences that he would like. The intelligent hedonist accepts some discipline in life as a necessary evil or sometimes just as a necessary inconvenience, but he does not renounce his belief that hedonism is the best life. If he succeeds in becoming rich and powerful, he might be able to achieve his fantasy life after all.

In remaining committed to maximizing his self-indulgence, he neglects to recognize—much less to cultivate—inestimably valuable potentialities of the self that are incompatible with hedonism. Indeed, hedonism is predicated on the shallowest conception of human nature.

There are internal demands and resources that make hedonism a simpleton's quest, and it will take pages to provide a full summary. To begin with, we human beings have an emotional *need* for internal constraints, priorities, and committed allegiances. Otherwise, we are in the condition of normlessness: a shapeless, directionless, and confused state of being, where nothing is ordered or meaningful, and the powers of effective conduct are radically diminished. This is a condition of torment, for which one would vainly seek a remedy in hedonism, where nothing is sacred; nothing is reverenced. To our bewilderment and consternation, hedonism only looks good until we succeed in it. A succession of instant gratifications could give meaning only to a creature unendowed with a moral nature or without dedication and ideal aspiration—in Plato's language, a being with nothing in the soul yearning to be born—no eros to couple the mortal and the divine. Hedonism is precisely a repudiation of such devotion. Immediate pleasure-seeking forbids us to store and discipline the energies of the spirit that might lead to ideal goods. Where such an impoverished nature occurs, we should feel contempt and pity. At even a modest level of aspiration, we recognize that to establish a semblance of order in the self is invaluable, and it is the prime condition of establishing an enduring order of goods in the world. Such is our hope and ambition.

Even the hedonist wonders whether life can be somehow "meaningful." Anyone pleads to know the meaning of life. Usually, this is the cry of a sufferer whose ambitions have failed and who seeks some wholesale consolation or redemption. The question can take a less morbid form, however: What are the meanings *in* life? For an intelligent and embattled creature such as man, to determine the meaning of events is essential: What does any occasion in my environment, whether animal, vegetable, or mineral, portend for my benefit or disaster and for that of my associates? This is our native form of thought, and we naturally exercise it in reference to the events of our experience. Events are taken out of isolation and are recognized to be constituents of an inclusive field of activities. Thereby they become significant, and they are meaningful in the honorific sense when they imply precious events or forms of experience.

For the hedonist, events cannot be meaningful as they are for one who possesses a moral nature. Meanings are often moral. That is, the moral qualities of human character and conduct have great import in our lives. Honesty, responsibility, and sacrifice are revered; pettiness, evasion, and cruelty are detested. This is not a condition incidental to human existence. It is not merely conventional to ask of the moral meaning of events in the fabric of human endeavor. Our moral nature is essential to life. Admittedly, it is more pronounced in some individuals than in others, and the awareness of its indispensable functions is often lacking, as in our present culture. Still, we habitually think of activities as *unworthy*, *trivial*, *greedy*, *short-sighted*, and the like; we think of others as *noble*, *courageous*, or *life-sustaining*. We would, accordingly, think of the pleasures of the jet set or of the Hollywood elite as paltry or self-indulgent. They are unimportant, empty, shallow. They are *merely* pleasant, if that. They are not contributory to anything of moment. They do not and cannot sustain a life, friendship, or the moral order. For any creature whose life is perilous and insecure, for whom so many goods are transient and elusive, the stable and enduring are invaluable, whether found within the self or in the world, and we invest much—sometimes everything—in these orders. Cognizant of such necessities, our moral nature is often discriminating and powerful. Hence the meanings of the moral life are both potent and deeply satisfying.

To renounce hedonism is not a sacrifice but the first step in an intrinsically good life. To possess the powers that make us capable of resistance, renunciation, and fortitude makes us capable of much else besides—of ideal goods and ideal states of the soul. Rather than consider all desires equal and equally worthy, we discriminate those that are capable of noble fulfillment or beautiful form. Rather than think of life as a sum of atomistic episodes, we must think about the nature of the good life as a whole. No such resource is available to him who must "live without boundaries" or "have it all." Such a man has *less*, for he refuses to distinguish and cultivate those powers that are necessary for ideal goods, whose consummations are hidden from him. Listen to Nietzsche:

> What is essential and inestimable in every morality is that it constitutes a
> long compulsion. . . . [A]ll there is or has been on earth of freedom, subtlety,

boldness, dance, and masterly sureness, whether in thought itself or in government, or in rhetoric and persuasion, in the arts just as in ethics, has
developed only owing to the "tyranny of such capricious laws." . . .

What is essential "in heaven and on earth" seems to be, to say it once
more, that there should be *obedience* over a long period of time and in a *single*
direction: given that, something always develops, and has developed, for
whose sake it is worth while to live on earth; for example, virtue, art, music,
dance, reason, spirituality—something transfiguring, subtle, mad, and divine.[5]

It is unmistakable in the nature of things that the requirements of life
include tutelage, discipline, and renunciation. In a complacent society, it is
equally true that resistance to the constraints of wisdom will lead to their
wholesale repudiation. Of course (contrary to Nietzsche's suggestion) the
ventures of the dedicated lover of the ideal are often disappointing, and they
might bring bitterness. It is wise not to substitute grandiose dreams for fundamental, but difficult, goods. To take responsibility for a child and raise him
to an adult—now *that* can give meaning to your life. A man has certain priorities, matters he regards to be of greatest importance—perhaps that man
who would bring his child to honorable manhood. This is an end for which
he will strive and sacrifice above all others. If he succeeds, with the aid of
wisdom and luck, he would be deeply gratified. He has had to endure much
for this result: deprivation, inadequacy, disappointment, discouragement, but
in an obvious sense he has triumphed over these sufferings; he has mastered
them. With dedication, and even joy, he has done what really matters, however humble it might appear. He might even be happy.

Moralists have always distinguished happiness from pleasure. Only an
oaf thinks that happiness is an accumulation of pleasures. Still, "happy" and
"happiness" are imprecise. There is a variety of qualitatively distinctive experiences that are coveted, sought for, and welcomed. It will be helpful to distinguish two broad classes: the episodic and the abiding. The first is an event
that might be highly enjoyable in itself—it is "divinely sweet for the
moment," but it is but a spasm in time. A sampling of episodic pleasures
would be such as these: orgasm, having sex at will, going for a swim, sitting
in the sunshine, a massage, a fine cigar. The abiding, on the other hand,
should be thought of as a state of mind, an underlying condition, a more or
less permanent and ambient characteristic of the self. It might not be conscious, for the most part, but somehow it qualifies many, if not all, of our
experiences and judgments. Here is an assortment of conditions that can be
more or less prevalent and enduring and their effects varyingly powerful:
cheerfulness; serenity; peace of mind; confidence, optimism; feeling loved,
needed, appreciated; feeling that God loves you. It might be a sense of order
and strength within yourself that provides the desired condition: a sense of
self-sufficiency regarding the values of one's life. The goods vitally embodied

in one's own life are not in jeopardy regarding their nature as good, and they are not wanting. One is neither fretful nor insecure about the organizing principles of his life, which have become deep and habitual in his nature, and he steadily draws nourishment and fulfillment from them. The Socratics developed such a conception superbly, and I will turn to it shortly in the form provided by Aristotle. In any case, what we seek is an abiding sense of well-being, something durable and sustaining within the psyche, informing all our experience, in good times and bad. This is beyond the hedonist.

Anyone modestly endowed with experience and intelligence would prefer the positive and enduring states over the merely transient and episodic gratifications. This distinction seems to capture the difference between happiness and pleasure. The pervasive state by no means precludes episodes of pleasure, though it might make them less episodic. The Greeks are always telling us, too, that the pleasures of the virtuous surpass those of the vicious. To them, this claim is equivalent to saying that the pleasures of those who are happy are intrinsically more pleasant. Just as we prefer these blessedly nourishing subjective conditions, we favor external goods that tend to be staying and unfailing, such as a friendship. Friendship does not exist for the hedonist, who will not work and sacrifice for the would-be friend, but who must seize whatever transient good captures him for the moment.

Contrary to the conviction of the hedonist, the question is not that of amassing pleasures. No sum of atomistic enjoyments could compensate for the lack of a fundamentally satisfying state of being, and they could hardly appease a distracted and driven soul for more than a moment. As I have just suggested, there are also ambient conditions that are not happy but wretched: fear; anxiety; depression; insecurity; loneliness; being unloved, out of control, bitter, resentful, consumed with hatred; and so on. Pleasures will never compensate for their torments, but he who enjoys a form of inner calm and certitude is much less needy for pleasure. It is a further matter, of course, to speculate on how such a condition might be attained. It might be attributable to various causes or even to causes unknown. In most cases, one's temperament is a crucial factor, and temperament is largely determined by heredity.

Moralists have offered us a variety of ideas of happiness in the soul. I will focus on the Socratic legacy, which has the greatest pertinence to the moral life. The desired state is that of virtue—moral and intellectual virtue, in the distinction given us by Aristotle. The exercise of virtue is *eudaimonia*, which has usually been translated as happiness, until very recently, when liberated translators have given us the appallingly permissive "human flourishing" to assure us of a properly up-to-date Aristotle. A point lost in translation is that *eudaimonia* suggests *well souled*. It is not far from a literal translation of *eudaimonia*, and the Greeks had a very definite idea about what it means to be well souled.[6] The term can be virtually equated to happiness, nevertheless, on the understanding that the condition denoted is of a highly definite nature and equips us handsomely for the contingencies and opportunities of life. Even so, it seems less than axiomatic that a virtuous soul enjoys the qualitative feeling that we refer to with "happiness."

It is important to notice that happiness has an ineliminable *moral* dimension. Following his forebears, Aristotle could not conceive of *eudaimonia* apart from moral excellence. The possession of moral and intellectual virtue, he says, makes life complete and self-sufficient. This is the enduring and pervasive state of soul that he distinguishes from pleasure. It consists of both theoretical and practical wisdom, which are intellectual virtues, and courage, justice, and temperance (*sophrosyne*), the primary moral virtues. Theoretical wisdom contemplates the eternal and unchanging, approximating to the life of the divine. Practical wisdom knows the nature of the good life for man and how, in general, it is attained. In specific circumstances, armed with this knowledge, the man of practical wisdom displays both experience and excellence in deliberation to determine the most virtuous act of which he is capable in respect to these circumstances. This is the mean between the extremes of excess and defect, "but in regard to goodness and excellence it is an extreme."[7] Aristotle shows no indecision on what the nature of the good life is, but he does express reservations about the best form of political life, where he is more pragmatic than his teacher. It is intriguing that he says rather little to explain *why* the virtues are equated with happiness. He just says that they are our proper function and we are happy when we fulfill that function. I will provide my own understanding of their merit, concentrating on the moral virtues.

Courage is an indispensable trait. Aristotle never questions its worth. Would one *want* to be a coward, to be ruled by fear? Could one endure the myriad adversities of life and effectively face its dangers without it? Could the polis survive without courage? Can there be any good life without it? True, the man of courage will put himself in dangerous circumstances as his wisdom requires, where the coward might draw more breaths over a lifetime, but all breaths are by no means equal. The coward, moreover, is thereby parasitic upon the works of the brave. It is no wonder that to be thought a coward is supremely disgraceful. The base and ignoble cannot be weighed against the blessings of courage and of *eudaimonia*.

Aristotle, as we have seen, has a precise definition of justice, but he also uses the term more loosely to cover any issue of moral rectitude or transgression, as Plato had also done. "[T]heft, adultery, poisoning, procuring, enticement of slaves, assassination and bearing false witness" are forms of injustice; likewise with "assault, imprisonment, murder, violent robbery, maiming, defamation, and character-smearing."[8] (Plato had included temple-robbing and religious desecration.) The most inclusive use of "justice" is to equate it with whatever is lawful, where "lawful" is understood normatively. In these passages of the *Nicomachean Ethics* (1129a–1130a), Aristotle, in effect, makes duty a part of justice. Lawfulness is the disposition of the citizen to do whatever is required of him to support the welfare of the social and political community. In other words, he has duties to perform. A just man, accordingly, does his duty.

Aristotle's analysis of *sophrosyne* is not precise. Sometimes he confines it to moderation of the bodily appetites of touch and taste (1118a). But then he refers to the entire spectrum of appetitive nature, saying of the *sophron*, "For the aim of both his appetite and his reason is to do what is noble. The appetite of the self-controlled man is directed at the right objects, in the right way, and at the right time; and that is what reason prescribes."[9] The latter formulation best expresses the level of excellence that Aristotle has in mind. *Sophrosyne* goes well beyond the suppression of inapt desires. The fully virtuous individual, presumably, does not *have* inapt desires. Aristotle distinguishes virtue from moral strength. Those with moral strength suffer temptation and wrestle with their desires, but they succeed in choosing the right thing after all. The virtuous man, on every occasion, not only does the most virtuous deed of which he is capable; he also experiences the right feelings. He has no temptation with which to struggle. "[I]t is moral virtue that is concerned with emotions and actions, and it is in emotions and actions that excess, deficiency, and the median are found. Thus we can experience fear, confidence, desire, anger, pity, and generally any kind of pleasure and pain either too much or too little, and in either case not properly. But to experience all this at the right time, toward the right objects, toward the right people, for the right reason, and in the right manner—that is the median and the best course, the course that is the mark of virtue."[10]

Whew! No one, I am sure, has ever possessed *sophrosyne* in the full sense described by Aristotle. All the same, he describes an ideal limit to which a few persons approximate. They tend to have emotions and feelings appropriate to the occasion and in proportion to it, and they desire what is good and abhor what is evil; these characteristics are deeply embedded in their nature. They are at the opposite extreme from those who are ravaged by unruly lusts, hatreds, obsessions, divided allegiances, inner turmoil, and conflict. The difference is between heaven and hell. No wonder that *sophrosyne* is among the greatest assets any human being could possess. The possession does not mean that one is opposed to pleasure. Far from it. Aristotle even says that of all acts, those of virtue are *most pleasant* (1099a). One is opposed to those pleasures that are base or that are unsuitable for the occasion, but some occasions properly admit of revelry: Socrates spends the entire night drinking with his friends at the home of Agathon, and during the party Alcibiades reports that Socrates amply indulges himself with pleasures during the respites of military campaigns.

The absence of self-control is a great deficit for the individual. He is incapable of any good that requires focus and persistence, and when he finds himself in unusually trying circumstances, he discovers that he is without inner resources to contend with them. He likewise finds that others cannot rely upon him or trust him. He must be a parasite and an object of suspicion and contempt. It is obvious that in associated life each of us tends to benefit from the *sophrosyne* of others. Instinctively recognizing the need for elementary good behavior and reliability, we are alarmed by those who show little sign of self-restraint or moral discipline, and we neither trust nor respect them.

The human individual is in fact generously fitted for occasions of delight—even for sustained joy and affirmation, but he is also terribly susceptible to emotional failure and destructive passion. In consequence, he often cripples or nullifies his own treasure. Some pettiness of soul or ravenous need intrudes to sabotage his good. Thus the capacity for gladness and rejoicing is typically ineffectual and frustrated. If only we had *sophrosyne*, we would be less prone to self-ruination. We might sustain what is lovely and joyous. To be sure, we are also beset with powerlessness in response to the fancies and tragedies visited upon us by the world, whatever our virtue. Our competence is easily outmatched. Even so, there are myriad possible responses to our finitude, and here we may be left to wail like an infant or to bemoan the injustice of it all, or we may be fortified by wisdom and virtue and thereby less dependent upon the vagaries of fortune. Excellence of soul is difficult and rare, and it is not omnipotent, but it is our worthiest comrade in fulfilling our capacities for a persistent good. Willfully to make hedonism the ideal, by contrast, is consummate unwisdom.

The moral virtues are perfections of the desiring part of the soul, as Aristotle says it. Accordingly, one who is just will not simply do just deeds—just as one who is courageous will not simply do courageous deeds—but he will *desire* to do them. He will do them as an expression of his nature. The truly virtuous act issues from "a firm and unchangeable character." An elaboration of Aristotle's thinking about the nature of moral virtue will gain intelligibility if we focus for a moment on the function of desire. An object of desire is something for which we have some kind of need, affection, loyalty, or love. A virtuous man would be defined, in part, by the nature of his loves. It is needlessly abstract just to say that he loves courage, justice, and self-control. He loves those *things* that are noble and beautiful: his friends, his polis, his comrades. He loves excellent states of character, institutions, and actions; he loves virtuous ideals and principles. His allegiance is powerful and unswerving. To have such a love implies that he has dispositions of a fairly definite sort: virtuous dispositions; he is disposed—strongly disposed—to love and to do what is excellent.

The possession of vital tendencies of this sort is owing in some significant degree to inherent potentialities in one's nature, but their specific *objects* might not be innate. A youth must be *provided* with appropriate objects of love. His eros must be furnished with worthy exemplars and goals—presented, perhaps, with the force and beauty that a Plato commands. Aristotle is incorrect, then, in describing moral education as just the repetition of virtuous actions. It must also include the effort to offer to the soul of the learner the most praiseworthy persons and ideals, in the hope that they would ignite his love and focus his aspiration.

There are lesser virtues reviewed by Aristotle, and one could add some that escape his notice. Charity, for example, can be distinguished from justice; so can kindness. The ability to give and to receive love, moreover, is rare and precious. We should also speak of the special qualities suitable for the nurturing of the young, and we could properly add some bourgeois virtues: hard work, patience, dependability, and personal responsibility. I would especially emphasize the latter. With the expression "*personal* responsibility," I mean to describe the individual who will not be disposed to shirk his duties or shift them to someone else. At the same time, more than being dutiful, he will disdain the idea of depending on those who contribute while he is willfully idle. He supposes, still more, that it is up to himself to take the initiatives that are appropriate for his prosperity and well-being. Perhaps Aristotle would incorporate this notion of responsibility into his expanded sense of justice.[11]

It is also worth noting that one could possess the cardinal virtues and still be humorless and a bore—not a dancer, no twinkle in the eye. The virtuous man by Aristotle's definition could also lack the power to see into the very heart of human beings. Discounting the trait of *sophrosyne*, we could also notice that one could have virtue and still have, say, a morose temperament. To notice such lacks—and there are still others—is not to diminish the consummate importance of the cardinal virtues. Without them, in fact, these other gifts would come to little. One would be eminently well-souled with the powers of virtue, but they are not exhaustive of all desirable human attributes.

For Aristotle, as for his predecessors, the cardinal virtues are interdependent: none can be perfected without the complementary powers of the others. Without practical wisdom, courage, and temperance, for example, the disposition to be just is impotent: one would not know what the just act is, or he might be afraid to do it, or his resolve might give way to some overbearing impulse. In the same way, *sophrosyne* without the other moral virtues and intelligence is mere sentimentality—mindless "caring," perhaps, to use the current expression. Such feeling, of course, would not be a virtue; it would not be *sophrosyne* if not in the company of the other excellences. Courage, too, without justice and wisdom is dangerous, and practical wisdom, likewise, is morally ineffectual when it is not animated by desire for what is good. When the moral virtues are not present, indeed, there can be no practical wisdom: there is mere cleverness, as Aristotle says, and it is apt to be put to ill use. The unity of the virtues, then, is not only a moral ideal. Insofar as it specifies conditions without which certain excellences could not exist, it is also a statement of fact. It is an extraordinary ideal in every sense: it is an expression of superb moral excellence (without any of our contemporary sentimentality), and its fulfillment must be rare. This is the "happy" soul. It is harmonious; its powers developed, unified, always available, and morally concerted. It is without inner disturbance from the discordant or ignoble, and this nature is gratified above all in virtuous actions. *Eudaimon* indeed!

We need not summon a neatly itemized table of virtues selected for each distinctive occasion. What we are looking for is an individual who is disposed to act in predictably moral ways whenever demands, of whatever sort, are made upon him. He is a lover of *to kalon*, that which is highest and best. He will be resolute and steadfast; he will wish to do right by every man; he will have loyalty and forbearance, gentleness and patience; and he will be unambiguously trustworthy. There will be a marked integrity and toughness about him—he won't give way to sentimentality, blandishment, or intimidation. If he truly has virtue (in distinction from moral strength), it is not problematic with him to direct his powers to the good. He has no temptation for either the petty or the vicious; his virtue is neither superficial nor occasional.

It is helpful to have a general name that encompasses all such precious qualities collectively. Call it virtue, integrity, nobility of character, honor, or justice in the soul. There are other names, too, but the point is that we need not invariably refer to a list of virtues fitted to the specific differences of each occasion. This is faithful to the spirit of Plato and Aristotle, who frequently refer to noble deeds that are not readily defined by reference to a specific virtue. When we are speaking of actual individuals, we will use the terms of highest praise sparingly, for such people are rare. Still, it is possible to approximate to heroic levels, and sometimes we do.

To understand the nature and rewards of the virtuous life, we must pursue at greater length some of the themes that Aristotle introduces. I have in mind at present to examine two inseparable points. The first is his remarkable claim that acts of virtue are the most pleasant. The second is his belief in the equation of virtue and happiness, which he shares with Socrates and Plato.

It seems implausible to say that virtuous acts are the most pleasant, but there are conditions under which it might be true. It could be true for that person who loves virtue above all else, and we derive the greatest pleasure, Aristotle had said, from doing that which we love most. There are at least a few people who answer to this description. Socrates is presented as the consummate lover. The object of his love is *to kalon*, which is variously translated as the fine, good, noble, or beautiful—all the terms we use to express the highest and best. *To kalon* is inclusive of all such goods, and it includes virtue. Socrates, Plato tells us, thought nothing in the nature of things is more important than virtue. It is plausible to say, then, that acts of virtue were the fulfillment of his great love and hence most pleasant. But how many of us are like Socrates? Still, there are lesser men who also love *to kalon*, the noble and beautiful, and they would also feel gratified and fulfilled in the exercise of virtue. It is a commitment satisfied and celebrated. In each specific case, there is satisfaction of a deep and vital disposition in the achievement of a noble end. A lovable state of affairs indeed! Attending this commitment there is also a felt revulsion for weakness, cowardice, and self-indulgence. We turn from them as from the foulest objects.

Still, there is something inadequate about this argument; it can be only a lunge at the truth. There are many acts of virtue that are not pleasant and are sometimes painful. I noted in the preceding chapter that duties are sometimes onerous, but the virtuous man fulfills them in any case, pleasant or not. One feels no pleasure in speaking plain truth to those whom it will grieve; there is no pleasure, but dismay and fatigue, in resisting on every hand the incessant pleading for lower standards. The superbly heroic Admiral Stockdale felt no pleasure while he was being tortured.[12] The virtuous man will do the right thing, seemingly at all costs. He will not grovel; he will not pander; he will not take unfair advantage; he will not betray, no matter what the sacrifice. Is he invariably deriving pleasure from such acts? Would he say they are invariably *most* pleasant? Aristotle's position is most indefensible when we recognize that many virtuous actions *fail*, no matter how virtuous. If you dedicate yourself to rescuing a friend in danger of drowning, devoting your every resource to the task, you still might not succeed. Your friend might die. And so it is with many virtuous actions: there is defeat; the cause is lost. We cannot say that these failures are pleasant.

Aristotle's assertion about virtue and pleasure is an incautious generalization, and it might lead the hasty reader to conclude that Aristotle was so oblivious to experience as to suppose that the excellent of soul never suffer. Part of his praise of virtue, however, is to observe that when met with misfortune and adversity, the virtuous endure them better than others, so he acknowledges that the virtuous life will hardly be free of torments. Still, clarification is needed. It will be much worth our while to consider further the nature of noble actions and thereby to gain further insight, perhaps, into their motives and rewards.

An additional distinction will help. It is that between pleasure and satisfaction. Pleasure can be construed very broadly, of course, to allow for any satisfaction being called a pleasure, but there are such noteworthy differences between "pleasant" experiences that they must be remarked. The ordinary hedonist, I suppose, most commonly thinks of pleasures in terms of the gratification of bodily appetites—mere sensual indulgence, or he thinks of them as fulfilling basic lusts, such as those for power, wealth, fame, status, and sex.

But there is often profound happiness in experience that cannot be called *sensual* in the usual sense nor that caters to the most excited agitations of the psyche. These I will call satisfactions. I am hugely satisfied, for example, in taking my morning coffee with Chrys, the two of us talking of diurnal events, sharing delight and dismay. I find great satisfaction just in tilling the soil in my garden, for that matter. Neither of these activities is accompanied by screams of ecstasy, but they are irreplaceably satisfying all the same, and—somehow—they give a wonderful meaning to my life. They are life-sustaining and life-affirming as physical pleasures, as such, are not.

We could offer a variety of examples of satisfactions, conduct experienced to be of singular worth and of high priority, yet unaccompanied by overt excitement: the discovery and acquisition of knowledge, perhaps, or listening to the opera, friendship, the fulfillment of sacred obligations, writing lucid and forceful paragraphs, family activities. Acts of virtue can be of that nature. A few pages back, I distinguished the merely frivolous from the morally significant—another instance of pleasures distinguished from satisfactions. Those who know the difference at first hand will never suppose that satisfaction is only a meager substitute for sensual thrill. To the contrary! This fact testifies to the existence of profound needs and capabilities in the human soul that are not reducible to quests for pleasures, mere fun, in the sense I have distinguished. We are capable of aspirations, loves, and allegiances that dwarf the allure of routine pleasures.[13] I am not speaking of the power to *delay* gratification, which is obviously of great importance. I am suggesting that there *is* gratification but of a qualitatively different sort. Its existence by no means negates the frequent need to delay reward. We often have to put up with drudgery and unpleasantness as such.

These remarks suggest a further distinction, imprecise but of notable consequence: a human being is capable of establishing fairly definite priorities in respect to what it is *important* to do. He also has, more or less, a scale of sensual enticements. The priorities of what is important do not correspond to the order of delights provided by the nerve endings. There are practices of great moment that must take precedence over entertainments and other indulgences, or we will perish, and we are evidently fitted for such tasks in a manner that makes them oftentimes rewarding, highly rewarding. For a creature struggling for survival, it would be an inestimable resource to be of a nature to be positively reinforced by doing deeds that promote his fitness along with that of the moral order that he inhabits. I do not say that all satisfactions are derived from such demands or that they are equally rewarding for all persons, nor do I say that the urge for animal indulgences must be irrelevant to survival. (Consider sexuality.) Still, we cannot be incessantly engaged in it; there are frequently more important matters to attend to.

The capacity to embrace the important in preference to the indulgent is surely one of the most precious and morally fertile assets of human nature. It seems plausible that the instinctive basis of our moral nature consists in part of this aptitide for according priority to the important relative to the hedonistic and to finding satisfaction in it. This conjecture lends support to the classical idea that we have a natural propensity to virtue. To be sure, the aptitude seems to vary substantially from individual to individual, and it evidently requires learning to give it development and form. In contemporary life, the learning is decidedly in decline, and the cultural cognoscenti seem to wish to abolish the distinction altogether.

Even in regard to what I have called satisfaction, there are differing sorts of it available to differing natures. A character with affinities to deep and noble satisfactions is greatly preferable to appeasing the urges of the hedonist. Surely this distinction between pleasure and satisfaction does not preclude delectable forms of sensuality in the conduct of life, but one would not find that aggregated fragments of pleasure constitute the good of his existence.

Just as satisfaction is distinguishable from pleasure, it must likewise be distinguished from happiness. A satisfaction is apt to be more enduring and fertile than a pleasure, to be sure, and it is owing to a fundamental disposition or capacity of self, but it does not possess the enveloping and perduring quality that I have referred to as happiness. As we shall see, moreover, the virtuous have profound satisfactions of their own, but there are many other satisfactions that lack moral quality, as well as vicious ones.

In due course, these clarifications might help us grasp the nature and merits of the life of virtue. If we speak only of pleasure, on the other hand, we might lose a great prize. We are not feeling pleasure when our virtue brings failure and suffering. Moreover, we do what is virtuous under extreme duress and even under conditions of hopelessness. If virtue were always pleasant, indeed, there would be nothing extraordinary when an individual retains his virtue even under the most threatening circumstances. Even in pain, he does not violate his integrity. How does he do it? We will be helped to fathom such marvels by thinking further about the nature of a virtuous act. It is not done for the sake of pleasure. One of the characteristics of a virtuous act is that it is done for its own sake (1105b), but what does "for its own sake" mean? That it is done simply because it is virtuous? Perhaps that is what Aristotle was thinking, but if so, he was mistaken. *The act itself* is done for its own sake. When the virtuous man sees his comrade in peril, he thinks, "I must come to his aid!" and he might do so at great risk to himself. The *rescue* is needful, and *that* is what he recognizes. Assuredly, he does not think, "It is virtuous to rescue a comrade in peril" and then and for that reason undertakes the risk. He simply must aid his comrade. The act at issue is the dangerous *rescue*, and precisely *that* is what one wills to do. One wills it, to be sure, if he is virtuous, *because* he is virtuous, but cogitating about virtue does not enter into the actual deliberation nor does thinking about *eudaimonia*. The rescuer is denominated "virtuous" because he has such a disposition in regard to such acts. The gratification he will enjoy in consequence of the rescue is *in the rescue*, not in the fact that he was virtuous.

In a preliminary sense at least, this is the paradigm of virtuous conduct, and it does not compel us to suppose that there must be an intrinsic connection between virtue and pleasure. Why, then, is the act done under even the worst of circumstances? It seems to come from the necessity of one's own nature, to appropriate the words of Spinoza. Let us entertain some further conjectures about the virtuous nature: What are its necessities? And how—if at all—are they conjoined with pleasure, satisfaction, or happiness?

If we grant that to possess the virtues is to be well souled, then it still remains to question whether to be well souled is to possess the abiding well-being of happiness. Aristotle obviously thinks so, but his analyses are more suggestive than systematic. His view is wise, just the same, if the idea of happiness is treated with care. Surely one is blessed to possess virtue in the manner described by Aristotle, but (as he recognizes) that does not mean that one must be invariably jolly, optimistic, and smiling, or that he never be in anger, anguish, and suffering. Aristotle had nothing so foolish in mind.

To pursue the exploration, I return to the idea of the virtuous man as lover of the good, who is so devout that he will not be stayed by any threat in his pursuit of it. The idea gains credibility by considering a common but nonetheless telling example. Consider the case of parents: it is extremely admirable but usually not surprising when they defend their young heroically and even to the sacrifice of their own lives. Evidently, courage and devotion of a like nature can sometimes be found in other forms of attachment. Such loyalties inform our motivations to do acts that are virtuous. The crisis before us, accordingly, is not judged or felt in atomistic loneliness, nor is it measured by its episodes of pleasure. It is vibrant with meanings that we love: friendship, honor, and integrity. Intense allegiances and fundamental goods to which we are sworn wait upon our action. The meaning of life is before us; we are at the point of a life-affirming or life-denying act. All these goods are in the balance, along with the loyalty we have pledged them. We are bonded to them as to our own flesh and blood.

At a given turning point, we might not rehearse such thoughts explicitly; we act instinctively, as in the case of the parents who protect their child or the man who comes to the rescue of his comrade. At any moment in his ordeal, consciously or not, Admiral Stockdale is profoundly attached to his fellow prisoners, to his duty as a military officer, to his nation and its principles, and to the meaning his life might have in the lives of others. He cannot let these persons and principles down. Inestimably valuable spirits, comprehensive of his very life, animate his soul and strengthen his love.

Wisdom and virtue will often put a man at odds with his environment, not in harmony with it, when it is corrupt, weak, or uncomprehending, and he might be hated or killed. For his part, Stockdale might have perished in agony; his comrades might have capitulated, and his enemies would have triumphed. His integrity might be "rewarded" with contempt from supercilious critics. Still, he tells us of a profound and all-important satisfaction. Speaking of their ordeal as prisoners of war, he writes of himself and his comrades,

> For us, the deprivation from the physical side of the good life and even the pain and the loneliness were shallow complaints compared to finding yourself stripped of all entitlements to reputation, love or honor at home. . . .
>
> Americans in Hanoi learned fast. They made no deals. They learned that "meeting them half way" was the road to degradation. . . . [O]ne soon finds himself taking his lumps with pride and not merely liking but loving that tapping guy next door, the man he never sees, the man he bears his soul to after each torture session, . . . Then he realizes he can't be hurt and he can't be had as long as he tells the truth and clings to that forgiving band of brothers who are becoming his country, his family. . . .
>
> It comes down to unselfish comradeship, and it comes down to pride, dignity, an enduring sense of self-worth and to that enigmatic mixture of conscience and egoism called personal honor.[14]

The preservation of integrity and loyalty to the good—the Greeks would say the preservation of virtue—comes to be of the highest importance, and it enables Stockdale to triumph. These are objects of his love, as are his comrades. Notice especially the remarkable words *"he can't be hurt and he can't be had"* as long as he retains his integrity. Such a remark might have come from Socrates, who said that no harm can come to a just man. "Harm" means harm to the soul—not physical pain. Just so, Stockdale has asserted that when he and his comrades were able to maintain their integrity, their captors couldn't hurt them. Just because you can crush my body does not mean that you can crush my spirit, my virtue. Though you kill me, I die with my virtue intact. Though you have killed me, you have not defeated *me*. Here, "I" or "me" *is* fundamentally my virtue, so you have not harmed me. We do not identify with our bodies but with our virtue, and to betray it is to destroy what we love best. The preservation of integrity surpasses the preservation of mere life. An ideal good is maintained and honored, and something of ultimate worth has been accomplished. It would be misleading to call this experience a pleasure, but we can say that it supremely vindicates the most precious meaning of our life. That, to be sure, is a supreme *satisfaction*. The spirit has survived against the greatest odds and has preserved what is most important to it. This is one of the ways in which acts of virtue can be deeply satisfying and ennobling, if not always pleasant. This satisfaction eminently surpasses that of episodic pleasure, for we are fulfilling our greatest and noblest loves.

Integrity means a wholeness and consistency of self that is preserved under all conditions, but it also has reference to a particular *kind* of self: one that aspires to *to kalon* and holds it in reverence. In more specific terms, the self of integrity also loves definite institutions and individuals: the corps, his comrades, his nation, his family, his principles, and his ideals. This is neither a transient love nor a merely intellectual assent but a love definitive of fundamental dispositions. To maintain such integrity is a satisfaction that could not, without a distortion of the usual sense of the word, be called *pleasure*. It comes of the fulfillment of that which we regard as supremely good, even in the midst of pain. The satisfactions of the virtuous, even when they are without pleasure, might be abundant with this gratification. There is a form of satisfaction that one finds in being virtuous even when he is undergoing physical agony. Even if you are killed, you have not succumbed, and that which is best in you has not been defeated.

This is a triumph of the noble spirit, but not all virtuous conduct is laden with satisfaction. Just as there is no pleasure in failed acts of moral integrity, there can be no satisfaction in them either, rather: sorrow, frustration, bitterness, and agony.

I have expressed hesitancy about the equation of happiness and virtue—that is, of the identity of feeling happy and being well souled. Would not a virtuous and perceptive individual in typical human surroundings be apt to feel decidedly alienated and ill-fitted to the world? Might not he especially suffer from it—from its stupidities, cruelties, pretenses, vanities, and incomprehension? To have a virtuous and discerning soul might prove to be a sort of liability: Would such a one not be unusually vulnerable to suffering due to his singular awareness of the world's gross insufficiencies? To be sure, such questions are not to be found in Platonic writings; they sound more like Nietzsche. Although he is a plebeian, Socrates displays an aristocratic disdain for "the many," who are unable to ruffle his soul. Aristotle would be apt to say that alienation exhibits a failure of *sophrosyne*: such unworthy objects merit no such concern. Surely, in any event, to be *obsessed* with the world's inadequacies betrays a distinct lack of wisdom. It is a form of sentimentalism, and it is patently unnecessary as a motive for doing acts of virtue. Even so, the simple *equation* of being well souled and feeling happy continues to be highly problematical. It is complacent in its way, but I have defended the idea that there is a sense of happiness that is exclusively associated with virtue, with love of what is best and the will to pursue it under all circumstances. Pleasure does not attend every act of virtue, and neither does satisfaction. Just the same, there is profound satisfaction in gratifying our noblest loves—when, indeed, they *are* gratified—even when attended with great personal sacrifice.

These are by no means devastating concessions. What one must do is judge alternative ways of life—such as that of moral excellence or that of the hedonist. A man would never be virtuous or share in its blessings if he performed his exemplary acts only at his convenience. We should likewise be mindful of the fact that one who is well souled has a range of pleasures available to him that is foreclosed to the mean-spirited and self-indulgent. Most of his acts of virtue *are* pleasant. The man of virtue is not always being tested by torture, after all. He has most moments free of such torments. It is also worth a reminder that Socratic *areté* is not puritanical; it has no inherent disdain for the pleasures of the body and will find joy and delight in them. It will not be ruled by them, however. In addition, as I will urge momentarily, goods in the custody of virtue are apt to surpass those that are not secured in this way.

The satisfaction that accompanies the preservation of integrity under the most adverse conditions, once more, is not exhaustive of *eudaimonia*. *Eudaimonia* is an ambient state, self-sustaining, and incomparably worthy. It is also most efficacious in the conduct of life, through all its promise and peril, pleasure and pain. Misery and failure might befall anyone, even the virtuous. He who has justice in the soul, nevertheless, is most apt to bear the hardships of life well and often to master them, and he is most apt to enjoy a pleasant, noble, and abiding happiness. Or so the Greeks have taught. It would be no mean result.[15]

Such are some of the conditions that attend acts of virtue, but there is more to consider to give intelligibility to this remarkable phenomenon. The man who is fully virtuous from the Socratic standpoint must be a lover of wisdom, courage, temperance, and justice. The love of virtue, nevertheless, is surely a derivative affection. Initially, at any rate, we love it for what it makes possible. The fundamental goods of life are typically in jeopardy, and we fear for them. The security of life, home, and family is unsure; the stability of the social order is likewise at risk. Enemies and other hazards abound. The social conditions that might assure defense and the pursuit of happiness are fragile, and behind all these worries is the endless threat of corruption in ourselves and others that would devastate our substance and our hopes. Under such conditions, virtue is the greatest resource: more than any other factor, it holds the world together and sustains life. *That* is its value. The sorts of fundamental goods that I have suggested are not mere interests or preferences; they are necessities of nature, and the threats to them are by no means just one fashion distinguished from another: they are real evils. We first of all love the primal goods, and we fear and detest what endangers them. Then, we love what sustains the goods and combats the perils to them. We are moved to do acts of virtue because of our devotion to the protection of fundamental goods. We become in due course lovers of wisdom and virtue and sustainers of them, doing homage to their universal value, because we have recognized their supreme merit in the conduct of life. In the best of cases, we attain virtue in the self: strength, order, and a composedness of soul inform every experience.

For the maintenance of good communities, virtue is required above all else. Love per se is ineffectual and limited. To believe that all we need is love is the thinking of ignorant sentimentalists. Or, we might remain intact for a brief time as an equilibrium of selfish egos, but the first obstinate conflict that occurs will shatter the balance. Individuals might be united in consequence of sheer hatred of others, fanaticism, and relentless indoctrination, but—in addition to their other failings—such groups cannot retain their particular bond upon the failure of these unhappy devices. A dictator might preserve a kind of order with nothing but terror, but in war and politics, in work and the family, in education and in the "little platoons" of civil life, the absence of virtue means the growth of irresponsibility, crime, cowardice, intrigue, and treachery. The center will not hold. There have been durable tyrannies, but in the absence of virtue in private associations, life becomes intolerable—as if tyranny were not bad enough in itself. To be sure, there are many sorts of community, and there are many and varying conditions that sustain them. I am saying that virtuous moral qualities are most important. Consider the hell of living in a society where virtue is everywhere lacking: men without justice and self-restraint—irresponsible, untrustworthy, deceitful, predatory, destructive, and ruthless—and tell me that virtue is not one of our supreme blessings.

Virtue causes the center to hold. It sustains and invigorates fundamental goods. That is the main reason for loving it. Surely whatever capacity we have for virtue has evolved for this reason and not because it constitutes happiness in the soul. In the worst of cases, its presence in the soul might bring rather little happiness. That particular outcome in an individual is incidental to natural selection, but the preservation of fundamental goods is not. Indeed, much of the reason for virtuous conduct is surely that our propensities to it are deeply inbred, *eudaimonia* or not.

To the hard-core Aristotelian, this might be a repulsive doctrine, but here again, as in most matters, there remains the substratum of gold in the ancient wisdom. For those somewhere in the vicinity of Socratic eros, the soul might well become virtuous and happy. For them, virtue in the soul is more comely than all other suitors; cultivation of it surpasses all other goods. Some portion of that legendary strength, gentleness, and serenity might be theirs. Hence, for the Socratic lover, the priorities of life bear little resemblance to those of the hedonist or to the ambitions of those who would vanquish the world through the accumulation of external power. Inner strength and order, sureness, and steadfastness are at the same time intrinsically precious and of the highest service in the conduct of life.

It is a mistake of the greatest magnitude, a tragic mistake, to think of the virtues only in heroic proportions, modeled on the scale of Socrates himself and in service only to the most exalted goods. It is most plausible that virtue arises from the demand to preserve the elementary goods that are essential to any moral order. All of the seemingly commonplace goods of daily life are highly dependent upon the exercise of moral virtue. *Moreover, these ordinary goods are capable of radical betterment in its company.* The ordinary becomes the extraordinary. Marriage is the best example. With few exceptions, there is no greater blessing than a good and loving marriage, no greater good than to share life and responsibility with a true soulmate. The sense of unity with another in love compensates for much hardship and despair, and the happiness that comes from steadfast affection, appreciation, and support surpasses all understanding. The one who gives such things to you needn't otherwise be a special person, but love from her is more desired and more precious than any commendation and affection from the greatest personage.

The effect seems out of all proportion to the cause. John is an ordinary man and Mary is an ordinary woman, yet their love for each other transfigures their life like a heavenly visitation. And marriage is a state available to almost everyone, so its great good would seem to be almost universally available. But it is not. Its blessings are rare. Most marriages are mediocre to miserable. There are many reasons for the poor showing: foremost, presumably, the absence of affection, but after that the principal cause is lack of virtue. It takes good character to make a happy marriage. If John and Mary lack it, their love alone will not carry them through, nor will caring and sensitivity. Even for individuals who are well disposed to each other, there are seemingly endless emotional and practical incompatibilities, and these can easily reduce the union to quarrel and silent desperation. The man and the woman become a torment to each other. There are great challenges to be met to accomplish a good marriage, and to do it requires virtue. Abiding devotions, sacrifices, loyalties that surpass failure and disappointment, and the determination to see it through together can bring a happiness that the undemanding pleasures of cohabitation will never produce. The union of two *good* people is a thing of life-sustaining beauty, a sacred bond. The combination of two hedonists can make no such achievement nor can that of persons of weakness and vice. All the marriage manuals in all the bookstores are worthless without good character.

The rearing of children is another "routine" practice. It can be a source of bitter disappointments, anger, recriminations, exhaustion, and the ruination of youth, or it can be a source of accomplishment, pride, and massive gratification. Being a good parent preeminently requires sacrifice, character, and sagacity. And thus it is across the full array of ordinary human activity. We must contend with folly, wickedness, incapacity, deprivation, heartbreak, and death. No need for integrity, wisdom, and fortitude? We are not possessors of the complete and perfect virtue described by Aristotle, but we are capable in varying degrees of good dispositions and good conduct, yet most people fall well short of their capabilities. The failure is felt in our infirmity with all manner of weakness and vice and in the sacrifice of goods, great and small, through all phases of human experience.

Socrates and his students believed that virtue exists according to nature. There are several components of this position: The very order of nature itself is constituted by perfections of form, and the nature of man possesses the inherent aptitude to achieve its own perfection. The achievement of form is the completion of our nature, and it assures man an essential harmony with the natural order. Man and nature are made for each other.

It is puzzling at first to find such a congratulatory view of nature coupled with a recognition of the difficulty and rarity of these completions and an unflinching acknowledgment of the turmoil and corruption of human endeavor. How could virtue be regarded as a natural outcome when it is difficult and atypical? In the popular sense of the term, it is more "natural" to be underhanded, greedy, and irresponsible or to be a hedonist. Our perplexity vanishes when we see that this is, in effect, a *normative* definition of nature: the nature of a being, as Aristotle puts it succinctly, is the characteristics it possesses in its completion and perfection. Never mind whatever monsters and deficiencies nature otherwise produces; such matters don't enter into the essential definition. Nature *is* the perfections and not otherwise.

The important matter, nevertheless, is that such perfections are real possibilities of nature. For us Darwinians, of course, it cannot be said that man and nature are made for each other. The best we can say is that man has been made for nature, but the construction is flawed and the fit less than ideal. All the same, our trials in nature have resulted, not surprisingly, in some fine selections. There are marvelous specimens of humanity, and there is in some a high capability for moral and intellectual virtue. Our moral virtues might be the consequence of a happy combination of martial valor, impulse control, the herd instinct, the tendency to reciprocate, sexual love, and the urge to reproduce, all of which have their origins in natural selection. Perhaps the combination also includes an innate capacity to find satisfaction in works that sustain the moral order. And surely by such virtues, in their completion, we are "well souled" for life. Amidst all the contingencies of the universal flux, good character is a singularly valuable asset. When we think of virtue in its unrivaled capacity to sustain communal life, it is difficult to imagine how it could be rejected by the forthright use of moral considerations. In the sense that I have given to the expression, it is appropriate to say that virtue exists according to nature. In some cases, at least, we have a natural aptitude and propensity for it, and in any case it is our most effective instrument of conduct. Its absence is a calamity.

The existence of virtue according to nature as I have characterized it is not wholly unlike the Greek conception. Plato and Aristotle say a creature exists according to nature when it fulfills its proper function. How maladroit would it be to say, today, that we fulfill our proper function in virtuous conduct? "Proper" is the pivotal term. For the ancients, it means to fulfill a role determined by the very nature of being: the forms of human completion replicate antecedent forms in the constitution of nature. I cannot sustain the archaic sense of "proper," but I do accord it an intelligible meaning nonetheless: Given the traits of the environment that we occupy, given the natural tendencies and potentialities of human nature, and given the requirement to sustain a flourishing moral order, then there is no hesitation to say that virtuous conduct is our proper function—or one of our proper functions. The Greeks exemplify that philosophic misadventure that designs the universe in terms of moral biases. They transferred back into the cosmos as constitutive form those features of natural life that they most admired. Without recourse to such a maneuver, I have no embarrassment to say that virtue exists according to nature; I insist on it, indeed.

Although virtue is a supreme good, it is not widely pursued, and it is even derided. The immediate appeal of hedonism is typically potent and the disciplines of virtue typically forbidding. In the absence of effective influences to the contrary, most individuals will follow the less demanding course. There are many ways of getting through life, and we might try it in a more-or-less slovenly manner and still come out, with luck, tolerably well. Even the vicious man, unless he is nagged by a persistent remnant of moral feeling, might revel in his own version of success—though the criminal life is a very bad bet on the whole. Those, too, who suppose their principal resource is that of external power might, if their supply of it is sufficient, get some good out of it. Still, even leaving aside its victims, power without virtue is apt to be a disaster—like the life of a spoiled child is a disaster: the little monster is everywhere detested, and he can't figure out why all the indulgences granted him fail to make him happy. In the event, I have no wish to do more than acknowledge the existence of such alternatives. I do not admire or recommend them. They cannot be supported by moral considerations, and they cannot support a moral order; they are parasitical upon it.

We should not be surprised at how corruptible we are—wealth, power, sex, and status being so consummately alluring, and the flesh so weak. Given the necessities of mere survival to the next day, integrity seems a fatuous luxury. Accordingly, Plato's almost ceaseless emphasis on the importance of moderating the passions is wisdom itself. One who is mindful of Plato's cautions will recognize that a civilization that does not persistently emphasize the difference between the high and the low will expire.

When conditions are right, nature produces its occasional perfections. I have referred to moral dispositions *in their completion*. "In their completion" is the fateful qualification. How do we complete these propensities? That is, how are they distinguished and cultivated? And who will take the responsibility to do it? Who will teach attachments to values "as to our own flesh and blood" that will nourish the virtuous imagination? Few today seem interested in undertaking such tasks, or even in thinking about them.

A first step is to ponder the environment that seems appropriate for effective moral learning. I remarked earlier that Aristotle (whose full writings on education are lost to us) had neglected to tell of the role of eros in the education of virtue. Another imperative that he might have emphasized (which he perhaps thought too obvious to mention) is that moral education must take place in a context in which the necessity of the exercise of moral qualities is vividly evident. These are not academic or hypothetical requirements. They have been distinguished for their functions in attaining and protecting fundamental goods in a perilous world and bringing harmony to social life. The young should not simply be advised of the existence of such necessities; they must experience them. Their thought and action must be chastened by some experience of the real hazards that steadily beset our lives. Elementary awareness of the always precarious and corruptible world would be typically instructive. When our children do not become palpably sensible of the actual consequences of vice and virtue—witness them and suffer them—and when they are not required to recognize and contribute to the needful works of common life, they will attain to worthy character only by a miracle.

Such tutelage can be ignored, to be sure, or simply dismissed, or the young can be protected from such realities by foolishly indulgent parents, but to attain even a minimally functional level of morality is a demanding and perpetual task. It is a continuous and urgent duty of civilization, yet we can plausibly read the culture of the last half century and more as a steady deterioration and rejection of life-sustaining norms. The beliefs, duties, and ambitions foundational to a proud and sustainable moral order are in retreat. Increasingly, "morality" has had little to do with virtue. People are assured of their "virtue" by supporting what they are told are virtuous allegiances: abortion on demand, environmentalism, affirmative action, pleading the cause of the homeless, denouncing sexism, and so forth. They also believe that their goodness consists in "caring," "openness," "sensitivity," and a recognition that the dominant culture and its traditional virtues are both antiquated and corrupt. Anything that was once esteemed great, superior, or distinguished is to be mocked.

There is sometimes enough trace of validity in some of these causes and accusations to convince the credulous of the perfect rectitude of their crusade. Yet the crusade is mostly rhetorical. That is, whatever your burning issue, it can be supported at virtually no expense to yourself. The taxpayers provide the money and the bureaucrats provide the management. The universities will take care of removing those archaic and repressive books from the curriculum. All you do is express outrage, engage in an occasional demonstration, denounce the establishment, and feel righteous. With this cost-free position, you have satisfied your obligations and certified your virtue. In personal morality, hedonism, coupled with arrogance, reigns supreme.

The intellectuals and their camp followers (commonly in the media and universities) assure these blessed souls that they are indeed at the forefront of human decency. Psychobabblers, for their part, strive for reputation by conveniently substituting emotional categories for moral: Are you *comfortable* with yourself, no matter what, and with any form of deviancy? Are you *non-judgmental, laid-back, free of hang-ups, sensitive, open, accepting?* Then you're OK, a perfect person. Continue as you are, with our (authoritative) blessing. Those who are susceptible to this song come to believe that they are morally superior just because they sing it too.

At the same time, these righteous persons have little compunction about lying at their own convenience, neglecting their children, compromising their loyalty to their friends, defaming the innocent, being unscrupulous in work and in school, manipulative and deceitful in politics, and being irresponsible in the performance of duties. Irresponsibility—not to mention incompetence and corruption—is epidemic throughout all institutions. In the home, at the office, the insurance agency, the hospital, the plumbing company, the school, city hall, the boardroom, the executive suite, and the government: indifference and negligence are rampant. For all their compassion, moreover, our moral exemplars have little inclination to sacrifice anything at all for god, man, or country. Any request for an adjustment in their priorities they regard as an assault on their dignity.

"Hyperbole!" "Diatribe!" "Caricature!" you cry. Yes, these are sweeping generalizations. Only a minority of persons—but a very powerful minority— satisfies them fully in every regard, and there are some saving exceptions to these descriptions. If virtue is indeed what holds the world together, however, then these exceptions must be joined by legions more. Virtue is in peril in any culture of cheap and instant pleasures. *Sophrosyne* is out of reach. Eros, likewise, will never transfigure a life where there is no reverence for the highest possibilities. Teachers and preceptors betray the generations when they deride our entire heritage and are tolerant of incivility and self-indulgence. A soul more appreciative of excellence is no longer thought to deserve respect and authority. The task of educators and parents is no longer to elevate the youth but to entertain them. The prophecy of "The Second Coming" expresses our situation well. And who today exemplifies the new morality best? The former president of the United States, of all people, much loved by millions, William J. Clinton.

The ethics of caring and self-indulgence that oozes through society is disabling. We require little of the young; we only sympathize with them for the few demands that are made upon them. Thereby we keep them infantile, egocentric, and helpless. They wander the landscape, vaguely trying to "find" themselves, but there is nothing there to find, for the greatest sources of direction and inspiration have been denied them. A moral philosophy that exhausts itself in "caring" must be a disaster. A moral philosophy must provide order, limit, and discipline, and aspiration must be defined in terms of what nature and morality make possible.

Among the enlightened, words like "order," "limit," and "discipline" unfailingly bring forth accusations of oppressive intent, not liberation. Freedom *is* a treasure, but not invariably, and sometimes the users of words like "order" and "discipline" really are up to no good. In the preceding chapter I spoke of the division of moral responsibilities. I recall that notion in order to draw attention to the sorts of institutions that seem fitted by nature to address the problems of moral decay and recovery.

b. The Law of Mediocrity

Plato's critique of democracy in book 8 of *The Republic* is directed against freedom. If there *is* freedom, there *is not* authority, order, or direction—whether in the state or in the soul of the individual. When authority and direction are lacking, men do not use their freedom well. They squander it in dissipation and destruction. What good is freedom if no one knows how to use it or cannot combine it with virtue? The question is as urgent today as it was in ancient Athens. Everywhere we see individuals pursuing self-indulgence according to the passing whim, and no excellence of any sort is achieved; no surpassing goods are acknowledged or accomplished; and the lust for uninhibited gratification masquerades with the rhetoric of rights and freedom. Incapacity, lassitude, and anomie prevail, and resistance to vice becomes increasingly scarce. Freedom feeds upon itself, demanding ever more of the same and petulantly resisting any kind of authority as an imposition. Then, lo and behold, with all this freedom, we are still unhappy. "How can this be?" we demand. "There must be one or two hitherto unrecognized impediments lurking somewhere. Find them and extirpate them and *then* we will be happy! Maybe it is the presence of sexist language that is oppressing us, or maybe it is the shortage of unisex bathrooms. Find these horrors and others like them and destroy them! The reign of happiness will follow at once." Such is the thinking of those who are beguiled by unlimited freedom. Their wisdom is that of the hedonist. Their adolescent philosophy might seem an isolated, harmless, and even amusing matter, were the apostles of this freedom not so tyrannical and ruthless; the consequences are apt to be much worse than first suspected.

When the fully committed adherents of the philosophy of instant gratification find that happiness does not follow the overthrow of this or that obstacle to self-indulgence, they do not reconsider the wisdom of their fury. In its advanced form—commonly witnessed in the moral avant-garde—their frustration turns to an indiscriminate rage of destruction: destroy all limits, everything!—all norms, traditions, arts, institutions, and authorities! Death to it all! Hence the tyrannical nature, fated to be most miserable, would bring down the world in a fit of self-righteousness.

The milder forms of this philosophy are more insidious. Their followers believe that if there is anywhere the mildest frustration, pain, deprivation, or suffering, any impediment, any discipline, then something is wrong in the social order, and we must turn to the state for the remedy. The idea that life will have its irremediable hardships is unacceptable. No distress need be endured. Equally unacceptable is the notion that private groups and individuals might themselves take responsibility for their fate and introduce their own initiatives to contend with both adversity and aspiration. With such thinking, they become highly susceptible to the lures of demagogues, who are thereby enabled to expand their power.

Following Plato, I have used "freedom" instead of "rights," but the variation in diction should not disguise the fact that the problem of which he speaks could be formulated in the terms I used in the preceding chapter: I spoke of the folly and excess that might proliferate in the exercise of rights. Plato's response to the excesses is to denounce democracy. Rule must be in the hands of the wisest and best, who will direct the lives of everyone else for their own benefit. This is a "solution" that many of us find abhorrent. Those who have a monopoly of authority are rarely if ever the wisest and best, and their monopoly will make them worse. Anyway, freedom is not that dangerous—so we would like to think. The autonomous man postulated by Enlightenment philosophers, such as Locke, is rational and industrious. Leave him to his own pursuits and he will flourish; just don't let him get away with interfering in the freedom of others. In the event, he's not apt to be obsessed with doing so, because he is not markedly evil or even immoderate in his passions.

Plato's conception of human nature is much closer to the truth than Locke's, yet we aren't going to sacrifice our precious freedoms anyway. Are we deluded once again by a childish fantasy? Well, we often are, to be sure, but even so, freedom has not turned out to be nearly as mad as it might seem. This is because liberal regimes have had some unanticipated resources that are profoundly beneficent.

Locke conceives the atomistic individual in radical juxtaposition to the state. Let the state stay out of private affairs, leaving individuals to themselves. Actual liberal regimes, foremost among them the United States, did just that. The rights enumerated in the American Constitution pertain to the rights of individuals. The result, however, was not to produce a mere aggregate of separate persons, but to facilitate the exuberant flourishing of private associations. Left to our own devices, we do not exist separately but in communities—groups of every size, composition, and function. These orders have given an astonishing vitality and fertility to civic life, and they have been well motivated to care for the moral character of their members. Almost by inadvertance, the liberal philosophy authorized, by most measures, some of the most successful societies in history.[16]

We rejoice in our freedom and offer thanksgiving to its founders. In accordance with this lovely arrangement, we think of self-rule not simply in terms of democratic government but also, more profoundly, in terms of the autonomy of civil society: the remarkable facility of private institutions in various forms of association with each other to rule themselves in an orderly and prosperous manner without need of extensive authority from the state. The success of this self-rule, to be sure, required the cultivation and practice of civic virtue and personal responsibility.[17]

Why didn't the liberal regime founder in the manner dramatized by Plato? Because the essential constraining, forming, and directive influences on the population come from associations whose purpose and rationale are not freedom. These associations have potencies that had escaped the attention of both Plato and Locke.[18] Of the numerous institutions of civic life, the most important have been family, church, school, and commercial enterprise (most of which have been on a small scale), and we might add neighborhoods, small and stable village communities, and cultural/ethnic societies. In all such forms of society, authority over the membership—especially the young—tends to be exerted in a manner that is direct and personal, as distinguished from remote, bureaucratic, and legalistic. There is personal attention to specific individuals in order to introduce them to the norms of the group and to require their observance of them.

The purpose of the family—at least until very recently—has not been freedom. It has been to nurture the young into decent, responsible, productive adults, capable of contributing to the welfare of the kinship group and to the ongoing life of the community. No generation can be raised to be dependent upon the largesse of charity or the ministrations of the state. A permissive family environment was regarded to be antithetical to these worthy goals. Husband and wife, in fulfilling their duties, must curtail their own choices and abide by their obligations as head of the family. The aim of family life might be said to be the *autonomy* of its members, if we use that term to mean persons who are *mature, capable, and responsible*, but then the goal of autonomy must be distinguished from that of freedom in the sense of fewer duties and more rights. The family might gladly permit freedom, but only where it did not threaten duty or moral propriety. Otherwise, freedom would be antithetical to autonomy. Parents will also encourage personal initiative and self-reliance but still within the bounds of good conduct. Certainly the aims of religious life (again, until recently) have not been freedom. Common worship, indoctrination into the dogmas of the church (with a heavy emphasis on moral instruction), and contributing to the good works of the church have been paramount. Participation in commercial endeavors requires that one learn the disciplines of hard work, reliability, cooperation, and following directions. Schooling, too, is not aimed at freedom per se, nor at self-esteem or self-expression. It is aimed at learning and at the acquisition of skills in learning. Here, too, autonomy as distinguished from freedom would be a major goal. Many schools would commonly impart particular moral, religious, and sometimes ethnic teachings, but any school would be a scene of moral training in the sense that punctuality, honesty, civility, self-discipline, and hard work would be rewarded, and cheating, causing disturbances, showing disrespect, and lack of application would be penalized. In some phases of schooling, independent ventures in learning would be promoted and praised.

In an obvious sense, these associations have no choice but to be teachers of virtue. The family, the church, the school, and the business concern cannot tolerate bad behavior. For their very survival and prosperity, they must demand good conduct and energetic contribution of their participants. Otherwise, the system crashes. The necessity of moral tutelage is according to nature, and, in the main, these arrangements in civil society proved rather successful in establishing habits of responsibility and good conduct.[19] Accordingly, the freedoms that individuals enjoyed were not apt to lead to dissolute behavior. Plato's worst fears did not materialize. This is a classic case of distributing moral labor where it belongs by nature: Those who have the greatest motivation for teaching moral virtue and who most suffer the consequences of license are those in whom the responsibility resides.

Or will Plato have the last word, after all? These traditional and natural moral functions have not persisted well; they have eroded to the point of collapse.

Before looking into this woeful development, we must consider some further characteristics of liberal society. The function of autonomous associations, once more, has not been to expand the availability of unrestrained choices. In the original liberal tradition, the praise of freedom was directed elsewhere: to the limitation of state interference in private life. With cheers of triumph and salvation, intrusive government is abolished! The conduct of private affairs is left to more congenial, well-motivated, and competent authorities. In the natural and constitutionally mandated division of moral labor, a free man cannot be conceived as dependent upon the generosity of the state, much less upon the ambitions of politicians. Such dependency is slavery.

The government of a free people is also praised for prohibiting unwanted intrusions by private groups and individuals into the lives of other groups and individuals. There is precious freedom, moreover, in respect to the ways that individuals may participate in common life. In principle, the individual will decide his religious affiliation, his philosophy and politics, his vocation and recreations, the place where he lives, his friendships, his spouse, and voluntary associations. In these vital matters, however, the very freedom of private associations stands as a sometime obstacle to the freedom of the individual. You cannot, for example, go to college and join a learned profession at will. Apart from the matter of having to pay large sums of money for these opportunities, you can't go to Harvard and become a doctor if Harvard won't admit you and the medical profession judges you unqualified. You can't join the country club if its members won't have you; you can't get a job if no work is available or if the owners don't want you; regardless of your wealth, you can't buy a house in a certain neighborhood if no one there will sell to you; and a landlord can forbid you space on his premises for any reason to his liking.

In most instances, the criteria for participation in these groups and activities are determined by the members of the group itself. Harvard decides who will be admitted to Harvard; the country club decides who will be accepted in membership; and the landlord decides to whom he will rent. You might judge the criteria to be just and good in some instances and arbitrary and oppressive in others. It makes no difference. The criteria are not up to you. This condition is inseparable from the freedom of private institutions. I'm not speaking here of the rights of citizenship or of the impartial rule of law that ought to govern the conduct of the state. The question is that of the autonomy of private associations, by which I mean their right of self-governance.

In cognizance of both the opportunities and limitations of civil society, individuals decide for themselves what they will or will not attempt with their lives, and they might pursue their ambitions with enthusiasm and resource. It has been an arrangement especially well suited to those with a strong sense of responsibility and a willingness to take the risks of personal initiative. If you choose to go to college at all, and Harvard will not take you, then you look for other possibilities, and you might have to work at the same time that you study. For many persons, this has proved to be a great success story. American civil life provided opportunities unprecedented in human history and likewise yielded unprecedented social mobility and prosperity. Countless individuals celebrated their chance to participate in a free society.

For several reasons, nevertheless, the autonomy of civil life has been subject to criticism. Autonomous groups can confine their membership and services on the basis of race, religion, sex, ethnicity, wealth, class, and anything else, and they typically do. Unrestrained business interests will construct a strip mall next to an old established neighborhood; they can sell shoddy products; and they can provide abominable working conditions, to which even children might be subjected. The bounties of civil life, moreover, will not be equally available to all. Various groups and individuals will lack the cultural or financial wherewithal to pursue education; they might be unable to afford school or medical care—perhaps even food and shelter. There has been, accordingly, much agitation to set these situations right, and the state has been almost universally regarded as the only agency that can do it. The general welfare requires the activist state.

Still, morality according to nature requires that we be alert to conduct and dispositions that enfeeble the moral order. With this caution in mind, it is wise to assume in all matters a tendency to the expansion of dominion. Politics and governance are just of the more conspicuous demonstrations of this compulsion, aspirants and officials of every sort looking to absorb into their jurisdictions powers and prerogatives hitherto beyond them. This is to be expected and hence always a matter of concern. A considerable literature has gathered around the the merits of innumerable policy variations. The following is not a contribution to that collection. My comments are intended to introduce and to emphasize moral considerations that might help in weighing the import of the alternatives. My position is not value neutral, but defends institutions that are vital to the moral life.

The immediate topic is the steady inflation of the state. Its power and the scope of its jurisdiction have relentlessly enlarged. It has also grown for reasons additional to those recited: the demands of waging war, for example, but not least, by any means, because of the avarice of politicians and bureaucrats. Like most persons, they lust for power and reputation. Bureaucrats can expand their jurisdiction because they are largely free to interpret their legal mandate in a manner that permits them to regulate ever more of hitherto autonomous operations. The politician can gain power by means of bribery and deception: he has priorities of his own, and he has no more love of responsibility than anyone else. He makes every promise to have the state take over whatever unpleasant work that used to be done by private individuals; he pledges to provide the remedy for every irritation. (This is his preferred form of bribery.)

The tax collector is insatiable, and the career lawmaker spends to the limit of public endurance and beyond. There is no mystery: politicians and bureaucrats become delirious at the prospect of sharing in the command of many billions of dollars and sharing in the regulation of millions of human activities. Virtually anyone with massive amounts of money at his disposal will develop grandiose plans for spending it; and when he has the power to collect still more cash, his grandiosity will expand. Today, the very meaning of life to political aspirants is to establish or to enlarge public programs; and glowing reputation is secured as champion of such munificence. The self-aggrandizing politician comes to think of taxpayers as nothing but instruments of his social policies. He does this not with the welfare of his constituents foremost in mind, but with thought for the glories of reputation: defender of the downtrodden! author of benevolent services to the disadvantaged! He is indifferent to the failure of the programs in themselves, so long as they succeed in promoting his lustrous image.

Hence there arises the disabling and alarming condition of more and more people becoming beneficiaries of public expenditure, on which they depend for their welfare and sometimes their survival. A few politicians escape corruption, and some of this group strive to expand state beneficences because they sincerely believe it is the right thing to do, and occasionally it is. Public support for education at all levels is a fine example. Either way, there is extension of state power and contraction of private and local authority.

Politicians of today are only intermittently constrained by an ideal of service to country. Rather, engagement in politics per se, exercise of power, and basking in glory have become ends in themselves. Are these such unusual motivations? Integrity in public life is the true rarity. The politician shamelessly manipulates the public just in order to attain or retain office, and he is always eager to expand the scope of his control. Let nothing escape politicization! The ideologies of the political left are particularly well suited to sustain these base ambitions, but so-called moderates and conservatives are hardly untainted. The politician will not go away, of course, but must we give him so much to do? The mischief he can cause will be reduced as the scope of his dominion is kept under vigilant surveillance. At one time, we could rely on the federal judiciary to keep his lusts under control, but that day seems to have passed. The courts have been ingenious in finding new ways to permit continued expansion of government jurisdiction.

Much of the local flavor and responsibility are disappearing. The reduction in autonomy and individuality is in part owing to the massive disposition of state monies to all manner of "private" institutions. A condition of the receipt of these gifts, for example, is to relinquish any sign of sectarian distinctiveness. An adoption agency that had the purpose of placing Catholic children in Catholic homes may no longer do so, if it receives taxpayers' money, for discrimination on the basis of religion in publicly supported agencies is prohibited by law. Likewise, no charity may be extended to individuals on condition of their receiving religious instruction, giving up alcohol, or (until recently) accepting work. Any school with public subsidies of any form may not offer a denominational prayer on the premises or display sectarian symbols. Universities must adhere to affirmative action in admissions, staffing, and faculty development or risk bankruptcy. It is not within the jurisdiction of the Professional Golfers' Association to prohibit the use of golf carts to any and all members of the association. The Boy Scouts of America have been under judicial pressure to abandon "under God" and "morally straight" for fear that some individuals might feel offended or excluded by such phrases. The government even finds a way to keep its finger on the membership of many private clubs. Week after week, year after year, insensibly to the average citizen, the march goes on: small programs become very large; temporary expedients become permanent; and new crises for government activism are discovered daily. Politicians, lawyers, judges, and bureaucrats make decisions and policy and manage affairs in more and more areas of common life from which they once would have been run off by citizens brandishing firearms.

The division of moral labor memorialized in the Constitution has been reversed. The original idea was that our freedom would consist fundamentally in freedom from intrusions from government and from each other. The self-appointed custodians of the common weal, however, think it wise that the state should intervene more and the family less. They want government control and familial permissiveness. This is an inversion of the natural order of moral responsibility. We slip toward the antithesis of the founding ethos: the government regulates more and more of life; our freedom relative to the state diminishes steadily, while private associations, in contrast, fall all over themselves to offer more freedom. Nothing seems to be more important to the family, the mainline protestant churches, the Catholic Church, and the schools than to relax requirements, offer more choices, and to teach non-judgmental compassion. Even the military has been gravely infected.

Anyone who is uneasy about the strength and vigor of the moral order must be concerned about the revitalization of civil society, especially the family. The dimensions of the problem are complex and perhaps intractable. A common and well-documented charge is that welfare programs undercut the necessity of a family to meet its basic obligations. Indeed, they discourage the very formation and endurance of families.[20] If this seems an implausible scenario, it is essential to be reminded that it is rather easy for human beings to neglect their duties. We have a natural inclination to evade them, if possible, and we have a spontaneous inclination to self-indulgence.

The more affluent segments of society, too, seem lulled by the availability of welfare. "Entitlements" and services for the middle class continue to expand. Still, the lives of these folk do not depend on such largesse. Why are *they* increasingly irresponsible as parents, citizens, employees, and managers? We may be sure that explanations for such phenomena would take us beyond that of the overweening state alone. As it may happen from case to case, there are several eligible accounts of our "cultural meltdown," and I would not attempt to track them all down. One of the more systematic analyses comes from Fukuyama.[21] He observes that our decline "is readily measurable in statistics on crime, fatherless children, reduced educational outcomes and opportunities, broken trust, and the like."[22] "And the like" includes "rates of crime, family breakdown, drug use, litigation, suicide, and tax evasion."[23] Our "social capital," as he calls it, is dissolving. In a subtle and thorough analysis, he concludes that these problems stem primarily from family breakdown, which, in turn, is principally owing to the sexual and feminist revolutions.[24]

In his review of Fukuyama's study, J. Q. Wilson dissents. According to his judgment, the main source of our moral deterioration is the influence of cultural elites, who have long been urging permissive and antinomian ways of life. Their influence has been marginal until recent decades, during which the normal resistances to such decadence have been dissipated.[25] Wilson's view is not altogether unlike that of Bork in *Slouching Towards Gomorrah*, to which I have already referrred. Bork puts the blame on the philosophy and practice of liberalism, which fails to provide the requisite opposition to the lust for self-indulgence.

In *The Marriage Problem*, Wilson pushes the sources of decay back to the Enlightenment and before. The rising demand for personal autonomy in all spheres of life brings prominence to the notion of individual rights, which, Wilson agrees, is a highly desirable change. But the notion of rights weakens the authority of custom, tradition, and religion, and this development is of mixed value—having, after all, its own ill effects on marriage and the family, for example. The increasing demands for autonomy and rights have had the general effect of converting marriage from a sacred and (almost) irrevocable bond into an arrangement of convenience, and the obligations of family, likewise, lose their sanctity. Various historical occurrences have served to support these trends, which are especially accentuated by leaders from the intellectual and artistic communities.[26]

A particularly striking example of the poisonous influence of our cultural preceptors is provided by Robert Weissberg in his *The Politics of Empowerment*.[27] Noting that "empowerment" seems to be an all-solving idea for today's intellectual, Weissberg surveys the literature to determine what the idea is about and to see what good it might portend. Empowerment, after all, ought to be a fine thing. Nothing would seem more eligible for the disadvantaged than to attain education, skills, character, and positive goals. His computer search disclosed thousands of entries on the topic, and presumably Weissberg made a manful attempt to discern and digest their message, which is presented, analyzed, and evaluated in his study. The results are flabbergasting. In his own words, published elsewhere, he reports: "An expedition through untold scholarly accounts across varied disciplines, with hardly an exception, reveals a truly dismal picture. . . ." "In sum," he concludes, "this academic-taught gospel *never* entails arduous work at self-transformation to ultimately exert mastery; empowerment *always* means escaping the imposition of social conventionality on behalf of self-indulgence."[28] What a betrayal of the powerless! And what a disclosure of the vacuous uniformity of the presumably radical mind.[29]

Evidently the self-righteous morality of the 1960s, propped up by the tradition of individual rights and exploiting normal but treacherous human tendencies, has taken root, and the moral indolence of the populations of civil society must be in some significant measure owing to that. It is not improbable, too, that our ambitions and successes in materialistic pursuits have displaced our moral energies. Distracted parents can't spare the time and effort to make elementary requirements on their children. Supported by the intellectuals, they allow themselves to believe that routine social observances are "merely conventional" and hence disposable. It is certain, however, that toleration of seemingly lesser matters—like personal slovenliness and insolence—is disastrous. Such indulgence leads to contempt for parents and for standards of good conduct in general. Assuredly, initiative and responsibility are further eroded by the spread of bureaucracy, whether it is that spawned by government or by huge private enterprises. This impersonal monster gradually subdues the qualitative distinctiveness and vigor of local custom, and with it the autonomy and authority of these one-time centers of life. All told, it is a menacing array. Whatever their disagreements about causation, each of these theorists shares the conviction that a reinvigoration of ethical rectitude and responsibility is a necessity.

Many conditions have contributed to the lapse of moral decency and sense of duty, and there are several that I have not even suggested, most notable among them the current state of popular entertainments. The cesspool of television programming, for example, is both symptomatic of our degradation and contributory to its furtherance. Perhaps it is now the most corrosive element in the entire culture. Again, these matters do not permit of exactitude in judgment, and we should also observe that different forms of association are vulnerable to different forms of seduction. The liberal religious denominations have not hesitated to embrace every radical philosophy circulated in the last fifty years. Most of the schools have done likewise.

The family is one of the institutions most vulnerable to decline. Not only is it subject to the forms of decay already mentioned, but it is also beset with the weaknesses of adventurous sexuality and the stresses of intense emotional need. At the same time, it is the most important of civilizing institutions. It is odd, perhaps, that an institution so crucial to our well-being is at the same time unusually subject to failure, but we must in any case recognize this extraordinary wedding of vitality and frailty. It is likely that the incessant rantings from traditional moral authorities about the disciplines of marriage have their origin in this recognition: the family is at the same time essential to life and always threatened with dissolution. This is a precarious condition of human existence, but there are ways to resist and lessen the threats.

The decline in moral self-reliance combines with the increasing readiness of the state to right all wrongs. For centuries, we have taken for granted that individuals must learn to cope with most of the affronts that we routinely receive. But now insensitivity is prohibited by law and a new censorship is thriving, while the informal and customary ways of rectifying bad manners have been replaced by the courts. In the same way, individuals used to be taught to look out for themselves—not to fall off ladders or to be burned by coffee, but this simple form of responsibility has been largely eclipsed by blaming the builders of ladders and the sellers of coffee and hauling them before an obliging judiciary. What delicate race of creatures is forthcoming? Can we depend upon them to be teachers and learners of virtue?

The failing self-reliance of private associations is in large part due to the growth of the state, but their failure is a cause in its own right, for it facilitates continued appropriation of power and prerogative by government. To what extent has the appropriation of power by the state caused the decline in private life? Or is it more a matter of the decline facilitating government expansion? When there is less willingness to fulfill our duties, we look to someone to do them for us, and the politicians, bureaucrats, lawyers, and judges are happy to accommodate. Hence we are less willing to resist encroachment; we acquiesce to it and even welcome it. Given the frailties of human nature, it is less surprising that responsibility diminish rather than thrive. In any event, it is incontestable: the primary institutions of society have lost much of their vigor and are redefining their mission, while we also redefine that of the state. Until we restore something like the original division of moral labor, we are apt to look more and more like the people depicted in book 8 of *The Republic*. We become inept in the exercise of freedom.

Although I am not equally sure of all the hypotheses about the sources of social breakdown, I am confident of two positions regarding it. The first of them is this: It is always difficult to sustain morale and commitment; there is always a wavering line separating dedication and capitulation. *We can take it as a law of nature, indeed, that it is very difficult to drive standards upward and to keep them up, while it is very easy to let them decline.* (We can call this the law of the tendency to mediocrity—or simply *the law of mediocrity*.) There is immediate gratification in relaxation; the short-run pressures are almost always downward. To sustain long-term discipline requires special conditions. There is little excitement, for example, in keeping academic and moral standards at a high level; there is no intrinsic thrill in it. It is hard work. The elevation of standards is more apt to occur as a necessity of survival in a difficult environment. Security and prosperity, while fine things in themselves, tend to make us lax and complacent in respect to moral priorities. Pursuit of material gain and indulgence in hedonistic ambitions become more conspicuous.

If we are to contend with the causes of descent into mediocrity and then corruption, we must be cognizant of both the promise and the peril of any relevant form of association. To assure clarity on such a critical issue, we must distinguish two senses of mediocrity. There is first the inevitable form of it: nature disburses her forces such that the most numerous representation of individuals must be at the mean, and these individuals will be an average of those few at the extremes. This is the so-called normal distribution. The second sense is the more pertinent in the present context: the entire curve can move higher or lower—in some cases much higher or lower. The mean moves higher or lower while remaining indomitably a mean. The distribution of moral conscientiousness, for example, must have a mean. In a highly conscientious population, the mean represents much more responsibility than in a less conscientious one. Accordingly, we can speak of a tendency to mediocrity in two senses, but the crucial one here is in reference to whether the mean is ascending or descending. The law of mediocrity says that in respect to standards of thought and conduct, ascent is difficult and uncommon, while descent is both easy and usual.

I speak here of the tendency to mediocrity not as the inevitable regression to the mean but as the tendency for standards to fall from excellence. Apart from life-threatening conditions, standards tend to weaken and are less diligently observed, and the mean of the normal distribution sinks ever lower. Every standard, every aspiration, every norm of character and conduct tends to be drawn toward mediocrity, and the measures of mediocrity themselves decline. There are so many occasions when we ought to stand firm, when we must resist the immediate way out, but it is easier to adjust, to compromise, to give in. Every demand for lowering of standards is difficult to resist. It is so easy to say yes and so difficult to say no. When we are accommodating, there is no conflict, no resistance, no hard feelings. Everybody is happy, so why make an issue out of standards?

The facts suggest that men are naturally drawn to reduced tension and lessened effort; they are drawn to ease and comfort. The necessities of life normally require substantially more than this, and we typically respond aggressively to them. As always, however, there is ambiguity and ambivalence in human nature. We are naturally competitive and naturally seek status and dominance. Even so, when security seems assured or when someone else is available to do our duties, there is a relaxation of our moral vigilance and intellectual rigor, and our competitive side tends to spend itself in materialistic obsessions, adventitious entertainments, and corrupt ambitions. Our strenuous attention to the conditions of excellence in life-sustaining endeavors will diminish. The current state of American politics and government illustrates this condition exactly: What in principle ought to be a peripheral and subsidiary activity has moved to the forefront. It monopolizes the attention and energies of millions, and it incorporates more and more of national life. At the same time, the standards of behavior in political life are debauched. The Clintons, their accomplices, their countless hangers-on, and apologists are of course the prime example but by no means the only one. There are many politicians who are morally despicable, most of them on the left. If other institutions functioned at a similar level of degeneracy, they would become quickly dysfunctional and at the point of anarchy, or they would descend into tyranny—just as Plato predicted.

There are cases where government intervention is justified. The pragmatist and policy wonk will say, "Well, we'll act in those cases only." Which cases are those? It is hard to find agreement—which is not to say that we should give up. In contending with these questions, the wonk should be mindful of the fact that the state never rests. It is always looking for an opportunity to extend its reach. It happens quietly and insensibly. Titanic efforts are required to contain it, and they usually fail. "Eternal vigilance is the price of liberty," but the price has become higher than we wish to pay. The pragmatic wonk is hardly aware, moreover, of the abundant resources of civil society, and he bridles at institutions beyond his control. He confines his accounting of benefits and harms largely to economic terms. He is ignorant of the blessings of local autonomy that do not have a cash payoff. Income transfers accompanied by political rhetoric look good, while there are invisible losses of far greater consequence: losses in moral qualities. He is probably ignorant of the nature and conditions of a flourishing free society, and he is oblivious to the law of mediocrity. Finally, the wonk, when he is not merely self-serving, unreflectively presupposes that the only morality is that of compassion and caring. I am defending a more vigorous and ambitious morality, in which the distribution of responsibilities appears to be in accordance with nature.

High standards and high levels of performance are always under threat from our tendencies to sloth, hedonism, and complacency. These tendencies are encouraged by determinable variations in social conditions and resisted by others. I am not tempted to engage in argument with the wonk on this or that policy issue. I am concerned with the moral functions of civil life, a momentous issue that receives little attention. Which institutions solicit moral vigor, and which ones discourage it? Why do these institutions decline, and how can they be restored? The second of my confidently held positions is this: The remedies for our moral weariness must come from the institutions of civil society—the family above all. Civil society must somehow become morally rejuvenated. Responsibilities for the conduct of life should be more widely distributed, not more centralized, and failure to discharge them properly should, on the whole, be corrected by local authorities.

I am also concerned with the *qualitative* value of private community life, which I will consider later on. I will conclude the present phase of things by mentioning an underappreciated, if not unrecognized, asset of self-reliant private life: the competition between independent institutions.

The state believes that it raises standards of, say, education, law enforcement, and public health if it requires all the relevant agencies under its jurisdiction to conform to standards that will be issued and enforced by the state and will be uniform to all parties. That way, whoever is remiss in the pursuit of excellence can be called to account. With such reasoning, we think to remedy an evil, and at the same time, once more, we expand the powers of government—a familiar pattern. The clear historical lesson, however, is that centralization and standardization lead to mediocrity or worse. Due to the incessant demand for a relaxation of requirements, and due to fatigue, indifference, and corruption, there is always a steady downward pressure on standards. Public officials and bureaucrats are ill motivated to resist this pressure. They have nothing to fear from competing institutions, for there are none. They have little to gain for their efforts, and they can retain their power by political means. In response to the query regarding the ineffectuality and decline of their institutions, the chorus of bureaucrats and politicians is unfailing: "We must have more money! Put the tax collector to work night and day, and then you will see results."

Economists teach that monopolies create worse products at higher costs. That is the nature of monoplies, while competition stimulates the opposite tendencies. Accordingly, when state regulation minimizes or eradicates competition, its functionaries will be more susceptible to irresponsibility and corruption. In its willingness to expand its power and often to abuse it, the state is not unlike most other institutions. Many of them—such as commercial enterprises—also overreach and abuse. Businesses tend to deceive and cheat to the limit that they can get away with. Businessmen are limited in their dishonesty by government, in one of its valid responsibilities, but the principal limitation is the existence of competition (which is also preserved by the law). The greatest restraint on the expansion and abuse of power, in business and elsewhere, is the existence of competition between jealous centers of endeavor. At the same time, within the framework provided by law, this competition and rivalry encourage strenuous efforts by these centers to raise their standards of performance and to improve their services.

Our political philosophy was once a model of the antimonopolistic ethos. At the beginning, there were sternly defined limits to government authority. The principle of subsidiarity, which nourishes competition, was deeply respected, and local institutions were zealously protective of their autonomy. There was also the original separation of powers between the executive, judicial, and legislative branches, and there was an active and passionately defended federal system by which the states maintained their own sovereignty. That system and ethos are now moribund. The citizenry have not proved effectively resistant to the debilitating tendencies of the state: they are politically and morally apathetic, and the ballot is degraded. Hence the highly salutary effects of competition are steadily disappearing. Recognition of the pivotal importance of autonomy in both public and private institutions is fading. At the same time, we are less heedful of the deadliness of uniformity and enforced standardization among them. One wonders whether the will to sustain a self-governing civil society was not an anomaly, a historical fluke—a noble but unusually evanescent eddy in the universal flux.

Now, to look for elucidation, it is not precise to say that families, as such, are in direct competition with each other, and their members do not typically inquire how they can subdue other families. Still, each unit must strive to ensure that its own members prosper and are capable of contributing to its well-being in a competitive environment. As I have observed, a major part of this endeavor is to inculcate moral responsibility, not only for the general welfare of the family but also because good moral character is—or was—regarded as a paramount asset for the entire society. The unit of immediate kin, accordingly, desired respect and respectability in the eyes of the rest of the community, which once honored moral rectitude.

A more straightforward example is that of the schools, now in deplorable condition. Competition between them for students and for public funds would be apt to improve them significantly. Competition might also be created through privatization of many public services,[30] but a more fundamental form of competition is consequent upon the mobility of families and businesses. Whenever possible, they will move to localities where they find life more attractive. Hence they tend to exert an upward pressure on standards: municipalities must work to attract and retain good citizens and enterprising companies if for no other reason than to safeguard their tax base. Local jurisdictions, in effect, are in competition with each other. In each of them, schools, business conditions, law enforcement, public services, and the system of taxation must be improved if the locale is to prosper. The limits of government intrusion will also be keenly watched. If, on the other hand, a supervening state apparatus has seen to it that all localities are the same, then pressure on standards reverts to the retrograde. If competition is essential, we must *resist* centralization and uniformity. We must let local institutions flourish according to their lights.

Competition encourages independence and vigor in local institutions, and we might anticipate that the imperative for high moral requirements would be resuscitated by them. Personal freedom would tend less to descend into self-indulgence and irresponsibility. Our fundamental rights would not be excuses for the pursuit of hedonism but would be sources of energetic pursuit of excellence in a society that demands it, in effect, and rewards it. Thus we might hope, at any rate. It has happened before.

Modern publicity and mobility give additional efficacy to the constructive features of competition. It is typically difficult, of course, for a family or business to move, and it is often done with reluctance and even pain. Even those who lack mobility, however, are benefited by those who can relocate with relative ease, for the politicians are on warning that their works are under surveillance where it matters. The effectiveness is not first of all in the voting booth, where the citizen is often bamboozled, but among those who vote with their feet: when a man contends with his own vital responsibilities—his work, his home, his family attachments—he is prompted to be as rational and constructive as possible, and he is less susceptible to demagoguery, emotionalism, and misinformation. But when, by contrast, he is confronted with the extravagant blandishments that fall within political persuasion, if he pays attention at all, he does well not to become a blithering idiot.

Mobility is far from being an unmixed blessing, nevertheless. It is one of the conspicuous phenomena of modern life that the willingness to pull up stakes disrupts and dismembers traditional forms of association. Individuals move away from home to improve their financial condition. They also migrate to the big city in order to enjoy a way of life where they will not be under the surveillance of moral tutors and familiar faces. Mobility, then, is decidedly ambiguous. It disrupts families and communities. I have no idea what the prospects are for the resurrection of autonomous community life in some form. It is under siege by the state; it is seduced by the bright lights of the city; and it might even be the victim of its own material success. One cannot be optimistic. The dismemberment of the community, on the other hand, is resisted by the instinct to move with the herd, which is responsible for both blessings and curses.

This brings me to a discussion of morality according to custom, which might flourish in autonomous civil society. The topic is both subtle and difficult.

NOTES

1. Plato, *The Republic*, 2d ed., trans. Allan Bloom (New York: Basic Books, 1991), pp. 239–40.

2. Ibid., p. 236.

3. Robert Bork, *Slouching Towards Gommorah* (New York: HarperCollins, 1996).

4. Charles Reich, *The Greening of America* (New York: Random House, 1970).

5. Friedrich Nietzsche, *Beyond Good and Evil*, trans. with commentary Walter Kaufmann (New York: Vintage Books, 1989), pp. 100–101.

6. A *daimon* is a spiritual agent, somewhere between man and the gods. (The "voice" that spoke to the mind of Socrates, and which he unfailingly heeded, he called his *daimonion*.) The prefix *eu* means "well." Does it then obscure the meaning of *eudaimonia* to translate it "well souled," or might not that catch the basic import of the word? Might not the Greeks have taken it as redundant to say that to be well souled

is to be in a state of surpassing benefit? To their minds, *of course* it is a surpassing benefit, so there is an identity of "well-souled" and "happy"—so much so that in their dictionary they are not listed as two separate words, nor in their philosophy are they two separate ideas. *We* say, vaguely, "happy"; the Greek has only to say "well souled."

7. Aristotle, *Nicomachean Ethics*, trans. intro., and notes, Martin Ostwald (Indianapolis and New York: The Bobbs-Merrill Company, Inc., 1962), p. 44 (1107a). Aristotle's account of excellence in deliberation is neither complete nor altogether clear. With some indeterminate promptings from Aristotle himself, deliberation is widely interpreted to incorporate deductive reasoning. I believe that is an untenable reading. As I decipher it, deliberation is not essentially different from what I have called moral appraisal, but with these differences: deliberation presupposes an end, where the end is the virtuous action appropriate to the conditions. The man of practical wisdom will do the virtuous deed, but he requires deliberation to determine what it is. Inasmuch as he is already bent on virtue, excellence in deliberation also presupposes the presence of moral virtue. My notion of appraisal allows for it to be done well or ill; it is still appraisal, and the end might be highly indeterminate or provisional.

8. Ibid., p. 117 (1131a).

9. Ibid., p. 82 (1119b).

10. Ibid., p. 43 (1106b).

11. If we were generous in our hermeneutics, any of these supplements might be incorporated into Aristotle's original list, but it would be childish to insist that he must have thought of everything.

12. James B. Stockdale, *A Vietnam Experience: Ten Years of Reflection* (Stanford, CA: Hoover Institution Press, Stanford University, 1984).

13. Moralists, Aristotle included, often make a distinction between higher and lower pleasures. Hume tried to capture this distinction by his reference to "the calmer passions." Mill struggled with it by differentiating *happiness* and *content*, where Socrates is happy but not necessarily content.

14. Stockdale, *A Vietnam Experience*, pp. 126–28. In addition to being a military man, Stockdale is philosophic and educated. In a manner that would delight Plato, he insists that the best military men *must* be educated and philosophic, and so must anyone of complete virtue. His reflections are highly instructive to those who love wisdom and good character—and who are concerned about their disappearance in contemporary life.

15. Perhaps the intrinsic link between virtue and happiness did not exist for Socrates himself. In *The Apology*, he affirms the equation of virtue and happiness, and then, in effect, denies it. In giving several reasons why he is fearless of death, Socrates entertains the possibility that death might be simple annihilation, likened to a perfectly dreamless sleep. "Now if you suppose that there is no consciousness, but a sleep like the sleep of him who is undisturbed even by dreams, death will be an unspeakable gain. For if a person were to select the night in which his sleep was undisturbed even by dreams, and were to compare with this the other days and nights of his life, and then were to tell us how many days and nights he had passed in the course of his life better and more pleasantly than this one, I think any man, I will not say a private man, but even the great king will not find many such days or nights, when compared with the others. Now if death be of such a nature, I say that to die is gain; for eter-

nity is then only a single night" (40d–41a, Jowett translation). Socrates has said that few if any of his days were as good as a dreamless sleep! This is from the man who is consummately virtuous, but can it be from a man who is happy? This is one of the most troublesome passages in world literature, and I have never found a scholar who can explain it away.

16. I have no mind to argue the details of the variations that a liberal regime might take, nor will I take up the wholesale denunciations. According to Marx and his followers, the liberal regime is the greatest disaster in human history. Though Marx was wrong, it is and always will be important to consider his arguments. Every generation should be educated to know the virtues of a free society, but it should also know what can be said against it, and it should be able to assess the legitimacy of opposing views.

17. Democratic government, to be clear about the matter, is not self-rule after all, but, in principle, *representative* or—better—*responsible* government. Whether politicians are in fact responsible is another question.

18. It did not escape the genius of Tocqueville, who recognized the vital role of private associations in democratic culture.

19. I am not supposing that moral tutelage is omnipotent. Individuals vary in their moral capacities. But the endeavors of moral learning are not impotent either. As Aristotle put it, we require education in order to make the potential actual. It doesn't happen automatically, and many corruptions lie along the way.

20. The now-classic source for these analyses is Charles Murray, *Losing Ground: American Social Policy, 1950–1980* (New York: Basic Books, 1984).

21. Francis Fukuyama, *The Great Disruption* (New York: The Free Press, 1999).

22. Ibid., p. 5.

23. Ibid., p. 23.

24. See esp. *The Great Disruption*, chap. 5. Fukuyama is not inclined, nevertheless, to bemoan these revolutions or to take a reactionary view of them. The remedy for our disruptions lies, he says, simply in the instinctive human capacity to form stable communities; but he has nothing specific to add to this general nostrum.

25. James Q. Wilson, "Cultural Meltdown," *The Public Interest*, no. 137 (fall 1999), pp. 99–104.

26. See esp. chap. 4 of *The Marriage Problem*. Wilson's argument is intriguing and forceful. Surely, as Wilson says, the notion of individual rights presents a powerful intellectual rationale to those who would repudiate all limits, and this repudiation has occurred most conspicuously in cultures where individual rights are most prominent.

27. Robert Weissberg, *The Politics of Empowerment* (Westport, CT, and London: Praeger, 1999).

28. Robert Weissberg, "The Vagaries of Empowerment," *Social Science and Modern Society* 37, no. 2 (January/February 2000), p. 16. (The first and second quotations are not inconsistent with each other. The rare exception occurs in nonacademic work, such as the trenchant studies of the decay of civil society in Peter L. Berger and Richard John Neuhaus, *To Empower People: From State to Civil Society*, 2d ed., ed. Michael Novak [Washington, DC: AEI Press, 1996].)

29. Weissberg's theme is supported by the splendid analyses of Myron Magnet

in *The Dream and the Nightmare: The Sixties' Legacy to the Underclass* (San Francisco: Encounter Books, 2000). The dream is the granting of full civil rights to blacks. The nightmare is the poisoning of their emancipation by communicating to them (and others) disdain for such values as delayed gratification, education, hard work, and personal responsibility.

30. I am not one of those who believes in the automatic effectiveness of private enterprise, which is often corrupt and incompetent, but it is much better than the state, and it possesses self-corrective tendencies that are lacking when government holds a monopoly on the provision of services.

| 8 |

Custom and Morality

T he will to belong is so great that philosophers have twisted every fact of life to assure themselves that we are at home in the very universe itself. The longing has its origins in modest, but still fateful, conditions. It is beyond serious question that human beings, like most other mammals, have an innate desire to belong to the pack, to bond with its members. It is a necessary condition of survival. The phenomenon is everywhere in evidence, and students of human nature have never failed to notice its prevalence and strength. In addition to the benefits of the common defense, the sense of belonging, solidarity, and commonality is irreplaceable, and to be excluded is torture. The morale and vitality of the family, the tribe, the team, the fraternal association, and the regiment depend upon this sort of cohesion.

Many of our virtues are largely owing to this instinct, loyalty to the pack, but so are both xenophobia and the demand for unthinking conformity. To think of human behavior in the context of the herd animal is offensive to many, but wisdom requires that we be candid about this fundamental instinct. It is by no means the only innate drive in our repertoire. Counterpoised to it, as one case in point, is the will to autonomy, independence—the will to be truly your own man, and this yearning too is funded with both threat and promise.

Whether formally or informally, the herd is organized in a hierarchy—normally but not invariably with the dominant male at the peak; sometimes the lead is shared by additional individuals. Groups without a hierarchy do not endure well: there is confusion and quarrel, and effective leadership is lacking. We *desire* a leader, and a durable solidarity requires such a person, around whom the others rally. Good leadership, just the same, does not mean that those who are led will be passive hulks; the best leaders encourage the development of talent and virtue among their people.

Those in lower echelons of the order might struggle, by various means, to replace the leader, and eventually one of the aspirants is successful. In general, this is a salutary process, for it tends to result in a high quality of direction for the group. Most of those in subordinate positions of the hierarchy, however, prefer to keep that status. They do not have the strength to risk a challenge to the alpha male, and they enjoy the security of being in an unambiguously established position in the whole. When the leader overtly recognizes and rewards their loyalty, they are deeply gratified. An individual is likely to belong to more than one intimately bonded community. He might be a member of a kinship group, an athletic team, and a neighborhood gang all at once. These allegiances are apt to conflict with one another, more or less, and they are apt to change over time. The youngster yearns to be free of the leading strings of parents and joins a circle of friends—his peer group—where he conforms with a passion to *their* mores.

Not every aggregate of persons is a pack, and we should not want the situation to be otherwise. The desire for a leader, for example, can be hazardous. It is effectively exploited by the Hitlers of the world. We have learned to select our political leaders in other ways and to place limits on their powers. In our sanity, we hope that political order would not be herd-like, but it still tends to be that way. Our sanity, nevertheless, does not negate the instinct, which has many invaluable functions. It is also important to remember that members of a human pack have moral dispositions and are susceptible to suasion by moral considerations, which might even lead them to diverge from the prevailing mentality.

The life of a people is organized in customs. Customs are adaptations—great and small, innumerable and various, saturating common life. They have arisen and evolved in the struggle for survival, prosperity, and happiness. The love of customs owes much to their success as adaptations, but such affection also goes deeper. It owes much to the herd instinct. The customs one loves are those of his particular herd. To participate in a customary way of life satisfies the need to belong, and therein lies much of the strength and attractiveness of such a life. Individuals naturally bond with the group into which they are born. They are taught the norms, traditions, arts, and religion of a specific community—in brief, its customs. It begins with family, kin, friends, and neighbors. Here are bonds of love, dependence, loyalty, and authority. All of these bonds are *personal*, and hence they are particularly affective. Proudly and solicitously, specific individuals initiate us into a way of life, with its own unique and treasured qualities. Every hour of every day we live in and through the customary. Here we learn to be human, to use the cliché. It is intimate, familiar, and comfortable. One is at home. The very substance of one's life, it seems, is made up of customs.

Some grasp of the nature of customary life is essential both for the purpose of appreciating its qualitative value and for understanding the nature and import of morality according to custom. Ignore for the moment the fanaticism, stupidities, cruelties, and tyrannies that distinguish many customs, and ignore the fact that custom tends to be intolerant of individuality that threatens the sanctity of the prevailing order. Think, rather, of custom as a natural and almost universal way of life, regardless of its failures and savageries. The idealized portrait will display what is admirable about custom and the source of affection for it. Then we will be able to get some sense of its functions in the moral life.

I mean by customary life not only that of ancient or primitive tribes but any society with a living history and thriving traditions, with its own character. Such a tradition, moreover, functions as *guide* and *authority* in the conduct of life. Tradition is a revered, distinctive, and persistent form of life. It functions as guide and authority simply because those who are responsible for the preservation of custom must initiate each generation into what it means to be a part of that tradition: What are the practices, norms, obligations, and ideals that give it definition and life? What must one do to be a member? What is the behavior proper to a Marine? To an American? A Christian? A member of a particular school or family? These are the considerations that appeal to fledgling members of such associations or to those who would belong. The norms and ideals embodied in a tradition are those that have emerged and endured in the history of a group, an institution, a people. Acceptance of them is a condition of full membership in a community. Precedent is honored and authoritative.

The affection for custom has a temporal dimension. The culture is a heritage, the gift of our ancestors: heroes and wise men—and gods, too. The lands and seas that have sustained us are part of the heritage. Our mythology and laws are recorded in ancient and sacred documents. Our forebears labored, sacrificed, and died that we might prosper. We honor them; we are beholden to them, and we dedicate ourselves to preserving and expanding their legacy. Such a heritage is a revered authority; it stays our wayward impulses. To be accepted into such a tradition and to be a part of it is a holy experience. One is part of an enduring whole. This is the way in which the human race has been educated. We are beings who are very well suited to living according to custom.

A variety of associations can be customary in the requisite sense: not just an entire civilization but also an extended family, a guild, a church, a village, a fraternal organization, a school, a university, a local business. Most of the autonomous groups in civil society have been customary in this sense. The opposite of a customary society is a bureaucracy, which is governed entirely by principles of administrative efficiency and impersonality. Likewise antagonistic to custom are those theoretical utopias and moralities that pretend to be entirely rational: constructed, presumably, out of the whole cloth of impartial and autonomous reason.

Its peculiar customs define a given civilization in distinction from another, and its inhabitants learn it is *their* community, in contrast to others. Concomitantly, there is a powerful in-group/out-group dichotomy. Like it or not, communities that don't observe it will dissolve into the confines of those that do. Our clannish exclusivity, in fact, is a large part of our communal good. This is *our* culture and heritage—something distinctive and distinguishable, something uniquely the possession of our group, which we must defend against others. It has a unity and individuality that are not held in common with others. Distinctive customary life helps to establish and preserve social solidarity. In large part, the members of a group are bonded to each other in virtue of protecting and contributing to a shared way of life.

Not custom per se, but *specific* customs arouse attachment, loyalty, and a willingness to sacrifice. The customs that constitute a particular culture are celebrated by its members, and observance of them is rewarded. The culture is an object of piety. There is a process of initiation to be accepted as a full member, and the young ardently wish to pass the tests and to belong without reserve, to bask in the warmth of established status. In these circumstances, the authority of the customs is not in question. The problem is to be accepted by that authority and to become in unity with the whole. The unity, to be sure, is always imperfect. It is a ceaseless task of the leaders to encourage conformity to law, to contain antisocial impulses, and to punish lawlessness.

Customary groups can be responsive to change, and they do change. They undergo revision in consequence of serious internal disturbance or because of major disruptions in their environment: a way of life is somehow in crisis. Response to the threat is *adaptive* and *evolutionary*; there is a great will that the deeply accustomed way of life be preserved as much as possible. Customs are revered as mother and father; we have piety to them. Change, then, is not radical departure nor based upon a systematic and "rational" blueprint for a new order. Customary life is inherently conservative. Established orders are precious just in being *established*; in a precarious and threatening world, we revere the trustworthy and the enduring. More than this, customs are conditions of human identity, attachment, and solidarity. The family does not lightly repudiate mother and father.

The customs of a people are also conservative because they are manifestations of nature, as it has been distilled within the conditions of their particular tradition. In no small part, the wisdom of a people is a consequence of their respect for the stubbornly persistent traits of reality. Their patterns of conduct are a synthesis of the experience accumulated across generations and the demands of human nature adapting to local circumstances. Universal dispositions are fulfilled in the forms of custom. At the begining of this section I reviewed a few of the main features of the herd and the behavior of its members. Expressed through customs of great variety, these properties of communal life are found in all societies governed by tradition. The norms, rituals, and practices of a customary culture are unmarked by the rational, in the sense noticed above, suggesting that custom is in large part a revelation of nature.

I am not endorsing the view that custom creates our nature, forms our very soul. The rapidly accumulating evidence belies such a position. The truth, evidently, is that we are of such a nature that we are instinctively attached to the tribe and to the features that constitute its identity. Variations from one culture to the next do not bespeak fundamental differences in human nature. They speak of the ways in which human nature has adapted to a specific environment. Accordingly, though cultures are distinctive, they are not irreducibly singular, and we find that people behave in much the same ways across variations in culture. One of the common features of behavior from culture to culture is the attachment to the local group, its own authority, institutions, arts, and rituals. It is not tribe per se to which I am attached, but *this* tribe, which has nurtured me in its ways and protected me and accepts me on condition that I in turn accept its demands upon me. Our good must be concrete and specific, and for us humans it is the good of local custom and attachments. It is our natural way of life.

The modern cosmopolitan state is not a unitary customary regime. There are many subcultures, each with its own traditions, and even these tend to be fragmented. Many in a resident population are mobile and transient; families disperse; cultures mix; and their respective identities become less discernible. Alienation, loneliness, and normlessness are common. There is still the yearning to belong to identifiable communities, each with its own unity, its distinctive membership, and its own ceremonies and memory. We find it highly congenial to participate in institutions that are bearers of long tradition, with their own lore and customs, and with some hope of persistence in the flux of change. Such customary orders give us an identity and a sense of belonging, and in their endurance through the generations they give our efforts and loyalty a lasting significance. Being a part of them is an end in itself; they are institutions that one could love. Universities, for example, have been much of that nature—until recently. Trendiness, bureaucracy, and government regulation are killers of custom and tradition. Their apologists have an agenda of their own.[1]

When the associations of civil society are durable and somehow retain their autonomy, each might sustain and celebrate its native ethos and morale.

Local community, with its own intrinsic ways, might be something that one could love; it can be an object of solicitude and devotion. Did anyone ever have a sense of belonging in an association that is merely useful as an instrument of personal advancement or that is defined by abstract efficiency and technological rationality—possessing all the ambience of a Soviet tractor factory?[2]

The mind is comfortable and secure working within an established and venerated order. Radical reformers, on the other hand, have no respect for custom. In fact, they detest it. It is not that they protest this custom or that; they protest its very existence, which stands obstinately in their way—in the way of a truly new and rational social system. Accordingly, their program includes the eradication of the prevailing order. Perhaps some customs will, incidentally, survive, but only because they meet the "rational" test. Hence we have the distinction between a putatively rational philosophy and the hodgepodge of traditions. The latter seem ludicrously inadequate.

What is meant by a rational system? The familiar historical prototypes have been diverse. Perhaps there is a supreme and absolute good known to reason, or perhaps there is a single theoretically established principle from which all other norms are derived. In either case, there is an intuitive or self-evident certainty—some form of a priori knowledge. Consequently the principles are universal and rationally incontrovertible. They are neither contextual nor experimental; they transcend custom and history. Or divine law might be rationally discerned, or knowledge of human nature might produce the desired deductive progression. A recent strategy is to systematize our presumed moral intuitions in a manner to yield a "moral geometry." In all these cases, the system is produced by a philosopher, of all people, who announces his rational doctrine to a less-than-expectant world.

The "rationality" of these systems is dubious. Not only are there distinctly different and mutually incompatible modes of arriving at them, but their results are starkly different in content. Each and every mode, I would argue, is essentially flawed; there is not a correct one to be distinguished from the rest—though each author intransigently believes he has done just that.

Maybe our rational system could be constructed in some other way, as some philosophers have in fact attempted. Why not provide a definition of principle in terms of whatever it would be that a truly rational individual would choose? Then we set about to define that individual. Are we speaking of one who would choose to maximize utility over the long run? Do we have in mind the man who would always choose safety first behind the veil of ignorance? Is our man one who can learn one form of behavior as easily as another: one who can be sensitive, caring, perfectly impartial, gender neutral, and egalitarian to the core? Obviously, definitions of "rational" are already morally biased, each in its own way, but even if we produced the miracle of an inherently uncontroversial definition, why in the name of heaven should this chap constitute the norm for creatures with no discernible resemblance to him? Real people are notoriously driven by a medley of firm and intense passions having little to do with rationality in the postulated sense: love of family, tribe, and traditional identity. There is also love of power and distinction, as these would be fulfilled in the customs of one's own world, and there is hatred of anyone or anything that threatens their goods. Abstractly rational plans do not excite real people, for whom ties of nature, sentiment, piety, custom, and loyalty give meaning to life. Indeed, as I will propose, just these ties are essential for moral authority and learning.

Although beings of nature and history do not readily fall into place with recondite thinking, theorists are tireless in telling these creatures what it is rational for them to do, and then they express amazement that some fellow is obstinately incapable of it and rebels against it. Some saucy philosopher might teach that it is "irrational" to be attached to local custom, but it is likewise "irrational" to be attached to mother regardless of what her other distinguishing characteristics might be. Instinct has no regard for rationality of that sort. It is truly rational, after all, to deal with the realities of human existence rather than to hypothesize scenarios more congenial to the mind of a haughty intellectual.

For the sake of clarity, contrast two stark models of rationality. The model I have been presupposing is familiar and widely accepted in common practice, but the oversimplified version might seem repugnant. Rationality is conceived as functioning well with our actual resources and limitations, both in regard to the world and within the psyche. If both psyche and world are insistent in their nature, then rationality must respect that insistence. The competing model of rationality, beloved of utopians, takes little or nothing as insistent, and declares that what is reasonable is the remaking of human nature and the world in a manner to achieve some grand and glorious result. Hence it is "reasonable" to establish a perfectly cooperative society, let us say, egalitarian in all respects, and perhaps even with unlimited freedom. To achieve such a marvel, to be sure, we must rid the population of the effects of benighted forms of socialization, and then in a collective crusade we shall transform the world. Our parochial desires will vanish and will be supplanted with something different in kind: untainted and impartial benevolence. Thus would we become perfectly rational. Unlimited freedom could not then be noxious, for no one would desire anything that could be injurious to another.

In contrast, rationality might be at once more modest *and more productive*. Think of it as trying to attain goods and to avoid evils where the goods and evils are for the most part given by the typical range of our natural inclinations, as these are embodied in custom. Now, an individual might try any form of force or fraud to attain his coveted ends, but these strategies are unmistakably destructive of social life. Rather than undertake a redefinition of human nature and custom, we promulgate severe warnings against using destructive strategies and impose effective penalties for their actual use. There must also be rewards for the observance of nourishing and constructive norms. Lucidly aware of these contingencies, we are much less apt to engage in bad behavior and more apt to abide by the rules. To a significant degree, our antisocial tendencies are muted and weakened in the process, while our natural tendencies to accept constructive participation are fortified and invigorated. That is, there is learning in the soul in consequence of the requirements of conduct, but the requirements must be appropriate to our nature. Then the enforcement of laws that establish punishment and reward for typical behavior becomes a principal agency of teaching. Thus are we made more rational.

For the stark version of rationality, there are urgent goods and evils—both for ourselves and others—immediately dependent upon the fulfillment of normal responsibilities, and our cognizance of them, once again, concentrates the mind wonderfully. The contingencies of personal responsibility make us more rational. Such encouragements of practical intelligence do not presuppose a systematic redesign of human nature but a sharp recognition of its tendencies. Many natural inclinations are ordered, cultivated, and praised, and their fulfillment is usually gratifying. Thus we encourage moral steadfastness and justice, courage, integrity, service to family and associates, preeminence in achievement. Capitalism and patriotism tend to exhibit this kind of rationality, where our typical impulses are turned to good account, while socialism is an example of the other kind.

This has been the stark model. It should by no means be taken as a denial that discourse is sometimes persuasive, that moderation of the passions is possible, or that basic human drives cannot be developed into virtues. *But they are virtues of our peculiar nature;* they are not fashioned of sentimental reveries. It is wise to acknowledge that human beings act in certain characteristic ways; they act out their inner needs, loves, and ambitions; and rationality consists in recognizing them, discouraging their shortsighted and destructive tendencies, and supporting those qualities that are conducive to benefit. Human behavior is not rational in the utopian fashion. Men do what their nature demands, but the priorities and expressions of these demands are normally adjusted when the world is inhospitable to some and rewarding of others, and the manner of their execution is varied in response to perceived means and impediments. At the same time, the inner promptings of a man are often of a sort to make him a moral and constructive citizen, and sometimes they lead him to great and noble achievements, expressing the finest potentialities of the species. A form of morality according to custom will prove to be the best way to realize these precious results.

The incoherence of rational theory and common reality has been remarked in a number of forms by some shrewd observers, such as Hume, Nietzsche, Santayana, and Dewey. Each of them points out that these putatively pristine principles do not have a virgin birth. They are in fact derivative of customary experience. A thinker has, in effect, selected what he regards as paramount in the moral life and has proceded to absolutize it, concealing the imposture with spurious credentials.

When the self-deceiving deception is exposed, is there anything left? The absolutistic philosopher will say there is nothing, and so will the antifoundationalist, who is persuaded by the absolutist that in the absence of invariant foundations there is only relativism. Dewey's pragmatism, however, has been widely thought to be adequate to fill the void. I will not review the reservations about Dewey that I stated in chapter 3, nor will I recapitulate my critique of relativism. (My defense of virtue in the preceding chapter will withstand any relativism, yet it is neither an abstract rational system nor a guarantee that all moral perplexity and disagreement will vanish—even among the virtuous.) Still, it is worth referring to Dewey once more, for there are features of his pragmatism that are in fact conspicuous in the philosophy of custom. Dewey himself, however, is inflexible and unforgiving in his repudiation of custom. He always speaks of it as rigid, dogmatic, ignorant, and tyrannical. It must be replaced with intelligence.

He was seriously mistaken. There are, to be sure, customs and customary societies that answer to his description, but there is no necessity for this in the very nature of custom, and there are many contrary examples. Many traditional groupings have been able to retain their identity only because they have been able to adapt and evolve. Private associations detest revolution, but they might improve and strengthen themselves through revision. It will be helpful to distinguish *customary morality* from *morality according to custom*, where the former term denotes the intransigently rigid form.

Morality according to custom can be highly pragmatic, but it is a wiser pragmatism than Dewey's. Inasmuch as he rejects the idea of innate predispositions in human nature, he cannot acknowledge that nature is potent in custom; he must dismiss any notion of a native affection for the customary; and he must recoil at the authority of tradition. He is one of those who believe that education is virtually omnipotent; so custom must crumble before it.

The most desirable moral condition in Dewey's terms is democracy as a way of life: social intelligence. Individuals who have acquired some semblance of the democratic virtues will collectively address their shared problematic situations, thereupon to construct their shared good through cooperative action. Democratic man, as Dewey conceives him, is flexible, open-minded, experimental, collaborative, and egalitarian, and there is nothing clannish about him. Most notably, he is not bound by precedent: attachment to tradition is the incubus that denies entry to a free and progressive future. The democratic man habitually looks *forward*, ever willing to change and innovate, even to the point of continuing revolution. Admittedly, Dewey acknowledges, the requisite virtues are not widely in evidence, but through appropriate education in home, school, and voluntary associations, we can learn consultative intelligence and its attendant habits.

Education is not omnipotent, however. It cannot create democratic man, and it cannot eliminate our selfish, partisan, and destructive propensities. Rather than reinvent human nature, it must develop the antecedent natural aptitudes of human beings. The maturation of such powers is typically given morale and direction by prevailing traditions, but it will often have to give way to simple authority and force to contend with the antisocial aggressions characteristic of the species.

Although democratic deliberation and conduct in the manner proposed by Dewey are possible in some environments and for limited purposes, they cannot be the norm throughout the moral world, not least of all because they make unrealistic demands on our nature. We humans are very protective of our goods and willing to struggle for them, and we are typically ambitious for more. We recognize these traits in each other, so we are justly wary of the designs that others might have on our possessions. We would be foolish, accordingly, to assume that we might trust them wholly to the outcome of social intelligence. Our dearest goods, surely, we would not put in such jeopardy. Those, moreover, who would practice democracy as a way of life are vulnerable to exploitation by others who merely pretend to be observant. Those who have no such pretense, but who are openly devoted to the pursuit of their own advantage, will commonly have contempt for negotiation, and they will judge that the will to be accommodating is indicative of fear and weakness—and that judgment is often correct.

In addition to his failure to take sufficient cognizance of our abiding susceptibilities to weakness and vice, Dewey is unaware of the natural affection for habitual and enduring modes of life, and he is insensitive to the great educational potency of tradition. He did not realize that the life of custom is an inherent good, so he was likewise unaware of our native conservatism—of our bias in favor of the forms of life that are constitutive of our culture. A customary society shares its own distinctive objects of identity and piety, composed in a manner unique to itself. Inherited objects of solidarity, security, attachment, admiration, and ambition give real substance to life. Such an order cannot be manipulated this way and that on a daily basis without losing its very soul, and the individual who "rationally" casts aside familiar customs will find that the body of his life has actually withered. An entire nation can be eviscerated in this way.[3]

In brief, he was unaware of the *authority* of custom. *Custom is an invalu-*

able force both in moralizing the young and sustaining the morale of adults. By its nature, making the most of native propensities, it is uniquely capable of limiting the destructive impulses of its participants and enlisting their enthusiasm in noble ventures. It will not be fully successful, by any means, but it brings to bear on our unruly tendencies deep loyalties to tribe, tradition, and hallowed practice, and the tribe is not reticent to make its requirements known. This very conservatism is exploited in restraining our anarchic proclivities. Dewey has little to offer against the same threats: faith in democracy and assurances that cooperative intelligence will emancipate us from the failures and oppressions of the day and transport us to qualitatively superior experiences.

Morality according to custom, as I advocate it, would unite the authority of custom with elements of Dewey's contextualism, but it would not be dependent upon his utopian thinking about human nature and democracy as a way of life. The union of these features—custom and contextualism—is far less uncomfortable than one might think at first glance, and it might in fact be an ideal marriage. The matter of *authority* addresses the means by which individuals acquire moral character and norms, and the ways in which standards of conduct are taught and enforced. *Contextualism*, as I will explain, pertains to the assumptions in terms of which moral assessment and deliberation are carried on, and here pragmatic moral theory has much to teach.

Moral values are adaptations—particularly important ones. They are to be understood and criticized as such, neither as absolutes nor as arbitrary conventions. They might exist in various combinations, so moral appraisal necessarily requires analysis of how these varying adaptations are adaptable to each other. Ideas for adjustment and innovation might come from several quarters, and some of these proposals might be brilliant, educated, and informed with virtue, but they must be appraised in reference to exigent realities, and they must be subject to test and revision. According to this sort of analysis, moral standards and practices arise from the common experience of actual communities, not from the brow of Zeus. They are appraised from the standpoint of their functions in those communities. A particular practice or precept that is evaluated is considered not from the empyrean of abstract reason but in relation to other values that inform the life of the group.

For illustration, consider the development of the institution of human rights. There are those, sure enough, who believe that there is some sort of supreme principle in terms of which all legitimate rights are defined and justified, but let's not be overawed by such claims. The rights in our Bill of Rights, for example, emerged from centuries of political experience, principally in England, and these rights were incorporated piecemeal into British common law. If we examine each of them, we see that there is not a single and invariant principle behind each case; the moral considerations are not the same. Indeed, the original framers included no such bill, self-evident or not, but added it to appease the antifederalists and to appeal to wavering and reluctant states. Rights, that is, are introduced as a means of contending with living political problems. The introduction might be wise, and the outcome might be celebrated. Our experience—rather than a self-evident principle—will determine whether the institution of one right or another contributes to the welfare and vitality of the community.

The resultant bill is something of a melange, containing some very important rights and others that are less so; some that are listed separately might logically have been subsumed under others. Article 1 is most fundamental in defining a free society, providing for freedom of religion, of speech and press, and "the right of the people peaceably to assemble." Freedom of religion originated in our heritage, however, not to define a free society but to limit religious intolerance so great that it led to persecution and war. When state-mandated religion, moreover, is both intensely enforced and intensely resisted, civil discord and conflict are a certainty. It makes very good sense, accordingly, to call religious practices a right, that is, a protected form of activity. They achieved that status when social experience made it clear that such an arrangement was necessary. You could say that the defense of religious freedom is a utilitarian argument, but, actually, it has moral weight primarily because we reject needless and undeserved persecution and killing, even if only a minority of persons are thereby rescued and a would-be persecuting majority are consequently angered. The will to persecute in this manner is not morally admirable (and we found, too, that the anger did not in fact persist). Still, there are strong utilitarian considerations that are also pertinent to evaluating several of the clauses of the first Amendment, for they tend to be supportive of the general welfare.

The question of rights in various phases of legal proceedings receives attention in more of the articles of the Bill of Rights than any other issue. We are entitled to the due processes of law. This entitlement was insisted upon by individuals who had bitter experience of arbitrary authority and were deprived of the impartial rule of law, especially the laws that would guarantee their rights as English subjects. The principal rationale behind such a right could be construed as a matter of justice, rather than utility. We have an abhorrence of punishing the innocent or imposing on them needless rigors in legal proceedings. They don't deserve such treatment, and we rebel when subordinated to law and authority from which others are exempt.

What of the protection against self-incrimination? You could make an argument that it is counterutilitarian, for it stands in the way of determining who is guilty and sending him off where he can't hurt anybody. You could also argue that it is not defensible on grounds of justice: if the accused is innocent, there is no harm to himself in testifying, and if he is guilty, he deserves the harm. Nevertheless, the privilege against self-incrimination is thought to be a safeguard of the citizenship of free people. There is something inconclusive about testimony that a person is required to submit against himself, and there is also something demeaning about it. Confession, if it does occur, must be uncoerced and freely given; otherwise it is suspect; and to withhold from an individual the very possibility of declining to testify against himself can be taken as a negation of the dignity of citizenship.[4] On no account, according to these assumptions, can one who refuses to testify be judged guilty just because of his refusal. He might be standing up for the very principle that a citizen cannot be forced to incriminate himself. What kind of moral argument is this? Insofar as a right is at issue, could we say it is predicated on the dignity of the individual? As a matter of general moral priority, we wish to accord a high level of respect to a human life. This seems to be a rationale distinguishable from both justice and utility.

To take up a question unrecognized in the Constitution, what is the rationale for the right to abort a fetus? A woman's right to control her own body is sometimes invoked. As such, this is hardly a compelling argument, for there are many ways in which we deny people the right to do as they wish with their own body, such as using it to kill someone, but the point is that we see yet another form of moral justification for rights. It seems to assert that it is nobody else's business what a woman does with her body, and sometimes it isn't. John Stuart Mill had made this sort of principle conspicuous in *On Liberty*, where he declares that in self-regarding actions, the freedom of the individual "is, of right, absolute."

It is also commonly accepted that when one individual swears an oath to another, the other has a right to its performance. Being true to one's word is typically supportive of the general utility, but more fundamentally it establishes a division of moral responsibility: the obligation to keep faith means that the possessor of the right counts as more than one. He has a *right*. Both the obligation and the right are created by the promise. Some of the social contract theorists have (mistakenly) generalized the nature of this transaction to declare that promising is the basis of all rights.

The lesson in these many examples is that there is neither a unitary, wholly unambiguous, nor entirely unproblematic principle underlying all rights. Rather, the defense of rights invokes here utility, there justice; here promising, there the privacy or sanctity of the individual. As I have commented before, there are many features of the moral life that are important to us, and they are important for different reasons. There are irreducible types of moral consideration, and we use different combinations of them to defend various institutions.

There is not even a unitary definition of rights: all rights are not instances of a common essence. There are rights created by promising, one of the sacred bonds of social life. Our traditional enumerated rights, on the other hand, are mostly protections from intrusion, but the right to due process of law mandates that certain acts toward us be required of others. These varieties are not exhaustive. What all these cases do seem to have in common is that there is a *guarantee* of some state of affairs, something precious, something we want to preserve even at high cost, though the rationale for preserving different conditions is not identical from case to case. In any event, we have learned the worth of these guarantees through experience, not by pure reason.

The treasured conditions are not all of an identical nature, nor are they defended with identical moral considerations. In the actual history of a people, accordingly, these guarantees—these rights—are instituted to meet a variety of exigent conditions that arise in its common life. They are formulated and observed in a manner that would be compatible with the other esteemed values of the community, but perfect compatibility is impossible. All goods are not in harmony with one another, so difficult adjustments are made.

Like other conditions of social life, in brief, rights are adaptations—sometimes wise and priceless. It would not be inaccurate to call them *customs*, but that word is apt to be misunderstood, for we are apt to think of custom as invariably a mindless and automatic practice. Regardless of questions of diction, these pivotal modes of behavior function in a larger context of practice and aspiration in a problematic environment, and they must be assessed as such. A vital network of adaptations (or customs) requires mutual accommodations and searching appraisals of priority. Wisely discriminated rights are apt to be given very high priority. More precisely, in being regarded as a matter of high priority, a given form of practice is denominated a right (if not an obligation or a principle).

Similar circumstances are apt to arise in other societies, so it is unremarkable that similar responses are made to them. *For that reason*, it is intelligible to speak of universal rights and principles. Their universality is not a product of a priori reason. It is derivative of the common experience of the race. Universal law is a means of contending with universal conditions. Justice as proportionate equality, for example, is universal because the need for reciprocation of value for value is universal. Such practices as telling the truth, keeping promises, and refraining from gratuitous harm are likewise honored in any durable society—which is not to say that exceptions to them are always wrong. Where conditions are not of substantially the same sort, however, it is vain to speak of invariant law.

The discussion of rights has been intended to illustrate the contextualism of morality according to custom. A similar analysis might be made for any of our institutions and principles. The moral virtues too are vital adaptations, not the product of abstract speculation, and their proper analysis is likewise contextual. I will give further illustration momentarily by examining some of the claims of radical feminism.[5]

Contextualism is the form in which morality by custom closely resembles Dewey's pragmatism. Moral arrangements are introduced, elaborated, qualified, strengthened, and perhaps abandoned in order to satisfy the needs and demands that typically arise in a given community. Some of them attain a very high priority; we do not readily compromise or sacrifice them, so they are given special status as rights, obligations, or principles. But even these are not exceptionless or absolute, and they are integrated, more or less, with other goods of the community. Even with their high priority, they are not uniformly applicable within the same society. Different rights and freedoms are granted by different associations for different purposes under different conditions. I have urged the importance, for example, of distinguishing the responsibilities of the state from those of civil society. The state provides the conditions that protect freedom, but such groups as family, church, and school have distinctly different functions. When they take their prime duty to be the proliferation of freedoms, they endanger the moral order. Even freedom of speech is not a universal principle. It has massive value in reference to some institutions, but it may be properly limited in others. The military, for example, does not function well as a debating society, and any family has excellent reason to prohibit various sorts of talk or to censor the media within the home.

In addition to its contextual form of appraisal, morality according to custom is defined by its understanding of moral authority. Given the frailty and self-seeking typical of mankind, the question of authority must be given sustained and honest attention, and here is where I especially diverge from Dewey. Appropriate authority provides indispensable qualities to the moral order: there must be effective motive and sanction for conduct. There must be a pervasive willingness to observe the elementary requirements of social life. There must, in truth, be a morale that stimulates the teaching of virtue and that resists moral sloth and mediocrity. Contextualism alone does not provide these qualities. The mere fact that one engages in pragmatic moral analysis does not mean that he does it well and honestly, and his participation by no means guarantees that his *conduct* will improve—that he will become more responsible and virtuous.

To the heirs of the Age of Reason, just the same, the question of authority is embarrassing. There is something so distasteful about the whole business! But the sanity of life hangs by only a few strands. One of them that might keep life intact is authority. No doubt the longing for it has many sources, including our inclinations for selfish and destructive behavior. We are, moreover, bewildered, frightened, weak, and unsure of ourselves. Our survival as a species owes much to powerful leaders who surpass these deficits: men and women who are intelligent, strong, unambiguous, sure of themselves—*authoritative*, in a word. No wonder that it is so human to follow someone who will lead us through the ordeal. There is a vast lot of irresponsible and dangerous authority in the world, but a wise and good authority in the affairs of life is of inestimable value.

The customary initiation into law and authority has great hazards, to be sure. We can be confident they will give tremors to both the apostles of rationalism and the followers of Dewey, but these folk are insufficiently appreciative of both the moral force of tradition and our typical resistances to good conduct: hedonism, greed, penchant for violence, the will to dominate, irresponsibility, and the like. Given that human nature is so well endowed with antinomian and rebellious tendencies, and given that order is so difficult to maintain, such a status for authority is needful, if not always indispensable.

What means are there, after all, for establishing habits of moral conduct? Propaganda and mindless indoctrination are widely used. The method of threats, curses, and beatings is familiar, likewise with lies and misrepresentations. The most esoteric pretender to authority is abstract ethical theory, which claims to discover or determine the criteria in terms of which any moral bafflement may be dispelled, and it claims to appeal to reason. More presentable than any of these are the teachings of recognized authority: the church, the family, the corps, the elders of the tribe, the leaders of thriving private associations, the spokesmen for long-standing traditions. The traditions remain vital in the ongoing life of the group, and they are typically transmitted by personally engaged and trusted authorities. Distinctive centers of vital life have what abstract reason does not: *morale*. Moral teaching carries the force of treasured identities: A *Marine* does not abandon his buddies; a *Christian* does not abuse women; an *O'Shaugnessy* takes care of his family; a *Turk* keeps his word; an *Emory professor* takes his teaching seriously; a *Hill School man* does not lie or cheat; an *Iroquois chief* serves his people faithfully; *folks around here* treat others with fairness—and so on. The lapse of a Marine lets down the members of his unit, who were counting on him. Moral failure is a form of betrayal of those with whom one is intimately bonded. Loyalty to the group is an intense inducement to good conduct.

Notice that these examples are teachings of elementary moral practice, and we would be apt to find most of them in any culture. In fact, morality according to custom can require conduct that applies equally to persons outside the culture as well as within, while nonetheless appealing to a tradition characteristic of the home culture. ("People in this family treat everyone fairly," for example.) There is no reason to suppose that morality according to custom must be defined as conduct that is wholly idiosyncratic to a given society or that respects only the denizens of that society.

Custom is the source of the necessary authority. In morality by custom, moral learning and enforcement are not undertaken with the authority of abstract reason or that of creative intelligence, or of voting, nor by reliance on virtues that nature will not endorse. The authority is that of the customs of the people, honored in solidarity, taught and sustained by individuals vested with that authority. The lore, traditions, and the very fate of a community are brought to bear on conduct. The herd instinct is our ally, expressed and fulfilled in the expected forms of behavior. A powerful and fundamental trait of human nature is employed to resist our tendencies to self-indulgence and vice and to inspire dedicated conduct.

To be morally effective, an authority must be trusted and respected in his own milieu, to be sure. He is, and is perceived to be, responsible and unwavering in his duties. At best, he is regarded as the bearer of the revered legacies of a people, the keeper of cultural memory. He is the teacher of ancestral tradition and wisdom, by which an entire people, perhaps, are identified and steadied. The teachings of authoritative leaders have become lore—perhaps divine lore. Then, invested with deep and powerful emotions of loyalty, custom is vastly more authoritative than emancipated "reason," which is unhinged from human reality.

Who are these preceptors, the bearers and executives of the morale of the group? National leaders of various description, to be sure, but more typically they are those who are responsible for conducting the apprenticeships that routinely initiate the young into all phases of common life: parents above all, but any individual who is entrusted with the care and direction of the young in any of the phases of civic life. They would speak less in the accents of abstract justice than in terms of the rules, virtues, and ideals that preserve their common life in the face of persistent challenges to it. Just as ancient Greek youngsters absorbed the great teachings of Homer, other cultures treasure the lore of their own sacred books and moral sages.

Moral initiation is neither a cultural afterthought nor a matter of periodic sessions in a classroom. It is the continuous preparation for assuming the obligations of communal life; and the associations constituting that life share a measure of responsibility for carrying on this vital work. It includes an emphasis on the threats to a thriving community: a life girded with necessities that the customs of the people attend to, and it honors the goods that such a community attains. The elders must demand proper behavior from the young. The preservation of the group must continue, and breaches of proper conduct will not be tolerated. The young are apt to acquire a vivid sense that the entire culture is united in taking good conduct seriously. A chastening recognition!

Socialization is not the artsy-craftsy formation of a flower child. The wise educator will suppose that the moralization of youth is a serious and demanding project. He will know that it is difficult to sustain an entire culture, that there are many resistances to preserving a flourishing civilization. He will not suppose that moral transgressions are usually the consequence of a failure of *understanding*; he will not conclude that the culprit simply does not *know* what he is supposed to do. Instruction is not just a matter, then, of teaching right and wrong, with a good dose of explanation why right is right and wrong is wrong. Most moral failure is a consequence of simple neglect to do what we know we ought to do, or perhaps we willfully do what we know we should not. The child shatters the limits imposed on him by his parents, knowing that they are limits. The adolescent knows that he should not lie and cheat or indulge in arbitrary violence, but he lies and cheats and is violent. The youth defies established forms of decency, saying that he doesn't care about them. To be sure, he resorts heavily to rationalizations in behalf of these moments, but the need for rationalization presupposes that one is conscious of being morally out of order.

Teaching people basic rules of conduct is far from self-sufficient; they will dash such rules anyway. Neither will it be of great consequence to catalogue reasons for good conduct. The catalogue will be breezily cast aside. In short, mere reasoning or lecturing does not suffice to assure good behavior from recalcitrant and passionate flesh. In sober fact, the appeal to rationality without practical discipline is extremely injurious to emotional maturation. It engenders moral weakness and endless feelings of guilt. For creatures of rebelliousness and self-assertion, simple authority is also needed: "This is what you must do, whether you like it or not, and if you don't do it, you will answer to me." Don't be trapped in the sophisms of the truant; just insist that he behave well, and be sure that he pays a price for his lapses. Don't appeal to his understanding alone—as if he didn't know full well what he is supposed to do. Of course the child or the recruit must be taught the rules. That's essential. The rules are easy to understand, but just teaching them over and over again is futile and irresponsible. When necessary, just put your foot authoritatively down! Then you are more apt to attain compliance, and you will be taking the first step to help the initiate develop emotional order and good character.

I do not mean to suggest that moral education is nothing but a struggle with refractory nature. We should not forget other capacities of youth: pride, loyalty, eagerness to please, respect for authority, and above all the readiness to be inspired and to seek heroic tasks. The young aspire to be honored in the community, to be a credit to it, to gain distinction there and even beyond. It is part of the duty of the wise tutor—and one of his joys—to excite eros and to prompt it to what is fine and estimable.

Great demands are made on the time and patience of teachers—especially the parents, once more. Such teachers are regarded and perceived as authorities, so the normal inclination to follow those who occupy positions of status would be more or less activated. The tendencies to conform and to imitate would likewise be productive, so far as leaders and authorities themselves display excellence of character. Neither the encouragement of nonjudgmental compassion nor catering to the demands of youth will be among the highest priorities of such education, we may be sure.

More fundamental than the authority of any particular individual is that of the law, which is a crucial legacy of a people. Whether it be in the form of customary norms of the family, the common law of the university, or the Constitution of the United States, whether it be precedents of an institution, the traditions of a profession, or deliberate legislation enacted according to long-established procedure, the law is possessed of majesty. It is venerated authority. Wise leaders teach, "These are *our* laws, the laws of our people; they have guided us through our perilous history. They transcend the personal ambitions of whatever group finds itself at the head of state. We hold them in highest honor." At best, the blessings of rule of law will be widely recognized and defended, shielding the people from the designs of those who happen to have the most power at the moment.

Am I saying that the laws are beyond judgment and criticism? Nothing of the sort. But the very event of evaluating the law should be regarded as an occasion of gravity and moment. It should be accompanied by ceremony and solemnity. If one is a Deweyan, however, he will criticize the laws every day, day in and day out, and he will be obsessed with correcting them. He will say, of course, that he is trying to *improve* the law, to make it better. Apart from the fact that he often fails to do that, the most serious difficulty with this perpetual revisionism is that it reduces—if not negates—the *authority* of law: the law is there to be changed, if not repudiated. If law is made to be changed, it has lost its authority. It just sits there, as it were, trembling, waiting to be done over, its authority transferred to trendiness and sentiment or to the loudest voices. Soon, the very idea of the rule of law loses its sanctity. Our "wisdom" consists in having contempt for wisdom. We see the results of this now-habitual demeanor throughout every institution in America. Let us judge our laws, but let us judge them as revered beings, never to be subordinated to the passions of the day and altered only by the most conscientious appraisals and deliberations.

The customary educator will find that his project is often crowned with real successes. In the process of moral initiation, his pupils can deeply learn good conduct: justice, integrity, honesty, and the like. Eros might be enlisted in the service of great deeds and sacrifices. But will this in fact be the crown? What sort of morality will be taught? It might be of a highly oppressive and intolerant sort, to be sure. This is a serious question, and I will continue with it, but first attend to this crucial distinction: *Any* environment of moral education might degenerate into weak, cruel, or misguided modes of conduct. The question at the moment concerns the most effective *manner* of imparting moral habits—habits of virtue and wisdom, we would hope, and the claim here is that teaching according to custom, when it is not corrupt, is more potent than others in producing those individuals who will reliably defend and invigorate a morally demanding social order. *For those who are devoted to the formation of the virtuous character with which to sustain a moral order*, their principal resource is to avail themselves of the inherent powers of customary life. Other individuals can and do exploit the same resources to perpetrate oppression and evil.

The young wish to be accepted into full manhood or womanhood in their society, and to become morally responsible and virtuous is both a requirement and a challenge. To demonstrate honesty, courage, loyalty, trustworthiness, steadfastness, and a willingness to sacrifice is a prime condition for admission to full status as a member of the group. Powerful incentives! There is the real threat, however, that such initiation will take the form of uncritical indoctrination, and a wise society will be alert to such corruptions. Clearly, I do not mean to say that a morality of custom is good just because it is custom, for there are many objectionable ways of life, traditional or not.

In this context, bear in mind the difference between customary morality and morality according to custom. Morality by custom does not forswear intelligent discourse and deliberation. Distinguish also the *exercise* of moral authority, which might well dispense with explanation on critical occasions, from the antecedent process of *evaluating* the norms and policies to be enforced. Evaluation is one of many customary activities that require intelligence and wisdom. Contextual moral appraisal is, after all, *intelligent* appraisal. Moral appraisal might be united with wisdom according to nature, and it might be authoritative and effective, but it must be formulated in terms of the distinctive qualities of the culture, and it must address the specific values of the milieu in which it occurs. Appraisal must recognize the values deeply embedded in existing practices. Otherwise, in fact, it would not and could not be effective. Such wisdom itself might come to be honored; it is a part of the tradition absorbed by each generation. Morality according to custom might prove in many cases to be adaptable and innovative.

We cannot overemphasize the importance of wise appraisal. Hence we must also be cognizant of the sources of the needful virtues and habits of thought. One of the prime requirements for a flourishing society is the advancement of learning and the development of rigorous intellect. Disciplined—not fanciful—intelligence is always a great resource. In fact, most of our great institutions of learning and research are themselves creatures of custom, having evolved from modest and uncertain beginnings. They have protected their integrity by appealing to another product of the adaptive powers of custom, academic freedom.

To discourage the bondage of propaganda and to pursue the functions of informed and penetrating intellect, it is necessary that classroom teachers desist from partisanship that violates academic truthfulness. There is education that is not directed specifically to conduct but to acquisition of knowledge—from reading, writing, and arithmetic to extensive learning in the arts and sciences. It has moral import, but it is not taught as an instrument of tribal loyalty and moral strength. The teacher who engages in willfull misrepresentation for political purposes not only deprives the student of knowledge; he also betrays the obligation to stimulate powers of judicious inquiry and criticism. His aim, in effect, is to make his students into loyal followers of his own ideas, not independent thinkers. Yes, school teachers must insist on good conduct, and they will teach, in effect, the rewards of hard work, responsibility, and intellectual excellence, while the liabilities of dishonesty and lack of application will also be manifest, but intellectual breadth, rigor, and honesty remain their ultimate aim.

Academic integrity must include the teaching of the history, political principles, arts, and culture of their civilization. At best, students would also learn of the nature and works of other civilizations. For the sake of an exacting intelligence, none of these teachings should be undertaken in a tendentious manner. In other words, academic freedom—including its attendant obligations—is a precious asset in the adaptations and evolution of customary life. (Academic freedom is also precious for those blessed with the simple love of knowledge and truth. Those who are devoted to ideal goods, moreover, will heed this ancient idea: The moral virtues cannot be completed without intellectual virtue, and full intellectual excellence is impossible without moral virtue.)

We must disabuse ourselves of the idea of the inherent juxtaposition of custom to vigorous intelligence and moral decency. Custom and intelligence can become congenially and effectively allied with each other. There are customary associations plentiful with intelligence and decency. Where, as a matter of fact, do we find the wisest and most virtuous peoples? Not in the vast bureaucracies, which notoriously numb the minds of their occupants. And surely not in our universities, which are the self-appointed leaders in "rational" morality and at the same time a carnival of moral disgraces.

Where authority of the sort I have been suggesting is in evidence, and where it transmits a vigorous and honored tradition, the result is typically salutary. The well-led and cohesive association is apt to be characterized by dutiful behavior and spirited loyalty. In vital and autonomous associations, such as those that once animated civil society, customary moral teaching is potent. The normlessness of disjointed industrial and urban societies is less in evidence. So, once again, we are returned to self-governing and responsible institutions as the source of moral virility. Morality might live in autonomous orders of common life. Routine daily intercourse in a vigorous civil society nurtures good behavior. Loyalty to the teachings of family, church, school, and fellow workers becomes the nurse of virtue and love of the ideal.

The condition of lively customary practice is not altogether to be envied, nevertheless, for it is easily united with a high degree of rigidity and irresponsible authority. Distrust of outsiders and antagonism toward nonconformists are also prevalent. Intolerance to the point of fury is common. The impartiality and amiable relations with other groups that cosmopolitans admire are sometimes all but nonexistent. As resistance to these tendencies, the pluralism of modern civilizations has its own benefits: it is less apt to nurture insular and fanatical tribes. When individuals do not isolate themselves in just one group but participate in many, they might be less inclined to mindless parochialism, while remaining loyal to their roots. The respect and sense of justice that are imparted by the family and other authoritative groups, moreover, can very well be taught in a manner that extends their scope to all people. As I remarked earlier, a local and well-defined association can make moral demands that are largely common to all persons. In the name of their own traditions, such a group can also demand good behavior in regard to those not in the group. The leaders of a given community might insist, "We require our members to treat everyone with respect." Civil society is not of necessity a seedbed of provincialism. If, with its plentiful and variegated associations, it could regain its life and responsibilities, we might enjoy something of a beneficent mixture of local authority and intergroup concord. Moreover, the force of knowledge and intellectual integrity can be deployed to expose and criticize moral outrages and stupidities.

No one should suppose that moral education is easy or without its ominous possibilities. Extravagant hopes are unwarranted in even the best of cases. Human beings are ambitious, competitive, jealous of their goods, and wary of rivals. Even our professed universalists and cosmopolites can be as ruthless and implacable as any tribesman. Just stand in the way of their plans: you'll see. Much as I cherish the autonomy of civil society, moreover, I judge that its restoration is something less than imminent. Just some renewed vigor in the family, somehow, would be a hopeful sign.

There are both intellectual and practical threats to the authority of private groups. I have considered what seem the main practical threats. From the intellectual standpoint, as we have seen, rationalisms are the nemesis of morality by custom. The rationalist strides to center stage, denounces the prevailing morality, and announces the new order. Fortunately, he is not typically influential, for those who do the work of the world tend to be practical sorts. Nevertheless, the purported rationalist is sometimes effective—not because he is rational, but because he succeeds in mobilizing widespread and sometimes legitimate discontents, while intellectual onlookers applaud. The massive influence of Marxism is a case in point. First, given the absolute justice and rationality of our cause, we demonize the opposition in its entirety. Then, we call for the tearing down of everything and build paradise from the rubble. Lesser, but still potent, examples are sweeping theories of women's rights, which are parasitic on a few legitimate grievances. It is a simple proposition: any rights available to men must also be available to women. Why not? It seems perfectly rational. Why should anyone be privileged because of gender? Accordingly, any activity open to men must be open to women. Again, we demonize the opposition: anyone who doesn't go along is a sexist pig. This is a most effective strategy. It has brought out the coward and sycophant in legions of men and women (mostly men), most of them in high places.

To consult morality according to custom in such a controversy does not mean that the custom has always been to keep women out of men's work, so we'll keep it that way. (That would be customary morality.) It means that we must conscientiously look at the demands in the context of our contemporary institutions, to many of which we are justly attached. We would be alert to the fact that the putative absolute goods of the rational philosophy are nothing of the kind: however important, they are discriminated from within an intricate web of values. We would also be reminded that not all goods are agreeable to one another. We would, to go on, be mindful that universality is not an a priori good. Similarity across dissimilar conditions might be foolish and even disastrous—as might be the case in saying there are no morally relevant differences between men and women.

The result of such an appraisal is to conclude that there is no good reason that women should be excluded from politics, business, and the professions, and simple observation confirms that they make excellent contributions to them. Still, we would expect that the arrangement would not be an unmixed good. We might have profound anxiety about the denigration of motherhood and about the increasing reluctance of professional women to have children. We should likewise be concerned with contempt for fathers and even for masculinity as such. We would have the intense concern that careers for women would result in serious emotional deprivations for their children and neglect of their moral development, and we would become deeply fearful that unmarried women who become mothers will be regarded as heroines. Further, we might conclude that women *ought* to be excluded from partcipation in some traditionally masculine practices, such as the combat operations of the military. Fighting wars is fatal business, and our adversaries are not sentimentalists. Women cannot fight as well as men. More important, the presence of women in combat units seriously vitiates the essential bonding of men to each other. Collateral effects of this absolutism include the admission of women to military academies, which have consequently undergone a marked lowering of their standards. The effeminization of the military is anything but rational; it is shortsighted self-indulgence. The same can be said of some forms of police and firefighting operations.

Radical women want choice even when it deprives men of choice. A man wants to attend an all-male academy: the Virginia Military Institute, let us say, but he can no longer do so, for the state has required sexual integration. Part of his attachment to the idea of a military life was the fact that it has been a singularly masculine career. That choice no longer available; perhaps he will decide on a different sort of life altogether. He is not the only one deprived. Many men who once desired to take up what have hitherto been the masculine forms of work now turn to something else. This is far more than a personal disappointment to them. The most important matter is that men who would have given distinguished service to the challenges of defense and war are somewhere else. (The feminist will retort that the male psyche is through and through conventional. Good luck with that idea!)

A further triumph of the rationality of women's rights is no-fault divorce. One effect of this "right" is that women and their children are being abandoned more commonly than they used to be. In addition, and more subtly, men are more reluctant to enter into marriage when they feel that they would enjoy no distinctively masculine status there. Or, once in a marriage, when they have no uniquely manly role, their loyalty to the bond diminishes. Thereupon, some of them become more abusive; others leave the union. I do not say that women must be kept barefoot in winter and pregnant in summer. Callous and abusive men are despicable. I do say that the question of women's rights ought to be approached within the context of morality according to custom. There, its absolutistic pretensions would give way to a more discerning and judicious inquiry. The inquiry must be vexed, because not all goods are mutually compatible, but it might also be creative: we might develop some alternative practices that would minimize tension and quarrel, while preserving essential goods. In private and in public life, moreover, we would neither disparage nor discourage accustomed feminine roles, as we now do, for example, with endless propaganda and a tax code that discriminates against women who wish to maintain a traditional home life.

The two fundamental characteristics of morality according to custom are separable, to the detriment of each. The authority of custom might be unaccompanied by the pragmatic qualities of moral analysis; it can easily be enlisted to the cause of intolerance and oppression. The pragmatic side, in turn, might be undertaken without respect for custom and without its sanctions, tending in consequence to be rootless and ineffectual. It could give way to anarchy or to a version of moral rationalism. As matters stand today, customs that would animate contextualism are largely in retreat. As custom is attenuated, loses its confidence and vitality, so too is there loss of vigor and authority in its moral teachings. The appeal of rationalistic theory is especially strong when the steadying influence of traditionally autonomous associations is diminished. Likewise, with this weakening, a morality predicated on nothing more than hedonistic feeling will be received as wisdom. The young are told that their every radical utterance is genius incarnate. In truth, the philosophy the student thinks up in college, to the applause of his professors, is typically the product of a fevered and ill-taught imagination. More and more, arrogant individuals set forth their own self-evident philosophies. The old communities and the old divisions of labor are assaulted by appeals to everything from abstract reason to gross self-indulgence. Soon, everything one has believed in seems to have been discredited and cast down.

To repeat: traditional groups are by no means without sin. They have been guilty of wrongdoings of many sorts. (The feminists have less cause for complaint than have blacks and other minorities.) But what is the appropriate response to such injustices? The remedies are not indubitably obvious, but appraisal according to custom is distinctly more promising than the way of pure reason. The lovers of theoretic certainty may fully enunciate their claims, and they are deserving of a hearing, but their particular prescriptions are not to be taken to be self-certifying absolutes. (Even the relativist and historicist must be included in the conversation. Whether due to mindlessness or willful deception, an irony pervades their pronouncements: Under the guise of being nonjudgmental, they offer dogmatic absolutes! At this point it is difficult to see how their philosophies, as such, have anything to contribute, but their demands for this particular policy or that are open to contextual analysis.)

There are many practical obstacles to a vigorous life of private associations, principal among them the state and the devotion to efficiency and standardization that emerge with technological genius and economic demand. Consider the viral growth of bureaucracy, which incorporates many of the characteristically alienating features of modern life, and which is becoming our way of life. The aim of bureaucracy is regulation according to a rational and efficient plan. It seeks standardization, uniformity, and centralization where once there was autonomy and distinctiveness. The worst of it is not the labyrinths of paper, the corruption, incompetence, boring routine, minute and invariant specifications of procedure, the proliferation of regulations, and complete impersonality. The worst of it is that bureaucracy is neither efficient nor adaptive. To become one with it, as we witness daily, anesthetizes the powers of thought, initiative, and personal responsibility. Yet every day, like the relentless destruction of the Amazon rain forest, more and more of what had been autonomous and customary falls to the jurisdiction of a bureaucracy.[6] In the same process, the fertile sources of virtue become effete.

People succumb to this tyranny insensibly. It happens gradually; they are numbed by it; and then there seems to be no way out. But human nature is such that we might somehow recognize and resist this suffocation. Government, whether federal or state, is probably the main offender, and there may be a growing recognition of the insidious evil done to a society in which more and more of the population become clients of the state and more and more activities are regulated by bureaucrats. Somehow, we might find a way to reinvigorate civil society. Such a turn would go far to diminish the torpor and moral indifference that currently imperil us. It might revive our sense of responsibility, and we might rediscover the abundant and commonly benefi-cent resources of being a free people. To aspire to be such a people is worthy of eros, and perhaps eros will inspire us. Now we turn to further erotic objects: those of the individual whose soul longs to give birth in the service of *to kalon*.

NOTES

1. The multiculturalism that flourishes in the contemporary university is, in its way, a symptom of the desire for customary life, but this is a multiculturalism that refuses to make value judgments about the comparative merits of different cultures—except for heterosexual white male culture (as if that were a unitary being). The refusal to make value judgments is a protection against high standards. Multicultur-alism as it exists in the university denies that that there is anything that transcends culture, such as methods of inquiry, knowledge, science, human universals, or moral criteria. The nature of mind itself, they say, is exclusive to each culture.

2. The phrase, "all the ambience of a Soviet tractor factory," comes from Robert Weissberg (in personal correspondence).

3. For a case in point, see Peter Hitchens, *The Abolition of Britain* (San Fran-cisco: Encounter Books, 2002). England has eroded, if not abolished, "the very cus-toms, manners, methods, standards and laws which have for centuries restrained us from the sort of barbaric behavior that less happy lands suffer" (p. 296).

4. The earliest version of this argument that I know of is found in Hobbes, who does not frame it just as I have. His reasoning is that the nature of citizenship is unin-telligible if that very status requires the citizen to injure himself.

5. Another illustration, in effect, is provided in Wilson's *The Marriage Problem*. From the thirteenth century in England, if not sooner, a more individualistic and morally egalitarian society began to develop, for reasons specific to that culture. In due course, accordingly, the notion of individual rights became focal and was articu-lated in various media. But the nature and function of rights were not therefore unproblematic, and appraisal of them is a continuing need. See his chap. 4, "The Rise of the Modern Marriage."

6. When I arrived at Emory in 1971, the dean of the graduate school, Charles Lester, had one assistant dean, one administrative assistant, and about a half dozen secretaries. When I would go to see Charlie in his office, he would have his feet up on the desk as though he had nothing else to do, and we would happily talk of all manner of things relevant and irrelevant for several minutes. At such times I learned much of the lore of the university. There was never anything hurried about these con-versations. When we got down to business, we would reach a verbal understanding—

no forms to fill out, nothing in triplicate, no committees to satisfy. Charlie would say, "Send me a memo about this so I'll remember what we did." The staff of the graduate school today easily exceeds one hundred souls, with layer upon layer of deans. When a recent Dean was asked what he thought was the principal need of the graduate school, he replied, "More administrative personnel." Charlie Lester spent his life at Emory, and he gave his life to it. There are no more Charlie Lesters at Emory and no doubt very few of the sort in universities anywhere. That is an irreparable loss. The ethos of the school today bears almost no resemblance to what it was in Charlie's day, but we do have innumerable committees, subcommittees, boards, panels, councils, workshops, retreats, and task forces, all of which produce voluminous reports. To my knowledge, no one has inquired whether any of these has improved the quality of education and scholarship.

| 9 |

Uncommon Goods

Animal vitality and spontaneous exuberance! Life would be unbearable without them. What a waste to dissipate them in hedonism! Isn't there a way to preserve and enrich these energies and to give them form? Wouldn't that be a matchless adventure and consummation? Thus have many wondered. They tremble at the prospect, gaining inspiration from a Plato or a Nietzsche—or from an artist, a writer, or a poet. And great music, as Allan Bloom suggests, intimates the transfiguration of passion into ideal form. The ambitions of animal spirit might take a more practical bent, the aspiration to great deeds: heroism, glory, worldly accomplishment and conquest, inspired by the lives of masterful men.

In philosophic parlance, these are ideal goods, ideal ends. They require unusual passion and perseverence and a peculiar genius of one form or another. We can place them in two broad categories. One is a certain condition of the self—whether it be justice in the soul, holiness, *apatheia*, self-creation, or mystical oblivion. The other is to establish an overt state of affairs, whether an empire or works of art. These two sorts of outcome are not apt to occur separately. To achieve a certain state of soul requires that one undergo some sort of worldly discipline, and the man who would have overt achievement must have talents, learning, and the appropriate character. A certain perfected state of soul, moreover, would link one in a blessed way to things external: union with God, contemplation of the perfect forms of being, or with acts of virtue in the presence of *to kalon*.

Men bet their lives on ideal ends, and it is a perilous bet. The conditions that must coalesce to produce such a nature, and then to bring it to completion, are rare. There is an appalling rate of failure and disappointment. There are typically agonizing torments of the soul, and fatal misdirections, and even the attained reality of the envisioned end, if it occurs, might turn out to be vain and empty. Ideal *goods* is an unduly seductive term for something so elusive. The poet or painter might produce works of surpassing beauty and never cease to suffer. It is an abysmal thought, but the erotic youth will not be turned aside, and sometimes the end will truly satisfy him and provide a meaning resonant to his life as a whole. It is true, after all, that some souls are possessed by divine madness. Must they not try to make something divine of it? Let us review powerful philosophic interpretations of ideal goods. Then it will be occasion to be specific about some ideal goods that appeal to the "free and disillusioned spirit"—to return to the apt expression of Santayana.

a. Ideal Goods: Plato and Nietzsche

Both Plato and Nietzsche are connoisseurs of the life of eros. It would be difficult to find two thinkers more brilliant and influential on such a matter, but they are frequently in striking contrast to each other. To examine the differences will be instructive.

Recall some themes in Plato's philosophy: The erotic life is superbly portrayed in the person of Socrates, the lover par excellence, and the Socratic quest exemplifies the very nature of nature. The forms of perfection characteristic of human nature exist potentially in the soul. On this account, the fulfillment of the self is not a creative venture. In a cumulative process of education, one realizes an antecedently given form. This is the way in which all of nature functions: Each being is driven by an inherent thrust to attain its peculiar perfection. In a complacent view of things, these perfections, as such, are regarded to be in perfect harmony with each other. It is also complacent, in its way, to affirm that the inherent nature of man is to possess wisdom, courage, temperance, and justice, but it is an admirable complacency in the sense that Plato accords highest priority to the formation of moral qualities.

There is also a difficulty in explaining how the forms, which transcend the world of becoming, nevertheless inform all processes of change. Indeed, it is not clear from the nature of the theory why all changing things so constituted do not achieve their perfection, if any do, but Plato the unfailingly realistic observer of human affairs is under no illusions about the incapacities of nature. His discussion in *The Republic* about the corruption of the philosophic nature presupposes that even the best natures fall well short of their excellence, largely owing to the allure of political reputation. The allegory of the cave tells us that most men will remain in their subterranean state, ignorant of the light and contemptuous of attempts to seek it. The analysis of the degeneration of the state is predicated on the assumption that human beings are all too eager to follow a corrupt way of life. For the realistic Plato, then, the potentiality for *to kalon* is scarce and the actuality scarcer still. He who completes the highest potentiality, on the other hand, enjoys the highest goods: a nature that is both unified and master of all occasions, immortal works, and rapturous unity with the essential nature of being.

Many students of ancient thought have been critical of the Socratic idea that there is one and no more than one form of perfection. There are three parts of the soul, says Plato, each with its definitive virtue, and each individual approximates more or less to each of these functions. He also seems to say that the whole measure of a man is taken by determining how far he has come on the scale from natural to complete virtue. That is your measure as a human being. Such matters as your distinguishing traits of personality and temperament—your individualized needs, wants, and talents, for example—or your personal artistry and charm are not included in the reckoning. Not only might one argue, then, that there are worthy virtues that escape Plato's attention (or that he might have greater flexibility in defining), but one might also insist that there are powers of soul that are not of inherently moral quality, such as creative genius, that are nonetheless human marvels and excellences, and they might be particularly definitive of the nature of many individuals. We could also remark that there are profound satisfactions and fulfillments in life, such as marriage and family, about which Plato can seem to be disdainful.

Most conspicuous, perhaps, is this disregard for individuality. The ancient world gave forth prodigiously of greatly distinctive individuals, but Plato's account of the excellence of the soul provides no room for what is singular. To be sure, he dramatizes several remarkable individualities, foremost among them Socrates himself, and including Alcibiades, Agathon, Thrasymachus, Protagoras, and several others, and he was a student of the Greek literary heritage, which swarms with remarkable characters. He recognizes the existence of individuality in his observation that a democratic culture would be especially notable for its proliferation of distinctive personalities, and he has Alcibiades emphasize that Socrates is by far the most unique man of whom he has ever known. It is clear that Plato recognized and appreciated what is distinctive and unusual in individuals, but individuality seems not to be an erotic goal. Is this oversight, or is it deliberate? Is this Plato's bias in favor of what is universal—his conviction that what is individual is *therefore* inferior? Universal form, not individuality, defines perfection. Whatever the answer to such criticisms and questions might be, they give us no ground for dismissing the Platonic philosophy. If there were any book that I would read in my dying hours, it would be *The Symposium*.

With the crucial proviso that not all individualities are of equal worth, we must admit individuality into the pantheon of ideal goods. Individuals, however virtuous, do in fact differ markedly from one another, and we treasure what is singular in ourselves and in others too. We do not wish to be just like everyone else or to be absorbed into the herd as an undifferentiated unit. We want to be what we are and not what someone thinks we ought to be, and what we are is reducible neither to virtue alone nor to traits that are common to all or even most individuals. We might be a curiosity and a misfit in any conventional form of associated life. If so, *that* is the self that would be expressed and fulfilled. We might even believe, as Nietzsche did, that morality in many of its forms is impertinent to the realization of individuality or is even destructive of it.

Most men, to be sure, have neither the desire nor the courage to be unusually individual. That would be stressful and would distinguish them too much from the crowd. Still, we want to develop and protect some semblance of individuality, leaving the Emersonian or Nietzschean forms to hardier and more adventurous souls. Not least because the herd stands opposed to it, the uncompromising forms of individuality are rare, and they are seldom carried out well, but occasionally they are superb. For the handful who, in spite of all obstacles and conventions, are determined to define themselves and their works according to their inner genius, for those who are alienated from all that is safe, secure, and accepted, individuality is their ideal good. Their author is Nietzsche. There is no better way to examine this good, with its raptures and catastrophes, than to take up his thought.

Nietzsche's idea of the true individual is set in the context of a philosophy of nature, which, unhappily, is never more than adumbrated. Unlike the tidy order characterized by Plato, tending to predetermined forms, nature according to Nietzsche is, in his own term, Dionysian. Nature is chthonic, convulsive, without fixed order, and without purpose.[1] Zarathustra says,

> Verily, it is a blessing and not a blasphemy when I teach: "Over all things stand the heaven Accident, the heaven Innocence, the heaven Chance, the heaven Prankishness."
>
> "By Chance"—that is the most ancient nobility of the world, and this I restored to all things: I delivered them from their bondage under Purpose. This freedom and heavenly cheer I have placed over all things like an azure bell when I taught that over them and through them no "eternal will" wills. This prankish folly I have put in the place of that will when I taught: "In everything one thing is impossible: rationality."[2]

Zarathustra draws the proper inference: "O my brothers, is not everything in flux *now?* Have not all railings and bridges fallen into the water? Who could still cling to 'good' and 'evil'?"[3]

Nature *attains* order from time to time, but it cannot *re*tain it. As Dionysus is the god of flux, Apollo is the god of form. Typically, Apollonian order stands as a defense against the wild and lawless energies of Dionysus, but in human life the great project is to unite the two gods in one: turbulent and powerful passions taking form, while sacrificing none of their inherent force. The form is not antecedently given, nor is it enduring. Nature destroys order and goes on to create new forms, and so does the Dionysian individual. "And life itself confided this secret to me: 'Behold,' it said, '*I am that which must always overcome itself.*'"[4]

Nietzsche's philosophy of nature is anti-Cartesian as well as anti-Platonic. As we have seen, a Cartesian metaphysics can allow for no qualitative change or difference, and no values of any sort lurk in the precincts of nature. Ideal goods of either the Platonic or Nietzschean sort are unintelligible. For Nietzsche, the Dionysian and Apollonian are not inventions of subjective mind; they are characteristic of nature. Hence they constitute a repudiation of Cartesian philosophy. Treating all human powers as derivative of animal instinct, moreover, Nietzsche ridicules the notion of thinking substance. It hardly needs to be said that he also repudiates the idea of philosophic idealism that the entire cosmos, in its real being, is irreducibly rational and harmonious. While an idealist believes that the mind ultimately is fully at home in the universe, Nietzsche tends to think of nature as our antagonist. It offers no home, no comfort. Yet this very antagonism is celebrated by the higher man, for he thrives on whatever makes his life difficult. Comfort and complacency are the enemies of self-overcoming.

In a crucial sense, Nietzsche's expression, self-overcoming, is a substantial improvement on the Platonic idea of cumulative advance to a pre-established end, for Nietzsche knows that our advance requires confrontation with our own internal failings and weaknesses.[5] When he describes the process of becoming a self-created individual, he is always acutely aware that some of the most formidable obstacles lie within. There are massive and obstinate characteristics of the self that have to be faced and defeated. One is painfully conscious of incapacities, dependencies, and complacency, and he struggles against them. The inner life is also plagued with self-doubt: when your thinking is in opposition to everything taken to be holy and good, when everyone else, high and low, finds your ideas insanely unacceptable, in your loneliness and isolation you endure periods when you wonder whether you are not mad; you wonder whether you are losing your mind. Surely all these intelligent and sturdy folk standing together cannot be mistaken! For all his awareness of human frailty, Plato shows little or none of this subjective torment.[6]

The consciousness of the free spirit owes much, in Nietzsche's analysis, to the Christian heritage, in which tortured souls are always aware of their pride and their sinfulness, their backsliding and their subterfuges—no matter how cleverly and subtly they would be disguised, and they are full of woe and suffering for their incapacity. Whoever would be truly strong and free must be mercilessly honest. He will not protect himself with illusions, and he will become stronger by overcoming his dependency. One is obsessed with overcoming all such disabling features of the self. The hostility that men normally turn on others is pointed by the free spirit at himself. One's self becomes his favorite adversary. Whatever the newfound release, strength, and exultation, they are not a resting place. Life is that which must *always* overcome itself, and self-overcoming in itself is an exuberant and joyful experience.

Merciless honesty extends beyond self to world. The world is not friendly to human hopes, and it holds no sanctuary for the soul. One is not comforted, but the yearning for comfort has destroyed most philosophies. Least comforting is the truth about man, a weak and mendacious character, who prefers the easy satisfactions of the herd. Yet he throbs with resentments and hatreds, which he does not acknowledge, and which inform his moralities. Zarathustra, speaking for Nietzsche, suffers agonies of nausea, disgust, and pity for man, and one of his greatest triumphs is to overcome these feelings in himself. He does not change his judgment of man, but his nausea gives way to the conviction that the *Übermensch*, by his very existence, will redeem the pain and folly of all eternity. Zarathustra repeatedly teaches that man must go beyond man. The dignity and honor of man is that he is the being who is capable of overcoming man. This is the "arrow of longing" of Zarathustra, precursor of the *Übermensch*.

Life is so difficult that the characteristic response is to stop fighting, to give up, to seek solace and comfort in the herd and in religion, and to deny life itself. Then one would be in the throes of slave morality, more specifically, Christianity.[7] There is the ubiquitous herd instinct, which is jealous of all distinction. The will to conform is extremely difficult to overcome. "The human beings who are more similar, more ordinary, have had, and always have, an advantage; those more select, subtle, strange, and difficult to understand, easily remain alone, succumb to accidents, being isolated, and rarely propagate. *One must invoke tremendous counterforces* in order to cross this natural, all too natural *progressus in simile*, the continual development of man toward the similar, ordinary, average, herdlike—*common!*"[8] The herd instinct is not a mere annoyance; it is profound, and the higher man can easily succumb to it. He must ruthlessly establish and preserve the singular conditions needful for his own life and thought, or he will perish. Especially for the man whose art or ideas are utterly foreign to the milieu in which he subsists, these are rare, fragile, difficult, and at the same time *necessary* conditions. Nietzsche repeatedly uses metaphors like the desert, mountain peaks, and icy tundras to express the needed removal of the creative self from all that is ordinary, pacifying, and destructive of freedom. The same metaphors express the fact that his ideas and his experience are far removed from all that is common and acceptable.

Nietzsche's most characteristic position is that the life of the authentic individual is a boundless and exhilarating voyage without a terminus. There is no ultimate telos; there are no resting places; and there are no rules to determine what forms Apollo will create. There is no completion. Self-overcoming is succeeded by more self-overcoming. The process is one of sudden increments of freedom, power, and exultation as one is rid of the constraints, in all their variety and insistence, of the frightened herd animal, and the consequent release of powers propels him to even greater acts of creation. Let it never be supposed, however, that this is a life without discipline, restraint, and sacrifice. Few if any moralists are the equal of Nietzsche in his insistence that the erotic life is one of deprivation, rigor, and torment, a life requiring the utmost in courage, strength, and single-mindedness. The discipline and sacrifice are self-imposed. It is not a life for the timid, the self-indulgent, or the uncertain, but for those who are justly called to it, it promises an affirmation of life not hitherto conceived, much less experienced.

Nietzsche insists—Nietzsche above all insists—that eros requires objects of reverence and longing. What are such objects? Do they violate the principle of endless self-overcoming? The evidently all-sufficing object is the *Übermensch*, who does not yet exist, and Nietzsche is tortured by the uncertainty of the coming. We are told little of his nature, but presumably he, too, will not exist in a state of stasis. Presumably, he will also require dreadful obstacles and enemies. Yet there is at least one point in the corpus where the tone is decidedly different. It seems to speak of a terminus and a sort of finality. It is from "On Those Who Are Sublime" in *Thus Spoke Zarathustra*:

> He subdued monsters, he solved riddles: but he must still redeem his own monsters and riddles, changing them into heavenly children. As yet his knowledge has not learned to smile and to be without jealousy; as yet his torrential passion has not become still in beauty.
>
> Verily, it is not in satiety that his desire shall grow silent and be submerged, but in beauty. Gracefulness is part of the graciousness of the great-souled.
>
> His arm placed over his head: thus should the hero rest; thus should he overcome even his rest. But just for the hero the *beautiful* is the most difficult thing. No violent will can attain the beautiful by exertion. . . .
>
> When power becomes gracious and descends into the visible—such descent I call beauty.
>
> And there is nobody from whom I want beauty as much as from you who are powerful: let your kindness be your final self-conquest.
>
> Of all evil I deem you capable: therefore I want the good from you. . . .
>
> You shall strive after the virtue of the column: it grows more and more beautiful and gentle, but internally harder and more enduring, as it ascends.[9]

These words are gentler than most, and perhaps they have less appeal than those of the Nietzsche of titanic and endless self-overcoming. Either way, Nietzsche's is a message to ignite the erotic soul. He appeals to the romantic, restless, and heroic, those who yearn for the highest and would create it in themselves against all resistance. It is a recruitment of those who feel wholesale alienation from conventional society, those who have seen through its pretenses and evasions, the pettiness, smugness, and pomposity of normal life, and have contempt for them and who crave honesty and liberation. Everywhere they see all things tending to the average and the common, all standards kept at the levels of easy comfort. Against this, they are offered hardship, uncompromising honesty, and high calling in the face of an uncomprehending mass of mediocrities. They are offered the greatest challenge, the highest promise, and the highest affirmation. The clarion call continues: it is a demand to see cruelly into one's own soul, to do battle with demons, to endure rejection and ostracism, and to do without the intellectual and emotional comforts upon which others depend for their very lives. Out of all this will come a singular self-creation. It is a call to those who love what is brilliant, individual, uncommon, iconoclastic, bold, hard, and joyful.

Heady stuff! Intoxicating! Who has not had some inkling of these revulsions and aspirations? Who has not wearied of a stodgy life and longed for a rebellion against it all? Yes, there are truly uncommon goods offered here, and many a life has been devoted to them. They are, nevertheless, swollen with folly and excess. Nietzsche is mistaken in his assumption that all constraints on conduct and aspiration are merely conventional. He assumes the extreme flexibility of nature and more particularly that there are no morally normative structures inherent in human nature. Both of these beliefs are difficult to defend, as I have been arguing. One needn't be a Platonist to challenge Nietzsche here, but the mounting scientific evidence about human nature is substantially more congenial to Plato. That is, each of us is endowed with inherent dispositions that tend to suit us for one calling rather than another, and we also possess innate dispositions that equip us for moral judgment and conduct. Justice, for example, appears to be according to nature, and the herd instinct—categorically detested by Nietzsche—is a prime source of much that is noble and heroic.

For his part, in his contempt for the static and for what he regards as mere convention, Nietzsche repeatedly cries out for "the transvaluation of all values." Notice: *all* values. In effect, he calls for a rejection of all established forms of life and a complete revolution in the moral practices of Western civilization. This is so, at any rate, for the higher men, the philosophers of the future, whom he always calls *creators* of value. One of his prominent themes, moreover, is that morality is one of the most potent inhibitors of greatness, so morality must be overcome. He typically means *slave* morality: Christian morality, democratic or egalitarian morality, but not invariably; he had called for the transvaluation (*Unwertung*) of *all* values.

These are not harmless ideas. Any would-be genius reads such words and thereupon supposes that he is not bound by the same morality as everyone else. Often enough, the genius *does* tend to be neglectful of customary responsibilities, but he should not escape blame for his behavior. In the same way, Nietzsche routinely dismisses *every* form of human greatness hitherto known: "Naked I saw both the greatest and the smallest man: they are still all-too-similar to each other. Verily, even the greatest I found all-too-human."[10] Such remarks in themselves are indiscriminate enough, but coupled with his denunciation of man, as such, they are incendiary and dangerous. Yes, it's true: Nietzsche does not always talk in this way. There are several individuals—Socrates above all—for whom he expresses almost worshipful admiration, but he seems to have believed that even such a man would look paltry next to the *Übermensch*. Again, the fault with such pronouncements is to sanction a thundering denunciation of the entirety of human custom and achievement. The intellectuals—those of the impoverished and resentful soul—love this stuff. Nietzsche has been the exemplar and inspiration for the intellectual who *must* denounce every sensibility of common life, no matter how solid, how stable, how productive. The intellectual will stop at nothing to root out everything that makes life happy and durable. He urges the young to condemn and dismiss everything in sight. The young are deeply flattered and are happy to oblige. (There is rich irony in the intellectuals' love for Nietzsche, who despised them and always wrote of them with scorn and condescension.)

One who is carried away with Nietzsche's philosophy will miss much of the best that life can provide. Much that is "common" and "ordinary" is in fact precious, and natural satisfactions can, indeed, become extraordinary, as I have urged. The goods of human bonding can be holy and celebrated, and love between a man and a woman might surpass any good. The feeling of human solidarity is not always an abomination. Local custom enshrines and preserves such goods. An individual under Nietzsche's sway, on the other hand, readily becomes derisive of fundamental duties—such as maintaining home and family, defending the institutions upon which life depends, and cultivating the virtues without which the center will not hold.[11]

It is Nietzsche, actually, who tends to be the nihilist. He sought objects of reverence that would pass the test of pitiless honesty. So what does he come up with? His surpassing object is the *Übermensch*. Over and over again, Zarathustra pleads that without this being, all life is without meaning. His "most abysmal" thought is that the *Übermensch* will not happen.[12] So, your greatest and indispensable object of love is something that does not and might not ever exist, while all around you are palpitating possibilities of happiness and meaning. But they aren't good enough. Even self-overcoming, presumably, will not suffice without the promise of ultimate success in the overcoming of man by the *Übermensch*. No Christian ever denigrated the meaning of the earth more effectively than this. How can one be at the same time "faithful to the earth" and reverent when even the greatest individuals are hardly distinguishable from the most paltry? How can one be reverent when he seeks the transvaluation of all values?

One last question: Why must individuality be defined as that which is radically different from everything else and in opposition to it? It does imply distinctiveness, independence, and strength but not necessarily total alienation. The differences between one man and the next might be rather slight in some respects and pronounced in others. To turn difference into individuality, one must nourish the facets of his nature in a manner that is suitable to him for his own reasons, rather than simply respond to the demands of the flock. Individuality does imply, then, a willingness, if need be, to be a nonconformist, but the purpose is not to *be* a nonconformist. It is not eccentricity for the sake of eccentricity. Nonconformity is incidental.

When the differences tend to be pronounced, it is more difficult to sustain them, and virtue is required. Distinctiveness, if not utter singularity, in conspicuous traits implies strength and autonomy. This is in contrast to the person who always wishes to please, to be accommodating at all cost, and for whom nothing is more important than being accepted. This account of individuality by no means precludes, however, a man accepting and embracing his duties and being loyal to his community, but he is not this way because he is so timid and flaccid that he can't do anything else. We must distinguish blind or cowardly conformity from discerning affection and allegiance. In considering the ideal possibilities of our nature, we must remember that one can be a man of individuality and at the same time be a man of strength and dependability in comradeship with others. Individuality does not necessarily require you to be antinomian and contemptuous. To suppose that it does is to encourage adolescent stupidity. Indeed, what I have affirmed is not altogether unlike the individual described by Nietzsche himself in "On Those Who Are Sublime," quoted above. Without the transvaluation of all values and the overcoming of man, Nietzsche's philosophy would still be rare and exalted, and it would permit many objects of piety and enchantment without sacrificing freedom of mind.

In general terms, Nietzsche's thinking, unlike that of Plato, lacks respect for finitude. Like any romantic, he has no sense of limit. He abhors the idea, yet it is in fact deserving of being conceived as a great good. One of the virtues of the recognition of limit is that it implies the possibility of a definite sense of completion: there is a point that one might reach that constitutes both a finality and fulfillment of nature. It is not an imposition; it is *your* completion; yet such consummations are typically scorned by Nietzsche.

Quite rightly, from his standpoint, he perceives morality itself as constituting a limit, so, for him, morality—so far as it imposes limits—is something to overcome. To approximate to virtue, however, is to approach a limit and to seek—perhaps to find—completion. Nietzsche's tendency to neglect or even exclude moral qualities from his accounts of human greatness distinguishes him dramatically from Plato, and it blinds him to an ideal good.

Nietzsche's excesses damage a philosophy that is otherwise brilliant. I spoke of the needs of the perceptive, independent, and aspiring nature, the one who is cruelly alienated from the shams that make most lives bearable—including those of his own weakness and pretense. Across what seas must he sail if he is to be a true philosopher? Where Plato seems not even to recognize the existence of such a nature, Nietzsche seeks him out. He braces the soul driven from all coastlines, yet yearning to mount up spiritual treasures, to become free, whole, and with integrity. It is necessarily a lonely voyage, which others do not even conceive, much less undertake. Nietzsche appeals to the congenital but brilliant misfits of the world, for whom there is no prospect of comfort and acceptance in ordinary life.[13] The stimulation and development of such natures is surely an ideal good. They have produced plentiful works of genius, and to succeed calls forth strength and courage. Great individualities are both unusual and wonderful to behold, and life without yearning for what is rare and free would be dreary. Gratitude to the fates that such natures occur! It is true, as Nietzsche teaches, that the herd instinct works against them. Where it prevails unimpeded, we commonly observe mediocrity, pettiness, rigidity, intolerance, fear of the unusual, and cruelty. Even when these conditions are moderated, it is extremely difficult for the erotic soul to find the conditions suitable for his freedom. To create them and preserve them in a world of prosaic obsessions and duties is nearly impossible, and to succeed in such a task is an achievement of heroic proportions. There are many forms of morality, moreover, that do indeed discourage and even condemn worldly aspiration and distinction or simply leave them aside. In brief, there is much to admire in Nietzsche's profoundly ambiguous legacy. There is much to learn from him. His is a stirring account of freedom and power of soul. His description of this ideal good will always rouse the spirit and beckon to it.

The next two sections could be thought of as Nietzschean meditations. Before advancing to those topics, I return briefly to the general theme of ideal goods.

There ought to be nothing obscure or esoteric about ideal values of the soul. Just as Plato said, they are perfections of natural promptings and capacities. Such powers do not exist in a worldly void; neither are they subject to unlimited creativity. They can be made only out of the hard stuff of reality. Without self-knowledge and a good sense of natural limits and resources, reality will confound our ideal goods. It might well do so in any case, and a far-fetched ambition will almost surely become a curse. Aristotle distinguishes natural virtue and complete virtue—the difference between our native capacities and their developed fullness. That development is anything but guaranteed; it is hazardous and uncertain; it may well be frustrated, distorted, or incomplete. The great quest of life lies in traversing that passage with success. It can be informed with eros and wisdom, but, on the other side, the quest might never be recognized. We can easily waste our powers and remain in the ordinary. Many a soul that might have yearned to couple the mortal and divine remains in a humdrum existence.

The forming and directing of the spirit occur in various ways, and a form of self-overcoming is among them. Self-overcoming actually happens: if the words or the example of another can influence your thinking and feeling, then your own thought and imagination can be effective in the same way— perhaps even more so in many instances. We should not underestimate the potency of subjective life. In some individuals, as in many children, it is so vivid and forceful that the difference between imagination and reality is sometimes lost—or reality even recedes. Subjective rehearsing, appraising, urging, advising, aspiring, despising, and denouncing have efficacy in shaping one's character—directing and strengthening some favored tendencies, while feelings of intense shame for traits that one detests will tend to make them less insistent.

The mind achieves a new level of power when it masters a crucial challenge. This sort of elevation is not an increase in IQ; it is a release of other mental powers that are invaluable for the work of the mind. Consider growth in intellectual independence. You wish to think your own thoughts, but you find yourself always wondering whether your ideas will please this person or displease that one: the anticipated pleasure or displeasure controls not only what you are willing to say but even what you are willing to think. Someone other than yourself has established the order of business. This bondage, once detected, is hated; it is a violation of your freedom and integrity. It does not go away at once—we're not dealing with magic—but now it haunts the mind as it could not before. Occasionally, you find yourself asking, "Who gives a damn what Smith or Jones thinks about my ideas? Who are they to decide what I will think?" Gradually, the influence of Smith and Jones subsides and finally disappears. The importunate mob is dismissed. Now you think thoughts, entertain them, and appreciate them as you never could before. You become friendly to the muses, and they to you. There are new thoughts, hitherto disgraced or forbidden, that take you to insights, ideas, and values that otherwise would be closed to you. New frontiers, new continents, open before you, and with them a great sense of increment of power and independence.

There were thoughts that you couldn't think and feelings that you couldn't feel because they were somehow phobic or emotionally foreign to you. Incrementally, or perhaps in a flash, the barriers start to collapse. What was once forbidden becomes friend and ally. Defensiveness and evasiveness are reduced. The powers of the herd instinct, let us suppose—the need to be acceptable, to please, not to give offense—gradually fall away. You have cast out tyrannical inhibitions, and you are a far more effective thinker, though your IQ is unmoved.[14] You are a different self and a better self.

In company with such a wondrously liberating process, one develops and reinforces desired qualities by *engaging in overt activities* that call forth the traits of the soul that you would nourish—just as Aristotle said. You would be apt to become ineffectual and even mad if confined to the subjective process alone. With your emerging freedom, you try yourself as never before, eliciting and forming what had been quiescent and hidden. Success emboldens and strengthens the self still more. To demand much of yourself, to face great challenges, to endure, to be unabashed by unpopularity—that is the regimen for the emergence of your ideal self. Sustained exertion with intimidating and difficult works propels the faculties to unexpected power and grace. Eros, born of Poverty and Resource, works his transformative wonders.

To be sure, there are innate limits on what might be accomplished, and nothing will happen if you do not already possess the desire to overcome and to surpass. You must be a Platonic lover. Then progress is possible, refinement is possible. It might go far toward completing those dispositions that are most precious to you.

The pursuit of a better self need not be wholly in vain. Speaking of a better self, nevertheless, carries the possibility of a fateful seduction. We should not think of virtue of soul as a self-enclosed good, simply enjoying its own excellence as such. The self is not an encapsulated entity but a being functioning in a world, difficult and multifarious. The environments in which we act run the gamut from unbearable to blissful, from utterly chaotic to orderly and integrated. Most of them include antagonistic—perhaps overwhelming—powers, as well as potent resources and amiable goods. Blessed, then, is he with the personal powers and self-knowledge to establish and maintain a milieu in which he can satisfy his loves, ambitions, and obligations. His works and allegiances might be expressive of a unified nature and hence in some degree be well ordered and mutually supportive.

Some ancient sects believed that they could attain inner peace in any environment. In fact, however, they were typically ingenious and diligent in seeking the rare circumstances that suited their sensitive and reflective natures. Some individuals, to be sure, are graced with virtues that enable them to contend unusually well with adversity and misfortune, and they are to be envied. Aristotle, as I noted above, speaks eloquently of such persons, but he does not deny that they suffer from the pains inflicted upon them by

the world. Only the self-deluded suppose that the world of practice is immaterial to virtue and to happiness.

According to the native bent of a mind, it will seek activities and objects
of a certain sort, and some of these are known as "higher" or "superior."
What is denominated higher is some object or condition that satisfies superior capacities. Someone of high intelligence must have appropriate objects
of thought or suffer boredom or even madness. Likewise with poems, paint-
ings, literary or musical compositions: what is called higher or best is that
which satisfies the most powerful, educated, and accomplished faculties requisite to these forms of expression.[15] So it is with moral ideals and ideals of
individuality. Not all ideal ends are equal, assuredly. The forms of excellence
of which nature is capable admit of differences in scope, fecundity, intrinsic
satisfaction, and moral blessings. Still, eros drives us beyond the common
and the normal. The ordinary cannot answer to the demands of a mind in
love with the good. As one's sensibilities and talents take form, he discriminates his ideal goods, or perhaps—for various reasons—he curtails his ambitions. Perhaps his affection for the ideal is wavering, after all, or perhaps he
dissipates his energies in frivolity. There is much to be said for simplicity of
character and aims. The alternative is dispersal and artificiality of self, loss of
power, failure to achieve, and the temptation to mere pretense.

b. The Scientific Ideal

"All men by nature desire to know." Well, yes and no. We love knowledge,
understanding, and theoretical intelligibility, to be sure. But we are highly
passionate, vulnerable, and prejudiced beings, too, and life is hard, demanding
many expedients. So we want to "know" the world in a way to suit our hopes,
biases, and preconceived opinions. Much of our "knowing" is of this sort, and
truly dispassionate love of truth seems contrary to nature. In fact, a genuinely
honest and independent mind is one of nature's great rarities. Our astonishingly powerful brain evolved not for love of truth, but as an instrument of survival. The brain and central nervous system are programmed to take care of
their host, to help it survive.

When the interests of the organism are conspicuously dependent upon
knowledge of fact, we do tend to think scrupulously with a mind to truth. For
an animal otherwise weak in survival equipment, it is an invaluable asset to be
cognizant of minute variations in the behavior of the animate and inanimate
beings in the environment and so to anticipate their behavior. It is likewise
invaluable to be able to outsmart your competitors, especially fellow humans.
It is common, therefore that the mind be often employed in seeking the truth,
and it often does so very competently. Just the same, the powers of denial

extend even to situations where evasion of fact will be disastrous. Consider, for example, that for many years perhaps a majority of Israelis could not bring themselves to acknowledge the genocidal intentions of Yassir Arafat.

We suffer countless and excruciating deprivations. How we wish that things could be otherwise! Innumerable facts of life offend us, and we are distinctly more comfortable whenever we can get away with ignoring or denying them or when we can reinterpret them to make them more palatable. There is such fathomless suffering that any way to diminish it is a godsend. Your child dies. Unceasing pain, unspeakable despair. Perhaps you are able to think, "Though I don't know how, even this must be somehow for the best. My son is better off now; he is with God, and someday we will be together again in paradise." Life becomes possible with such a belief. The intolerable has become almost tolerable, and every day and every hour you look forward to the joyful reunion. The illusion works a miracle. Any set of propositions that threatens our happiness, our self-esteem, our treasured ideology, our religion, or our comforting philosophy is easily rejected or explained away. We would much rather maintain the evasion than suffer truth. Only when the threat is obvious, perilous, and immediate, it seems, are we disposed to drop our made-to-order reality and bow to the facts.

Both the dependence upon antecedently treasured ideas and the refusal to accept unpleasant truth testify to our remarkable capacity to believe what we most want to believe. Astounding ingenuity and doggedness are everywhere in service to this need. We witness its presence universally, even among those who boast of their transcendence of it.

The world allows success, of sorts, to living with illusions. Some of them, at least, carry little in the way of adverse consequences and much in the way of comfort and consolation. It seems fanatical, then, to protest such comforts, unless they bring intolerance or oppression to others. The typical reply to such permissiveness is that truth-seeking is a habit, a fixed way of behaving, and those who lack the habit will eventually fall upon some unforgiving facts. The answer is not empirically warranted. A person can in fact be wildly irrational in his metaphysical beliefs, for example, and consistently expert in, say, the practice of medicine. Another's wild irrationality might be in political thinking, while he is the very model of reason in regard to agriculture or biology. Recognizing our gift for compartmentalization, we might tolerate irrational meditations in religion without necessarily risking a similar illogic in regard to economics, business management, or history. This is not to deny, nevertheless, that it is normally of the greatest consequence to face the facts of our worldly predicaments, for illusion and error in these matters can be life-threatening. Neither is it to deny that we are rarely inclined to do so.

Such reflections suggest that truth is by no means an unmixed good, and one must wonder why anyone should pursue it at the expense of his innocent hopes. Even so, we proclaim a reverence for truth; we declare it one of the greatest goods. We profess to be fearless seekers of knowledge, and we pride ourselves on being independent thinkers. *We* are not seduced by paltry or self-serving considerations, and we are persuaded that true freedom of mind is constituted by our resolute acceptance of reality. To practice such proud acceptance might be called the scientific ideal.

But might the ideal be something of an imposture after all? Our devotion to truth is ambiguous, perhaps rightly so. Should we, then, reconsider its lofty status? I think not. What we might reconsider are the reasons for thinking it an ideal good. To be sure, it is an uncommon good; it is one of nature's most rare and precious. It is so not only because our tendencies to intellectual sloth and evasion in worldly practice are often calamitous. *It is also an ideal because its achievement requires the development of unusual and remarkable virtues in its possessor.* Potent disabilities within the self are overcome. In contrast to unflattering weakness of mind, self-possession and self-command are achieved in a manner befitting a free and disillusioned spirit.

For only a few tough and unyielding souls would there be reason to overcome the will to protective and consoling conviction—but these are the souls with whom I would sit and speak. Their happiness is not dependent upon the comforts of illusion, nor are they in the thrall of typical sources of reassurance. One may be intellectually irresponsible about matters worldly or otherworldly. In either case, there is a certain sacrifice of virtue involved in the posture, and there is an increment of virtue in taking the undaunted path. As a prelude to further such reflections, we must survey some of the quintessentially human traits that encourage moral and intellectual laziness, self-deception, and mental bondage.

Note first that unfounded thinking need not be deliberate. In most inquiries, no matter who we are, we come to a point where we are satisfied with the evidence, or we are satisfied that a given hypothesis is necessary to account for the observed phenomena. If we are sophisticated in logic and scientific method and the history of science, we recognize that this point is often hard to attain, and we realize that questions of method are themselves subject to intelligent controversy. We might suspend judgment on a question, or we might tentatively take a stand, remaining well aware that further inquiry might demand a reconsideration. The most conscientious will prefer uncertainty to premature conviction. They struggle to retain a treasured belief, but when the evidence will no longer support it, they give it up, however sadly or reluctantly.

If we are unsophisticated and untutored, on the other hand, we might be honestly satisfied with decidedly inadequate evidence. We are easily contented in this way. We unwittingly take into account only the evidence that seems to confirm our belief, disregarding all the evidence to the contrary, as people commonly do when confronted with the problem of evil, for example. Perhaps we suppose that one seemingly confirming instance—of God's goodness, perhaps—is sufficient, and we might lack the imagination to realize that many other explanations for the events in question are possible. We might not have the least idea about what sort of evidence would be needed to confirm a belief. What sort of evidence would be sufficient to prove the existence of an omnipotent, omniscient, infinitely good, and just being? We are always ready, too, to accept a proposition on the word of a trusted authority. That seems honest enough. None of these strategies is necessarily dishonest. They might simply be predicated on ignorance of the nature of rigorous inquiry or failure to give the matter much thought. Any topic might fall to this fate: politics, economic policy, morals, religion, and so on.

Hence one holds unsubstantiated convictions without deliberate intent to hide or to misrepresent, but how do we account for the recurrent phenomenon of even highly sophisticated individuals holding fast to a badly supported or even patently unwarranted proposition? The pattern is familiar: clutch to yourself the ideas that are dearest to you and subsequently do whatever seems necessary to make them intellectually respectable. The explanations for such conduct are many. The one most commonly advanced—but hardly the only one—is wish fulfillment. The human being is willing to believe—*demands* to believe—whatever is essential to sustain meaning in his life. He holds on to it as to life itself, and whoever would threaten it threatens his very existence. Whoever would undermine such beliefs is fit to be burned at the stake.

Our understanding of the desperate fear of contrary ideas will be given fuller intelligibility if we inquire more specifically into the temptations of the animal psyche. It does not seem to be noticed how much the cognitive powers of mind are subordinated to elemental instincts. Sheer possessiveness is a simple instance: ideas are like property; we defend them because they are *ours*. We have the all-too-familiar emotional need to be right. If someone gives reason for doubting our idea, we do not easily cast it aside or revise it. Rather, we smolder with anger and resentment, and we are obsessed with how we will take our revenge. In the meantime, we will redouble our efforts to defend our dogma: there must be some way we can preserve it, and you may be sure that we will. Partisanship surpasses dispassionate intellect. *My* idea, or that of *my* religion, or *my* political group is irresistable for just that reason.

Consider again our tribal inheritance. It is massively important to the survival of the tribe that its members be conformists, that they be obedient to the leader and devoted to the welfare of their group. Otherwise they perish. We witness everywhere the overwhelming tendency to conform, and this tendency conspicuously includes the will to conform to the *beliefs* of the herd. It is a virtual certainty that such a propensity has been selected in the evolutionary lottery. Natural selection or not, the will to please, to be acceptable and to be accepted, to think with the others, to congregate with the like-minded, to spurn the outsider or misfit, is universal. The process begins very early in life, when the young naturally imitate their elders and then their peers. They want to be like them, and it is essential to the life of the group that there be a drive to imitate.

Not quite so widely noted is the fact that we demand conformity from others. We not only want to imitate our fellows; we will not accept those who do not want to be like us. Both the leader and the led demand conformity of everyone. Disagreement and nonconformity are lethal to the tribe. It is anti-social and disloyal to criticize or to resist the lore of the people. Those who do it are untrustworthy. There must be solidarity and unity of purpose in all things. Thus nature must have it. Unanimity, not truth, is demanded. The impartial seeker after truth and justice must be punished, expelled from the group, or otherwise repudiated.

Both our will to believe and our demand that others share that belief are forcefully illustrated in religion. It is an instructive fact about the human condition that religion provides the foundation and meaning of life, yet it is unfounded in reasoning and evidence. Still, as a general human phenomenon, it is unshakable, and those who challenge it will suffer. The lesson is not only that one must have meaning in his life. Our tribe *requires* that we believe. One *must* believe, and he must believe in just the manner specified by his superiors. Belief is demanded and enforced by an array of terrifying threats and extravagant promises. The transports of heaven and the inconceivable pains of hell are contingent upon proper belief, and temporal tortures are visited upon those whose faith seems to waver or deviate. Such is the strength of the demand for conformity, and almost everyone feels it intensely.

Any number of further examples could be adduced. We would ill understand the conduct of officials, administrators, politicians, and bureaucrats if we left out of account their impulse to get our lives organized for what they think is best for us. The herd exerts its solidarity in still further ways. Whether within the tribe or outside of it, the in-group/out-group opposition is effective. We all think alike in the in-group; that's part of what makes us an in-group, while the ideas of the out-group are alien. We are naturally partisan: we must reject the ideas of our adversaries *because* they are those of the adversary, the foreign. "These people are not on our side," we think, "they are against us. Their agenda excludes our wisdom and our good." Henceforth, intransigence and accusation displace judiciousness and discernment.

That's fine, you say, for primitive tribesmen, but what does it have to do with, well, the modern university man or the intellectual, who is learned, sophisticated, emancipated, wholly independent in his thinking? Oh, my!

What naivete! No such independence exists, of course. It is nowhere to be found. The herd instinct reigns as forcefully as ever. The entire politically correct mob of professors, deans, provosts, university presidents, and advisers to the students will tolerate no deviancy: they insist on orthodoxy. They teach it in the classrooms; they transmit it in freshman orientation; they enforce much of it with speech and harassment codes that protect only the certified victim groups. Freedom of speech abates quickly. Radical student groups may disrupt incorrect gatherings with impunity; radical women's conclaves allow no dissent, no diversity. The august executive board of the American Anthropological Society will censure Derek Freeman for daring to question the religion of Mead. Distinguished sociologists will threaten James Coleman with official condemnation for his heresy that there is little correlation between the quality of education and the money spent on it. On it goes; it becomes a stampede. The president's Task Force on Racial Issues will not invite speakers who are opposed to affirmative action. The president of Dartmouth College will lie in public in order to carry out a vendetta against the *Dartmouth Review*. He is not humiliated, ridiculed, despised, or removed from office. Why not? What climate of repression must be the norm on campuses that such incidents occur without outrage from the entire community?[16] Elite journalists follow suit, as do editors and publishers. Many editors will refuse a manuscript, however meritorious, if it is not written in gender-neutral language.[17] If they exclude manuscripts just because of their (grammatically correct) pronouns, then of course they will do so if the content, regardless of its truth, is offensive to their sensibilities, and they will publish any trash if it is ideologically avant-garde. The pettiness and unmanliness of it all are stupefying.

Many members of the faculty are not defenders of these juvenile but tyrannical orthodoxies, but they keep their peace about them and go along with them. They are fearful to offend the revolutionary vanguard, who will jeer them, show contempt, charge them with crimes, and even get them dismissed from the university. Tribal law dominates intellectual life. *Such conduct is not anomalous. It is a reversion to form for human nature.* If the arguments of a John Stuart Mill do not take deep root even in the university, what is the source of any real attachment to freedom of inquiry and freedom of speech? Of course, those whose freedom is being suppressed don't like it. *They*, and the genuine student and inquirer, are the ones who suffer from a "hostile learning environment." But the censors are numerous and militant, and they have intimidated the rest.[18] The law of mediocrity is in full sway.

A tribal creed is a wonderful bonding device: belief in "diversity," for example, is a credo around which a community of the faithful is united. What a treasure! Woe to him who would spoil the party. The rewards of belonging, acceptance, security, status, and reputation surpass those of intellectual integrity. Rejection and exclusion are unendurable. There are still further rewards for the faithful: think of the distinction of being in the intellectual and moral vanguard. Imagine an intelligent youth who wants status and pre-eminence. He is taught in college that he is superior to bourgeois values, so he can't pursue any of the conventional paths to reputation. He must be an intellectual! In graduate school he learns that his superiority to bourgeois values can be extended to the entire Western tradition, the appalling work of dead white European males. Hence he does not lead the life of the mind—the pursuit and transmission of knowledge. He leads the life of an ideologue and revolutionary, and he does it in the university, of all places. There he has the status and preeminence he craved. There is wonderful status in being a theorist in a manner that surpasses the very comprehension of ordinary mortals, and it can be done at such little cost to oneself. According to the rules of status, in fact, you cannot even entertain ideas from people of low status or from the out-group; they must be ignored.

The greatest glory goes to the leaders of the elite. Consider the philosophic theorists who would conquer the thinking world by dismissing every form of intellectual rigor and accomplishment. At first glance, it might seem a humbling idea that philosophy has no cognitive value. In fact, neither does science. We might as well read tea leaves or the entrails of a sheep. It seems the ultimate in a self-deflating posture, but far from it. Think of the glory of bringing down the entire intellectual heritage of the Western world. What mastery! And won't it bring any number of eager new recruits into the fold? But caution, those who would have freedom of mind: very few corruptions are as insidious as craving to be a leader. Rather than take no thought for disciples and popular acclaim, he casts about for a way to collect them, whatever it takes. This is not a free mind. The outcast or recluse is more apt to be free.

I do not say that the entire intellectual capital of the West has yet been squandered in this way. My immediate intent is to illustrate the ease with which the mind is debased by normal human impulses. Still, the dishonesty and ruthlessness of politically correct culture pervades American life and puts it in peril. Is the corruption of cultural elites surprising? It should not be. True science extended to all matters of inquiry is the exception. One should be surprised and delighted where inquiry and discourse tend to be conscientious. That is an ideal good and an uncommon good.

Regardless of his participation in the culture wars, the scholar tends to do his thinking in reference to a peer group: the prevailing luminaries in his field. Their issues and their paradigms must be his. He thinks and writes with them always in the back of his mind: "Will this argument get their attention and approval? How will the eminent Professors X, Y, and Z react to what I say? What will please them? What will offend them? What will convince them? Will they reject me if I bypass the forms they have given to the recent literature?" And so on. This is the discourse of a slave. It is pursued insensibly, subliminally, and one is hardly aware of his subjection, yet the conclave of voices is a jury that you must satisfy. Your fate, you believe, is in their hands. They own you.

I do not ascribe the prevailing weaknesses of intellect to our tribal heritage alone. There may be innumerable causes of weakness and dishonesty, including a young man's wish to impress his girlfriend; but further sorts of causes must be mentioned. One is the colossal force of ideology, which becomes religion and invulnerable as religion.[19] Surely, one of the reasons for clinging to an ideology is that it is the accepted and required view of an admired group. You display your superiority by subscribing to their program and by being accepted into their confidence, but that needn't be the only reason. It might even be that one so loves the outcome promised by the ideology that he is blinded to its defects. In any event, it is indisputable that such attachments distort, weaken, and bias the mind, and they are common.

Ideological bias fosters scientific decrepitude in two ways, only one of which is morally blameless. A system of thought is so appealing that one unconsciously neglects to test it in crucial ways. Take the case of Rawls: there is no reason that I know of to think that he is dishonest or otherwise willing to deceive, yet it does not occur to him to examine—much less test—one of the assumptions from which the entire theory is suspended. He declares that his theory is derived from "our" moral intuitions—the intuitions of persons inhabiting liberal democracies. There is, however, no evidence presented that anyone holds these intuitions, and Rawls makes no attempt even to consider how we might go about determining what the moral intuitions of the population are. I take it he is so admiring of his idea of justice that it does not occur to him that the prerequisite intuitions might be no more than fantasies.

Lest one suppose that those engaged in the hard sciences are free of ideological deformations, we should be reminded that all manner of mistaken conclusions have been reached by them when they are ideologically committed or are panic-stricken by what they suppose is an impending doom—regarding, for example, scarcity of food supply, depletion of natural resources, nuclear winter, population growth, global warming, or pollution.[20] This is not a recent phenomenon. Corruptions of character have distorted science throughout its history. Scientists have struggled for reputation and preeminence, and they frequently engaged in dogmatics, dissimulation, lies, and character assassination in order to attain them.

Then there is the ideologist who willfully conceals and distorts—a very familiar case, unhappily. Presumably, such behavior is justified by assuming that those who are unsympathetic to the ideology are mentally handicapped in some way—victims of false consciousness, perhaps—so we needn't take their objections seriously. This is blatant question-begging, to be sure, but who cares? One typically assumes, in addition, that the end to be obtained by fidelity to the ideology is so glorious that telling a few lies on its behalf is an inconsequential sacrifice. One such ideology is the theory that all variations in the behavioral traits of individuals are a consequence of variations in socialization. This is the egalitarian's religion. Then, when someone puts the faith in jeopardy, the very spine of their cosmos is cracked. The shock is unbearable and the furies are loosed. This is what happened to *The Bell Curve*, a work of science very widely supported in the community with the scientific preparation requisite to judging it.[21] Most of them have kept their support to themselves, for the ideologues have been successful in galvanizing opposition to it and in demonizing its authors and anyone who might share their views. The popular media have been happy to share in the execution. Characteristic of most attacks on *The Bell Curve* is deliberate misrepresentation and willful disregard of its arguments.[22] Here, ideological fervor cares nothing for truth. Today, if the IQ controversy were to be addressed with competence and integrity, one would have to take up Jensen's *The g Factor* in detail, but our intellectual climate is such that it is ignored, misrepresented, or ridiculed rather than studied, and people who happen to hear of it will be sure it is nothing but the work of a racist.[23]

However dismaying, there is nothing inherently baffling about this behavior. Intelligence functions to take care of its master, and the master might judge it best to put his brains out for hire. Any clever fellow who is underhanded never thinks of truth. He thinks of how he can get ahead. Intelligence resembles the political consultant, many of whom are brainy but unscrupulous. When a politician seeks elective office, there is any number of persons who are willing to advise him how to do it. Their aim is not to tell the truth or to be purveyors of political science. Their aim is to deceive, misrepresent, conceal, make false promises, and so on in a manner that is not apt to be widely detected. Intelligence is gleefully utilized in a patently immoral way, and the politician is all for it. Power is commonly more important to the political class than integrity. Granted, there are many who must behave this way hypocritically—those who declare themselves to be dedicated to impartial deliberation. But if their partisanship, pettiness, love of power, fame, money, and acceptance are more urgent than their commitment to truth, then so much the worse for impartial inquiry.

In addition to temptations of the flesh, there are more innocent and subtle psychological impediments to intellectual strength and self-possession. There are forms of intellectual servitude that are unconscious but not necessarily unwelcome. The content and forms of thought with which we think are not a priori truths. Nobody's reflections begin ex nihilo. Problems of philosophy, for example, are expressed in definite terms, with definite categories, distinctions, definitions, and aims, and there are prevailing preoccupations and agendas in the milieu where the introduction and apprenticeship occur. To a great extent, one thinks in those terms, even if they happen to be effete and diversionary. They are more likely to constitute a prison for the mind than its piercing weapon, yet they are used to interpret and evaluate present and past thought, present and past thinkers. It is a closed circle. The study of ethics has been mired in this way for well over half a century. It is a nearly superhuman task to transcend these forms of thought, to be able to evaluate them, and to recast their very assumptions and aims. The intellectual climate might well be—as it commonly is—moribund and scholastic, and that is what the learner inherits and inhabits. He has some intimation that the whole business is sterile, but it is quite another step to find his way through it so as to be rid of its oppressions. He is more inclined simply to abandon the subject altogether.

The circle encloses others. The ideas of any collection of thinkers are apt to become snarled in a single mass, tangled in mutual dependency, with diminished access to the world outside. Nobody is able to function apart from this snarl. It constitutes their universe of discourse; it is their reality, so no one becomes untangled and breathes free. No one even realizes there is a problem. Instead of trying to think independently of the entire mass, they try this way or that to analyze some of its themes and to thread them together again in what seems a more becoming way. It amounts to a sort of communal autism. The communards insist, of course, that all roads to the truth must travel through their exclusive domain; anything else is furiously rejected.

A more entrancing form of bondage comes from our attachment to a great mind. His surpassing power and breadth captivate us, and they prevent us from thinking our own thoughts and forming our own philosophy. To be sure, one's philosophy ought to be formed in consequence of pondering many thinkers and reflecting upon a wide range of knowledge and experience. Though in the end there might be little about it that is original, it still might be authentically one's own, a genuine and forthright completion of that peculiar system of energies we call ourself. So one plays with fire in contemplating great minds, for they can capture us completely, and we are no longer able to think for ourselves. Like a candidate for initiation, a young man becomes obsessed with the thought of Kant, or he would possess the mind of Heidegger or Peirce or Leo Strauss, and soon enough he cannot think in any way but theirs. He is joined by others; the great thinker becomes a cult figure, and it is betrayal of the cult to criticize his ideas in a fundamental way. A true philosopher will *apprentice* himself to one or more of his elders, but he will *attach* himself to none of them. It is for other men to seek a protector.

Still another impediment is our addiction to theories and theorizing *as such*, chastened only rarely by critical experience. The joys of living in the imagination have much to do with this addiction. The imagination is apt to be a more pleasant abode than experience, so we remain there as much as possible. Ideas are among the charmed inhabitants of this "inner landscape," as Santayana calls it. In the imagination, we love ideas! An individual falls in with the charming seducer, falls in love with it, cherishes it more than hearth and home, and defends it against all odds. He thinks of the idea as giving definition to his being. He notes with gratification any incident that seems to confirm it; he concocts elaborate theories to safeguard it. He repeatedly verifies the fidelity of his beloved simply by *imagining* conditions that would attest to her virtue, and the test of imaginative verification is not itself put on trial. One's visceral reaction is to resist any and all threats to favored beliefs. Even those individuals who are committed in principle to testing theories with experience rarely do so. If one has little experience of interest, or if it is uncongenial, or experience doesn't matter much to him, he tends to live in the imagination.

There is a common psychological propensity, especially among males, to *shut out* experience, to focus on one thing alone and not to be distracted from it. At many critical junctures, this is an invaluable asset—concentration is essential, but it also means that one is susceptible to strangulation by theory at the expense of experience. Theory alone becomes one's preoccupation. It easily distracts from experience and substitutes for it. A man might cling tenaciously to a theory concerning the nature of a good life, and he might even believe he was living that life, and he might take his theory and his counterfeit good to the grave and never have had any particularly decent moments throughout his entire life, but his precious theory remained intact.

The distinguishable causes of dreamful thinking typically occur in combination: to adopt an ideology is inherently pleasant, especially when it issues from an acknowledged master, and when it is the preferred mode of thought of a distinguished coterie. Then it may be repeatedly confirmed simply by imagining the delightful state of affairs that it would put in place, reinforced by the mutual admiration of the initiated.

Ideas are more loved or hated than tested for truth. Any bodily system sends out shocks to the brain when it is in jeopardy, and the brain replies with an emergency response for the beleaguered part, or perhaps the whole system crashes, as in fainting. Just so, there are ideas that constitute unbearable shocks to the individual, so the brain obliges by shutting down the impertinent neural nets. The offending ideas are passed by; we will not fix upon them. It is a defense mechanism; it is protective of the psyche. Just as we jump from a threatening reptile, we will remove ourselves from this danger too.

I have been speaking of ways in which the mind evades reality for itself and misrepresents it to others, and I have suggested how our experience can be diluted, concealed, and prepackaged in a way to lose its honesty and vitality. Again and again I am struck by how words and theories get in the way of experience, rather than illuminate it. The result is that one does not think his own thoughts. He is not the possessor of his own mind, which has become insensibly occupied by others. Perhaps the drive to imitate is the main cause of merely formulaic thinking: the mouthing of words, solemnly affirmed as one's very self. We are naturally driven to imitate and absorb the thinking of our tribe and accept it as our own, and under many conditions, perhaps, this is as it should be. It is a condition of survival, but it is also a huge obstacle to freedom and self-possession, and it leaves the pursuit of the scientific ideal to others. One doesn't realize that he is merely imitating, but there is no vitality here, no conviction from life and experience, and no autonomy. One is no more than a deputy for the thinking of someone else.

The corruptions and incapacities of cultural elites are not surprising. Observance of the scientific ideal is difficult, and it is exceptional. It is a near certainty that any well-established and prevailing intellectual climate will be moribund, and it will be so precisely because it is well-established and prevailing. The tendency to scholasticism is virtually inevitable. A period of genuine intellectual vitality and accomplishment is quickly spent, and its successors occupy themselves with interminable analysis of the ideas that have already been generated. Their primary subject matter, as Dewey liked to say it, becomes the texts of their predecessors, and reflection is drawn away from experience itself. Working from life experience is more difficult and demanding than poring over the logic of existing documents. Allegiance, conformity, and imitation will naturally prevail. It is not in the least surprising that the vital periods of the mind flicker only briefly; they are the exception. The comatose state is normal. It will not be recognized as such by its adherents, to be sure, all of whom believe they are cutting edge.

A review of mental incapacities would be deficient without mention of arrogance. I mean moral and intellectual arrogance: the certitude of the perfection of one's own thinking and the disdain for the beliefs and moral values of others. One who is arrogant in this manner has no reservations about discarding ways of life cherished by others and imposing his own upon them. "They are idiots and fools," he thinks, "and I know what is best for them." Such a one might be an intellectual, say, or a leader among political liberals, a smart undergraduate, an elite journalist, or a member of an activist judiciary. Normally, he is greatly reinforced in his arrogance by belonging to a coterie that is likewise assured of its own superiority. Hence the jurist bent on reforming the law according to his own conceits, for example, is congratulated by judges and professors of a like mind, and together they praise themselves for their wisdom and virtue. Thus each becomes the more smug and self-important.

Such, of course, are very dangerous minds, for they are closed. They will accept instruction neither from their designated inferiors nor from experience, and they do not hesitate to impose their will on others. Arrogance can exist in union with any of the weaknesses already surveyed, making them always more noxious and disabling. Without arrogance, many of our worst tendencies might remain more or less dormant, remaining fearful of expression, but with it, almost any of one's deplorable traits might attain a halo of preeminence. Arrogance, then, as the Greeks always taught, causes much hurt; it is a dreadful vice. We should beware and condemn it rather than applaud and teach it.

I have been discussing distinguishable problems: comforting self-deception, hiding from the truth and even attacking it, tribal solidarity, bondage to existing forms of thought, and the oppressive fancies of arrogance. All of these might be called *intellectual* weaknesses, but such a characterization would cloak a crucial point: strictly speaking, most are not intellectual failures. Independence of mind is not congenial to the usual sort of person, and incapacities of thinking occur for many reasons in intelligent people. Their debilitation is often of a moral nature: they lack moral virtue. Where courage, discipline, and integrity are lacking, the quality of reflection on moral issues must languish. Where the will to be accepted and approved in the inner circle of the intelligentsia is paramount, there will not be conscientious and autonomous thought. Such is the state of most academics and intellectuals. They are deficient in moral virtue. Their deprivation is moral, not intellectual, but that deficit is virtually a precondition of success within the ethos of a self-absorbed culture. Due to some assortment of the weaknesses I reviewed above, they seek celebrity and status above all, and when their peers are likewise impaired, the road to fame and power is also the road to corruption. Their society produces all manner of theory and criticism unencumbered by honesty or fact.[24] They congratulate each other while excoriating the turpitude of their adversaries. They have succeeded in persuading countless others of their moral superiority, and it is the fervent wish of many to win the approval of such elevated beings and even—heaven itself!—to be accepted into their company. To be sure, intellectuals always speak in the name of the people. They are as shameless as politicians.

One is reminded of Aristotle's discussion of practical wisdom. Intelligence without moral virtue, he says, is mere cleverness, and he adds that the individual who is most threatening to the polis is he who is both highly intelligent and morally wicked. Moral propensities, he observes, cannot function well apart from intelligence—that is manifest, but neither can intellect function well apart from moral virtue. Both in practical affairs and in cherished theorizing, there can be little intellectual virtue without moral virtue. As already reported of Aristotle, they occur together or not at all.[25]

Those who fail to satisfy the scientific ideal are not always guilty of distinctively moral incapacity. The normal mind develops fairly definite intellectual habits and expectations, and its understanding of virtually any topic depends on these predispositions. Such bias is difficult to recognize and set aside, and even for the receptive it is penetrated only with sustained effort. Unaccustomed ideas, accordingly, do not readily accommodate the norms embedded in the typical mind. In the way that I prefer to speak of the matter, such minds—however learned—are not *individual*. They have no idea of what it is to *be* individual, and they cannot grasp the import of what is individual.

There is the further question of how one should think about all the baseless ideas that provide comfort and solace to suffering minds without causing serious injury to anyone.[26] There is a seemingly endless list of persons who declare that their lives would be unsustainable without their religious faith, and there are many others who have lost their faith while feeling at the same time that the loss is irreparable.

No candid observer can assume that such dependencies can be significantly diminished. Those who look to a "rational" reconstruction of the social order that would free everyone of such irrational fevers do not understand human nature—and often they do not shrink from trying to brainwash the people into "rationality." Looking past the emotional needs of average people, it is clear that many individuals of exceptional integrity, courage, and intelligence live (in part) by faith and depend upon it. I will comment in the final chapter about meanings in life. Here I speak to a preliminary topic. For some individuals, at least, the loss of illusion needn't be traumatic, and there are particular benefits in becoming disillusioned. To become willingly disillusioned requires personal traits that provide their own rewards. For some few souls, there might be a Nietzschean self-overcoming and a variant of Aristotelian *eudaimonia*.

When one takes the measure of the human soul—his own above all—he is not edified; he must keep many secrets—not only from others but from himself. It is a strange mentality that wants to penetrate the snares and lures of his own mind and to make them his adversary. It must come from a man who despises sham and weakness, who loves courage, struggle, and conquest. It is a contest, taking yourself as opponent. You become your own prey, and the hunt is exciting. There is much to overcome: I have touched on some of our entrenched incapacities. Think of all the forces that sustain our composure and divert our integrity—all those instinctive needs: acceptance, conformity, imitation, reputation, and status. Think as well of pettiness, pretense, smugness, complacency, vanity, insecurity, fear, hope, the will to popularity, the need to enlist followers. The list goes on: the seductions of ideology, imaginative theorizing, and the consolations of philosophy. The thought of overcoming such obstacles is too demanding for most. They have some sense of their own debilitating tendencies, but they insist, too, that they must be accommodating of social realities: one has to get along and get ahead, after all, and they have a point. Hence they lead a sort of double life. Or is it half a life?

They see the rigors of Nietzsche's asceticism of the soul—the icy peaks and barren deserts—and properly conclude that they have better things to do. Think of all the things in your self that you would like to overcome; think of all the subjective resources it would take; think of the costs to a normal life. No thank you. But there is the odd character who lusts after the prey. The nature of that which he would subdue also defines the virtues he would possess: honesty, courage, independence, and the like. With Nietzsche, the acts that make you virtuous are acts to overcome the native tendencies of the psyche that stand in the way of discipline, self-determination, and freedom. They would be reinforced and confirmed both in thinking and in deeds.

Suppose some approximation to them occurs. What is the good of that? It is the attainment of a sort of *eudaimonia*, when we use that expression to mean *well souled*. Well souled for what? For becoming a free and disillusioned spirit—a reflective being who surveys existence to discover whatever demons and gods it possesses, to celebrate its authentic meanings and goods, and to rejoice in the possession and exercise of his own power. No more bondage, but genuine self-possession, might be his. We are thinking of a person who does not wish to be under the tutelage of alien forces, including those of his own weakness. Nothing devious or unworthy is tolerated. We could call this remarkable condition a state of intellectual and moral integrity. We are describing a person who has engaged in a mighty struggle. To succeed in it— or just to carry it out with recognizable victories—presupposes extraordinary talents, and the struggle itself refines and perfects them. They define him, these powers of soul; they are at his disposal for all contingencies. His trials have made him well souled.

This is the same progression from natural to complete virtue that is characterized in the *Nicomachean Ethics*, but there is more self-overcoming in the project than Aristotle recognizes. The telos of this process is simply postulated by Aristotle, but here it is defined in terms of the actual challenges the psyche and the world present to a resolutely thinking being—a being whose powers are called forth and consummated in a manner that could not come to pass for the faint of heart. This is for the erotic and courageous pursuer of *to kalon*.

This meditation would be incomplete if left in a distinctly Nietzschean tenor. Nietzsche's individualism is sometimes morally foolish and irresponsible, and it is grotesquely intolerant of immeasurably precious values that rest on no illusion. Still, it must be agreed that this sort of individuality does not always breathe easily in ordinary life. Much of it offends the protectors of conventional sensibilities, and it does not easily endure the hypocrisies and shams of normal existence. No doubt it is good that these sorts are not plentiful. They are ill suited to much of the daily existence necessary to a community, and the community is apt to be uncomfortable with them. Still, these unconventional beings, who range from the village eccentric to the productive genius, are necessary to the survival of any culture that becomes unable to think beyond its reigning customs.

I have already begun to blend the analysis of intellectual excellence with moral considerations. It will be best to discontinue discussion of the good of the scientific ideal until we look into the good of integrity.

c. Integrity

There are individuals who are steadfast in their commitments. They do what they say they will do, whatever distractions or temptations might arise and whatever the risks from undertaking an unpopular or hazardous course. Indeed, we assume of them that they will do what has to be done whether they declare themselves or not, for that is their character. That is integrity. There is still more implied by the term: one's individuality, whatever it is, is not created anew to meet variations in the environment; one does not present a different face to different people in order to make himself acceptable to them, whatever they might like from him. He is the same man summer and winter, fair weather or foul. He is, moreover, the same man inside and out: he does not have a public personality—or personalities—that belie his inner nature. This is not to say that he is given to expressing himself. He might be commonly unwilling to display emotion. It is to say that there is no duplicity, no pretense, so what we encounter in our intercourse with him is really true of him. He is *genuine*, as we say, or sometimes we express the same fact by referring to him as a real person. All of this implies inner strength: a man who has no wish to be accommodating to every solicitation that comes along; there is no wavering; and there is no need to pretend. Neither would he lower himself to responding in kind to unworthy remarks and actions. If he is the real thing, he persists in high moral conduct where others are apt to resort to the petty or base.

The character we are considering is rare. He is one of nature's uncommon goods. In this world where nothing endures, where everything vacillates, where everyone sways with the popular breeze, where the self is dissipated to every whim, it is reassuring and edifying to contemplate something that is constant and unyielding. With this inner force, as well as in other ways, the ideal form of integrity has much in common with the pursuer of the scientific ideal. The lovers of both of these goods have unusual inner resources, yet obstacles to overcome in themselves, too. Integrity is the more inclusive condition and is not reducible to intellectual honesty and courage, and it incorporates goods not necessarily found in the other. Still, the present section can be taken in part as an elaboration of the preceding. I will use *autonomy* to refer to a union of these two ideals. The scientific ideal and the ideal of integrity complete each other in autonomy.

In discussions of integrity or its equivalents, a distinction is sometimes overlooked, but it must be observed. This is the difference between integrity as the formation and preservation of *individuality* and integrity as *moral steadfastness*. One could have the steadfastness without much individuality, just as one could have individuality with little presence of moral integrity. Full integrity, which is my topic, combines them. In the preceding chapter I used "integrity" interchangeably with "virtue." Here I include the notion of individuality within that of integrity, so the similarity to the notion of *areté* is thereby diminished.

Begin with the enticing but troublesome idea of individuality. The attainment of individuality can be an ideal good, but the possibility must be entertained with caution. The idea of individuality is problematic and ambiguous; its ideal properties must be distinguished from its considerable but tempting perils. Only then might we see how it can be merged with moral integrity. I reject any notion of it as license. It is not hedonism and permissiveness. The attainment of a truly individualized self is a matter of protracted discipline, and it requires the incorporation of limits.

It is hazardous—but not atypical—to think of integrity and individuality unhinged from each other. Modern writers and poets, the romantics especially, tend to make the mistake of severing them and celebrating individuality just on its own, where it becomes a virtue unto itself, without constraint. The person of this disposition treasures what is individual and nourishes it. His distinctive talents, idiosyncrasies, and peculiar genius are celebrated as such. An individual is unique and cherishes his uniqueness. He is determined that his life not be an imitation. He is impatient with limits; there is a prominent element of rebelliousness in him. Fidelity to this sort of commitment is at least a version of integrity. It requires a certain nerve and persistence to refuse the temptations of the herd and to disregard the hectoring of the solid and staid.

A further noteworthy trait of the modern version of individuality is its tendency to subjectivism: one tirelessly scrutinizes his own soul, in all its expressions, and he basks in a rich imaginative life. With this, the constraints of the outside world become less insistent and their status diminishes. With enough self-absorption, indeed, such a person might be given to extravagances of impulse and feeling, and then he seems a rather formless soul, actually. Today, this sort of ideal thrives in the celebration of bizarre, brazen, and even self-destructive forms of self-expression. It has descended to brainless self-indulgence. Even so, there is much to be salvaged in modern individualism. Its corruption into self-absorbed idiocy is not inevitable, and it might produce superb specimens of distinctive natures. It will serve us to persist in distinguishing the true coin of individuality from its counterfeits.

The tormented soul, brilliant and striving and highly individualized, is hardly acknowledged in ancient literature, or he is treated as an aberration, yet he has his own capabilities for ideal fulfillment. His champions are correct to say that what is noteworthy and precious about the self is not reducible to certain enumerated and precisely defined virtues. They refuse to think of the individual as no more than a replica of an antecedent and universal form, and imitation seems the sacrifice of all individuality and freedom. They aim for the development of a uniquely distinguished nature—an idea that owes much to Nietzsche, obviously, and resonates with Dewey's critique of fixed ends and his characterization of growth. A commonly used description of this ideal of individuality is that of making one's life into a work of art. The commitment might be creative and exhilirating, and life as a work of art could be an ideal worthy of eros.

The comment that one's life ought to be his own creation can be simply glib, just the same, and a cover for sloth and self-indulgence. The youth who would incarnate this form of life is subject to progressive degeneration. *Real* works of art are notoriously difficult; they require talent, dedication, persistence, and sacrifice, and even so they are often failures. So it can be with an individual, and the inherent constraints on a *life* are far more portentious than those on a poem or a painting. We cannot set aside the all-important question of what manner of self is *worthy* to be preserved and defended—worthy not only in the sense of its capacities to contribute to the vigor and richness of the moral order but worthy also from the standpoint of personal *eudaimonia*. The absolute die-hard will say that no form of limitation or definition is acceptable, but that comment betrays a sort of adolescent derangement: the logic of the hedonist, once more. It is entirely possible to unite stalwart virtue with individuality. Moral exemplars, such as Socrates, are hardly interchangeable automatons, after all. Ideal integrity, then, would be the formation and persistence of moral qualities as well as other noteworthy and affective traits of self. Admittedly, there are some precious forms of individuality, such as those found in many artists, that are in fact uneasy and impatient with moral responsibility. We must gratefully accept their genius in spite of their constitutional failings, but individuality need not invariably or even commonly be severed from good character.

To establish and maintain individuality with integrity demands that we resist powerful instincts. The man of authentic individuality must overcome the inbred tendencies to conform for the sake of conforming, and he will not yield his self to the seductions of comfort, ease, popularity, or status. At the same time, he must develop a virile freedom that also acknowledges limits and imposes stern self-discipline. Here, too, he has much self-overcoming to accomplish. It seems a greater puzzle, indeed, that there is independence and individualism than there is conformity and compliance. The will to conform and the will to demand conformity are so great that there seems to be no means for some kind of individual to develop and prosper. We seek to belong, to find a home in the whole, and we yearn for an enduring and sacred order. Most men are so eager for acceptance and so willing to conform that the idea of following one's inner law, regardless of what others think, is terrfying.

On the other hand, there are actually abundant sources of individualism. Every child grows up eager to test his limits and those imposed on him. He is bold and adventurous, and he surges with new aptitudes and powers that must find expression. To the consternation of his parents, he seems always to want things his own way. There is a concomitant trait: he wants to be himself rather than what others expect him to be. Accept me for myself, he cries! Hence there is a dialectic of forces, from which we will occasionally see a true individual, and he might even be endowed with noble character and a sense of limit.

The young child displays both these tendencies. He wants the acceptance, security, and praise of doing what is expected of him, but he is also driven to challenge the constraints of authority, to assert himself, and to be adventurous. At any rate, he is eager to assert himself against *adult* authority, but he flees to a group of peers, to which he conforms with a passion. His adventuresomeness might be expressed in a manner acceptable to the group, and if he is fortunate, he will find one that suits his characteristic propensities. He looks for a group to which he can conform comfortably. Even this is difficult, however, and adult individuals find that their lives are largely governed by pretense: they pretend to be what they are not. Thus would they try to please or impress others. If you cannot accept me for what I am, then I will try to be what you prefer. Inner law, such as it is, does not withstand social pressure. Standing alone, all alone, is something else entirely.

In addition to the difficulties of standing alone, the one driven to be himself confronts daunting challenges: there is a problem of self-discovery and self-formation. Who am I, really, and what is the individuality that I would be? How well do I know myself, and how do I distinguish what is authentically me from what I have been taught to be? There is a danger that I will commit myself to a life that will be untrue. If eros truly finds its object, will I have the strength to pursue it to fulfillment? Many a trembling soul finds this an exciting and perilous search. Though he has much in common with the entire race, his nature is identical to none other, and it is impossible that he could be himself in any but a few forms—no imitations, no copies, but uniquely and quintessentially himself. He is inspired by exemplars in history and literature, to be sure, but his goal is not to become the same with any of them. Otherwise, he continues in the servitude of pretense.

Such a being, like the one who would embody the scientific ideal, must exert pitiless self knowledge in his self-overcoming. We are imposters and forgers, and we don't even know it ourselves, but a few individuals are alert to their own dissembling ways. They catch themselves in them, and they can't tolerate it. It is for others to shield themselves from the truth—those who seek the gratifications of reputation and self-display. It is for others to rely on numberless rationalizations—disguised, no doubt, as conscientiousness, caring, friendliness, and sensible adherence to duty. The discerning see this in others, less frequently in themselves. But they must see it if they are to achieve self-possession and force of character. Then one endures the hardships of being an individual; he is a threat to herd mentality: mediocrity, complacency, and easy adjustment, and the herd will not tolerate it. One is reminded of Nietzsche's portrait of "the last man." After Zarathustra's denunciation of this slavish and contented being, the attendant crowd cry as one, "Give us this last man, O Zarathustra, . . . Turn us into these last men!"[27] When Zarathustra proves unsympathetic, they threaten his life and run him out of town.

Nietzsche had an exaggerated loathing for mediocrity, but his fears were not wholly groundless. Mediocrity is comfortable and popular. It is easy, complacent, and self-congratulatory, and it reinforces our love of conformity. Conformists do not wish to be challenged or told the truth. "Give us the last man, O Zarathustra!" The individual constitutes a reproach to sloth and weakness, and he will not be tolerated. He will not conform; he will not be like the rest of us. Out with him!

Not surprisingly, then, the individual is constrained, and the romantics bemoan the obtuseness of his suppressors. Are the suppressors entirely without reason, nevertheless? Certainly not. Unlike the man of perfect classical virtue, there are decided weaknesses in this individualism; it is not only because it distracts the lotus eaters. Under many conditions, the demand for conformity is justified: the survival of the group requires solidarity of purpose and action. There may well be a tortured ambivalence between the claims of individuality and duty. Moreover, there is apt to be a considerable residue of wisdom in the tribal lore, whether it is observed or not. One should not repudiate it just because it doesn't originate with himself.

Individuality easily takes perverse forms, and any family or group must be on guard against them. It readily turns into routine self-indulgence. When the young are not required to behave, all manner of monstrosities are apt to appear. A child is endowed with such self-serving drives as greed and ruthlessness, and his individuality might take shape around such possibilities, or he could remain forever juvenile as a hedonist, or his independence could become stalled in narcissism. In the contemporary world, of course, his mere self-expression—whatever sort of self it might be—is elevated to the highest good, and parents and teachers applaud his every antinomian twitch.

I might have quoted Emerson repeatedly in the preceding discussion. He is one of the great despisers of imitation and mediocrity, and he finds that society encourages nothing so much as conformity. Few authors express the greatness of individuality as forcefully as he, yet he is inattentive to its dark side. "Nothing is at last sacred but the integrity of your own mind," he affirms.[28] Then he relates a conversation. "On my saying, 'What have I to do with the sacredness of traditions, if I live wholly from within?' my friend suggested,—'But these impulses may be from below, not from above.' I replied, 'They do not seem to me to be such; but if I am the Devil's child, I will live then from the Devil.' No law can be sacred to me but that of my own nature."[29] No surprise that Nietzsche had great admiration for Emerson, who wrote in *Fate*, "Every spirit makes its house; but afterwards the house confines the spirit," and in *Circles*, "The only sin is limitation."

Emerson elsewhere takes a more qualified position, but these remarks nonetheless display the tendency to take individuality as an unqualified good. It is wiser to be more discriminating, and we do so when we rejoin the idea of individual singularity to that of moral rectitude. Although the two sides of integrity are frequently separated in fact, they need not be so in principle, and it is dangerous to praise and encourage individuality without reservation. Moral virtue is one of the necessary constraints on it, but it is also a power and a fulfillment. Individuality becomes corrupt and even effete when it functions without limit, and it is prone to haughtiness, but we need not conceive it as a repudiation of discipline and order. In its wisely chastened form, individuality is much less apt to be offensive to the common man, for it is not condescending. Its contempt is more apt to be directed at pretense, frivolity, and weakness. When individuality is attended by virtue, indeed, its possessor is a champion of fundamental goods of common life. In this incarnation, the individual is less likely to be viewed as an antagonist of customary life.

We are not bound to accept the typical modern formulations. We can think of individuality in a manner that puts it in happy combination with virtue, yielding an enriched notion of integrity. I have offered Plato as an example of a thinker who evidently disdains individuality, yet there is more tolerance of it in his philosophy than one might suspect, and, in fact, Plato offers a splendid suggestion. Immediately following the first description of justice in the soul in *The Republic*, Socrates adds that acts of justice might be done "either concerning the acquisition of money, or the care of the body, or something political, or concerning private contracts."[30] This is a remarkable observation, for moral excellence can be possessed, he says, by those engaged in ordinary pursuits—even politics, law, and business! The exercise of virtue in the soul would seem to be compatible with a diversity of ways of life. It seems to allow for the life of husband, father, writer, artist, friend, and citizen *with virtue*. This gives me a range of persons I can be. I can be *me*, but it is a virtuous me. I remain a distinctive individual, but an individual made better, stronger, and happier due to the possession of virtue. This is a further example of how a good is enriched and secured when joined with excellence of character. Virtue is not the antagonist of individuality but its protector and enhancer. Who is more individual than Socrates?

In subsequent treatments of justice—most notably in book 6—Socrates characterizes the perfection of the *philosophic* nature, the nature that craves knowledge of the forms, and this love of knowledge leads inexorably, if incidentally, to excellence in all parts of the soul. Although the philosophic life is claimed to be best of all, it is not the exclusive repository of virtue, and justice in the soul is evidently a possibility for some different sorts of people. To be sure, Plato himself is preoccupied with the philosophic nature. The possibilities suggested by his earlier analysis were left unexplored.

Of course, a man might have integrity while falling well short of the ideal self characterized by Plato or Aristotle. He might be perfectly resolute in his duties but aspire to no more than that. A man of integrity is nevertheless apt to possess many real virtues. He is not a trembling, shapeless lump, moved at will by his surroundings. Functionally, many of his virtues will be much the same as those of his ancestor, for both of them inhabit a world where courage, self-control, justice, and wisdom are surpassing assets. Rather than push this topic further, I will turn to a related technical question, after which I will comment on the *eudaimonia* of integrity.

Men will give up whatever integrity they have for the sake of passing and trifling goods. They might be criticized for self-betrayal or for denying their true self. But how, it will be asked, can one self be more real than another? How is it that any act of self is more truly an act of self than another? Perhaps the moralist is an obscurantist, relying on a spurious distinction between the real and the apparent will, which is invoked in order to force you to be free or to claim that your objection to the regime is not really real. The questioner of this distinction might well ask in addition, "What is it that has integrity? In speaking of the true self, aren't you postulating some sort of supersensible entity that possesses such a trait?" He could go on to defend the genuineness of the conformist. He conforms, say, for the sake of popularity and security. Then it seems that the desire for popularity and security is an authentic expression of that particular individual, while independence is not. Is it not sophistical of the moralist to make the claim that this is not the man's true self? In the case at issue, it *is* his true self.

Such objections do not miss the mark if the moralist does in fact resort to such antique distinctions. Our experience, nevertheless, is such that we are convinced that expressions like self-betrayal are meaningful and important. The problem of the postulated moralist is that he does not accurately understand and characterize the phenomenon at issue. His complaint should be that the conformist has misjudged what is *most important* to self. Distinctions between different tendencies within the self have a fundamentally *moral* quality: one has better and worse dispositions within his own constitution, which does not function as a unity. He is entirely capable of making a bad or ill-informed judgment about the best possibilities of his life. In the case of the willing conformist, the moralist might really have made a bad judgment: maybe that is the best the imitator can put together. If so, we should let it go, if no further harm is done.

The experience of self-contempt (or self-sacrifice, self-betrayal, self-congratulation, etc.) is common. Such experiences occur when one makes a judgment about what is best or what ought to be his foremost priorities, but due to weakness he is unable to honor the morally preferred deed. There is nothing obscurantist in saying that an individual has clear moral propensities, but owing to the urgency of other passions or obsessions, he is unable to do what he sincerely believes he ought to do. He accordingly suffers from remorse and self-reproach. We use an expression like self-betrayal to denote such a condition. Instead of saying he has denied his true self, we should say he has denied his *moral* or *better* self.

The self that has integrity is a morally determined self, not a metaphysical postulate. Some kind of self, determined in a thousand ways, given content in a thousand ways, comes into being. No need to engage in the occult: it is a self that has in some measure been morally constituted. Moral propensities, experience, and teaching coalesce to establish a distinctive nature. One has reached a determination about what is corrupt and what is not, what is weak and slavish, and what is upright and ideal. Corruptions are disdained and virtues pursued due to the incipient dispositions and the learning of the individual. Moral integrity is the established strength and durability of such a condition.

It is to this self-in-formation that a moralist appeals; he seeks to reinforce the best tendencies and to provide objects of aspiration. He would display to the conscientious soul the way in which he undermines himself or is ignorant of superior possibilities. In the language introduced earlier, we engage in a wide-ranging and discerning moral appraisal. We attempt to distinguish the concatenations of values to be expected by pursuit of one sort of life rather than another.[31] In a given case, appraisal might come to little, or it might inspire.

In the current instance, what is the appraisal pertinent to such an aspirant? How does an imagined modern Socrates advise an imagined modern Glaucon who is uncertain of the virtues of integrity? There is much that might be said. Glaucon is not apt to be tempted to be a conformist, to follow the many, but it could be pointed out to him that he harbors impulses that could draw him in that direction. He might be reassured if it were also pointed out that mere conformity is distinguished from a friendship of virtue—discerning and deliberate comradeship leavened with ideal affinities. Merely instinctive conformity is distinguished as well from solidarity with others in support of revered institutions, so Glaucon needn't equate integrity with either radical individualism or slavish conformism. Wise loyalties and ideal affinities cannot be equated to blind acceptance of the herd. To deny any such distinction is to fall victim to typical reductionism, disclosing a philosophic ineptitude. In regard to the present reflection, what could epitomize the nonreductive philosophy better than this comment from Santayana? "Love is a brilliant illustration of a principle everywhere discoverable: namely, that human reason lives by turning the friction of material forces into the light of ideal goods."[32] Our Glaucon might be surprised but happy to be told, in truth, that from the bonding of the herd instinct emerge heroic levels of courage and devotion to what is noble.

Inasmuch as a Socrates prefers to study all the alternatives, the two might take up the merits of a life of imitation and pretense. What is the difference between the independent mind and the pretender? Consider first that our student has specific needs and characteristics, and he wants to be respected for himself, not for a facade. At the same time, he also lusts after some glittering rewards: in his case, the glories of politics, where pretense is apt to be a great asset. Still, there are weighty differences: the man of integrity actually possesses virtue, while the pretender engages in masquerade. Why not? A Platonic-like answer might run as follows: A *poseur* does not command his own forces; he devotes himself to mere imitating. He imitates some trendsetter, who is also a pretender. Hence the *poseur* is an imitation of an imitation. This makes him something of a hollow shell—twice removed (Plato would say thrice removed) from the reality of a being who is an originator, *archai*, of action.

The discourse naturally proceeds to a discussion of what it means to be master of yourself. The idea can be made intelligible by returning to the notion of one's best self, the self one admires and aspires to be, not a self that one is ashamed of or that spends itself in trying to ingratiate high-status persons. The man of integrity marshalls his own strength, virtue, and intelligence in accord with his moral self. His resources are not transient, intermittent, and insecure; they are stable and vigorous. In contrast, the powers of the promiscuous self, such as they are, are dispersed to every social drift and bauble. The self is a whore: it is diffused throughout the marketplace, pandering to any occasion of praise and popularity. Diffusion of self is dissipation of power. It is a state of dependency, a perverse form of self-denial.

Such a self is owned by its clients. In effect, one has admitted that the claims made on him by these triflers take precedence over the claims he makes on himself. The inner law is silent, if not nonexistent. This is a highly dependent self, and its happiness is in the keeping of the humors of others. The gratifications of a diffused and promiscuous self must be dispersed, insecure, and suffused with anxiety—and not without self-contempt. The self as whore, moreover, is known for what it is but not respected for it. This is the difference between self-command and being commanded by others. In this context, freedom is acting from inner law, and the law is not for sale. There is a propriety of self that is not available to those whose self is scattered in the winds of fashion and dependency. One's character has a hard edge; its priorities are not prostituted.

The conversation between Socrates and Glaucon has already assumed a vocabulary too modern, and it need not be continued, but let us take up some further considerations in our own tongue. When invested with wisdom, a person of integrity would be without complacent assumptions about the essential goodness of the world. There is much sentimental theorizing to the effect that the nature of things is somehow a form of perfection, and the individual can bring himself into unbroken harmony with it. As a matter of simple integrity, however, one cannot be in harmony with the whole of things. Too much of it is faulty, cruel, oppressive, dishonest, and miserable. He who retains his integrity will be out of sorts with much that exists. He cannot be at peace with the universe at large, and much as he might want to, he cannot feel entirely at home in his own community. His individuality, perception, and honesty guarantee alienation from many of the most common features of the world, and he might feel painfully unsuited to normal social life in most of its forms.

How, then, can such a being be considered *eudaimon?* If you define *eudaimonia* as perfect adjustment to everything indiscriminately, then you speak of it in terms of the soul of Nietzsche's last man. Perhaps the price for autonomy is too high; perhaps it is better to be the last man. Is that what you really want? No such resolution is possible for a free and disillusioned spirit. It is suitable then to ask whether the autonomous man is well souled for the world *as candidly known* and whether the goods available to him are of a high order. Surely we can affirm that there are ideal goods beckoning singularly to him. An ideal good, after all, is the product of *discerning* intelligence, virtue, and eros. It is a deliberate construction out of the flux of nature, much else of which is turned aside. His own self, indeed, is an ideal good of a particular sort, and he possesses powers to construct wisely and courageously. He has profound attachments, loyalties, and loves, which he has also discriminated from the world's motley assortment. He may be unsuited to much in existence, but he is not dependent upon all of it, either; nor does he feel obliged to affirm it all.

He cannot think of happiness as if it were a morally neutral condition, for it is not. His happiness can be attained only in a manner that will satisfy his individuality and virtue. He loves the courageous and honest, and he despises what is cringing and false. We should ask what happiness is suitable for *him*, for the man of true autonomy—not for just any man and not just any happiness. Self-possession and self-command have become intrinsic to such a man, defining his soul. They require strength. In the extraordinary case, one exercises it without struggle. His strength is a presence like a natural force: it permeates his thought and deeds as a matter of course, without having to be summoned or exhorted. Here is an impregnable love and an impregnable good.

Imitation and pretense are not disabling in every environment. Some people are without shame, and they might become rich and powerful in the world with such devices. The varieties of life are many. Moral integrity itself can take various forms. It might be narrow, rigid, dogmatic, ignorant, and unthinking; it might be laced with vindictiveness, cruelty, and needless intolerance. Even without these deficiencies, it might have more modest aims than those revealed in *The Symposium*. One can have integrity in the sense of being true to his moral self, yet that self might not be driven by eros for what is highest; it might not aspire to what is noblest and best. It simply does its duty with integrity. United with the virtues of the scientific ideal, however, it attains a splendid completion nevertheless, and that in itself is a most uncommon good. United also with divine eros, it becomes capable of an ideal happiness.

Insensibly, the treatment of integrity and the scientific ideal has moved us to a modern recapitulation of the idea of the unity of the virtues, with the notable inclusion of an ideal of individuality. The unique and singular become proper objects of eros. The scientific ideal cannot exist, much less prosper, apart from integrity, and the moral qualities of integrity can be fully engaged with the realities of existence only in the company of intellectual power and candor. The striving for individuality is apt to founder if separated from intelligence and moral strength. If one is to form his expectations and assessments of life with scope, honesty, and discrimination, if he is to pursue ideal goods in accord with the disciplines of nature, and if he would attain them in some measure, then he must be vested with such qualities. Such a vesture is itself an ideal good. It is what I have called autonomy. Autonomy is a calling. It is not a part-time job or a hobby, and one must have the stomach for it. It is for those who are determined to develop their individuality and who at the same time want tasks suitable for eros, those who yearn to give birth to what is fine and noble.

d. COMPLETIONS

Thinking about the good is difficult. The topic is submerged in a stew of human weaknesses: fantasy, vanity, sentimentality, neediness, and desperation. On the other hand, to make a classification of *types* of good is easier, and it is sometimes helpful. Philosophers have offered us various classifications, but no set of distinctions is without problems. To my thinking, it is useful to distinguish four sorts: fundamental goods, accustomed goods, ideal goods, and unbought goods, but the divisions between them are porous. *Fundamental goods*, as previously remarked, are those conditions that life depends upon, including those that are essential for pursuing a greater good. The security of home and family, the vigor of the moral order, and minimally sane political conditions belong in this group, so do health, shelter, clothing, and food. *Accustomed goods* are those that are inseparable from normal activities and duties: the satisfactions, such as they are, of work, recreation, citizenship, and family, for example, but I would enlarge the notion of normal activities to include events that occur intermittently but fatefully. These would be such goods as marriages, births, loves, and reunions of those who have been parted. Such events are so precious that they are called holy. There are also victory in war, celebration of conspicuous forces of nature, and consecrations of epochal events in the life and history of the culture. Learning, too, is an accustomed good, so is the enjoyment of works of art, which might be among the most rhapsodic and exalted of experiences. (Likewise, there are accustomed evils: defeats, deaths, partings, failures of all kinds—not to mention boredom, disaffection, and oppression.) Is there anyone so removed from reality that he thinks of such goods and evils as conventional?

Ideal goods constitute another class. I will not now add to what I have already said of them, but I repeat that ideal goods are not necessarily—or usually—esoteric. The goods of friendship and family, of art and science, and of social order are capable of ideal fulfillment, but they typically require genius or virtue for such a happy outcome. The ideal forms of such ordinary goods as family and friendship are uncommon because virtue is uncommon. Then there are *unbought goods*, by which I mean those uncomplicated but frequently wonderful experiences that we undergo in virtue of the simple constitution of our nature. To name them *unbought* is to say that they are there for the asking—indeed, for the taking, if only we will permit ourselves. (I do not suggest that to position oneself to enjoy such goods is always effortless.) To revel in a view of the seashore is an unbought good, to breathe the morning air, to stroll under the live oaks, to share in mirth, to dance, to hold hands, to hug your child, to enjoy the sunshine and the garden, to catch the bird in flight or in song—all such wonders are unbought goods. Nature works endless enchantments, and we are delighted by their moods and nuances, but only if we let them in. If one is of a sour disposition, or if he is ceaselessly preoccupied with obligations or with status, always distracted, stressed, and anxious, or if he is obsessively introspective, these priceless goods will escape him. It is madness to be forever striving, achieving, and proving yourself. There are times to let the joys of experience, scarce as they are, get through to our famished senses. Who knows where or when he might be visited with the blessings of an unbought good?[33]

I debate whether I should add a fifth classification: completions, but I think better of it. Any variety of good might be a completion. The unbought good is a completion in the sense of being self-contained, but it is by no means the completion of every sort of activity in your life. If we follow Dewey, we would call any consummatory experience the completion of a history, so accustomed goods also will attain their completion on occasion. Fundamental goods, though ongoing, are not there for the taking. They must be achieved and reachieved, and they can be lost, so again we could speak of the attained good of this type as a completion. What if we speak more broadly, however, and ask of the completion of a self or a life? Or suppose we speak of the good of one's life as a whole. What would such expressions mean? And would such goods be distinguishable from all other forms?

Again, a further classification is unnecessary. Goods of the latter kind are best understood as completions of ideal goods. Virtue, for example, is an ideal end, and it is a completion of our nature. The meaning of the idea deserves attention. We can speak with clarity about the completion of a project or a work of art, but what is the completion of a self or a life? To speak of a self being completed implies that it has limits, and one has approached them, but it also implies that distinguishable traits—not just any trait—achieve this condition. We have potentialities for all manner of behavior. Most of them are not funded with great promise, and many are unworthy of completion. In a lifetime, accordingly, we must focus on rather few potentialities. It is frivolous to speak of the completion of the whole self; we distinguish and select certain promising possibilities and concentrate on them: warrior, doctor, artist, mother, father, or scholar.

Rather than a specific art, suppose our aim is a certain state of soul—the scientific ideal, perhaps, or integrity and autonomy. Although I defend the idea that self-overcoming is needful for any such end, it is idle to think of its accomplishment as an exclusively subjective process. One engages in deeds. One *desires* to engage in them. They are fulfillments, and they help to form and confirm our tendencies and to reinforce them. We become inseparable from them, and their intrinsic demands lure and propel us further. In the best of cases, our deeds constitute an order of harmonious goods, a fulfilling and satisfying environment—sometimes, perhaps, a fine and noble one—in which we dwell.

The deeds that we do measure the soul. One could not speak of how just, courageous, and independent he is unless he has succeeded in performing acts of justice, courage, and independence. Don't congratulate yourself on your presumed courage and then crumple before the first threat to it. Don't boast of the independence of your mind and then produce a work that is merely trendy. To speak of a completion of self without being able to display the act is fanciful or vacuous. We can speak assuredly of a completion only if it occurs in act. The act tests and confirms the completion. If we strive to surpass ourselves, using all our wit and courage, and we fail, and we never succeed in further surpassing, then it is clear we have met our limit.

Romantic yearnings, in contrast, tend to be indeterminate. The romantic acknowledges ends, but they are all transitional. The transitions are thrilling and satisfying, but inasmuch as we are beings that do have limitations, life cannot be endlessly transitional. We would like to have some sense of abiding completion and fulfillment. This would be a feeling that some worthy goal has been achieved, perhaps over a long period of time. It demanded your every resource, and you satisfied the demand; you put everything of yourself into it without reserve. The work expresses your best self, and you say, "Behold: it is good."

The confirmed completion testifies to the possession of specific qualities of self, and, to be sure, the possession implies a distinctive quality of experience and depth of reward. Completion is not termination: the virtuous man continues to do deeds that are virtuous, testifying to an abiding state of soul. He is content that he has satisfied his nature to its limits. Some mass of human energies has been integrated and directed to a worthy end and has been completed therein. Insofar as the man regards *his* nature, not a Platonic essence of absolute moral nature, he might even speak of the perfection of his soul—or some approximation to it. When one acknowledges that his moral powers are not infinite, he might affirm without dishonesty that he has perfected his moral nature, *his* moral nature. Abandoning unsustainable notions of human nature, we are permitted to think of completions and perfections, and perhaps to achieve and enjoy them and to be at peace with them. Life has become fully actual.

To consider what might be meant by the completion of a *life* is more difficult. There are many and varied requirements of a "complete" life, depending on the natures of diverse individuals. Still, we might formulate some worthwhile generalizations. What would it mean for life *as a whole* to be good? Santayana speaks of what makes life "good, excellent, beautiful, happy and worth having as a whole."[34] He doesn't tell us what that is! He simply refers us to the Greeks, without indicating what their philosophy teaches on this topic. The mere suggestion is greatly helpful. Surely we do not suppose that to declare a life good as a whole means that everything in it has been good, and only a theory-stricken utilitarian would say that it is good to the extent that its pleasures have exceeded its pains. It is not in the least implausible to say that a life has been good on the whole even if its pains have exceeded its pleasures. Nobody is even counting. Somehow, appeal to the felicific calculus betrays a lack of wisdom. We are moral beings, defining ourselves by our ambitions and responsibilities, and their satisfaction might make life good as a whole.

Is this what Santayana had in mind? The characteristic of Greek thinking to which he refers is surely the ideal of the ordered soul, the life of *sophrosyne*, aspiring to what is fine and noble. Perhaps he was also thinking of this: the nature of anything is defined by its outcome. The properties of a being accomplish a certain fruition, a completion, and to this we turn to judge of its goodness. Accordingly, the goodness of a life would be measured by how it turns out. What is the goodness and excellence of a man at his completion? Once more in accordance with Greek philosophy, we suppose that the completion is not adventitious; it is, rather, the true measure of a man. "Character is destiny," Aristotle says. We must remain unsure of Santayana's intent, but Santayana or not, this seems an appropriate way to judge a life as a whole.

A critic will say that the success of the outcome is not a negation of antecedent miseries and failures, including moral failures. Quite so. The issue is the *appropriate* estimation of a life. It is simply fanciful to look for perfection throughout, but is there any deception or evasion in a man judging his life in terms of its consummation? In pursuing objects of devotion, everyone struggles, undergoes failures and stupidities, endures inadequacies in his nature and conduct, and suffers piercing losses, but if an individual nevertheless completes noble ambitions, or if he satisfies his most sacred obligations, then it would be fitting to judge these completions as triumphs. In the end, he has triumphed over all manner of adversity. In an obvious sense, he has mastered it. His life is a triumph. Maybe you don't want to call that "good as a whole." That is an argument about words. The real question is whether one may honestly judge his life to have been worthwhile in virtue of such mastery and nobility.

Without *sophrosyne*, to be sure, completion could not be self-sufficient. A man's life might be ever so much a triumph, but it could not be satisfying if he were in a state of emotional disorder. Soured by resentment, anger, or bitterness, a soul will find neither peace nor satisfaction in any achievement. It is part of wisdom to know that injustices of all kinds are to be expected. Let a man not be destroyed by their existence, even when he is their victim. Our hypothetical man has attained a great good. Let him rejoice in *that* and continue to love and enjoy the goods he possesses. Perhaps, too, he retains his fundamental decency. Whatever else may happen, *he* has not been vanquished.

A complete life could be more than this. To help with this idea, we can return to the distinction between completion of self and completion of life. To say my *self* is complete and to leave it at that betrays a failure of wisdom and a sacrifice of good. The declaration is a bit egocentric, and it sounds much like the acceptance of a consolation prize. What one would hope to declare is that his *life* is complete. Excellence of soul is a composite of virtues for *living*, for making a life. One strives to construct a world for the best life within his compass. In the company of others and of virtue, he assembles a preferred world of works, arts, family, friends, recreations, properties, places, and teachings. As a lover of *to kalon*, he not merely contemplates those things that are lovely and noble but attempts also to *do* them. He makes some mark, at least, on institutions and practices that greatly exceed his own powers. He suffers limits beyond himself and within himself, painfully and tragically so, but genuine and inclusive completions, with the blessings of the fates, sometimes happen.

Not every life is triumphant or complete. One might be defeated. He looks back on a life redeemed by little or nothing. There are many thinkers, moreover, who believe passionately that *any* life is spoiled and meaningless just in the fact that it comes to an end. We die. This and other questions remain to be considered in appraising the good and evil of life and the world.

Notes

1. In this and other ways, Nietzsche's conception of nature has some resemblance to that which Dewey would formulate half a century later, but Nietzsche never undertakes a systematic account. His principal *philosophic* ancestor is Arthur Schopenhauer, but he claims ancestry to the Homeric Greeks and the early tragedians. There are also distinctly Hegelian elements in Nietzsche in that conflict is regarded as an essentially creative force.

2. Nietzsche, *Thus Spoke Zarathustra*, trans. and preface, Walter Kaufmann (New York: Penguin Books, 1978), p. 166.

3. Ibid., p. 201.

4. Ibid., p. 115.

5. For that matter, self-overcoming is also a more apt expression than Dewey's "growth," which does not sufficiently acknowledge the subjective barriers to increasing strength and fluency.

6. There is a passing comment by Socrates in the *Phaedrus* that at least hints of some such consciousness. Socrates says he wonders whether he is truly of sound mind or whether he might not really be more like Typhon (the wildest monster in Greek mythology). This remark at least shows that Socrates recognized himself as a man of extraordinary passions. Had they been *entirely* focused and directed by his love of the good?

7. To state the matter more formally, slave morality is that state of affairs where the values of the lowest in the social order are taken as normative for everyone else—including the strong, masterful, independent, and joyful, who will be judged and condemned according to "slave" criteria. The weak and lowly would reduce the "master" to their own nihilism. (In matters of justice, Rawls fulfills the definition of slave morality by making the condition of the least advantaged the all-sufficing criterion, disregarding the values of everyone else.)

8. Nietzsche, *Beyond Good and Evil*, trans. with commentary, Walter Kaufmann (New York: Vintage Books, 1989), p. 217. The emphasis on "One must invoke tremendous counter-forces" is mine.

9. *Thus Spoke Zarathustra*, p. 118. The notion of an almost Platonic completion is also suggested in the subtitle to Nietzsche's autobiography, *Ecce Homo: How One Becomes What One Is.*

10. Ibid., p. 93.

11. It can be argued—and no doubt someone has done so somewhere in the literature—that many of the values that Nietzsche repudiates are in fact repeatedly invoked by him in his praises of higher man and the free spirits of the future. Courage, strength, honesty, independence, and perseverance, for example, are always celebrated. Supposedly, they will reach greater heights in the future, but that is not an *Umwertung* of these values. It is slave morality that he loathes, and there is great point and force in many of his critiques of it. At the same time, he *praises* master morality, which flourished in ancient days. The revaluation of all *slave* values would be the coherent position for him to take, and that might be what he really had in mind. (Nietzsche decidedly does not endorse master morality unreservedly. The morality of the future will evidently be a Hegelian synthesis and elevation of elements from both master and slave morality. Slave morality, remember, has given us a necessary inwardness and from it comes the power to utilize self-torment creatively. In any case, the higher morality of the future will always be open-ended. Limits are never acceptable.) I am not concerned about the presence of uncertainties and ambiguities in Nietzsche's philosophy. I am concerned for the deadly effects of his exaggerations.

12. *Thus Spoke Zarathustra*, p. 216. More precisely, his *most* abysmal thought is that of eternal recurrence without the overman. With the overman, eternal recurrence is his most joyful thought.

13. Plato might appear to be Nietzsche's opposite here in every respect, but appearances are deceiving: the contrast is by no means complete. I understand Plato to say that the philosopher requires a life removed from common concerns, and the denizens of the cave think that philosophers are decidedly weird. On the other side of this claim, we see that Socrates himself lived in the *agora*, and the philosopher is at home in the cosmos as is no one else. Most important, Plato evidently feels no hesitation whatever about the meaning of life, while Nietzsche agonizes about it obsessively. Moreover, the alienation from the common world seems not to be in the slightest way disturbing to Plato, and, unlike Nietzsche, he suffers no paroxysms of nausea over *man*. In fact, Plato does not seem to agonize over anything. Even when he must suspend judgment, he is a man of Olympian serenity. The agonizers apparently will not get much sympathy from him. Socrates never agonizes either, even in life threatening situations, and Zarathustra has more mood swings in a day than Socrates had in his life. Perhaps the sort of soul that finds its union with Nietzsche did not exist in the classic period. Perhaps Nietzsche is correct in thinking that there is an irreplaceably Christian element in the modern consciousness.

14. By the same reasoning, it is evident that someone of comparable IQ might have a mind that is little better than a lump of concrete when it comes to addressing existentially troubling topics. A good mind is composed of more than high intelligence.

15. The egalitarian, of course, rages at "superior." But for the fact that his hatred of excellence has become so lethal, I would not bother once more to turn on him. Regardless of his rage, the facts remain the same: standards are determined relative to capabilities, and capabilities are not equal. Just as only a mathematician can

be thrilled by mathematical thinking, only a man suitably prepared with powers of literary and psychological discernment will be captivated by a novel by Dostoyevsky. Most men are incompetent to share in advanced mathematical thinking, and most are incapable of getting much out of Dostoyevsky. This is not *"just* a matter of taste." There is a decided asymmetry of taste. The lovers of Gauss and Hilbert can comprehend elementary arithmetic, and the lovers of Shakespeare and Dostoyevsky can comprehend children's stories, but there is nothing there to satisfy their intellect, discernment, and sensibilities. If it offends to refer to Shakespeare as superior, it is nonetheless true that his work satisfies minds of much greater endowment than those who are content with simple tales and cannot go beyond them. It is a *subsequent* question—not the first question—to distinguish what it is in a work of a Cezanne, a Beethoven, or a Tolstoy that succeeds in eliciting the rapt and appreciative response. (A critic or teacher can help the beginner by drawing attention to these qualities. Finally, nonetheless, the qualities will elude many would-be appreciators.) Perhaps the egalitarian will produce an argument to the effect that the differences in endowment are not to be distinguished as better or worse. That is semantic sorcery; it does not conceal the fact that there are great differences in human capabilities, in the human capacities for accomplishment. A great work of art grasps powers and characteristics of the universal flux and stays them in a superb order. It delivers the depth, complexity, nuance, and ambiguity of its subject in a manner that not every mind can comprehend, while other minds are enraptured.

16. Freeman is the author of *Margaret Mead and Samoa: The Making and Unmaking of an Anthropolgical Myth* (Cambridge, MA: Harvard University Press, 1983), which devastates Mead's study of Samoan Culture, *Coming of Age in Samoa*. At issue were both the goddesslike status of Mead and the proposition underlying her research: all differences in human behavior are the consequence of variations in socialization. Freeman's research has been amply vindicated in the course of time, but he was initially vilified and defamed. He was officially censured by a vote of the American Anthropological Association. Coleman's research, in turn, exploded some cherished dogmas of sociologists and educators. Coleman showed, for example, that there is not a significant correlation between expenditure of funds per pupil and achievement in learning. He also noted that student busing for the sake of racial desegregation resulted in white flight to the suburbs, and he showed that racial integration of schools, as such, does not improve the academic performance of black students. He was ruthlessly attacked by the president of the American Sociological Association, who attempted to have him censured by that society. He was likewise attacked by several other eminent sociologists and was publicly likened to a Nazi. Freeman and Coleman have described these experiences and—more broadly—characterized the milieu in which such events could occur. One must weep for the pettiness, weakness of mind, and failure of integrity in the academic community. See Derek Freeman, "Paradigms in Collision," *Academic Questions* 5, no. 3 (summer 1992): 23–33; James Coleman, "Response to the Sociology of Education Award," *Academic Questions* 2, no. 3 (summer 1989): 76–78; and "On the Self-Suppression of Academic Freedom," *Academic Questions* 4, no. 1 (winter 1990–1991): 17–22.

A summary account of the appalling derelictions of Dartmouth's President Freedman will be found in "Dartmouth Reviewed" by Jeffrey Hart (*The National*

Review, June 22, 1998), pp. 42–44. Among many other displays of academic malfeasance, Freedman denounced *The Dartmouth Review* for deliberate unvarnished racism and anti-Semitism in the very company of the editor of the *Review*, who was black, and the staff members, several of whom were Jews.

17. The demand for gender-neutral language is nothing more than a requirement for compliance with a political crusade. Some women, it is reported, feel excluded by "man" and "he," but that is a terrible reason to exclude the works of an author from publication. The women, moreover, are far more harmed by the enforcement of ideological purity than they are by the traditional forms of the English language, in which the generic "man" and "he" are used to include both male and female.

18. An especially good exposure of the denial of free speech in higher education is *The Shadow University* by Alan Charles Kors and Harvey A. Silverglate (New York and London: The Free Press, 1998).

19. The irrationality of the ideologically crazed left has been studied at length by Paul Hollander. See especially *Political Pilgrims: Travels of Western Intellectuals to the Soviet Union, China, and Cuba, 1928–1978* (New York: Oxford University Press, 1981) and *Anti-Americanism: Critiques at Home and Abroad, 1965–1990* (New York: Oxford University Press, 1992).

20. Such scares have been catalogued and analyzed at length by Julian L. Simon in his *The Ultimate Resource 2* (Princeton, NJ: Princeton University Press, 1996). For a glimpse of the ways in which ostensibly reputable scientists will attack even their most well-meaning critics, see "The Mau-Mauing of Bjørn Lomborg" by David Schoenbrod, *Commentary* (September 2002): 51–55. Lomborg is the author of *The Skeptical Environmentalist: Measuring the Real State of the World* (New York: Cambridge University Press, 2001). He is both a committed environmentalist and a thorough and rigorous investigator. His inquiries led him to be sharply critical of the environmentalist "Litany," as he calls it. In return for his uncommonly fine studies, he has been willfully misrepresented and defamed.

21. Richard J. Herrnstein and Charles Murray, *The Bell Curve: Intelligence and Class Structure in American Life* (New York: The Free Press, 1994).

22. I attended a "symposium" on *The Bell Curve* sponsored by Emory's Department of Anthropology. Two of the four members of the faculty panel bragged that they had not read it and would not read it, yet they sentenced it to death, and then things got worse. You think lynch mobs at a major academy of learning are impossible?

The most famous and influential opposition to Herrnstein and Murray comes from the popular guru Stephen Jay Gould, who dismisses them flippantly. (See *The Mismeasure of Man*, 2d ed. [New York: Norton, 1996].) Gould's criticisms include the charges that IQ tests measure nothing, they are fatally biased, and the statistical analyses in *The Bell Curve* are at some crucial points incorrect. Herrnstein and Murray had already pointed out that Gould's characteristic criticisms ignore the pertinent scientific studies. Particularly instructive about this case is the fact that Gould had been pointedly provided with the relevant literature, to which he makes no reference. He did not refute these studies; he acted as if they did not exist. All of this is documented in the review of the second edition of *Mismeasure*, "Race, Intelligence, and the Brain: The Errors and Omissions of the 'Revised' Edition of S. J. Gould's *The Mismeasure of Man* (1996)" by J. Philippe Rushton, in *Personality and Individual Dif-*

ferences 23, no. 1 (1997): 169–80. It contains explicit charges of "several counts of scholarly malfeasance," documented in detail.

23. Arthur R. Jensen, *The g Factor: The Science of Mental Ability* (Westport, CT: Praeger Publishers, 1998).

24. Thomas Sowell has aptly remarked (in one of his editorials) that the mind of an intellectual is a "fact free zone." A more profound observation occurs in another of his editorials: "What political shibboleths do is transform questions about facts, causation, and evidence into questions about personal identity and moral worth" (*The Atlanta Journal-Constitution*, February 18, 2002, p. A13). The profundity is in the verb *transform*. Sowell's impatience with such duplicity is given scope, detail, and documentation in *The Vision of the Anointed: Self-Congratulation as a Basis for Social Policy* (New York: Basic Books, 1995). I have already mentioned the work of Paul Hollander on the escapades of intellectuals. Perhaps the best single piece that I know of in respect to this issue is a gem by Gary Saul Morson, "What Is the Intelligentsia? Once More, an Old Russian Question" (*Academic Questions* 6, no. 3 [summer 1993]: 20–38). I say *"perhaps the best"* because the prize might equally well be accorded to Dostoevsky's *The Possessed*, with its astounding insights into the mind of revolutionary intellectuals.

25. Aristotle seems not to have been aware of how *theoretical* wisdom is corruptible by emotional needs.

26. These ideas, in fact, are sometimes coupled with meritorious moral teachings, and the teachings are often effective.

27. *Thus Spoke Zarathustra*, p. 18.

28. Emerson, *Self-Reliance*.

29. Ibid.

30. *Republic*, 443e (Bloom translation). The passage occurs near the end of book 4.

31. This is the form of moral inquiry supported by Socrates in the myth of Er, recounted in book 10 of *The Republic*. It bears little resemblance to the formal educational regime described in the preceding books, but it closely matches the sorts of inquiry evidently pursued by the historical Socrates. I take this to be one more fact that discourages a literal reading of the politics of *The Republic*.

32. Santayana, *The Life of Reason*, vol. 2, *Reason in Society* (Triton ed., vol. 3), p. 231.

33. John Lachs is a philosopher who has ably strived to characterize the many values of immediacy, and efforts to contend with his ideas are always fertile. See, for example, his "To Have and To Be" (*The Human Search*, ed. Lachs and Charles E. Scott [New York and Oxford: Oxford University Press, 1981], pp. 247–55), *Intermediate Man* (Indianapolis and Cambridge: Hackett Publishing Company, 1981), and "Aristotle and Dewey on the Rat Race" (*Philosophy and the Reconstruction of Culture*, ed. John J. Stuhr [Albany: State University of New York Press, 1993], pp. 97–109).

34. Santayana, *Character and Opinion in The United States* (Triton ed., vol. 8), p. 51.

| 10 |

Meanings

I t is possible for a man to lie awake at night, staring into space, and to wring his hands by day, crying to heaven, "What is the point of life? What does it all mean?" If he could but find the answer, he believes, his existence would become miraculously clear and happy! "There has got to be a reason for all this suffering," he pleads. If he learns it, the answer will be a form of salvation, but if he fails, his fate will be nihilism, nothingness. For most people, I suppose, the question translates into "Does God exist?" where "God" means a being revealed in some sacred text, who presides wisely and benevolently over human destiny and the entire cosmos, who assures that everything happens for the best. The mystery needn't presuppose such a predetermined content for its answer, but it does seem to assume that somewhere and somehow awaits a definite answer to be discovered, if only we are a good searcher. Perhaps it is in the keeping of a bearded old man on a faraway mountain top. If we can find him, he will tell us the answer, and all will be well. We search and we search. The quest is undertaken by all manner of thinkers and ordinary men alike.

Such an obsession testifies to much about the human condition. We are vulnerable and needy; happiness is scarce; we are prone to suffering; and many of our torments have no remedy. We will grasp at whatever it takes to get by, and we struggle to carry on. There are joys and victories, too, but they are episodic, and we remain in much the same condition, overall. It is no surprise, then, that we are apt to look for a wholesale solution: a permanent release from suffering and a new day of happiness. Until we see the possibility of such a great day, we are driven to ask what the point is of our travail. The very fact that we suppose there *is*—somehow—a point testifies to a further trait: our miseries are redeemed by there being a comprehensive purpose whose accomplishment depends, in part, on our existence; we are part of a grand design. Then, if we conclude that there is no point to it all, we say that life is meaningless. We become cynics and nihilists.

This is the morbid way to think about the meaning of life, undertaken by those in despondency and desperate for rescue. Perhaps we should be honest: think of the question as no more than a cry of hopelessness; there is no reason to pursue it other than the morbid one. We should go along with the cynic and drop the whole matter. On the other hand, it is a perfectly natural question for a creature like ourselves. Endowed with astounding intelligence, we are able to *conceive* life, to conceive great stretches of time, place, and meaning—all interconnected and fateful for our self-understanding. We are capable of conceiving our existence as part of an enormous and comprehending whole. Just to do that is amazing and wonderful. We examine our existence in our experienced environment, and we likewise examine the existence of its other inhabitants; that's how we are able to function. Then we extend the analysis to the entire cosmos, as we understand it, but due to our native hopes and weaknesses, this understanding is certain to be highly inventive. With moral discipline, however, we might still address the question of meaning with insight and rigor. It is a portentous and insistent question. We should by no means assume that it must end with either the grand design or nihilism.

In the context of this question, "meaning" and "meaningful" are vague and emotive, but progress in the discussion will bring its own clarity. Answers to the question of meaning are not ready-made and preestablished. The (usually morbid) question, "What is the meaning of life?" might be thought to be a matter of discovering a transcendent truth, like a Platonic form, which might somehow be revealed to us. In a crucial and vital sense, however, answers are configured from our philosophic understanding together with our grasp of our remarkable possibilities as natural beings.

Any random person may decide this matter just as he pleases, of course, and satisfy his psyche with all manner of comforting beliefs, but a free man would not. He could proceed with self-respect only by posing some fundamental and difficult questions about the nature of things. What kind of world is it? What is man's status within it? What sorts of possibilities exist for such a being in such a world? Of what perils, limits, resources, and ideal goods does reality admit? Each of these questions is fateful and difficult, demanding disciplined study and reflection. The question of the meaning of life can be conscientiously answered only with such exertions. The question must finally focus on the particular individual engaged in the quest: What is *his* good and *his* meaning in the encompassing whole? He does not ask these questions as a passive onlooker. He must ask what directions and actions *he* can take. With his self-knowledge and knowledge of the world, he must *do* something to conceive and accomplish his meaningful good, instructed and chastened by the powers characteristic of nature. The meaning of his life will be contingent upon what he can do in and with the world so understood.

As I have commented periodically, philosophers are not apt to come up empty-handed when they embark on this quest. They exhibit the remarkably human facility to design their conception of the whole in a manner that suits their emotional needs. We should also allow for the possibility of a man who finds meaning in his existence precisely in consequence of the most unflinching assessment of his entire predicament, acknowledging that nature sheds no tears for him, and the universe has no ultimate compensation in store. His assessment might lead him to conclude that success in his venture might require the development and exercise of virtues that are suitable for just this condition, that he discern, secure, and celebrate some of its greatest goods.

The question of whether one is leading a good and meaningful life is not, then, a matter of simple discovery. It is a matter of knowledge, judgment, and action. We must *judge* what a good life would be, and we must judge what is meaningful and whether our life has achieved meaning. We might be a poor judge, of course, and we could easily succumb to fantasy. In any case, having reason to rejoice in life is not something that just happens to a detached spectator. It is an *achievement*, accomplished with discernment, courage, and effort. To establish our good requires *action*—wise, disciplined, selective, and sustained. We *make* something of our lives, in the familiar phrase.

Despite the vagueness of the idea, it is possible to give a working definition, a functional equivalent, of "meaningful." It would be the assurance, the inner certitude, that one's life has been worth all the pain and effort. Perhaps life is affirmed in the manner just given in "Completions," but there might be more. We want *gratitude* for life, joy for being alive, so it must yield joyful goods. We likewise yearn to be somehow in unity with things lovely and good. Typically, if not invariably, affirmation has a moral quality: our life must have significance in some larger order, whose worth is great and assured. Equally affirming would be the sense that we are bearers of values and virtues that are noble, and they have left some impress on the works of our life, and such works constitute a legacy. Our duties have been fulfilled. Our legacy could be in the arts or politics or some other form of enduring achievement. Finally, we might add this to the working definition: a meaningful life is that which makes death morally and emotionally acceptable. Perhaps there is a redundancy in this idea, because it might happen that the satisfaction of the preceding conditions is precisely what is needed to make a good death, but we should not take that assumption for granted. With all such functions satisfied, life would be radiant with meanings. To sum up all these provisions in a word, for the sake of convenience, let us stipulate that a meaningful life is richly *affirming*. Affirming *a* life is not the same as saying yes to any and all life in general. Such an ambition is mawkish. To conclude that a life is meaningful is a matter of *discriminating* judgment.

The meaning of one's life is a matter of wisdom, virtue, and conduct, depending on one's learning what can fulfill such functions and perhaps others as well, but it is misguided to suppose that the judgment is merely *subjective*, in the usual sense of that unhappy term. What one determines to be an ideal meaning should not be the product of whim, fantasy, or wish. It ought to be predicated on an unsentimental appraisal of oneself in the order of real powers and limitations of nature. It would be a disciplined appraisal. Admittedly, it is a most difficult inquiry, with no assurance of success. Its conclusion might be a form of reasoned nihilism. Nietzsche regarded life as a struggle against nihilism, against the absence of meaning in the universe.

a. Struggles with Nihilism

It is not fixed in the stars what will satisfy my working definition of "meaningful." When given free rein, the imagination produces glorious fantasies. Typically, when one asks of the meaning of life, he is searching for some great fact of the universe that will satisfy several needs at once: to be redeemed from suffering, consoled and compensated, to be swaddled in happiness, to be assured that justice will triumph, to believe that one's own life—however frustrated and paltry—is necessary for some greater good, to feel at home in the universe, and to be assured that we will live forever. What extravagant demands! And how extravagant to suppose that they may be met in one fell swoop. A truthful spirit might have only contempt for them.

It is not clear that these demands are entirely irreducible. There is a subtler need, a most powerful one, and to my knowledge it has never been recognized in its own name: *the need to affirm the whole—to affirm everything!* Call it the will to cosmic optimism. The will to believe in an infinite god—as distinguished from local deities—might be derivative: it might be a device for guaranteeing the goodness of the whole and everything in it or somehow to vindicate it all. One might suppose that the man who craves a cosmic meaning for his life need only find his purpose in a worthy human occupation, but perhaps that isn't good enough. Perhaps he has a profound emotional need to find his good in the perfection of the whole. The need as such is typically unrecognized; it is insidious, and it is corrupting of a candid mind.

It is not clear why such a need exists, to affirm the whole. Any individual has the normal if pathetic wish that everything in his own peculiar circumstances be just right—that they answer flawlessly to his every desire, and the juvenile mind might believe that somehow this might be acccomplished. Perhaps when he conceives the totality of things, however vacuously, he would like to believe the same of it: that it could be perfect—or *is* perfect. In reflective souls, the need becomes urgent and oppressive. Whatever: the need is there to be witnessed.[1] Plato had no real grounds to believe that the world is in essence perfect nor had his successors. Most of them, however, display remarkable brilliance and ingenuity in explaining how the perfection is not compromised by all the appearances to the contrary. The result, nevertheless, is that their philosophies in the most generic sense are not as wise as they are in reference to more circumscribed topics.

I do not deny that others have held out against cosmic optimism, and they are to be congratulated for that, but in many cases their resistance is unwittingly half-hearted. They stay away entirely from the question of meaning in life on the assumption that it could only be found in some sort of cosmic affirmation. They have, in brief, retained the archetypal sense of meaning, so they have at the same time neglected to discern finite meanings. Dewey observed this failing in the case of Spencer:

> Merely because Spencer labeled his unknowable energy "God," this faded piece of metaphysical goods was greeted as an important and grateful concession to the reality of the spiritual realm. Were it not for the deep hold of the habit of seeking justification for ideal values in the remote and transcendent, surely this reference of them to an unknowable absolute would be despised by comparison with the demonstrations of experience that knowable energies are daily generating about us precious values.[2]

Two philosophers who indulge themselves in forms of cosmic optimism while disclaiming any attachment to "faded metaphysical goods" are Nietzsche and Santayana. Each is contemptuous of sentimental theorizing, yet in each the need to affirm the whole is so great that he betrays his philosophic courage and integrity.

I made passing reference to this failure in Nietzsche in chapter 9. By recourse to the idea of eternal recurrence, Zarathustra finds that the overman redeems all eternity. Because of eternal recurrence, the future is also the past—it is an exact repetition of the past, and the past is the future—everything that has happened will occur again in precisely the same manner. "And this slow spider, which crawls in the moonlight, and this moonlight itself, and I and you in the gateway, whispering together, whispering of eternal things—must not all of us have been here before? And return and walk in that other lane, out there, before us, in this long dreadful lane—must we not eternally return?"[3] Eternal recurrence abolishes any qualitative difference between future and past. Consequently, if the overman comes, the event will do more than redeem what is to be; it will redeem all that has been. (Zarathustra calls this "willing backwards.") In affirming both eternal recurrence and the coming of the *Übermensch*, Zarathustra thereby also affirms all that has been, however hideous. Indeed, he affirms it with unspeakable joy.[4]

Why must one so unsentimental and emancipated feel such a towering need to affirm anything and everything that has ever transpired in the universe—such a piercing need, in fact, that the alternative to meeting it is an abysmal nihilism? The "redemption" accomplished by the overman, indeed, seems to apply only to Nietzsche. How are the excruciating miseries *of those who suffered them* redeemed by *Nietzsche's* belief in the overman? Their pains are as real as ever, and for them the compensations of knowledge of the *Übermensch* and eternal recurrence are forever unavailable. This is a scandalous argument in ways too numerous to mention. It exhibits the intensity of the need to affirm the whole and the lengths to which one can go to do it.

The case of Santayana is similar but more modest in its ambitions. He knows of no way to redeem all suffering. After what he called his philosophic *metanoia*, he developed a conception of spiritual life in stark contrast to what he had formulated in *The Life of Reason*.[5] He regarded it to be a religion of love after the manner of Socrates, and he pronounced it to be suitable for "a completely free and disillusioned spirit." It is not after the manner of Socrates, however, for Socrates (or perhaps only Plato) held that in their *real* nature all beings are in harmony with each other. Now, actually observed natures, as Santayana frequently points out with vehemence, are very rarely in harmony with each other. More commonly, they devour one another, and many of these natures are vile and despicable—certainly unworthy of love. Yet Santayana contrives a way to believe that *as essence* all these natures really are lovable and really are in perfect harmony. The price he pays for the contrivance is that essence has no correspondence to existence. Accordingly, what he loves is no worldly thing at all but ideas *merely*, representing nothing. That is not an unusual conclusion for epistemologists, but the consequence should be nothing but skepticism.[6] In that case, this could not be a religion of love or redemption for *the world*: the real nature of worldly beings has been left out of account. We inhabit the same hideous place, but Santayana seems not to recognize this. He describes this religion as loving the love in all *things*.[7] In several writings, he goes into transports over this religion, which in fact cannot affirm what he believes it does. What such a philosophy displays, again, is the deep and gnawing yearning to affirm the whole in some vestment, whatever it takes.

I hold Santayana's wisdom in reverence. It is owed to the earlier and more discriminating Santayana. Such are the differences that can be made in philosophy by the perhaps inexplicit but nonetheless compelling need to be reconciled to the whole without exception and even to love it. Must we be nihilists if we cannot affirm the whole?

In contrast to such as Nietzsche and Santayana losing their grip on reality, the metaphysics sketched in chapter 3 would be a helpful corrective, for it insists on the full reality of the negative. It is a metaphysics that permits no distinction between good and evil to be transmuted into differences between reality and unreality. Even so, the first corrective for emotionally protective theorizing is the simple recognition that we are in fact possessed of this debilitating need. It is difficult to recognize and even more difficult to overcome, but it must be overcome by anyone who would be a free and disillusioned philosopher. Insofar as it is overcome, the mind is greatly liberated, and it discovers possibilities for breathtakingly rich meanings. When we are rigorously discriminating in our affirmations, we find much to love and to revere, and these affirmations lose nothing in being selective. Indeed, they gain, for they are achieved from within the limitations of a difficult and often tormenting world.

b. AFFIRMATIONS AND NEGATIONS

In the popular phrase, we need something to believe in. That is part of what it means to say that life has meaning. The expression does not necessarily refer to religious belief, and we can believe in something short of the entire universe. What else might we have in mind when we speak of something to believe in? There are several possibilities, including attachment to utopian theories. A particularly eligible source of meaning might be a real social order, institution, or other human movement that we judge to be eminently worthy and in which we share. When one of them has earned our allegiance, it sustains us in return. It has a distinctive function and identity, which endure through time: The institution has existed for generations before us, and it will continue for generations beyond. It is dependable and invariant in that it maintains its defining functions and unique identity, though surrounding it are inconstancy and flux. We have a purpose within an honored and beloved whole. Herein we find something that is bigger and better than ourselves in which we nevertheless play an integral part. Our littleness and our solitariness are banished by such a life. We are nourished by its heritage, and we contribute to its continuing worth and vigor. In an obvious sense, it transcends our own life. It is something to which we can be devoted, and in return it gives meaning to our life.

Suppose, for example, that one becomes deeply attached to a school or college. It is distinguished for its seriousness in educating, let us say. It has been in existence for generations; many students have attended it with pride and respect; they have a sense of gratitude to it, and they have fond recollections of it. People of the same lineage have attended for generation after generation. Members of the faculty devote their lives to the school. They have an abiding sense of the worth of what they do. They transmit treasured knowledge, and they are honored and appreciated for their service. Many of them have a profound sense of belonging in these hallowed halls—of being altogther at home in them. There is a felt rightness in being *there* and not elsewhere. "This is where I belong!" one thinks. Owing to the ethos of the school, they have no wish to be elsewhere or to be doing other than their accustomed duties. Life at the school is an end in itself, not a mere transition.

Such an individual is aware that he belongs to a long succession of its teachers, and he believes that many more will follow after he has died, sustaining the traditions and excellence that he himself helps to preserve and promote. He *believes* in the school; he *believes* in what it does, as he sees successive classes pass through it for decades. In its duration and worth, it transcends his physical existence: it was there before him; it will be there after him, and he is but one of its many teachers in whom education has been entrusted and accomplished. It is gratifying to him to think of it that way— to know it will be there, doing the same good works, after his departure, retaining its distinctive identity. He enjoys a sort of immortality in being a part of this history. The whole embodies his work and much of his nature, and the whole endures.

This is a form of life according to custom. It is an extremely sustaining experience. It might not be entirely atypical, but if it sounds like a fantasy, that is because such institutions hardly exist today. We have become too efficient, standardized, and interchangeable, and we are trendy. Institutions now exist in order to change, and we are each and every one of us on the lookout for the latest innovations in everything. By its nature, trendiness is a repudiation of what has gone before. Effectively, like hedonism, it is a form of nihilism; it has nothing to revere. Tomorrow, or the day after tomorrow, what has been our abode will be something else—more up to date, to be sure, more instrumental, more rational, more indistinguishable from others, and rid of any antiquated remnants of its history.

Somehow, not surprisingly, the inheritors of the once-hallowed halls do not believe in them, and they are not at home there. They are too cynical; they are hustlers for recognition and reputation. They think about "career moves" and status. They wonder how they look to their competitors in other schools— and how smart a figure they cut in the intellectual world. Their students, moreover, have changed greatly. They, too, are cynical; they are ill mannered; they believe it sophisticated to revere nothing, including the cultural heritage that the university might transmit; and it suits them best to be on a first-name basis with their professors.[8] While accepting and even encouraging the first-name business, the professors would nevertheless like to see as little of the students as possible. Morale is terrible. This is not a life-affirming experience.[9]

The general principle illustrated by this example seems to be this: We hunger for goods that are organic to an enduring and sustaining order. Even ideal goods are more meaningful as events within an encompassing framework of accustomed duties and ambitions. In achieving an ideal good, one contributes to a larger whole. As inseparable from a beloved and distinctive order, goods attain the stability of the encompassing condition that preserves them and gives them a larger meaning. The random, fragmented, and transient sorts of good do not make a whole or possess any unity among themselves, and for that reason they cannot support life and give it meaning.

Both the hunger and the means of satisfying it seem to be intrinsic to our nature. In a world where most changes are threatening and where security of life is precarious, it could not be otherwise. The ordering is not accomplished in imagination: it is a real order, inseparable from real institutions. Our fundamental forms of community intend such an order as a matter of course; it is their reason for being. Such an order, moreover, is more secure in its meaning if it is part of a definite history: our fathers and their fathers before them have made this order, and it is our duty to carry on their work. The repeated observance and celebration of the goods constituent of this domain are a potent force in distinguishing them from those that are isolated and ephemeral. Their greatest potency is probably felt in the family.

A family that provides a stable, consistent, and affectionate regimen accomplishes much in the way of elementary and assuring satisfactions, especially if it is integrated into the culture and continues through generations. This is far more than merely genetic transmission. I am thinking of intact intergenerational families, where the generations continue to live in connection with one another: grandparents, parents, and children. Such a process of continuity and renewal over the years is fundamentally supportive and stabilizing. The process itself, with its profound joys and satisfactions, and with the love and virtue that it generates, is its own good. It is an end in itself. Children conceived in joy and hope, nurtured with shared love and responsibility, become in turn the bearers of a beloved and honored tradition. It is the opposite of a simply transient and disconnected life. Admittedly, the process has all but vanished. Even where it survives, it has its characteristic torments, to be sure. Even ideal goods suffer from imperfections.

In recognizing the invaluable morale of a secure order of goods in human association, we also see that to provide meaning in life is in significant part a practical and social task. Today, however, even families are chaotic and ephemeral. Almost any customary arrangement provides such an order, but customary life is disappearing, and we cannot make ourselves believe in something by mere fiat or decision, nor can we believe in something transient, undistinctive, unworthy, and subject to easy change. This is not a cosmic, but a finite and practical, problem.

Later I will discuss additional sorts of orders in which goods are especially meaningful, but here I turn to a closely kindred question: that of a sense of belonging. This is another precious feeling: at its best, one of undisturbed comfort and acceptance. We are at one with our surroundings, in felt union with them. If that feeling could be extended to life as a whole, wouldn't *that* make life worth living! If that to which we belonged were the cosmos as such, wouldn't *that* be an affirmation! Once more, however, we are more honestly advised to seek the feeling in more circumscribed conditions, where it would be, again, a practical achievement. We still might attain that feeling of unity so profoundly that it could suffuse our experience with a fundamental reassurance and satisfaction, but there must be places or havens or groups that are worth belonging to. There must be places and activities in one's life that he loves and esteems and where he feels entirely at home. It is no accident that the fundamental metaphor for a feeling of belonging is "feeling at home," so home might be the place to begin. Amazing how effective home can be as a sanctuary from the cruelties of the world! Wonderful how the feeling of union between a man and a woman can seem all-sufficing. But it depends upon what kind of home and what kind of union it is. A good home can be so satisfying and reassuring that it becomes the very paradigm of belonging. A person can say that his home makes his life worth living, and he does not think to fret for the universe.

There are other sanctuaries of belonging: friends; gardens, lands, forests; arts and work might succeed, invested with things lovely and good, as would association with traditions and institutions that we believe in. But, if there is to be an *abiding* sense of belonging, it must be a place to which we can return; it must itself abide. This social order, this homestead, this work, this family, these shores and these oaks will abide beyond the day after tomorrow. When such rare and priceless conditions are met, they more than suffice as affirmations for a free and disillusioned mind.

One pursues many goods in a lifetime, and he might do so as part of a familiar and congenial order. His ideal mission might be to sustain and invigorate that very environment, and, if he is successful, he might enjoy a gratifying sense of completion. Perhaps he leaves a legacy not only of sustaining this order but of transmitting an example of nobility of character as well. Such a life ought to fulfill gloriously the demand for moral purpose and meaning. It might fail to do so, nevertheless, if one is mired in the demand for unconditional and universal affirmation, especially in the form of believing one must have a cosmic purpose. Part of the self-overcoming of a free and disillusioned spirit is to rid himself of such oppression. It is possible to love and affirm *selectively*, and the discriminated objects of love and affirmation might be of inestimable worth. Is it not good enough to live and die for them? It is a form of nihilism to think that such objects cannot be good enough.

There is just a grain of truth in the claim of philosophic idealism that the ultimate good consists in the correct consciousness of the whole. *Their* consciousness, however, is not correct, but obfuscatory, and it represents precisely that need for cosmic optimism that I have been criticizing. The grain is in the recognition that a given state of affairs can be experienced in markedly different ways. I am not thinking of a relativistic theory of truth; I have in mind the fact of great variations in evaluative response. Such variation is currently celebrated in order to support moral relativism and hedonistic self-indulgence, neither of which can survive an appraisal that is both thorough and candid. Few appraisals have that character, however. For many reasons, they are typically truncated and blunted; those who undertake them do *not* know better. Accordingly, there are innumerable goods that are underappreciated or neglected: great joys and meanings are foreclosed to the distracted, ignorant, or arrogant consciousness.

As I have suggested, our natural hedonism is crippling, and so is our sophomoric sophistication. When those of current stature and distinction ridicule all manner of sacred goods—fundamental goods, accustomed, ideal, or unbought—there are fools aplenty who will applaud them and follow them, for what could be worse than to appear to be a rube? What could be more exalted than to share the ideas of such superior minds? Those who ridicule have their own "sacred" good: their reputation as emancipated intellectuals. They feed off of that, "after the fashion of cattle, always looking down and with their heads bent to earth and table, . . . fattening themselves and copulating; and, for the sake of getting more of these things, they kick and butt with horns and hooves of iron."[10] The opinion leaders and the rubes live off each other. Either one without the other would bring an end to the travesty.

The goods that we call sacred deserve that name not because it has been so ordained by the gods. Moral authority moves from earth to heaven, not from heaven to earth; the gods confess what is already known to be holy. There are persons and experiences that we adore; they give us surpassing joy and satisfaction; we judge them to be of the highest virtue; and we will struggle and die for them. There are likewise forms of excellence in the soul and in conduct that we affirm unreservedly. In our vocabulary, the terms of highest praise apply to conditions of this sort. We speak of these goods in a vocabulary of ultimacy: they are eternal, immortal, sacred, or divine.

Such expressions express ultimacy in several related senses. We think of such goods as unsurpassed; we mean to say of them that they will not be compromised to transient considerations; our devotion to them will not be extinguished. The love for your child, the devotion to your wife, your respect for honor and integrity, your allegiance to wisdom and decency in common life, your loyalty to an established order of goods: such things will not be subordinated to trifles in your esteem and loyalty.

Metaphors of the eternal are also fitting because there is a clear sense in which our supreme goods are imperishable. That is, their *meaning* is eternally and invulnerably good, for their ascertained *worth* is imperishable. Their Platonic form, if you will, is eternal. Actual goods come and go; they perish, but their meaning does not. *As* meanings, they are our secure possession, and they survive the vicissitudes of fortune. It will always be true that an intimate relationship, or just an incident in that relationship, was the most intense and treasured good. This we would affirm forever. It is in that sense immortally good. We live now in the eternal when we feel, "This, now, is eternally good." There is both consolation and affirmation in possessing these meanings. Life accrues enormous value when we have them available to us. To speak of some goods as eternal or divine is not only fitting but necessary: there is no other way to convey the burden of experience.

I am not endorsing a form of moral absolutism. I am trying to convey the sense of ultimacy that attends our highest affirmations. Even these consummate meanings will not form a coherent whole. As Platonic Ideas, no doubt, they are harmonious, but in the crush of existence they will collide and rudely call for sacrifice. Devotion to duty and love of family, for example, are not invariably compatible. Yes, these supreme goods sometimes conflict with each other, and we are forced to choose between them. Life is tragic: some goods are invaluable and yet sometimes in friction with each other. It is tragic, too, when the meaning we ascribe to an event is mistaken. That is, we make misjudgments—sometimes catastrophic misjudgments—of particular cases and of ways of life.

The expressions of human ultimacy are naturally incorporated into religious thought and observance, and soon their usage is judged to be original to some theological doctrine, from which it is bestowed on worldly beings. But for two considerations, the confusion would be harmless: Individuals come to believe that these sacred goods have that status only because of supernatural authority. Failing to recognize that such authority is derivative of experience, persons who do not subscribe to religious dogmas might more easily conclude that nothing is sacred. The use of such terms, moreover, suggests that one must be a confessor of some religious system. Without such expressions, however, our moral language is impoverished—and our moral experience suffers as well.

Within intellectual circles, the impoverishment of evaluative discourse is at an advanced stage, and the degradation is also due to a beggarly experience. "Get a life!" as ordinary people say. Contrast the language of Santayana, a materialist and atheist, who routinely speaks of the divine, the eternal, the immortal, and the perfect, and thereby imparts a vivid sense of the most hallowed qualities of experience. What a mindless deprivation it is to proclaim, with pride and superiority, that nothing is sacred! The juvenile attractions of relativism and the pleasures of quibbling would be eclipsed by love of the ideal. At bottom, these petty obsessions are symptoms of incipient nihilism.

My interest is to discern what might give meaning to our existence. When we pursue and possess goods that we would call sacred or eternal, surely we grant that they give meaning. They make life worth living; we think of them as justifying travail, sacrifice, and devotion, and they satisfy our yearning to cease our moral wandering. The true sequence of experience, no doubt, is that values are called sacred *because* they are of a sort that justifies any renunciation. If we would die for them, we declare that they are more precious than our own vital signs. Their worth transcends the value of perpetuating our own life. One who is unwilling to die for anything is the nihilist. How empty the life of a man for whom no sacrifice is acceptable!

There are intensely meaningful values in experience, but that is not to say that they are widely noticed or shared. It is not to say they occur with fecundity and regularity in the lives of most individuals. There are negations as well as affirmations, and they are often overwhelming. Due to weakness in ourselves and defeats inflicted by the world, a life can be one of suffering, bitterness, and unredeemed labor, and many lives are of that sort. Those who are better fitted and more fortunate still endure frightful pain and loss, and they suffer acutely with the pain of those they love. They also contemplate the massive scale of human misery, incapacity, and corruption, and that is a trial in its own right. Nietzsche suffered from his contempt for *man*. There are those who are more discriminating but are nonetheless revolted by dishonesty, smugness, pretense, imitation, pettiness, and the like, and they find them everywhere. They might be unendurably oppressed by daily and unavoidable contact with them. Who can count the ways in which the meaning of a life might be assaulted? It is wise to remember that we need not—and should not—affirm the whole. We must exclude much and reject much, and we must be selective in what we hold sacred.

I remarked earlier that it is very much a matter of judgment—discerning judgment—to determine whether one can affirm his own life—to affirm that it has been worth living, perhaps joyously so. Many a man would judge that his life is a sorrowful failure, but he is typically retrieved from such a nihilistic conclusion by an illusion. I simply assert that natural conditions for a highly satisfying life *exist*, and sometimes they are realized, even to plenitude.

There are those who would deny any such assertion simply by reference to the fact of death. Death nullifies everything, they say. Such a rejoinder gives death too much credit. I am drawn to the wisdom of Epicurus, who observes, "When I am, death is not. When death is, I am not." A being who once existed but no longer exists is now nonexistent; there is only nonentity. The nonexistent cannot suffer, cannot experience. Only an agent can do that. Where there is no agent, there can be no regret, terror, suffering, or loss—

nothing of any kind. Nonexistence, then, ought not to be feared. Fear of it is baseless. Death, moreover, saves us from the putative wrath of the gods in an afterlife, according to Epicurus. The consequence is that we are liberated to enjoy the goods of life untainted by dread.

That is an argument that requires much meditation, as Epicurus advised, and surely the meditation will not be uniformly effective. Apart from the possibility that he might have been mistaken to believe that the soul is mortal, the imagination tends to spoil the appropriate reflection. One obsessively tries to do the patently nonsensical: to imagine what it would be like to be nonexistent, and he is apt to conclude—absurdly, once again—that it would be the utmost in terror and wretchedness. But nonentities are not alive; they do not exist. The effort of the imagination is inherently vain and destructive, to be sure, but sometimes it seems there is no constraining it. It is its job, its compulsion, to put itself in circumstances other than the here and now. That is normally an invaluable function, but here it does one foul to persist in it.

Perhaps the imagination can be satisfied with its inherent limitations. If you want to know what death is "like," consider the nature of a similar and familiar condition: being knocked out by total anesthesia. When you are anesthetized, you experience nothing; there is no experience. The anesthesia works so quickly that you don't even know it when you pass from consciousness to unconsciousness. When you wake up, you have no memory of anything that occurred during the period of entire deprivation of sensation. That interval is a perfect blank. For you, there is nothing *to be* remembered. For you, in the relevant sense, that time did not exist. *That* is what it is like to be dead: a perfect blank, absolute nonentity, just as it is under the ministrations of the anesthetist. The candle has gone out; the flame is no more. Epicurus's own example to the identical effect is to ask whether one had fear, sorrow, or some other form of awareness prior to his birth. Once more, "When I am, death is not. When death is, I am not." Even a fevered imagination might be satisfied.

Such reassurances by no means exclude fears and regrets of another nature. A dying man might suffer agonies over the welfare and happiness of his unattended family, or he reproaches himself, let us say, for his failures to have done well by his obligations. Perhaps he aches for the failures and cruelties of his life, which can never be set right. Any such torments are possible, but they are not the fear of being dead. In death as oblivion, there is nothing to fear.

But what is logic to desperate emotion? Surely this is a case, like so many others, where our virtues, or lack thereof, will be crucial. There are individuals who are especially fearful and anxious. Their fears are constantly excited, and they have dread for even trivial matters. On the other hand, there are those who by nature are not easily worried or intimidated. They have contempt for terror; fear is typically beneath them. These differences are also shown in their regard for death. Such observations suggest that there are different ways of thinking about death and of overcoming our natural—if not universal—dread of it. The way of Epicurus is neither exhaustive nor all-sufficing. A more comprehensive reflection is appropriate.

The Caesar imagined by Shakespeare helps with such thinking:

> Cowards die many times before their deaths;
> The valiant never taste of death but once.
> Of all the wonders that I yet have heard,
> It seems to me most strange that men should fear;
> Seeing that death, a necessary end,
> Will come when it will come. (*Julius Caesar*, 2.2.37–42)

It is good to be a fatalist about death. It is good to acknowledge that death will happen. We must die. The only question is *how* will we die. Trembling? Cringing? Pleading? Crying? But why do that? It is going to happen anyway, so be noble about it. Be contemptuous of weakness and fear. Some men are that way: they have contempt for death. They despise whatever frailties would disgrace a soul of its justice and decency. Thus, if one has the appropriate virtue, his thinking will not be fixated on death per se, but he will reflect on good kinds and bad kinds of it, and he will conduct his life not to avoid death but a bad or ignoble death, and he will seek, so far as possible, to achieve a good death. A virtuous death, indeed, is one of the ideal goods of life.

If it be a man's highest and dearest priority to live well and nobly, then injustice, not death, is dreaded. Injustice in the soul, loss of those whom he loves, cowardice, or failure of principle are more fearful than death. He will sacrifice his life before his integrity. And then, when a man has learned to live well and he is satisfied that his way of life has an eternal virtue, his mortality is not a threat to the meaning of his life, and it can be graciously born. Such it must be for one whose priorities are deeply established: living nobly is more important than merely living, and it is vastly more satisfying. One cannot live nobly and freely if he believes that death is the greatest evil. Obsession with it diminishes much that gives life meaning, so the virtuous man has only scorn for such a demeaning fear.

The wise man ponders the *manner* and *meanings* of death more than the mere fact of death. Of the many ways that men die, most of them are bad: ignominious, groveling, dishonored, pointless, alone, far from home, in terror, in failure, in regret, in physical agony, in protracted deterioration, rigged up in a hospital bed, or—worst of all—too soon. And we have little control over the terms of our death. That, too, is one of the most threatening parts of it. Many men die well, but such a happy outcome is unusual, not least because many die before their time—aware that their promise is unkept, their responsibilities to their beloved left vacant, and probably feeling an agony of separation.

The distinction between good and bad deaths suggests that there is a kernel of truth in Plato's claim that courage is knowledge of what ought to be feared and what ought not to be: one ought to fear an ignoble or meaningless death, but he ought not to fear a death that consummates his life. Some deaths are fearful and some are devoutly to be wished for, but the distinction will be affective only for a man of virtue. It is sometimes said that one must overcome his fear of death in order to achieve a good life, but the saying has reversed the order of causation. The virtues for living well are the self-same as those for facing death with wisdom and acceptance, so one should learn the virtues of noble life. His hope should be to attain a measure of Socratic *eudaimonia*; if that is accomplished, then death, as such, loses its terrors. Rather, it loses its terrors for oneself; one can still be terrified at the prospect of death for others, who will be lost to ourselves and the world.

In the matter of our mortality, as in many others, there are few things of greater profit than to meditate on the person of Socrates. He is a man of such virtue that he will do what he believes is right as surely as water is wet and fire is hot. The necessity of his own nature excludes all considerations to the contrary as surely as heat excludes cold and wet excludes dry. He tells Crito that he will stand at his post without other considerations. Anything else is impertinent and unseemly. With Socrates, as I imagine him, these other considerations do not occur. He does not weigh them or otherwise struggle with them and consequently dismiss them. They do not occur. He is entirely agreeable to philosophize about these matters in moments of leisure, to be sure. He insists upon it, and he concludes that his duty requires that nothing matters but to man his post. When his duty is in fact given him, his mind is unclouded by reservations to the contrary.

The experience of going to your death is closely akin, if not identical, to the manning of one's post in the Socratic manner. Going to your death properly is like manning your post properly: it is something that one simply does, undisturbed by irrelevancies. Just as you stand your post like a man, you die like a man—without frills, fanfare, or grandiosity. The death of Socrates was not an act of courage. He was past that problem. It was an act of calm, serenity, and even gentleness—perhaps even an act of piety and a benediction. It has become one of the sacred meanings of our heritage. Given our normal animal psyche, however, a Socratic acceptance of death appears to be a mistake made by nature, which seems preoccupied with self-preservation. Still, such acceptance seems not to occur wholly at random. It is closely linked to the unqualified embrace of one's duty—or to the demands of one's virtue, and virtue is coveted by natural selection. We are capable of many different kinds of love, and a love of self-preservation for its own sake and above all else is beneath the contempt of the man who loves excellence. Such a base emotion precludes courage and every other virtue, and the human race would not have survived to this day if nothing mattered but keeping your own skin intact. Natural selection has helped to make us noble.

Socrates anticipated the Epicurean logic, but he remained (according to the *Apology*) undecided in regard to the possibilities of immortality. Although unsure of what follows death, he still showed the utmost equanimity, leaving us to believe that his virtue, as he regarded it, would suffice in any case. "My virtues have served me well and unfailingly thus far," he might have thought, "so if my self persists, they will continue to do so; I have no foreboding." A similar thought, inspired by the same virtue, might lie behind his contempt for fear of the unknown. If we do not know our future, it is idle and unseemly to fret about it. Such fretfulness could be a consequence of the same inappropriate exercise of imagination. We would be better employed to think about the ways in which we might, if possible, use our death to promote and secure some good.

The man who dies in completion also knows a form of immortality, for he sees that much in him survives in those domains of life in which he has believed, and they will survive him. They will carry on what is worthy of remembrance in his nature. The meaning of his life does not die with him. To expire with no such heritage would be a horrible death, and the man who thinks of his death as mere nullification has had an empty life. For whatever reasons, he has been unable to know his life as an integral part of a goodly order—perhaps a holy order—that will not be nullified with his death.

The recognition and acceptance of our mortality includes more than pondering death. We can also reflect upon how this dimension of our finitude can affect our living aspirations and experience. The question of how we can best live must be framed in terms of our limited years and those of others. Those who are obsessed with literally endless life are deprived of a fundamental wisdom: a life does not become any more blessed just in going on forever. It does so by virtue of the meanings embodied in it. To reduce the meaning of life to mere duration is nihilistic. A man conceives his life much in terms of ambitions and responsibilities. In some cases, they are wisely determined, and sometimes they are achieved. He might have pondered the question of what comprises a good and noble life; he might have reached an answer that satisfies him; and these conditions, too, he might have fulfilled. Such a man will not believe that mortality is a curse. He will have thanksgiving that he shares in it. He takes every day of his life as an occasion for satisfaction and gratitude.

There are certain graces of temperament that make the inevitability of death less imperious. In those of little greed, those who do not grasp and clutch at things and covet them madly, there is an acquiescence, finally, to the fatal. It is wisdom to acknowledge that to all things there is a season, and there is something unbecoming in pleading to the fates for more. One welcomes and cherishes the qualities of life in all their amiability. He feels thankful for them, blessed with them, without assuming that they are his in perpetuity or that he will be cheated when he loses them. He is their lover without being their owner. We depart the beings that we love, and the parting is also due to their own mortality. To love anything that is mutable and mortal is to make ourself vulnerable—susceptible to great suffering. We must recognize the inherently tragic character of life and love. So far as that be truly acknowledged, we may love things fatalistically, so to speak, and yet without reserve, unburdened by the extortionate demand that the relation be imperishable. While we live, we may rejoice in its imperishable meaning.

Death is by no means the greatest evil, and it need not be an object of terror. It can be accepted graciously and in confidence that one has bestowed an ennobling legacy upon his successors. The meaning of one's life survives in that legacy, and he is remembered and honored for it. In the moments before he drank the hemlock, Socrates offered a libation to the gods. He asked that his further journey be prosperous, but his libation might also have been one of thanksgiving—thanksgiving for his life and its meanings.

The forthcoming discussion of ideal immortality will include further attention to these themes, but I turn now to another question. A wholesale negation of the meaning of life, so it is thought, lies in the humiliating insignificance of man—not only in the universe at large but even on his own planet. The self-image of man is at stake. In many different ways, systems of thought have displayed an inflamed imagination by conceiving man as somehow the principal player in a cosmic tableau. The formulation might be altogether straightforward, as in the doctrine that the point of the whole of creation is to provide the setting for the drama of human sin and salvation. A subtler and more sophisticated version of placing man at the center of the whole is in those philosophies that translate the categories of the human mind into the constitutive order of the universe. There is a certain pathos in the yearning for such grandiose elevation of status. The pervasive quality of the yearning is demonstrated in the persistence of religions and philosophies that pander to it, but it shows most intensely in the trauma that is suffered when these doctrines are challenged. The challenge is deeply frightening; the challengers are detested and, if possible, hunted down and exterminated.

It is evidently of great importance to the human psyche to have an exalted sense of its status in the whole frame of things, and the advance of science has been most unkind to this need. With the advent of modern science and its steady acceleration, man has become progressively more miniscule in the whole—to the point of being infinitesimal. Sensibilities are staggered, and it gets worse. Darwin's idea was, and is, greeted with horror. The child of God descended from apes? Preposterous! Our noble soul inherited from simians? Never! But it seems to get even worse than this. According to classical Darwinian theory, either an individual or a group is understood to be the unit of evolutionary selection. The individual's success in his environment is owing to his natural powers, and they are exercised for his own benefit or—in some versions—the benefit of his group. But Darwin did not know about DNA, so, according to many neo-Darwinians, his account was insofar erroneous. The biological organism—such as a human being—is no more than an agent for its genes: their manservant, as it were. The gene is the unit of selection, and the function of these microscopic and wholly insentient beings is to replicate *themselves*.[11] From the standpoint of natural selection, the self-esteem of the organism that they inhabit is incidental. In the evolutionary process, all that matters is whether the organism succeeds in reproducing, and hence replicating its resident genes.[12] Scientifically speaking, we organisms are merely the tools of our genes. What could be more diminishing than that? The self-image of man is degraded. Nowhere does there yawn a deeper pit of nihilism.

There are other ideas that are thought to preserve our special status, such as that of free will, or the possession of godlike reason, or an immortal soul. Whatever else they do, all such notions have the function, allegedly, of constituting and preserving our dignity and establishing our position as unique and supreme within nature. Thereby our existence inherits a worthy, appropriate, and indispensable meaning, without which we are plunged into despair. Far be it from me to engage each and every one of these positions. For the sake of economy, I will concentrate on the putative humiliations attendant to neo-Darwinism. From that analysis it will be possible to draw broader implications about the meaning of our status in nature.

To think that our purpose is to replicate our genes is to confound one universe of discourse with another. Only if we are asking of the mechanisms of natural selection might we say, figuratively, that we are agents for the replication of our genes, and even that would be reductive, for it implies that genes are independent agents. There are numerous conditions that are necessary for the process of selection to occur, both genetic and environmental, but the genes are in no sense ultimate. The inclusive processes of nature are ultimate. The fate of any bit of chromosomal material is wholly dependent upon what its environment will tolerate or support, and environments have proven to be extremely discriminating and ruthless. Human beings are a product of that full-scale gauntlet and are the most intelligent participants in it. Hence it is more true and philosophical to say that *nature* has given us our form. Would anyone take this conclusion to mean that we exist *for the sake* of nature? Why, then, for our genes?

We typically desire to replicate *ourselves*, but our purposes never include the replication of our genes for their own sake. *We* use *them*, in effect, to

create more human beings. The replication of genes would be utterly meaningless—just another chemical process—unless it had the consequence of
contributing to the formation of conscious beings, such as ourselves. Otherwise, replication is pointless. Mere chemical processes, as such, have no purpose; they just happen. To think otherwise is to read back into nature a form
of existence that occurs in living agents only. Such a projection, to be sure, is
a common failing, but it is nonetheless nonsensical to say that the purpose of
a sentient and intelligent being is to be the vehicle for the replication of an
absolutely insensate one, as insensate as a rock.

If one were to take the reductionist view literally, indeed, he would never
use terms of praise, condemnation, or other expressions of evaluation in reference to human character and conduct per se. That is, he would never judge
of them in themselves alone, with no regard to goods other than human. In
order to remain logically coherent, he must not utter moral considerations
to evaluate, say, an issue of justice in its own right. Likewise, he would not
assess the policy of appeasement as an instrument of international relations
just insofar as it contributes to our own welfare and suffering. He couldn't
even exclaim, "Good for you!" If our "true" purpose in life were the reproduction of as many of our genes as possible, then we would always subordinate our moral imperatives—as well as our personal needs and ambitions—
to the proliferation of genes. Absurd, you say? Of course it is absurd. That's
the point. The supposition that we exist for the sake of our genes abandons
any distinction between the fully human and a set of the microscopic components of our being.

This is not to deny that genetic materials have much to say about how
we behave, how we turn out, and how we react to how we turn out. As I have
been insisting throughout, wisdom in the moral life requires knowledge of
the patterns of conduct and feeling configured by genetic information in
combination with other variables. Many of the features of a living being are
given definition by his inheritance, and much incapacity and folly are owing
to ignorance or denial of them.

It is essential to understand that one's nature owes much to his genetic
inheritance but that he is not identical to it. More than this, it is essential to
understand that the whole individual, the self, is more than a nature—more
than distinctive capacities and inherent powers. The self has a nature but it
is far more than a nature. The sources of one's being are plentiful and
diverse, many of them due to a cultural inheritance. The culturally acquired
materials that qualify our nature and that are served by native aptitudes are a
massive part of the self and its resources. Some of the men who lived thousands of years ago had the genetic endowment to be great mathematicians,
but none of them were, because sophisticated mathematics did not exist. And
so it is with most of the great workings of the spirit—in art, science, philos-

ophy, and politics: their greatness is achieved because of the treasures of their history. The self that possesses no such treasures is a near vacuity. The moral self, too, owes much to our nature. Our capacity for courage and loyalty are by nature, yet think of the massive differences in the selves in which these capacities live. Is it a self that has learned from only the most meagre and limited experience, or has it been nurtured in a wise and ennobling environment? Has it also learned from Plato and Dewey, or has it been kept out of school altogether? Our inheritance, accordingly, is vastly more than genetic: we live and thrive on a superb legacy of meanings bequeathed to us by our cultural ancestors. They, of course, are not the only source of the materials and instruments furnished to the mind. Any object of my love and any source of my learning helps to constitute my being. My being is also constituted by the fact that I am loved, hated, admired, depended upon (and much else) by others. Their particular relation to me contributes to who I am—how I think, feel, and act, and how I identify myself. Subtract any of this array of sources, and you subtract from me.

A person is the result, the outcome—above all, the *synthesis* and *unification* of these comprehensive sources, which lie far afield. This unification—this self—is what suffers, chooses, fails, and triumphs. It is possessed of inconceivably greater powers of living than any of the constituent biological forces taken singly, and *it*—not its biological members—exults or despairs over its knowledge, accomplishments, and loves. Whatever I think, feel, or do, there are causes of it, and effectively among them are my genes. Still, effects do not disappear into their causes. If they did, nothing but first causes would be real.

This is elementary Aristotelian thinking. The identity of any being is defined by its completion. This is not a quarrel about "identity," "completion," or "unification." It is the simple observation that what matters to us is our nature, resources, and experience as whole functioning beings, and our further adventures depend upon the powers intrinsic to *that* being. Only if one thinks of self as a separate and self-enclosed substance, radically juxtaposed to its many origins, might he plausibly regard his self as a competitor to its sources. Only then might he feel that their efficacy detracts from his. But that is a misconception of self. Our agency is no more in rivalry with its constituent members than a living organism is in rivalry with its heart, lungs, and brain. We are a unification of these several and various powers. My genes do not detract from my agency but contribute to it, and the agency is *mine*. By means of an immensely complex process, genes are replicated, but *I* possess meanings and aspirations that take precedence over the fate of this gene or that.

There are many who detest the idea of any genetic determination at all or of any sort of determinism. To me, I confess, the idea of having something of a direction but not literally a destiny, given by nature, to be discovered and pursued, is attractive. It is an uncertain, exciting, and perilous venture, where small variations in determining conditions might lead to great variations in consequences and where small missteps in judgment could lead to widely diverging paths. Ultimately, deep and abiding satisfactions of the self might occur. I do not thereby dance to the tune played by my genes: my genes help me to dance. They do not abolish the entirety of the self but furnish it with urges and powers. The form of determinism that would be dispiriting, if not annihilating, would be one in which our perceptions, thoughts, cognitions, feelings, loves, emotions, talents, and dispositions were literally superfluous; we would have no agency and no fulfillment of thought and effort.

Apart from that form, which has had an occasional defender, there are still those who persist in supposing that our agency is nullified in being composed of causal conditions. This concern, as I have observed, evidently rests on a mistaken conception of self, but perhaps there is a further way to relieve nagging discomforts. We need to be satisfied on two questions. (1) Are we capable of learning? That is, do we possess the capabilities to modify our present condition and expand its powers? Can we learn arithmetic, for example? Can we become a poet, an engineer, a soldier, a mother, or a cowboy? The question is whether we can do these things with our own faculties, in response to inner and outer promptings and with the assistance of advice and instruction and other forms of support. Are the faculties truly instrumental? Does learning actually occur? (2) Are we capable of deliberative and selective action? That is, do we possess the faculties to distinguish alternative courses of conduct, evaluate them, judge one as preferable to others, and pursue the preferable one? Might we possess the powers to conclude, say, that it is to our particular good to master physics rather than literature and then to go ahead with physics?

These seem to be stupid questions, because we engage in both of these activities all the time. If they really occur, they are not an illusion. To acknowledge their reality, however, is important in assessing the supposed obnoxious character of significant genetic (and other) sources of our nature and conduct. It is no objection to say that our capabilities of learning are largely derived from genetic materials, nor is it an objection to say that what we want to learn and are capable of mastering are in some large part derivative of them, too. If the capability is there, and if it is to the benefit and pleasure of self to use it, *then use it*. Our ability to distinguish, evaluate, and execute will be owing to various conditions. Fine! The point is, if we have the ability, and its exercise is greatly beneficial to us, then there is every reason to get on with it. The concrete organic whole enjoys and suffers, fails and triumphs. So apply yourself to joy and triumph! No gene or combination of genes philosophizes, writes poetry, sings, or builds bridges. It takes a vastly more complex being to do that, and it's vastly more exciting than being a gene.

Whatever our philosophic reservations, if we do not apply ourselves, we will promptly suffer and die, so the controversy seems to be eminently contrived and supercilious. If there is a remnant of sense in it, it might have to do with our self-image, of which there have been many, most of them merely sentimental. In effect, I have been trying to contribute to the human self-image. I have just done so in clarifying and expanding the notion of self, and I do so in articulating various ideal goods. One of them is what I called autonomy. Autonomy is real. That is, it really occurs: there really are individuals who satisfy that characterization. Their powers of conduct are distinguishable from those of others, and they might be objects of admiration, envy, and emulation. If autonomy is real, then it is another piece of philosophic obfuscation to ask, "Is it *really* real?" The only serious question would be whether it really is such a singular *good*. Perhaps it requires more appraisal, or perhaps for a given individual it is better to be mediocre and a conformist. These are questions about specific individuals and specific goods. The ways in which and the extent to which we can make a life turn out well is a matter of knowledge of resources and possibilities and of control over them. It is also a matter—as it has always been—of knowledge of the constraints, needs, and goods of human nature and the entire human condition. These powers and possibilities are unevenly distributed, as are the accidents of fortune. That is part of our fate. It must be part of any realistic image of man.

One might reply that it is still ignominious to be such a meaningless speck from the standpoint of the universe. I have no sympathy, I must declare, with such anxieties. I wonder whether they are merely compensatory, but perhaps they are not wholly so. I do not judge the meaning of a life from the standpoint of the universe. A life might be heroically significant from an earthly and human standpoint. The meanings of life must be determined in the terms available to us such as we are, and that is not a grudging concession to our cosmic insignificance. I have been suggesting some of the sacred values and meanings available to us as earthly creatures. To consider the dignity of man, look no further than to the occasions of his virtue and integrity and to the freedom of mind that he might achieve. These are marvelous and singular successes. Does it matter whether we are significant to the universe if we are cherished and supported by the ones we love? Such conditions are of ultimate meaning *to us*. *They mean everything to us*, and to achieve them is heaven itself. Part of the good of a free and disillusioned spirit is precisely self-sufficiency with respect to the real possibilities of nature. He is categorically distinguished from the wishful thinkers, and many of the goods in his life are a function of that distinction. At the same time, the degradation of man is not as a cosmic nonentity but as one who debases human decency.

There *is*, moreover, something of astonishing cosmic significance about our existence after all, though we are the only ones to know it and appreciate it, and it has not occurred as part of a grand design. Estimates of the occurrence of life elsewhere in the universe are highly problematic, but it is likely that extraterrestial intelligent life is extremely unusual, if it exists at all. And yet here we are: a sort of cosmic miracle in our mere existence. Even that life would be initiated on this planet, which has proven so hospitable to furious reproduction and variation, is improbable, and yet it has happened. Here we are, and we are *intelligent!* We acquire knowledge of our place on this miniscule planet in the infinite reaches of space, and from here we acquire more and more knowledge about the nature of the universe. You want special? *That* is special. The improbability of it all leads many to reject the very possibility of a naturalistic explanation. Apart from the fact that there are not at the moment any respectable alternative explanations—they are one and all mythopoetic—improbability is no refutation. Any highly improbable event, like being one in a billion, seems miraculous to that one, but somebody had to be the one. Likewise, we are that one (or more) in a universe where any real possibility, however remote, might occur. Not only is it amazing that intelligent life has occurred, but we—you and I: self-conscious and thinking individuals—are among their tiny number. We are *knowing* participants in the miracle! It is difficult to imagine anything more singular than that, and I, for one, sometimes enjoy that fact to the point of ecstasy.

It is a still further question to ask of the meaning of *the universe*, and I assume that the very asking of it typically presupposes a theological preoccupation. In any event, we can hardly help asking the question. It can be meaningfully posed within the context of scientific cosmology, where the matter of the origins and destiny of the universe (or perhaps universes) might be helpfully pursued. Who knows what strange and wonderful new things will eventually be learned—whether about the universe as such or about whatever occupants it might turn out to have? If they are *learned*, whatever they may be, they must be verified scientifically, not imaginatively.

Rather than speculate about the universe at large, it would be more suitable to the present inquiry to stay another moment with earth and its meanings, or, more precisely, with nature.[13] In thinking about the meanings of nature, we do well to be Aristotelians. We must think of its outcomes, its completions. We must think of our own lives in this way but also of nature itself. Men once believed that nature was produced by the divine, but that sort of thinking had it backward. *The truth is that nature produces the divine.* That is one of the reasons why we should feel piety toward nature. Originally blind and unthinking nature produces—along with much else—divine beings, such as love, knowledge, and virtue. Do not think it ignominious that divine beings come from unthinking nature. Rather, show piety to nature that it should produce such miracles. The blessed miracles have occurred; that is fact. Nature has become so ordered that intelligence, bonding, and loyalty have come from its bosom. The miracles of wisdom, imagination, beauty, heroism, and eros are real. We are the beneficiaries of this inheritance, in which we revel, and we celebrate nature's fecundity. If deoxyribonucleic acid is among the progenitors of the divine, why should we resent it?

The divine is a *discriminated* inheritance. Many of nature's bestowals are unwelcome and destructive, showing once again that we must be selective in our natural piety. To say that we ought to be selective does not mean that goods must be disordered or at random, and we do not wish for them to be. We have a natural affection for stability, continuity, and order. Novelty, change, uncertainty, and surprise provide their own worthy excitements, to be sure. Life without challenge and adventure would be awfully tedious, but we are terrified when they threaten the very existence of cherished and established orders. Life easily becomes unsettled and unsure, and abiding conflict wearies the spirit. We live in connection; we live as organic parts of orders, and we love those that are enduring. Isolated, disconnected, and fragmented experience is called "meaningless."

Goods that are casual and unrelated provide neither meaning nor abiding satisfaction, nor do goods that are irreconcilable with each other, but the objects of our love and admiration can exist and thrive in relative order and coherence, and they will be more cherished on just that account. The following section will not be a revelation of hitherto unremarked goods, but it will suggest congenial orders that they might take.

c. Immortal Goods

Santayana's *Reason in Religion* shows how religion has discerned and promoted a wide range of ideal goods—and ofttimes corrupted them. The book is remarkable just for distinguishing these many goods in the flux of experience, seeing what they demand in the way of discipline and renunciation and showing how religion exacts and celebrates these requirements. Orthodox religious beliefs and observances do not promote natural goods by inadvertence. The poets and prophets who founded religions were rich in wisdom. It was a wisdom drawn from the experience and needs of a people, and it ministered to those needs. Thus the word of god is highly indebted to the poetry of worldly wise men.

Three of the ideal goods widely associated with religion are piety, spirituality, and immortality. Some say they are *exclusively* associated, but Santayana has a thoroughly naturalistic rendering of each. *Ideal* immortality, for example, like any ideal good, is deliberately fashioned from natural conditions. For Santayana, it means life in the eternal, not eternal life. My intention here is not to follow Santayana to the letter, for I cannot do that, nor is it to provide an exposition of his views. He is my muse, but I speak for myself.

Nietzsche admired the condition of *gratitude*, when it is without illusion. To feel gratitude is to affirm life, to be grateful to be alive. But to what or whom would one be grateful? Here we are well assisted by Santayana in his notion of piety. "Piety, in its nobler and Roman sense, may be said to mean man's reverent attachment to the sources of his being and the steadying of his life by that attachment."[14] Almost everyone inherits a culture. We are taught its lore and customs; we become familiar with its traditions, history, religion, arts, and literature. Its native lands and seas and its cities and towns become familiar. Its gods and heroes are our progenitors and protectors. We mourn the honored dead and dedicate ourselves to furthering their mission. The heritage is regarded with affection and veneration. It provides much of our sense of who we are and of what is important, and it helps to tie us together as a community. Within such a culture, the significance of fundamental and accustomed goods and evils is largely understood in terms of sustaining and contributing to the life of the whole. Hence births, deaths, marriages, and the ceremonies of state are objects of significance for all the society. To follow Santayana, we call all such attachments a condition of *piety*. To be an object of piety is to belong to an identifiable and interconnected order of life-sustaining goods. In the first instance, the order might be that of a nourishing family, culture, tradition, or constitutional system.

If we are to be steadied by these attachments, their existence must be, in large measure, secure and abiding, and when they are transient, we may be upheld by their meanings, many of which would be recorded in our histories. For any particular individual, the sources of his being can be more precisely distinguished. Not all of them fall within a well-defined culture or during a definite period of his life. New sources of reverent attachment might occur at any stage of life—such as the birth of children and grandchildren or the late discovery of an author or a friend. Whatever these sources, they are not likely to have an atomistic existence. They have emerged and subsist as part of some organization of goods: the family, a community, a political tradition, a philosophy, a religion, the republic of letters, a school of art.

The formation of experience that becomes piety begins early. We look to parents, the center and foundation of our universe. Kin, friends, neighbors, persons, and places enlarge this universe, and we fondly remember schools and teachers that initiated us into the company of greater things; we have reverence for books and authors that have seized our intellect and imagination, endowing them with powers and riches, and for wise political principles. So do we revere masterpieces of art and science and their creators. Without them, the spirit would be diminished, life impoverished. As moral (and aesthetic) beings, we would also have piety to those forces that could be credited with the emergence of wisdom, moral virtue, and artistic genius, which have endowed the world with greatness and beauty. We would learn profound piety to those conditions that preserve and invigorate them. All such beings earn our honor and gratitude.

A wise man does not reflect upon the existence of goods as if they occur adventitiously; he would learn of their sources and interdependencies that he might know inclusive orders of life that are deserving of reverent gratitude. Piety is a discriminating affection. It is accorded to beings who are worthy of it, who have somehow nurtured, instructed, disciplined, and inspired us. There are many such beings and many others of a contrary nature. Still, there are individuals in large number who have no feelings of piety—no reverence, no attachment. Perhaps they are in a state of misery, connected to nothing worthy of reverence, or they might have an undiscriminating and sophistical alienation from their entire culture. Perhaps they are ignorant, cynical, or shallow—mere hedonists. Perhaps they have been denied a proper education.

Piety is the most elementary form of rootedness. A civilization that lacks it must be superficial and precarious. It is one of the duties of our basic institutions to inform the young of the existence and nature of objects worthy of a sustaining attachment, explaining why they deserve our loyalty and thanksgiving. To share these objects of piety is to establish a bond—perhaps a powerful one—between distinct individuals. A common piety is one of the conditions of community. At the same time, we would have institutions that also honor the scientific ideal and that teach critical discrimination. To be nonjudgmental is a form of idiocy. Much piety is misplaced: the product of mere sentiment, or of fanaticism, indoctrination, and regimentation, but there is also much in existence that truly deserves our veneration. A vigilant civilization harbors institutions where the difference between blind emotion and clear perception is insisted upon. It would make sure that each generation is introduced to such distinctions, and it would see to it that the young are more than superficially aware of the meanings of their institutions and heritage. Thus a wise and honest piety might flourish—and with it the civilization that nurtures it.

To decline to discriminate is to say that all things are equally deserving; everything is the same. Piety must be discriminating. Selectivity is essential to biological and intelligent life: if we do not distinguish friends and enemies, life will quickly disappear, and without powers of discernment, we will not attain the highest goods. Hence piety should not be accorded to the human race as such, to the universe as a whole, or to nature per se. Each of them is responsible for both good and evil. If the aim of a free and disillusioned thinker is to appraise nature truly and candidly, to form his reactions fittingly to the occasion, and to cultivate *eudaimonia* suitable to the real nature of things, then he cannot be reverently attached to all things indiscriminately.

I observed in the preceding section that divine things are the product of nature, observing also that we ought therefore to have piety to nature, but "nature" requires a discriminating eye. When we think of it at the highest level of abstraction, as the sum of all existing potentialities and actualities, we cannot regard nature as such as an object of piety. We must acknowledge that it produces decidedly mixed results, from heavenly to hellish. Teeming with all manner of powers indifferent to human sensibilities or crushing of them, it could not be otherwise. Nor could one feel a lively piety to the mere fact that nature has produced the divine, for that gives us no distinguishable object or symbol of reverent attachment. This seems an unsatisfactory conclusion, for it leaves us with feelings of gratitude and without any palpable being upon which to bestow them.

Could the remedy for such frustration lie in a form of poetic paganism? The pagan religions personified all manner of forces, both alien and beneficent, in their deities. Indeed, pagan piety often displays remarkable honesty in representing many powers as clearly ambiguous in regard to human fate. There are gods or goddesses of destruction and fecundity, of war, beauty, wisdom, art, and love, gods of fire and the sea and the sky and the underworld. The pagans tend to an honest pluralism: no single deity is regarded as somehow embodying the whole; their piety is both genuine and discriminating. Modern and monotheistic man is poor in poetic symbols of the fateful powers of nature, and he is insofar poor or uncritical in the experience of natural piety. It may happen in a given case, all the same, that an individual fixes upon this or that imaginative rendering, and this has the desired effect of inspiring piety and respect; he is deeply aware of the momentous conditions that undergird his existence.

There is much to commend in also having a form of piety toward threatening and destructive forces, for they too must be deeply acknowledged and respected in their way. Such a form would not inspire reverent attachment, to be sure, nor would it be steadying, but it could make us wiser, and it would not fall into the trap of mystic oneness with the whole. That is the night in which all cows are black—to borrow Hegel's phrase.

In a universe that is often cold and threatening, secure objects of veneration and thanksgiving are essential, and to revere them in common is a condition of human solidarity. We might distinguish them well, and we thereby accord them the honor they deserve. This would be the ideal form of the life of custom. Any individual shares many such customary objects with others, creating something of a union between them, but his particular combination of allegiances would be uniquely his own. They are the sort of thing that he would especially recollect in writing a memoir. In such a form of remembrance, he would find that the objects of piety are not a random assortment. They have a certain connectedness, first of all because they already exist, many of them, in an enduring order: the history of a people, an established culture, a nation, a religion, and protective institutions. They also have an order given by the fact that they are the specific sources of the being of a particular individual. These are the sources of *my* being. They have a coherence and even a symbiosis in being foundational to the good of *my* life. My life, to be sure, contains ambiguity, conflict, tragedy, and failure, all of which have sources, but my life is not chaos, and I try to distinguish within it what is best and most worthy. So far as my self has order and integration and worth, there are objects of piety that have interconnection and harmony. The people, customs, laws, authors, teachings, and traditions of my life are not disjointed; they have coalesced in their way, and so I may look upon them as an ordered whole. With appropriate reflection, the order can be distinguished and apprehended in thought. This is one sort of whole, at least, toward which one can feel reverent attachment.

Piety is largely retrospective; it pertains to things that have existed and sometimes endure. Spirituality has a distinctly prospective quality. "A man is spiritual when he lives in the presence of the ideal, and whether he eat or drink does so for the sake of a true and ultimate good."[15] To be spiritual is to be devoted to the formation of ideal ends; it is the life of eros, striving to give birth in the company of *to kalon*. Hence it is an active life: the effort to bring divine beings into existence and sustain them. These beings can be of many kinds, as we have seen: works of art and science, works of virtue, just and secure political institutions, the nurturance of loves, friendships, and families, the formation of a certain kind of self. Following the usage of Plato and Santayana, we call these goods eternal, immortal, or divine.

Ideal ends are sometimes achieved, and when they have been wisely discriminated and quickened by one's peculiar genius, eros is completed and justified. It might be an "end" that continues to bestow its own form of riches: justice in politics, happy union with those we love, works of virtue, art, or knowledge, or the inspiration to others of a noble life. Pursuit of the ideal might end in a completion, or an approximation thereto, but it can also be a failure and a frustration. Even so, there is a *meaning* in what one attempts: one is devoted to what is highest and best; one would embody such loyalty in the formation of his aspirations, in his self, in his works, and in his teachings.

Another form of spirit is suggested: one has an affinity for all that is fine and good. His soul is drawn to all that is excellent, whether or not he be its creator. Love for what is best would be embodied in his soul and in all he undertakes, and it would be transmitted in his teachings, though he never give birth to a great work or transcendent achievement. This needn't be its own form of fanaticism or the fussy and obsessive form of perfectionism. It is a matter of the ideals that one stands for and would embody in his thought and conduct, what he would think proper to aim for. Though no works of greatness result, this would still be a form of living "in the presence of the ideal," and this in itsef is a noble distinction. It informs all of one's experience and elevates his judgment.

Not infrequently, the ideal ends in one's life exist in tension with accustomed duties or with one another. One thinks of the impassioned artist or scientist who neglects everything for his master obsession; he is neither a loving husband and father nor a good citizen, nor even capable of supporting himself responsibly or looking after his daily needs. Such is the price that is often paid for extraordinary genius. Such cases illustrate the fact that *life in the spirit requires renunciation.* Our poet—who might be doomed to irresponsibility in any case—ought to order his life for the sake of his art without lusting after other goods that he would sacrifice to his muse. If, at the opposite extreme, one disposes his talents and passions across a wide range of attractions, and he accepts responsibilities indiscriminately, none of his endeavors will receive the energies worthy of eros. It is as shallow and futile as trying to be all things to all people. There must be self-denial.

When eros is selective and invested with wisdom, it might achieve a genuine ordering of its goods—goods in harmony and interdependence with one another, a product of unified moral affinities. In truth, such a harmonious order is rare and difficult. It is an ideal good in its own right—the making of a complete life. It demands self-knowledge, virtue, wise and disciplined renunciations, and dedication. So far as our virtues are an ordered whole and accompanied by wisdom, they will be expressed with a like coherence in our works and aspirations. Our friendships, moral allegiances, political ideals, arts, conduct, and teachings will be of a piece; our ideal affinities and our integrity will see to that. Integrity in the soul means integrity in the loves and works of the soul. The meanings of a life would tend to harmony and strength; they would establish a bright and persistent order within the flux.

When a life devoted to the ideal is somehow realized, it becomes an object of piety in its own right. Many of the objects of piety come into being as ideal goods: a nation's founding principles, for instance. Piety is rightly felt, indeed, toward present and living goods, the goods one has achieved and possesses: piety to the works of virtue, intelligence, and eros, such as a good and happy family, for example.

There are, accordingly, salient continuities between objects of piety and of spirit. A life has continuity from its sources to its completions: a continuity of piety and spirit. Objects of piety have formed one's being in a manner to stir the aspirations of spirit and give them content and direction. They contribute to the nurturing of cherished goods, which themselves are worthy of reverence and gratitude. The sources of our being fund the life of spirit, and the spirit enriches what it has inherited. Thus there is a fertile reciprocity between piety and spirituality. Perhaps, on the other hand, a chance and random inspiration seizes the spirit, which ventures in untried directions. In any case, the spirit must be nurtured. A perfect *dis*continuity of piety and spirituality, if such a thing could happen, would mean that spirituality had nothing to feed upon. It would be mere egotism and display—what is known today as self-expression.

The objects of piety and spirituality, so far as they exist in continuity, constitute an inclusive order of goods. They are something of a distinctive whole, which we might find in the renewal and growth of a vigorous culture or in philosophy or in works of art and science. Piety to our ancestors need not be an ossification of the spirit. With the intervention of eros, it could be quite the reverse. Just as a sound education celebrates objects of piety, it furnishes the soul with appreciations of the ideal, hoping to kindle love in the youthful heart for high and virtuous callings.

It is entirely possible, of course, that the ideals of a life will diverge from the meanings embedded in objects of piety and even conflict with them, as when one renounces his family, religion, or nation. Such discord will be a source of suffering, but it might also inspire works of intense creativity, in which one would strive to adjust or unify conflicting values. Conflict has its own virtues, but it more often evades reconciliation. Accordingly, I imply nothing so extravagant as a completely coherent life, without discontinuity and cacaphony, but surely, through the force of his character and works, one might approach a genuine order. The attempt to reconcile or surpass contradictions would be a motive of the ordering process. This would not be a form sheltered within the self alone; it is an ordering of one's world and its meanings. As noted a moment ago, integrity of soul assures some integrity of loves and works. We can call such an ordering of goods an ideal realm of being, which we inhabit. Life in this spiritual habitation is often interrupted, but it is a real habitation all the same, and a real life: the life of one who is reverent to conditions that have supported, formed, and inspired him and who appropriates these goods in the service of ideal objects of affection.

To live in the spirit means to *do* something, to distinguish, appreciate, and achieve these goods, enjoy them, preserve and protect them, teach and transmit them, and—the fates willing—to bring new orderings of nature to completion. These goods we call immortal, eternal, divine. To live in the spirit is to participate in the immortal, to share in *to kalon*, the noble and beautiful. This is the central idea in ideal immortality. "Ideal immortality," Santayana writes, "is a principle revealed to insight; it is seen by observing the eternal quality of ideas and validities, and the affinity to them native to reason or the cognitive energy of mind."[16] We have an affinity to the divine—to the highest and best. Man is not just a greedy and fleshly creature. For some men, their most urgent and gratifying affinity is to what is finest.

We share in and contribute to forms of being that earn the title "eternal." They are "eternal validities." In all such cases, we are loyal to many beings far beyond ourselves in time and place, and we support, create, and affirm beyond ourselves. Thus the meanings of what we do transcend our personal finitude: They are bearers of the highest values of spirit that have been inherited from others, and they are significant for further human life and aspiration. There is a felt sense of ideal life, of living in the eternal. We live in the ideal, and the ideal lives in us.

That is part of our immortality. There is also a form of it in the transmission of ideal life from ourselves to others. Biological reproduction in its own right is a precious form of immortality, and it is especially so when we impart our ideal values to our offspring, who might share them and feel piety toward them. We naturally cherish our works and values and wish them to endure, and this need can attain ideal meaning. What is most precious in one's heritage and spirit can be shared with one's own flesh and blood, who can bear it into the future. What a joyous idea! A similar heritage would be established by sharing our life in the spirit with anyone whose ideal affinities resemble our own and who would feel thanksgiving for these goods.

A man's life has a meaning, with its own piety and spirituality. In virtue of his words and works, this meaning becomes the inheritance of those who follow, who might exemplify it in their own lives. The ideal that lives in us might live in them. This, I think, is the most splendid form of immortality. We do not live forever, but we share in that which is eternal; perhaps we personify it in some measure, and we impart it to others who would live in the spirit. In this manner, the finest and noblest qualities of a person are preserved, perhaps to fructify. Santayana's summary is eloquent.

> Since the ideal has this perpetual pertinence to mortal struggles, he who lives in the ideal and leaves it expressed in society or in art enjoys a double immortality. The eternal has absorbed him while he lived, and when he is dead his influence brings others to the same absorption, making them, through that ideal identity with the best in him, reincarnations and perennial seats of all in him which he could rationally hope to rescue from destruction. He can say, without any subterfuge or desire to delude himself, that he shall not wholly die; for he will have a better notion than the vulgar of what constitutes his being.[17]

That is what the noble spirit knows, and it is one of the many truths that endow his life with meaning.

The failure to experience one's life as part of a larger and beloved reality is probably the main cause of meaninglessness. Recall—as Santayana did— that such "common" occupations as friendship and the family are capable of ideal fulfillment. They can, accordingly, constitute much of that inclusive whole that sustains ideal immortality. We will find meaning, and death will be accepted, with the awareness that our great and intimate loves do not perish with us. The beloved reality with which we have been one lives on.

Those who cannot accept death on any terms will be unmoved by these words. This is not an immortality for everyone. It is for the free and disillusioned, who know piety and spirituality at first hand and without reserve. Santayana one last time: "It may indeed be said," he writes, "that no man of any depth of soul has made his prolonged existence the touchstone of his enthusiasms. Such an instinct is carnal, and if immortality is to add a higher inspiration to life it must not be an immortality of selfishness. What a despicable creature must a man be, and how sunk below the level of the most barbaric virtue, if he cannot bear to live for his children, for his art, or for his country!"[18]

To live in the spirit is to inhabit an ideal realm—not fanciful but composed of the immortal goods of piety and spirit. These goods are an integration and consummation of our natural condition, and they express our ideal affinities. While this domain is a whole, it is far short of the entirety of all being, and it does not justify all existence. We might love it as we love any well-defined existence: our family, our lands, our country, a circle of friends, our art, or our work. This ideal realm, however finite, is inclusive of such existences. It is a capacious and congenial domain, whose meanings transcend the particular events of one's own life. It is populated by beings and ideals that have elicited our love, homage, and loyalty, and we willingly sacrifice for them. One can celebrate this ideal domain and affirm that its goods have made his life eminently worth living, even to giving it a feeling of sanctity.

The final affirmation, were one so blessed, would be a more comprehensive piety. It would be more than our gratitude to the sources of our being, generous though they might be. It is also a thanksgiving for ideal goods and other objects of the spirit that give to life a noble and eternal meaning. Piety becomes the most inclusive form of attachment—a reverence toward all good that has been brought to completion in the ferment of nature, and a gratitude to the fates that one has shared in it.

d. Conclusion

It is evident that men are highly dependent upon a favored view of the nature of things in order to find a meaning for their lives. A worldly metaphysics offers an intelligibility and discipline to the moral life that the more optimistic systems do not, but it offers no cosmic reassurance. The precarious and the negative, the pestilential conflicts and costs, and the limits of nature must be soberly acknowledged. In its candor about the nature of nature, a worldly metaphysics chastens the fancy and demands of us that we think about the meanings of life in a manner at once more realistic and resourceful, and it likewise demands that the meanings that we cherish be attained by wise and deliberate effort. There are powers, orders, and ends resident within nature with which we can become allied, and our own nature—evolved from within the inclusive whole—has its own great potencies for good that are organic to just such a world. Candor about the nature of things affirms that there are plentiful opportunities for life-celebrating goods, but we must be respectful of nature's ways and means if we are to glimpse them and possess them, and even then success is not assured. The fates are often unkind.

I distinguished the morbid from the healthy form of asking of the meaning of life, and the healthy form must begin with some such realistic context, but this legitimate form itself becomes unwholesome. If you continue to ask it, if it becomes an obsession with you, then you are failing: your life is rather vacant and unsure, and there are no great goods within it that you enjoy and celebrate. Satisfy yourself of your finitude, ponder well what affirmations are suitable to the life of a free man, distinguish what is most worthy and precious, and enjoy and rejoice in the values that can be made good in the universal flux. Then you will not be thinking interminably about the meaning of life but consorting with nature's erotic fertility. Then, in moments of reflection, you will be steadied and reassured by thinking of the meanings achieved in your existence and marveling at them. You will know ideal immortality, and you might know piety in its most inclusive sense.

Nature does not give easily of her goods. A proper cognizance of the realities of the human situation leads us to acknowledge the supreme value of excellence of character. It must be placed above the ideal of individuality, which is parasitic upon it. Individuality is a luxury, a brilliant luxury, but virtue is not. The moral excellence of the soul is intrinsically strengthening and satisfying; it is the greatest power for securing abiding goods in a perilous and unsure world, and with it, ordinary goods surpass themselves.

The meanings of life are more important than the quantity of its pleasures. The quality of our happiness, such as it might be, depends upon the quality of our soul. The quality of our loves and our allegiances, pervaded by our affinity to the ideal, makes life worth living. At this stage of my life, I know of no better way to think honestly about the good than to consider what I wish most deeply for my beloved grandchildren. I wish them wisdom, courage, temperance, and justice, and if the idea of integrity is not explicitly implied by these virtues, then I wish them integrity, too. And I wish them, finally, the divine eros to pursue these goods with joy and vigor. Whatever might befall them, and whatever else they might choose, their lives will be much the better for possessing, so far as they can, these priceless qualities.

From within the tumult of nature, a supreme good emerges, and it is the greater for being achieved in a world that is threatening and corrupting. In her final words to Socrates, Diotima says that a person who loves the ideal will bring forth acts of virtue, he will be friend to the human and divine, "and be immortal, if mortal man may. Would that be an ignoble life?"

NOTES

1. In the *Phaedo*, Socrates offers a short review of his philosophic convictions (96a–100e). He concludes that the best explanation for why anything happens is that it is *best* that it should happen that way. He then offers a version of the theory of forms. That theory *pleases* him, he says, and he adds that he *assumes* that evidence to the contrary is false. He also adds that his belief is "no doubt foolish." Remarkable candor! We cannot be sure whether the dialogue states the actual views of Socrates or even of Plato, for that matter. Shortly after this admission, Socrates offers a series of further beliefs, the import of which is to express deep skepticism regarding our cognitive powers. In the text, these are his last stated philosophic opinions before he proceeds to the taking of the hemlock.

2. John Dewey, "The Influence of Darwinism on Philosophy," *The Middle Works of John Dewey*, vol. 4: 1907–1909, ed. Jo Ann Boydston (Carbondale and Edwardsville: Southern Illinois University Press, 1977), p. 12.

3. Friedrich Nietzsche, *Thus Spoke Zarathustra*, trans. and Preface by Walter Kaufmann (New York: Penguin Books, 1978), p. 158.

4. See *Thus Spoke Zarathustra*, esp. "On Redemption" in the second part and "On the Vision and the Riddle," "The Convalescent," and "The Other Dancing Song" in the third part.

5. See my "Ultimate Religion," *Overheard in Seville: Journal of the Santayana Society* 16 (fall 1998): 1–13. The first half of this essay is in criticism of Santayana, the second half in praise. The difference is between that which was written after his *metanoia* and that before it.

6. If Santayana shifts from skepticism to animal faith, as he calls it, then the object of experience is no longer *essence* as such. But it is only essences, not existences, that are harmonious and intrinsically worthy of love. There is no way out of this contradiction for a free and disillusioned spirit. (In an earlier chapter I quoted Santayana's remark that we love the beings of nature "in idea only." I did not at that time remark that as *idea*, essence has no reference.)

7. See Santayana, "Ultimate Religion," in *The Works of George Santayana*, Triton ed., vol. 10 (New York: Charles Scribner's Sons, 1937), pp. 243–57. It is unmistakable throughout this essay that the objects of religious devotion are real worldly beings— or rather, the love in them. Other writings are not so unambiguous.

8. The problem of being ill-mannered is neither marginal nor trivial. The point of manners is not the form of words, but the demeanor: you are deliberately aware of the existence and the sensibilities of the other; you are willingly responsive to his presence, prepared to take the next step in some form of civil and agreeable conduct. This demeanor has all but vanished, and life is therefore more harsh and insensitive and teaching distinctly less pleasant. This is also an ironic result, for every student is indoctrinated to the prevailing speech code, which requires him to be sensitive. Presumably, he is less apt to make racist or sexist remarks, but his demeanor remains oblivious to normal decency.

9. Harvard would seem to be the Valhalla of an educator's life. If you are at Harvard, there are no more career moves. I once asked a friend there if his colleagues had a sense of loyalty and belonging. He said they do not. Harvard has become a mere instrument to advance the egocentric interests of its faculty; it is no longer an end in itself.

10. *Republic*, 586a (trans. Bloom).

11. In my unsystematic readings on this topic, Richard Dawkins is the most forceful proponent of the theory that the gene is the unit of selection. See *The Selfish Gene* (New York and Oxford: Oxford University Press, 1976), and *The Extended Phenotype* (New York and Oxford: Oxford Univeristy Press, 1982). There is no shortage of evolutionary biologists who dispute his analysis. It is not gospel. But if we can show that the truth of his theory would not be a threat to the dignity of man, then we can do so with those of its rivals as well.

12. Dawkins writes, "If we wish to speak of adaptations as being 'for the good' of something, that something is the active, germ-line replicator" (*The Extended Phenotype*, p. 113).

13. There are pertinent distinctions between "universe" and "nature." One can speak helpfully of the *nature* of nature without commitment about the origin, age, size, contents, and end of the universe, for example. To ask of the nature of something is to inquire what *kind* of being it is, what *sorts* of powers and qualities it possesses. One refers to the characteristic potentialities and actualities of nature without being a cosmologist. The actualities will vary from place to place throughout the universe: man, for example, is a unique actuality. We can speak more aptly of the unity of man and nature than we can of man and the universe. It is not clear what "the unity of man and the universe" means, but a clear meaning of "unity of man and nature" can be provided: we refer to the continuities of the nature of man and the nature of the processes in which he is actually enveloped.

14. George Santayana, *The Life of Reason*, vol. 3: *Reason in Religion* (Triton ed., vol. 4), p. 132. The "Roman" sense is especially that conveyed in the poetry of Virgil, most notably the *Aeneid*. In a few instances, my phraseology in the following discussions is adapted from my essay "Ultimate Religion."

15. Santayana, *Reason in Religion*, p. 142.

16. Ibid., p. 159.

17. Ibid., p. 189.

18. Ibid., p. 181.

Bibliography

Aristotle. *Nicomachean Ethics*. Translated, with introduction and notes, by Martin Ost-
    wald. Indianapolis and New York: The Bobbs-Merrill Company, 1962.
————. *Politics*. Translated by T. A. Sinclair. Revised and re-presented by Trevor J.
    Saunders. London: Penguin Books, 1992.
Berger, Peter L., and Richard John Neuhaus. *To Empower People: From State to Civil
    Society*. 2d ed. Edited by Michael Novak. Washington, DC: The AEI Press,
    1996.
Bork, Robert. *Slouching Towards Gommorah*. New York: HarperCollins, 1996.
Bouchard, Thomas J. "Do Environmental Similarities Explain the Similarity of Iden-
    tical Twins Reared Apart?" *Intelligence* 7 (1983): 175–84.
————, D. T. Lykken, M. McGue, N. L. Segal, and A. Tellegen. "Sources of Human
    Psychological Differences: The Minnesota Study of Twins Reared Apart." *Sci-
    ence* 250 (1990): 223–28.
Buss, David M. *The Evolution of Desire*. New York: Basic Books, 1994.
Cohen, David B. *Stranger in the Nest*. New York: John Wiley & Sons, 1999.
Coleman, James. "On the Self-Suppression of Academic Freedom." *Academic Ques-
    tions* 4, no. 1 (winter 1990–1991): 17–22.
————. "Response to the Sociology of Education Award." *Academic Questions* 2, no. 3
    (summer 1989): 76–78.
Dawkins, Richard. *The Extended Phenotype*. New York and Oxford: Oxford University
    Press, 1982.
————. *The Selfish Gene*. New York and Oxford: Oxford University Press, 1976.
Descartes, René. *Meditations on First Philosophy* (1641). Many translations, many edi-
    tions.
Dewey, John. *Experience and Nature*. In *John Dewey: The Later Works*, vol. 1. Edited by
    Jo Ann Boydston. Carbondale and Edwardsville: Southern Illinois University
    Press, 1981.

———. "The Influence of Darwinism on Philosophy." In *John Dewey: The Middle Works*, vol. 4. Edited by Jo Ann Boydston. Carbondale and Edwardsville: Southern Illinois University Press, 1977.

———. *The Quest for Certainty*. In *John Dewey: The Later Works*, vol. 4. Edited by Jo Ann Boydston. Carbondale and Edwardsville: Southern Illinois University Press, 1988.

Emerson, Ralph Waldo. *Essays, 1837–1860*. Many editions.

Erasmus, Charles J. *In Search of the Common Good*. Glencoe, IL: The Free Press, 1977.

Flanagan, Owen. *Varieties of Moral Personality*. Cambridge and London: Harvard University Press, 1991.

Frank, Robert H. *Passions Within Reason*. New York and London: W. W. Norton & Company, 1988.

Freeman, Derek. *Margaret Mead and Samoa: The Making and Unmaking of an Anthropological Myth*. Cambridge, MA: Harvard University Press, 1983.

———. "Paradigms in Collision." *Academic Questions* 5, no. 3 (summer 1992): 23–33.

Fukuyama, Francis. *The Great Disruption*. New York: The Free Press, 1999.

Goldberg, Steven. *The Inevitability of Patriarchy*. New York: William Morrow, 1973.

Gouinlock, James. *Excellence in Public Discourse: John Stuart Mill, John Dewey, and Social Intelligence*. New York: Teachers College Press, 1986.

———. *Rediscovering the Moral Life: Philosophy and Human Practice*. Amherst, NY: Prometheus Books, 1993.

———. "Ultimate Religion." *Overheard in Seville: The Journal of the Santayana Society* 16 (fall 1998): 1–13.

Gould, Stephen J. *The Mismeasure of Man*, 2d ed. New York: Norton, 1996.

Greenberg, Jerald, and Ronald L. Cohen, eds. *Equity and Justice in Social Behavior.* New York: Academic Press, 1982.

Hart, Jeffrey. "Dartmouth Reviewed." *The National Review* (June 22, 1998): 42–44.

Hegel, G. W. F. *The Phenomenology of Mind [Geistes]*. Translated, with an introduction and notes, by J. B. Baillie. London: George Allen and Unwin Ltd.; New York: The Macmillan Company, 1955.

Herrnstein, Richard J., and Charles Murray. *The Bell Curve: Intelligence and Class Structure in American Life*. New York: The Free Press, 1994.

Hitchens, Peter. *The Abolition of Britain*. San Francisco: Encounter Books, 2002.

Hobbes, Thomas. *Leviathan* (1651). Many editions.

Hollander, Paul. *Anti-Americanism: Critiques at Home and Abroad, 1965–1990*. New York: Oxford University Press, 1992.

———. *Political Pilgrims: Travels of Western Intellectuals to the Soviet Union, China, and Cuba, 1928–1978*. New York: Oxford University Press, 1981.

Homans, George C. *Sentiments and Activities*. Glencoe, IL: The Free Press, 1962.

———. *Social Behavior: Its Elementary Forms*. New York: Harcourt Brace Jovanovich, 1974.

Jensen, Arthur R. *The g Factor: The Science of Mental Ability*. Westport, CT: Praeger, 1998.

Kant, Immanuel. *Critique of Pure Reason*. Translated by Norman Kemp Smith. London: Macmillan, 1958.

———. *Foundations of the Metaphysics of Morals*. Translated and with an introduction by Lewis White Beck. New York: The Liberal Arts Press, 1959.

———. "On the Supposed Right to Lie from Altruistic Motives." In *The Critique of Practical Reason and Other Writings in Moral Philosophy*. Edited and translated by Lewis White Beck. Chicago: The University of Chicago Press, 1949.

Keeley, Lawrence H. *War Before Civilization*. New York: Oxford University Press, 1996.

Kekes, John. *A Case for Conservatism*. Ithaca, NY and London: Cornell University Press, 1998.

———. *Facing Evil*. Princeton, NJ: Princeton University Press, 1990.

Kors, Alan Charles, and Harvey A. Silverglate. *The Shadow University*. New York and London: The Free Press, 1998.

Lachs, John. "Aristotle and Dewey on the Rat Race." In *Philosophy and the Reconstruction of Culture*. Edited by John J. Stuhr. Albany: State University of New York Press, 1993, pp. 97–109.

———. *Intermediate Man*. Indianapolis and Cambridge, MA: Hackett Publishing Company, 1981.

———. "To Have and To Be." *The Human Search*. Edited by Lachs and Charles E. Scott. New York and Oxford: Oxford University Press, 1981, pp. 247–55.

Lerner, Melvin J. *The Belief in a Just World: A Fundamental Delusion*. New York and London: Plenum Press, 1980.

Levin, Michael. *Why Race Matters*. Westport, CT, and London: Praeger, 1997.

Livingston, Donald. *Philosophical Melancholy and Delerium: Hume's Pathology of Philosophy*. Chicago and London: University of Chicago Press, 1998.

Locke, John. *Two Treatises of Government* (1690). Many editions.

Lomborg, Bjørn. *The Skeptical Environmentalist: Measuring the Real State of the World*. New York: Cambridge University Press, 2001.

Magnet, Myron. *The Dream and the Nightmare: The Sixties' Legacy to the Underclass*. San Francisco: Encounter Books, 2000.

Morson, Gary Saul. "What is the Intelligentsia? Once More, an Old Russian Question." *Academic Questions* 6, no. 3 (summer 1993): 20–38.

Murray, Charles. *Losing Ground: American Social Policy, 1950–1980*. New York: Basic Books, 1984.

Neville, Robert. *Recovery of the Measure*. Albany: State University of New York Press, 1989.

Nietzsche, Friedrich. *Beyond Good and Evil*. Translated, with commentary, by Walter Kaufmann. New York: Vintage Books, 1989.

———. *Thus Spoke Zarathustra*. Translated and with a preface by Walter Kaufmann. New York: Penguin Books, 1978.

Olasky, Marvin. *The Tragedy of American Compassion*. Washington, DC: Regnery Gateway, 1992.

Pinker, Steven. *How the Mind Works*. New York and London: W. W. Norton, 1997.

———. *The Blank Slate: The Modern Denial of Human Nature*. New York: Viking Penguin, 2002.

Plato. *The Collected Dialogues of Plato*. Edited by Edith Hamilton and Huntington Cairns. Princeton, NJ: Princeton University Press, 1971.

———. *The Republic*. Translated, with notes and interpretive essay, by Allan Bloom. 2d ed. New York: Basic Books, 1991.

Popenoe, David. *Life Without Father.* New York: The Free Press, 1996.

Rachlin, Howard, and David Laibson, eds. *The Matching Law.* Cambridge, MA, and London: Harvard University Press, 1997.

Rawls, John. *A Theory of Justice.* Cambridge, MA: Harvard University Press, 1971.

Reich, Charles. *The Greening of America.* New York: Random House, 1970.

Ridley, Matt. *The Origins of Virtue: Human Instincts and the Evolution of Cooperation.* New York: Viking Press, 1997.

———. *The Red Queen.* London: Penguin Books, 1993.

Rushton, J. Philippe. *Race, Evolution, and Behavior.* 2d ed. New Brunswick, NJ: Transaction Publishers, 1997.

———. "Race, Intelligence, and the Brain: The Errors and Omissions of the 'Revised' Edition of S. J. Gould's *The Mismeasure of Man* (1996)." *Personality and Individual Differences* 23, no. 1 (1997): 169–80.

Santayana, George. *Character and Opinion in The United States.* In *The Works of George Santayana.* Triton ed. Vol. 8. New York: Charles Scribner's Sons, 1937.

———. *Dominations and Powers: Reflections on Liberty, Society, and Government.* New York: Charles Scribner's Sons, 1951.

———. *Interpretations of Poetry and Religion.* In *The Works of George Santayana.* Triton ed. Vol. 2. New York: Charles Scribner's Sons, 1936.

———. *The Life of Reason,* vol. 1: *Reason in Common Sense.* In *The Works of George Santayana.* Triton ed. Vol. 3. New York: Charles Scribner's Sons, 1936.

———. *The Life of Reason,* vol. 2: *Reason in Society.* In *The Works of George Santayana.* Triton ed. Vol. 3. New York: Charles Scribner's Sons, 1936.

———. *The Life of Reason,* vol. 3: *Reason in Religion.* In *The Works of George Santayana.* Triton ed. Vol. 4. New York: Charles Scribner's Sons, 1936.

———. *The Life of Reason,* vol. 5: *Reason in Science.* In *The Works of George Santayana.* Triton ed. Vol. 5. New York: Charles Scribner's Sons, 1936.

———. *Realms of Being.* 4 vols. In *The Works of George Santayana.* Triton ed. Vols. 14 and 15. New York: Charles Scribner's Sons, 1937, 1940.

———. *Scepticism and Animal Faith.* In *The Works of George Santayana.* Triton ed. Vol. 13. New York: Charles Scribner's Sons, 1937.

———. "Ultimate Religion." in *The Works of George Santayana.* Triton ed. Vol. 10. New York: Charles Scribner's Sons, 1937.

Schoenbrod, David. "The Mau-Mauing of Bjørn Lomborg." *Commentary* (September 2002): 51–55.

Simon, Julian L. *The Ultimate Resource 2.* Princeton, NJ: Princeton University Press, 1996.

Singer, Peter. *Practical Ethics.* 2d ed. Cambridge: Cambridge University Press, 1993.

Sober, Elliott, and David Sloan Wilson. *Unto Others: The Evolution and Psychology of Unselfish Behavior.* Cambridge, MA: Harvard University Press, 1998.

Sowell, Thomas. "Affirmative Action: A Worldwide Disaster." *Commentary* 88, no. 6 (December 1989): 21–41.

———. *The Economics and Politics of Race.* New York: Morrow, 1983.

———. *Ethnic America.* New York: Basic Books, 1981.

———. *Preferential Policies: An International Perspective.* New York: Morrow, 1990.

———. *The Vision of the Anointed: Self-Congratulation as a Basis for Social Policy.* New York: Basic Books, 1995.

Spinoza, Baruch. *Ethics* (1677). Many translations, many editions.

Stockdale, James B. *A Vietnam Experience: Ten Years of Reflection.* Stanford, CA: Hoover Institution Press, Stanford University, 1984.

Turiel, Elliot, Melanie Killen, and Charles C. Helwig. "Morality: Its Structure, Functions, and Vagaries." In Jerome Kagan and Sharon Lamb, eds., *The Emergence of Morality in Young Children.* Chicago and London: University of Chicago Press, 1987.

Waite, Linda J., and Maggie Gallagher. *The Case for Marriage.* New York: Doubleday, 2000.

Weissberg, Robert. *Political Tolerance.* Thousand Oaks, CA; London; and New Delhi: Sage Publications, 1998.

———. *The Politics of Empowerment.* Westport, CT, and London: Praeger, 1999.

———. "The Vagaries of Empowerment." *Social Science and Modern Society* 37, no. 2 (January/February 2000).

Wilson, E. O. *Consilience.* New York: Alfred A. Knopf, 1998.

Wilson, James Q. "Cultural Meltdown." *The Public Interest* 137 (fall 1999): 99–104.

———. *The Marriage Problem: How Our Culture Has Weakened Families.* New York: HarperCollins, 2002.

———. *The Moral Sense.* New York: The Free Press, 1993.

Wrangham, Richard, and Dale Peterson. *Demonic Males: Apes and the Origins of Human Violence.* Boston and New York: Houghton Mifflin, 1996.

Index